THE FOREIGN POLICY OF
CZECHOSLOVAKIA
1918-1935

BY

FELIX JOHN VONDRACEK

AMS PRESS
NEW YORK

COLUMBIA UNIVERSITY
STUDIES IN THE
SOCIAL SCIENCES

426

The Series was formerly known as
Studies in History, Economics and Public Law.

Reprinted with the permission of Columbia University Press
From the edition of 1937, New York
First AMS EDITION published 1968
Manufactured in the United States of America

Library of Congress Catalogue Card Number: 73-76645

AMS PRESS, INC.
NEW YORK, N. Y. 10003

To
My Wife
OLGA MARIE VONDRACEK

ACKNOWLEDGMENTS

ALTHOUGH it is not possible to mention individually all who have assisted in the preparation of this work, the writer wishes to express his gratitude particularly to certain members of the Faculty of Political Science of Columbia University, to Professor Carlton J. H. Hayes, to the late Professor Parker Thomas Moon, under whose direction the work was begun, and to Professor Walter Consuelo Langsam, under whom the work was completed. In addition, the writer desires to thank also the various members of the Czechoslovak Consulates-General at New York and Chicago, and of the Legation at Washington, D. C., who, periodically for over a decade, have generously placed at his disposal materials not readily accessible to the general reader. Similar appreciation is felt for many favors received from the *Svornost* (Chicago) and from the Congressional Library, the library of Columbia University, and those of the Universities of Chicago, Iowa, and North Dakota.

TABLE OF CONTENTS

PAGE

ACKNOWLEDGMENTS 7

CHAPTER I
THE PROBLEMS OF INDEPENDENCE

General Considerations 13
The New Government 14
Peace Conference Preliminaries 24
The Territorial Settlement 27
Other Peace Conference Problems 43

CHAPTER II
DOMESTIC STABILIZATION

Interdependence of Foreign and Domestic Policies 60
Financial Policy 60
Economic Policy 76
Social Reform 89
Religious Policy 91

CHAPTER III
THE GREAT POWERS, 1918–1923

Objectives of Foreign Policy 98
Germany 98
The Western Powers 100
The League of Nations 105
The Russian Problem 113
The Siberian Campaign 114
Intra-Slav Cooperation vs. a " Western Orientation " 129
The Genoa Conference 139
The Rapprochement with Russia 144

CHAPTER IV
THE RECONSTRUCTION OF CENTRAL EUROPE, 1918–1923

Beneš' Central European Objectives 147
Boundary Disputes with Poland 148
The Formation of the Little Entente 162

9

PAGE

The Problem of Austria 173
The Attempted Rapprochement with Poland 178
Friction with Hungary 181
Central European Economic Cooperation 189
The Reconstruction of Austria 192
Early Little Entente Conferences 197
The Reconstruction of Hungary 205

CHAPTER V

The Search for Security, 1924–1926

"The Treaty of Mutual Assistance" 209
The French Alliance 211
France, Italy and the Little Entente 220
The Italo-Czechoslovak Treaty 224
The Praha and Ljubljana Conferences 226
The Geneva Protocol 227
Locarno 229
Security to the East 241

CHAPTER VI

Efforts to Maintain the New Status Quo

Commercial Treaties 247
The Debt Settlement with the United States 248
The Catholic Question 249
Fascism 257
Minority Reconciliations 258
Better Relations with the Soviet Union 259
Friendship with Poland 263
Franco-Italian Rivalry 265
"Irreconcilable Hungary" 271
The Austrian Problem Again 278
Little Entente Conferences, 1925–1929 288
Germany and the League of Nations 297
Peace, Security and Disarmament 299

CHAPTER VII

The Depression

Economic Conferences 305
The Proposed Austro-German Customs Union 312
Politics *vs.* Economics within the Little Entente 318
Hungarian Revisionism 326
Italo-Czechoslovak Friction 330

PAGE

The U. S. S. R. and Poland 334
Revisionism *vs.* the Status Quo 336
Reparations and Debts 341

CHAPTER VIII

THE NAZI CRISIS

The Causes and Importance of Hitlerism 351
Strengthening the Little Entente 356
Italy and Poland 360
1933 Little Entente Conferences 364
The Franco-Soviet Non-Aggression Pact 368
Disarmament Negotiations 369
The Germano-Polish Rapprochement 373
Debt Default 376
The Revival of Hungarian Revisionism 377
Austria 380
Friction with Germany 383
Attempts to Isolate Germany 386
The Henlein Movement 407
Göring's Balkan Tour 411
Amplification of the Modus Vivendi 412
Solidarity of the Status Quo Bloc 413
Renewed Friction with Poland 418
Italy *vs.* Ethiopia 420
Masaryk's Resignation 423

BIBLIOGRAPHY 426

INDEX 445

CHAPTER I

THE PROBLEMS OF INDEPENDENCE

GENERAL CONSIDERATIONS

AT the beginning of her independent existence, Czechoslovakia faced numerous problems inherent in her new status and the post-war conditions. The young state would require many years of peace in which to consolidate its position and complete the development of its resources. Hence, from the outset, its leaders appreciated that, viewed from the point of self-interest, a policy of preserving the post-war status quo would become a vital necessity. Extreme nationalism * would react, ultimately, against Czechoslovakia, which ought to adopt at least a generous if not an altruistic policy. Her geographic position between the recently-defeated Central Powers, with Germany on the one hand and with Austria and Hungary on the other, together with the close ties, particularly economic, that still bound her to these countries, created for her a precarious situation that could permit stability only when it existed to some degree also within the territories of her immediate neighbors. Nevertheless, a far-sighted foreign policy would be exceedingly difficult to put into effect, for the intense nationalism and hatred engendered by the recent struggle precluded the possibility of the late enemies seeing eye to eye even on matters of common interest, until bitter experience alone should teach them what measures must be adopted for their mutual advantage.

The problems that faced Czechoslovakia were complex, involving almost every aspect of human activity. Not only

* The term "nationalism" is used in the American sense, specifically as defined in C. J. H. Hayes' *Essays on Nationalism* (New York, 1926).

were there a large number of questions concerning the foreign relations of the new state that demanded almost immediate solution, but there existed domestic problems, perhaps even more vital, that brooked still less delay. Thus, while Czechoslovakia was attempting to clarify her relations with different individual friends and foes and to obtain a peace settlement that she deemed indispensable to her existence and safety, she was forced also to set her own house in order, to establish a government and to determine her future policies. These various problems had to be solved by newly elected or appointed officials, most of them with little previous experience in the higher governmental activities. Under such conditions, some mistakes and misunderstandings were inevitable, yet, on the whole, few steps had to be retraced.

The New Government

The question that demanded foremost attention was the creation of the new government. During the War, two Czechoslovak governments had been created, at Paris and Praha (Prague) respectively. The former, the Czechoslovak National Council, was the work of Czechs and Slovaks residing in Allied countries, led by Masaryk,[1] Beneš[2] and

[1] Thomas Garrigue Masaryk was born of poor parents at Hodonín (Göding) in Slovakia on March 7, 1850. Obtaining an education after a severe struggle, he became Professor of Philosophy at the University of Praha. For many years he was unpopular because he sought to teach his people to make Bohemia great in the present rather than merely to glorify the past. Shortly after the outbreak of the War he went voluntarily into exile, and from headquarters at Paris directed the Czechoslovak revolutionary struggle. As President of the National Council, he made trips to England, Russia and the United States on behalf of the revolutionary cause.

[2] Edward Beneš, after obtaining his doctorate at Paris in 1909, became Professor of National Economics at the Czech Business Academy

Štefánik,[2a] whereas the latter was the product of a movement inspired by Kramář.[3] The Paris government, after receiving de facto recognitions from the Allied Great Powers and the United States, proclaimed Czechoslovak independence on October 18, 1918.[4] The revolutionists at Praha, taking advantage of Austria's growing weakness, actually established Czechoslovakia by a bloodless uprising of October 28.[5]

Many uncertainties that had existed as to the political form of the new state at earlier periods of the revolutionary struggle were dissipated by 1918; even ardent former monarchists had been converted to the idea of a Republic.[6] The two Czechoslovak governments were merged without friction. The consolidation was effected at Geneva on

and was active in the national movement. In 1914, when only thirty years of age, he was entrusted with the leadership of the domestic revolutionary movement after Masaryk's departure. During the following year he came to the conclusion that he, too, could best serve the cause abroad. Hence he also went to Paris where he became General Secretary of the National Council, and, with Masaryk, a co-founder of the Czechoslovak Republic.

[2a] Before the War, Milan R. Štefánik left his native Slovakia to become an explorer for France. Subsequently, as a French general, he played an influential part in obtaining the support of the Western Powers for the revolutionary cause.

[3] Karel Kramář, the most prominent Czech leader who was not an exile, led the domestic movement against the Dual Monarchy, and, during the early years of the War, eclipsed Masaryk in popularity. The growing conviction that independence had been won through Masaryk's conversion of the Western Powers to the Czechoslovak cause brought about an eventual decline in the influence of Kramář.

[4] Beneš, E., My War Memoirs (New York, 1928), pp. 415-427.

[5] Opočenský, J., The Collapse of the Austro-Hungarian Monarchy and the Rise of the Czechoslovak State (Prague, 1928), pp. 93-147.

[6] On the question of republic vs. monarchy, cf. Masaryk's memorandum to the Allies of February, 1916, in Masaryk, T. G., Světová revoluce za války a ve válce, 1914-1918 (Praha, 1933, hereafter referred to as Světová Revoluce), pp. 476-478; Beneš, op. cit., pp. 444-445; Bielsky, E. (Edward Beneš), "Československé země republikou", Československá Samostatnost, vol. iv, p. 25, November 20, 1918.

October 31, by the Declaration of Geneva,[7] drawn up by delegates representing both groups. Masaryk became President; Kramář, President of the Council of Ministers; Beneš, Minister for Foreign Affairs; and Štefánik, Minister for National Defense. On November 14 the first units of the Czechoslovak Legions returned from France and Italy. Masaryk hastened from the United States to assume his new duties, reaching Praha on December 21, where he was duly inaugurated.[8]

The revolutionary leaders had to determine also the composition of the Provisional National Assembly, the body into which the National Council had enlarged itself. It was imperative that the National Assembly organize itself promptly; consequently it was not the product of elections, but an emergency body summoned hastily to conduct affairs during the period of transition. Therefore, when it met for the first time on November 14, its membership was based, proportionally, upon the number of votes polled by all existing Czech parties during the last elections, those of 1911 to the Austrian *Abgeordnetenhaus*. Its personnel was appointed by the executive committees of the various parties concerned.[9] Of the total membership of 270, the 54 Slovaks had to be selected arbitrarily, by the Slovak National Council, for no better method of selection existed, since the Slovaks had had virtually no representation in the Hungarian parliament.[10] In his inaugural address, Kramář proclaimed the

[7] Declaration of Geneva, in leaflet form (in Czech); reprinted also in Čapek, T., Jr., *Origins of the Czechoslovak State* (New York, 1926); cf. also, Opočenský, *op. cit.*, pp. 58-62; Beneš, *op. cit.*, pp. 440-443.

[8] Masaryk, *op. cit.*, pp. 383-384.

[9] *Cf.* Haskins, C. H. and Lord, R. H., *Some Problems of the Peace Conference* (Cambridge, 1920), pp. 233-236; Graham, M. W., *New Governments of Central Europe* (New York, 1924), p. 275.

[10] For details of the composition of the Provisional National Assembly, *cf.* Šedivý, K., *Sept années de politique intérieure tchécoslovaque, 1918-1925* (Prague, 1925), pp. 7-8.

establishment of the Czechoslovak Republic and the dissolution of all ties with the House of Habsburg-Lorraine. He
also invited the Bohemian Germans to participate in the
government, but both they and the Magyars refused to cooperate with the Czechs.[11]

These refusals were discordant notes in the establishment
of the new government: although expected, they indicated,
nevertheless, the dangers to which the new Republic would
be exposed from the hostile minorities that would, in
all probability, be incorporated after the Peace Conference
had established definitive boundaries. By contrast, they
indicated also the necessity to the Czechs of the support of
the other Slavic groups within the state. The support of
the Slovaks had been pledged as early as October 30,[12] thus
strengthening the ties already created by the Pittsburgh
Agreement.[13] Similarly, during November, the Ruthenes
organized three National Councils at Přešov, Užhorod and
Chust, which soon merged. On May 8, 1919,[14] the con-
solidated Ruthene National Council approved the action

[11] Papánek, J., *La Tchécoslovaquie, histoire politique et juridique de sa
création* (Prague, 1922), pp. 69-70; Borovička, J., *Ten Years of Czechoslovak Politics* (Prague, 1929), pp. 29-54.

[12] Loubal, F., " Slovenská declarace z 30 října 1918 s hlediška mezinárodního", *Zahraniční Politika*, vol. ii, pp. 1435-1440; Haskins and Lord,
op. cit., pp. 237-238; Čapek, *op. cit.*, appendix. *Cf.* also, Opočenský,
op. cit., pp. 153-168. On October 30, by the Declaration of Turčanský
Sv. Martin, the Slovaks associated themselves with the uprising in Praha
two days earlier.

[13] On June 30, 1918, Masaryk climaxed his earlier revolutionary activities in America by signing the Agreement of Pittsburgh between the
Czechs and Slovaks, whereby, in the Czechoslovakia-to-be, the latter were
guaranteed their own assembly, courts and administration. *Cf.* the Pittsburgh Agreement, reprinted in Paličkář, S. J. and Brož, A., " Czechs
and Slovaks at Odds", *Current History*, vol. xxii, p. 788; Masaryk,
op. cit., pp. 255-257.

[14] Masaryk, *op. cit.*, pp. 295-296; Mercier, M., *La Formation de l'état
tchécoslovaque* (Chartres, 1922), pp. 103-104.

taken in the preceding October by the American Ruthenes during the Philadelphia Congress of the oppressed nationalities of Central Europe, in favor of union with Czechoslovakia.[15]

During November and December, 1918, Czech forces occupied the German and Magyar areas that Czechoslovakia hoped would be included in her boundaries-to-be. Several skirmishes took place in towns with German majorities,[16] and the resulting agitation did not abate until checked by President Masaryk's conciliatory Christmas speech,[17] which promised equal treatment to both Czechs and Germans. Similar difficulties were encountered in Slovakia, from which were driven numerous detachments of Hungarian soldiers.[18] In an attempted defense of this region in January, 1919, the Magyars established a so-called Eastern Slovak National Council, which soon collapsed when repudiated by the Slovak deputies at Praha. An interesting sidelight was the fact that, throughout the occupation of Slovakia, the Czechs took care to curb anti-Semitic agitation, in spite of the fact that many of the purveyors of anti-Czech propaganda were Hungarian Jews supposedly subsidized by the government of

[15] The Amerikánská Národní Rada Ugro-Rušinov plebiscite at Philadelphia resulted in seventy percent voting for union with Czechoslovakia, twenty percent for union with the Ukraine, nine percent for complete independence and only one percent for remaining with Hungary. For full details, cf. *Svornost*, January 12, 1919.

[16] Cf. Molisch, P., *Die Sudetendeutsche Freiheitsbewegung in den Jahren 1918-19* (Vienna, 1932), for a complete account of the German agitation in Bohemia during 1918-1919.

[17] *Prager Presse*, December 26, 1918.

[18] On December 4, the Allied Powers authorized the Czech occupation of Slovakia and the expulsion of Hungarian forces. *Cf. Le Temps*, December 5, 1918; or Street, C. J. C., *Slovakia, Past and Present* (London, 1928), p. 33.

Bela Kun at Budapest.[19]   The new Slovak provincial government was actually inaugurated on February 1, 1919.[20]

The dangers to which Czechoslovakia was exposed indicated also the need for a comprehensive military policy. As a temporary measure, the government called to the colors on November 22, 1918, reservists of the classes of 1895-99,[21] and thereby raised many of the forces needed immediately upon the Hungarian frontier.   In a newspaper interview of January 12, 1919, Kramář made a fervent plea for a large army to protect the Republic against threats emanating from Germany and Russia.[22]   Masaryk, ordinarily an anti-militarist, expressed the same opinion to Professor Ernest Denis.[23]   On January 28, 1920, the Czechoslovak government announced the creation of a peacetime army of 8,000 officers and 141,910 conscripted men.[24]   Václav Klofáč, the Minister of National Defense, was largely instrumental in bringing about the adoption of the Defense Act of March 19, 1920.   Upon that date, the National Assembly approved unanimously the second and third readings of the bill.   By its provisions, a two-year period of universal military service was made compulsory for the next three years.[25]   For the

[19] Graham, *op. cit.*, p. 276; Šedivý, *op. cit.*, pp. 10-11.

[20] For full details, *cf.* Seton-Watson R. W., *The New Slovakia* (Prague, 1924).

[21] *Svornost*, November 28, 1918.

[22] *Le Temps*, January 12, 1919; *Svornost*, January 16, 1919.

[23] *Svornost*, May 3, 1919.

[24] *Ibid., Národní Listy*, January 29, 1920.

[25] When the bill had been presented for the first time by Klofáč to the National Assembly on January 25, 1920, the sole opposition to it had been voiced by the Social Democrats who had desired four months' military service rather than two years'. However, when representatives of the other parties pointed out the inadequacy of so short a period, the Social Democrats withdrew their objections. In time of peace, the ages of service are twenty to fifty years, and in time of war, seventeen to sixty. *Cf. Národní Politika* and *Národní Listy*, January 26, 1920; *Svornost*, February 1, 1920.

subsequent three years the period of service was reduced to eighteen months. At the expiration of these six years, if the number of trained militia would be deemed still insufficient, further periods of fourteen months' service each would be instituted. The control of mobilization and the summoning of trainees was vested in the National Assembly. Special additional resolutions of the National Assembly welcomed more publicity regarding military activities and a greater measure of civilian influence at the War Ministry. In this manner was the Republic provided with an adequate army, one which, in a major emergency, would number more than a million men.[26]

The concluding step requisite to the establishment of the Czechoslovak government was the adoption of a constitution. Wisely, the leaders refrained from attempting to draw a permanent one too hastily; therefore, a provisional constitution was put into effect on November 13, 1918,[27] and a permanent one deferred until the general situation of the Republic would become more clarified and the more pressing of its problems solved. Thus it was that the definite constitution was left to be framed and enacted by the first regularly elected National Assembly on February 29, 1920.[28]

[26] *Národní Listy, Národní Politika, Prager Presse*, March 20, 1920; *Svornost*, March 24, 1920; *cf.* also, Borovička, *op. cit.*, pp. 96-97.

[27] For an analysis of the Provisional Constitution, *cf.* Graham, *op. cit.*, pp. 279-281.

[28] Graham, *op. cit.*, pp. 292-313; Hoetzl, J. and Joachim, V., *The Constitution of the Czechoslovak Republic* (Prague, 1920) ; Brož, A., *Three Years of the Czechoslovak Republic* (Prague, 1921), pp. 18-21. It is beyond the scope of this work to attempt more than a superficial analysis of the Czechoslovak constitution, which is one of the most democratic in the world, imbued with the principle that the people are the sole source of authority. Every regulation attempts to express the popular will through the legislative bodies, cabinet and president. Although protecting racial minorities, it seeks foremost the unhindered expression of the will of the majority by permitting a three-fifths majority in parliament

The method of conducting foreign affairs is a vital matter in any study concerning foreign policy. The provisional constitution of Czechoslovakia provided specifically for the responsibility of the ministry to the National Assembly, a policy continued in the permanent constitution. Thus, to expedite matters, in actual practice, the Foreign Minister is required periodically to give reports of his activities to the Foreign Affairs Committees of the National Assembly. Article 64, Section 1, a, states that the President

shall represent the State in its relations with other States, shall negotiate and ratify international treaties. Commercial treaties, and treaties which for the State or its citizens entail financial or personal burdens, especially military burdens, as well as treaties affecting the territories of the State require the affirmation of Parliament. The affirmation of Parliament takes the form of a Constitutional Law (article 1 of the introductory law).

Czechoslovakia was particularly fortunate that Masaryk and Beneš were President and Foreign Minister, respectively, for so long after the establishment of independence. This assurance of continuity and consistency of policy was further enhanced by the close personal friendship of the two men. The conduct of Czechoslovakia's foreign policy is replete with instances wherein the major decisions were arrived at only after a conference between these founders of the new state.[29]

to accomplish almost anything—a prudent and necessary measure in view of the fact that thereby the Czechs and Slovaks have a sufficient margin of safety whereby they need not fear the obstructionist tactics of hostile Germans or Magyars. While universal suffrage was conceded, the conservative nature of the new régime was also assured by a bicameral parliament —a Senate of 150 members and a Chamber of Deputies of 300 members —and by a seven-year term for the president who is not eligible for more than two terms except for Masaryk, who was made president for life.

[29] Cf. Národní Shromáždění Československé v prvním roce Republiky (Praha, 1919); Jolly, E., Le Pouvoir legislatif dans la République Tchécoslovaque (Paris, 1924).

Czechoslovakia also faced the problem of obtaining a peace settlement that would guarantee her future stability and safety. Her prestige was high, because of the help afforded the Allies by her legions [30] in France, Italy and Russia, and because her leaders, particularly Masaryk and Beneš, had shown, by their actions and predictions, the most accurate understanding of Central European conditions and needs. Perhaps even more to the point was the fact that Czechoslovakia had already obtained the promise of a seat at the coming Peace Conference.[31]   Thus, certain of a sympathetic audience, she hoped to realize all her major contentions.

Before the Peace Conference met, Czechoslovakia was destined to suffer a considerable diminution of prestige because of the inexperience of her government. At the outset, the Provisional National Assembly attempted to direct foreign policy by appointing from its own members a foreign committee of sixteen to whom Beneš was required to send regular reports. It took little time to discover that this system was unsatisfactory. Not only was a committee of sixteen too large to work effectively, but it was found that many of the members, in their inexperience, were so naive as to inform foreign diplomats of internal affairs in which they

[30] At the end of the War, the Czechoslovak army included 92,000 men in Russia, 12,000 in France, 24,000 in Italy and 54,000 in the Italian so-called home guard, a total of 182,000 men. According to statistics compiled in 1923, these forces had suffered a loss of 4,500 men killed (*sic*) ; Masaryk, *op. cit.*, pp. 331-332. Later revised figures give slightly different totals; *cf. Svornost*, August 29, 1928. In the course of a trip through Vienna, Praha, Laibach and Trieste, December 28, 1918–January 14, 1919, to establish a United States courier service through Central and Southern Europe, Major A. J. Peaslee asked if Allied troops should be sent to Czechoslovakia to curb Bolshevik influences, protect the mines and give tangible evidence of Allied support. Masaryk stated that " he would not oppose it ", but preferred rather to have the Czechoslovak troops sent home from Allied countries. *Cf.* Miller, D. H., *My Diary at the Conference of Paris* (n. p., 1926), vol. iii, pp. 320-321.

[31] By the treaty of September 28, 1918, with France.

should have no concern. As an example, when Father Hlinka [32] organized his anti-Czech campaign in the rural non-partisan organization of the Czechoslovak Catholics in Praha, and was seconded by speeches of Juriga and Kordač,[33] information of which leaked out through members of the committee of sixteen, there came to Paris, about the middle of January, 1919, alarming rumors about the condition of the Republic, which was reputed ready for anarchy. Much was made of the friction between Kramář and other members, several of whom were alleged to be ready to resign. The fact was also brought out that Beneš wished to cooperate with the committee, but feared it was too often influenced unduly by party considerations. Things came to such a pass that he was finally compelled to protest that the domestic squabbles were creating an unfavorable foreign situation. His protest was heeded; two smaller units, the Foreign Affairs Committees of the Senate and of the Chamber of Deputies, which often met as one body (the Foreign Affairs Committee of the National Assembly), were created to receive his reports, and he was given a much freer hand in the conduct of foreign affairs.[34]

[32] Father Andrew Hlinka was an able, patriotic and popular Catholic priest who, during the War, was almost invaluable for his work in leading Slovak opposition to Hungary. After the War, neither he nor the other Slovak leaders were treated by the Czechs with the recognition they deserved. As a result of the neglect which his people suffered, he became embittered and began a campaign to free the Slovaks from the "oppressive" Czech rule. Cf. also, infra, p. 95.

[33] Juriga and Kordač were two Slovak members of parliament.

[34] Hrušovský, I., "Pět let zahraniční politiky československé za vedení Benešova", Anon., *Dr. Edvard Beneš, spoluzakladatel nové svobody a tvůrce zahraniční politiky československé* (henceforth referred to as *Dr. Edvard Beneš*, Praha, 1924), p. 126. For a comprehensive account of the organization of the foreign service, cf. Anon., *Deset let československé zahraniční politiky* (Praha, 1928). pp. 98-118.

Peace Conference Preliminaries

Beneš had not gone to Praha while the new government was in the process of formation, but had remained in Paris, maintaining contacts with the leading Allied diplomats. Before the Peace Conference opened, he had already secured important promises from the Great Powers. The exact methods by which the various Allied promises to further Czechoslovak claims were obtained have not been disclosed, but the results speak for themselves. In addition to the French promise of September 28, 1918, to attempt to obtain for Czechoslovakia her German-inhabited borderlands, and similar British and Italian commitments of January 7, 1919, Beneš obtained, by a note of December 20, 1918, a further French promise to support Czechoslovakia's claims on the Austrian frontier.[35] Thus fortified, he awaited with confidence the approaching Peace Conference.

In the course of the deliberations, questions of procedure became vexatious. One of the earliest problems was the point at which the small states were to enter the negotiations. Immediately after the Armistice, most of the proposals submitted by British and French statesmen regarding the Peace Conference specified that only the Great Powers could participate in the peace negotiations,[36] a viewpoint that was opposed by the small Powers and by the United States. This dissenting opinion was voiced best by D. H. Miller (November 22, 1918),[37] who recommended the participation of all the victor states in the negotiations. From the view-

[35] The best account of these activities of Beneš, while still inadequate as to specific details, is to be found in Vochoč, V., " Dr. Beneš a mírová konference pařižská ", *Dr. Edward Beneš*, pp. 85-92.

[36] *Cf.* Binkley, R. C., " New Light on the Paris Peace Conference ", *Political Science Quarterly*, vol. xlvi, pp. 339-350; Baker, R. S., *Woodrow Wilson and the World Settlement* (New York, 1922), vol. iii, pp. 56-63; Miller, *op. cit.*, vol. ii, pp. 14, 22-23, 81, 84.

[37] Miller, *op. cit.*, vol. ii, pp. 32-33.

point of the small states, this proposal was generous and fair, but it was open to criticism in that it excluded the defeated states from any voice in the deliberations. The question of representation was finally decided after an exchange of British and French opinions, December 11 and 13, 1918, by an agreement that each Great Power would be allowed five delegates; the lesser Allies, three each; the new states, two; states in the process of formation, one; neutrals, one; and that there would be no enemy representatives.[38] Subsequently, during January 12-17, 1919, procedure was modified further by a decision that the states with universal interests were the five Great Powers, and that all others had merely regional interests. The former might attend every session of the Conference, but the latter only those sessions in which their special interests were concerned.[39] Objections to this procedure on the part of the small Powers proved to be of no avail.[40]

Czechoslovakia was admitted to the first plenary session of January 18, 1919.[41] None of the new states had any better status than she: Yugoslavia was recognized as Serbia only; Albania, the newest pre-war state, was not granted any representation; and even Poland experienced greater initial difficulties because of internal friction between the

[38] *Ibid.*, vol. ii, pp. 295-296. *Cf. ibid.*, vol. i, pp. 379-446, for a list of all the delegates to the Peace Conference. Czechoslovakia sent a delegation of forty-six members, which included expert and technical advisors and other staff members.

[39] Miller, *op. cit.*, vol. iii, p. 274.

[40] *Ibid.*, vol. iv, pp. 68-77; Vochoč, *loc. cit.*, p. 85; House, E. M. and Seymour, C., *What Really Happened at Paris* (New York, 1921), pp. 16-17; Temperley, H. W. V., *History of the Peace Conference at Paris* (London, 1920), vol. i, pp. 236-278. *Cf.* also Baker, *op. cit.*, vol. i, pp. 177-180, for Allied fears that President Wilson and the small states would control the Peace Conference if equal representation were conceded.

[41] France promised such recognition in Article 3 of the treaty of September 28, 1918.

Warsaw government and the Comité National Polonaise at Paris.[42]

In view of the chaos in Central Europe, which was the scene of many small actual, if not official, wars, the Supreme Council, on January 24, 1919, issued a solemn warning to the world that no country should attempt to obtain its territorial claims forcibly, but should await a decision by the Peace Conference in every instance.[43] This warning was intended for the benefit of the victor, as well as the vanquished, states. For Czechoslovakia, having friction over prospective frontiers with Hungary on the south and Poland on the north, this warning meant a temporary reliance upon provisional agreements with the Allied High Command, an unsatisfactory procedure which kept the frontiers in a state of turmoil. Beneš stressed the point that the Czechoslovak question fitted into the framework of the new Europe. The sooner it was settled the better it would be for all concerned. As early as December, 1918, he had prepared a memoir [44] on the Czechoslovak program, and, early in February, 1919, had others ready in more detail on special questions.[45] These

[42] Vochoč, *loc. cit.*, pp. 91-92; Temperley, *op. cit.*, vol. iv, p. 131. The scope of this work does not permit more than a general discussion of only those aspects of the Peace Conference that are of particular interest to Czechoslovakia. The general uncertainty that still prevails today concerning the intimate workings of the Peace Conference can perhaps be best appreciated by a perusal of Binkley, R. C., " Ten Years of Peace Conference History ", *Journal of Modern History*, vol. i, pp. 607-629. *Cf.* also, Miller, D. H., *The Drafting of the Covenant* (New York, 1928, vol. i, discussion; vol. ii, documents).

[43] Temperley, *op. cit.*, vol. iv, p. 132; Thompson, C. T., *The Peace Conference Day by Day* (New York, 1920), pp. 137-139.

[44] *Peace Conference Delegation, 1919, Memoirs* (Official claims of the Czechoslovak Delegation, Paris, 1919); Miller, *My Diary at the Conference of Paris*, vol. xiv, pp. 211-225.

[45] By February 1, 1919, only Czechoslovakia, and Greece, in part, had submitted official territorial claims. *Cf.* Miller, *op. cit.*, vol. xiv, p. 161 *et seq.*

memoirs contained a general account of the place of the Czechoslovaks in the framework of the world, the reasons for their territorial demands, detailed accounts of the problems of the Germans in Bohemia, of Těšín (Teschen), of Slovakia, of Ruthenia, of the Sorbs of Lusatia, of the corridor between Austria and Hungary to Yugoslavia, of the region of Kladno (Glatz), of the southern frontier, and a statement of Czechoslovakia's rights in the matter of reparations. In presenting these claims, Beneš' chief concern was that, because of her newness, Czechoslovakia might have less weight than her power and resources would normally entitle her to have,[46] a difficulty that was being experienced by the other Succession States as well.

The Territorial Settlement

After receiving a tentative report on Czechoslovakia's boundaries on January 21, 1919,[47] the Big Ten took up the question officially on January 27,[48] and four days later authorized an Inter-Allied Commission for Těšín [49] because of the complex nature of that particular dispute. On February 5, the Supreme Council granted Beneš a hearing,[50] as a result of which there was created a special territorial commission for Czechoslovak affairs.[51] With regard to the boundaries of Czechoslovakia, the Conference came early to definite conclusions, usually favorable to the new state. It was soon found difficult to compel the other parties concerned to abide by the awards, for the disappointed states felt that they could not lose more by contesting unfavorable decisions.

[46] *Československá Korespondence*, February 25, 1919.

[47] Miller, *op. cit.*, vol. iv, pp. 230-232.

[48] Vochoč, *loc. cit.*, pp. 96-98.

[49] Temperley, *op. cit.*, vol. iv, p. 132.

[50] *Ibid.*, vol. i, p. 503.

[51] *Ibid.*, vol. iv, p. 132; vol. i, p. 257; Binkley, *loc. cit.*, p. 536.

When the historic and linguistic boundaries were not identical, which factor should prevail, history or ethnography? The former Kingdom of Bohemia was an excellent illustration of this conflict of principles, with the center inhabited by Czechs and the entire northern and western frontiers peopled by Germans. The strong mutual antipathy between the two races, productive of almost incessant friction for centuries, had been intensified as a result of the War. Should peoples whose relationship had been so exacerbated be compelled to live together in the new Republic? In spite of the general Wilsonian principle that, whenever possible, political and linguistic boundaries should coincide, Bohemia was recognized as an exception, as an instance where history was deemed more important than ethnic purity.[52] Bohemia proper was an economic and geographical unit, strategically protected in part by nature. To deprive her of her mountain frontiers would be tantamount to handing her over to Germany which would control all the mountain passes and be within thirty miles of Praha. The Czechs contended that the Germans had been installed artificially in Bohemia either as colonists, officials or bureaucrats, a contention that they had deemed proved even before the War, by the fact that there had become manifest, as an evidence of the economic interests that bound the country together, the phenomenon of a Czech counter-colonization of these same German regions.[53]

[52] Cf. Hazen, C. D., Europe since 1815 (New York, 1923), vol. ii, pp. 812-814; Haskins and Lord, op. cit., pp. 212-222; Scott, A. P., An Introduction to the Peace Treaties (Chicago, 1920), pp. 213-215.

[53] House and Seymour, op. cit., pp. 103-104; Pichon, J. E., " Les Frontiers de l'état tchécoslovaque ", Questions européennes, Travaux du comité d'études, tome ii, pp. 107-116 (Rapport présenté à la séance du 7 mars, 1919) ; Peace Conference Delegation, 1919, Memoirs, no. 3, " Le Problème des Allemands de Bohème ".

Shortly after the hearing of February 5, 1919, the Czecho-slovak territorial demands were submitted in detail to the Conference. Originally, Beneš' plans had contemplated strict adherence to the historic Bohemian frontiers, but later they were modified for economic, military, political or strategic reasons. Within Czechoslovakia there existed differences of opinion as to what the frontiers should be with Saxony and Prussian Silesia, whether to demand all Glatz or merely the southwestern portion.[54] The frontier rectifications fin-ally requested by Czechoslovakia included in Prussian Silesia a line incorporating Hlubčice, Ratibor, Rybník and Těšin, with the right bank of the Oder, and in Saxony, in the Krušne Mountains and along the Elbe, changes of two or three kilometers in seven places. For relinquishing Glatz, compensation was suggested in northern Opava, and a portion of the Rumberk salient was offered for an increase in the Frydland salient.[55]

Immediately after its organization in February, 1919, the territorial commission on Czechoslovakia began its labors; in common with other similar commissions, its verdict was to be announced by March 8, but it did not present any report until early in April.[56] As early as February 28, *Le Temps* announced that the question of the Bohemian Germans was settled, and by March 1 was positive that Czechoslovakia would obtain the historic frontier. The requested changes in the historic frontier were then con-sidered, particularly the cession to Germany of Cheb up to Falknov in order to obtain Glatz and a portion of Upper

[54] Vochoč, *loc. cit.*, p. 101.

[55] *Peace Conference Delegation, 1919, Memoirs*, no. 2, "Les Revendi-cations territoriales de la République tchécoslovaque"; no. 9, "Le Problème de la région de Glatz"; Beneš, E., *Problemy nové Evropy a zahraniční politika československá* (henceforth referred to as *Problemy nové Evropy*, Praha, 1924), pp. 16-21; Vochoč, *loc. cit.*, pp. 101-102.

[56] *Cf.* Miller, *op. cit.*, vol. vi, pp. 43-52 (date uncertain).

Silesia on the left bank of the Oder, the right bank having been refused by the commission. After due consideration, the territorial commission conceded the principal requests of Czechoslovakia, rectifying in her favor the frontier at Glatz, Hlučin and Hlubčice.[57] This report of the commission, approved on April 2 by the four foreign ministers and the American Secretary of State, was shortly afterwards rejected by the Council of Four which refused to change the historic frontier without further examination, for the reasons that the old frontier was the simpler and easier to maintain, would avoid friction with Germany, and would require no delimitation commission.[58] Even the Council of Four finally permitted some changes in favor of Czechoslovakia. On April 17, she was granted Hlučin and Hlubčice on the alleged grounds that these regions formed an awkward salient into Czech Silesia from Upper Silesia, which had recently been awarded to Poland.[59]

On the whole, the problem of the Bohemian Germans had caused much less grief to the Czechs than they had anticipated. Great Britain, France and Italy had already arrived at an understanding to create a Czechoslovakia with easily defensible frontiers and substantial economic resources, regardless of the fact that such a program necessitated the inclusion of large minorities.[60] The three Powers envisaged Czechoslovakia as an Allied rampart against the resuscitation of Pan-Germanism and desired to strengthen her by establishing direct contact with Rumania.[61] Beneš appreciated that any possible objections on the part of President Wilson to

[57] *Ibid.*, vol. xvi, pp. 11-16.

[58] House and Seymour, *op. cit.*, p. 100.

[59] Temperley, *op. cit.*, vol. iv, pp. 267-270; Miller, *op. cit.*, vol. vi, p. 353; Vochoč, *loc. cit.*, p. 104.

[60] Miller, *op. cit.*, vol. xvi, pp. 11-16 (April 1, 1919).

[61] *Ibid.*, vol. xvii, p. 94.

the violation of the principle of national self-determination would arise only if the Bohemian Germans could create their own state and if Czechoslovakia could exist without them.[62] Since such an alternative was manifestly impossible, the United States approved the Allied program. Consequently, when Austria proposed a plebiscite for German Bohemia, the Allies reiterated their intention to maintain the historic frontiers to the greatest possible degree.[63]

On the Austrian frontier, Czechoslovak requests included the railroad at Gmünd, the Czechoslovak minorities at Postorna and Valčić, and the river systems of the Morava and its tributary, the Dyje. Although the Big Four had arrived at a definite decision concerning the Austrian frontier as early as May 13, 1919, the terms were not made public until June 2. Czechoslovakia obtained most of the desired areas in Vitorazko and Postorna, with the right bank of the Morava, but in Gmünd was restricted to the station and railway across the Valčić.[64]

Another Czechoslovak request was for a narrow corridor between Austria and Hungary to establish direct territorial contact with Yugoslavia. Although some Slav minorities did exist in this region, the motivation for the request was strategic. Of all the Powers, France alone favored the creation of the corridor, for military reasons; the others objected with equal frankness: the United States, for ethnographic reasons; Great Britain, because of the indefensibility of the corridor in time of war, and Italy, as prejudicial to her own interests. Hence, the project was rejected first by the

[62] *Ibid.*, vol. xvi, p. 12; Vochoč, *loc. cit.*, p. 105.

[63] House and Seymour, *op. cit.*, p. 97; *cf.* also, Baker, *op. cit.*, vol. iii, pp. 249-252, for Clemenceau's note of March 31, 1919, to Wilson, in reply to Lloyd George's note of March 26, asking for normal frontiers for Czechoslovakia (i. e. to include the German-speaking areas).

[64] Miller, *op. cit.*, vol. xvi, pp. 234-235, 272; Temperley, *op. cit.*, vol. iv, p. 267; Vochoč, *loc. cit.*, p. 105.

territorial commission and later by the Council of Four. Czechoslovakia was granted a small bridge-head [65] on the right side of the Danube, as consolation and as a partial protection for Bratislava, but with the explicit condition that no fortifications were to be constructed on the southern side of the river.[66]

Two other extreme Czechoslovak requests were special pleas for the Czech minority in Lower Austria and for the Sorbs of Lusatia. It was evident that neither minority could be annexed, and doubtful what degree, if any, of autonomy would or could be conceded by Austria and Germany respectively. According to the Austrian census of 1910, the Czechs in Lower Austria numbered 122,329 (102,000 in Vienna), but the Czechs claimed fully 400,000. A compromise was finally reached when Articles 62 and 69 of the Treaty of St. Germain protected the rights of this minority. Czechoslovakia fared worse when she urged that the 160,000 Sorbs in the districts of Cottbus and Bautzen be removed from the respective jurisdictions of Prussia and Saxony, and autonomously united with the latter. The request met with an outright refusal.[67]

Czechoslovakia was no more consistent than other claimants in the arguments she advanced: in determining her frontiers with Germany and Austria, she had appealed to the doctrine of historic frontiers, but in the case of Hungary, she argued against the same doctrine in order to obtain Slovakia. In the realization that Hungary's claim to Slovakia was over a thousand years old, Czechoslovakia appealed instead to the right of national self-determination. Although separated for more than a millennium, the patriots

[65] Four square kilometers.

[66] Temperley, *op. cit.*, vol. iv, pp. 273-274.

[67] *Ibid.*, vol. iv, pp. 275-276; *Peace Conference Delegation, 1919, Memoirs*, no. 7, "Les Serbes de Lusace".

among the Czechs of Bohemia and the Slovaks of Hungary
had never forgotten their common origin, nor the fact that
they spoke practically the same language.[68] Few peoples in
all Europe had resisted more tenaciously efforts at assimilation on the part of their neighbors. Many of the leaders
of each deemed the War an opportunity for freedom and
union, and realized that union was essential to both; otherwise, each would be so weak numerically and so exposed
geographically as to be unable to maintain independence, even
if acquired. These leaders came to regard Slovakia as an
integral part of the new Republic.[69]

The northern boundary of Slovakia, between Galicia and
Hungary, was well defined both by history and by natural
mountain barriers, but the southern boundary remained in
serious doubt. Here, strong arguments could be advanced
against any line that might be suggested; many decades of
attempted Magyarization had left no well defined ethno-
logical boundary. Since the armistice of November 3, 1918,
with Austria-Hungary had drawn no southern boundary for
Slovakia, Beneš was anxious to establish one as soon as
possible. To this end, he began to negotiate with France.
In response to his request, a temporary military boundary
was drawn a month later by the Allied High Command along
the Danube to the mouth of the Ipel, along it to Řimavská
Sobota, then to the mouth of the Uha, and along it to the
Uzok.[70] However, Beneš still deemed this boundary insufficient, and, in January, 1919, requested instead the
Danube to Vacov and a southeastern frontier along the
heights of Matra, Buk and Tokaj, and the Bodrog and Uha

---

[68] *Cf.* Dominian, L., *The Frontiers of Language and Nationality in
Europe* (New York, 1917), pp. 150-151.

[69] *Cf.* Stanoyevich, M. S., *Slavonic Nations of Yesterday and Today*
(New York, 1925), pp. 267-322.

[70] *Svornost*, December 29, 1918.

rivers.[71]   The territorial commission pointed out that this line would include large Magyar minorities and would still leave considerable Slovak minorities in Hungary.[72]

Before the question of the Hungarian boundary came up for consideration by the Peace Conference in May, 1919, the situation was made more complex by Hungarian resistance.   Czechoslovakia found herself compelled to wage actual war if she were to hope to retain Slovakia.   To recapitulate, the armistice of November 3, 1918, had been drawn primarily with Italian interests in view, hence was incomplete in its provisions for the future.   To remedy this defect, another Military Convention for Hungary, signed on November 13 at Belgrade, provided for the occupation of a specified region in Hungary [73] and for the demobilization of all Hungarian forces except two cavalry and six infantry divisions.[74]   Serbia was thus protected, but Rumania and Czechoslovakia were neglected.

On December 3, 1918, the Peace Conference requested that Count Karolyi, who came into power in Hungary at the time of the armistice, evacuate Slovakia, and five days later Czech troops occupied northern Slovakia as far as the demarcation line, half-way between the Carpathians and the Danube.   Since the Czechs claimed all Slovakia, they announced they would not observe this line any longer on December 13, and advanced to the Danube.   The advance was aided by the arrival of French troops at Prešov and Košice on December 28.   On New Year's Day, the French gave over Bratislava to the Czechs, who occupied all Slovakia.   The final step was taken, apparently, with the draw-

[71] *Peace Conference Delegation, 1919, Memoirs,* no. 5, "La Slovaquie—le territoire revendique en Slovaquie".

[72] House and Seymour, *op. cit.,* p. 105; Vochoč, *loc. cit.,* p. 102.

[73] By the agreement, this region might also be extended, if necessary.

[74] Beneš, *My War Memoirs,* pp. 459-466; Temperley, *op. cit.,* vol. i, pp. 351-352.

ing of the southern boundary by the military authorities [75] on February 13, 1919.   Thus far, in obedience to Karolyi's orders, the Hungarians had attempted no resistance.[76]

In the meantime, Hungarian affairs came to a crisis that resulted in the overthrow of Karolyi and the establishment of a Soviet government on March 31, with Garbai the nominal President, but with Bela Kun actually in control.[77]   The new government proclaimed an alliance with Russian Bolshevism.   It also proceeded to utilize the services of numerous unemployed officers of the former German and Austro-Hungarian armies.   Although these officers probably abhorred communism, they apparently grasped eagerly at the idea of using it as an excuse for armed resistance and as a tool with which to recover lost territory.[78]   However, the new forces were for many weeks quite ineffective.   The Rumanians took advantage of this fact in April to advance to the Theiss River, beyond the lines permitted them.[79]

Similarly, the Czechs advanced southward and occupied Salgo-Tarjan and Miskolcz.   On May 1, at Čap, the Czech

[75] By Foch and Weygand, who were in consultation with Beneš, Pichon and Berthelot.

[76] Opočenský, *op. cit.*, pp. 193-214; Beneš, *op. cit.*, pp. 472-483; Masaryk, *op. cit.*, p. 486; Hrušovský, *loc. cit.*, pp. 143-145.

[77] *Cf.* Temperley, *op. cit.*, vol. i, p. 353.   An Allied demand of March 19 that all Hungarian forces be withdrawn for temporary military reasons behind a line representing Rumania's extreme claims was interpreted by Karolyi as a claim for frontiers impossible for Hungary to accept, and as the basis for his resignation, particularly after news arrived the following day of the cession of Transylvania to Rumania.   Baker, *op. cit.*, vol. ii, pp. 29-30; *cf.* Thompson, *op. cit.*, pp. 261-264, 273-275 and 279-280 for the various studies and investigations of the Supreme Council on the Hungarian situation during March, 1919.

[78] *Cf.* Kaas, Baron A. and Lazarovics, F. de, *Bolshevism in Hungary* (London, 1931), pp. 170-173; Jaszi, O., *Revolution and Counter-Revolution in Hungary* (London, 1924), p. 153; Huszar, K., *Proletarier Diktatur in Ungarn* (Regensburg, 1920), pp. 180-184.

[79] Kaas and Lazarovics, *op. cit.*, pp. 184-185; Temperley, *op. cit.*, vol. i, p. 354.

left wing established contact with the Rumanian right.   The imminent joint advance, which gave great promise of success, was prevented by the Supreme Council's orders that the Rumanians must not advance beyond the Theiss.   Thus protected, the bulk of the Hungarian army was transferred from the Rumanian front to Slovakia, where the Czech forces were scattered over large areas difficult to defend. In the estimation of Bela Kun, the prospects were favorable: a successful offensive in Slovakia would consolidate his domestic position, regain the valuable mining areas of Salgo-Tarjan and Miskolcz, separate Czechs and Rumanians, and possibly open the way for a Russian advance across the Carpathians.   In this crisis, the Supreme Council displayed little energy.   Instead of ordering Bela Kun to evacuate Slovakia, and of promising an equivalent Rumanian with-drawal, it ordered Rumania to withdraw beyond a new frontier that had been drawn secretly without her consent. As might be anticipated, Rumania refused to obey, where-upon the Powers again confessed their weakness and inde-cision by making no attempt to coerce her.[80]

During the struggle for Slovakia, one of the greatest handicaps of both contestants was the shortage of ammuni-tion.   The Škoda works had not, as yet, resumed full opera-tion, whereas Hungary had no munition works of her own, but was dependent upon purchases from Italy.   The Czechs demanded that the Austrian government turn over war material then in Vienna, and, after an initial refusal, Austria was compelled to yield the 60,000 shells in question under the threat of a stoppage of the coal supply.   Nevertheless, by the end of the first week in June, 1919, the position of the Czechs had become critical: the front had been pierced at several points, over one-third of Slovakia had been lost,

---

[80] Temperley, *op. cit.*, vol. i, p. 355; Dillon, E. J., *The Inside Story of the Peace Conference* (New York, 1920), p. 217.

Košice was evacuated as a result of an uprising of the neighboring Hungarian minority, the Czechs were in full retreat on the whole front, and even Bratislava was in jeopardy and was falsely reported to have fallen. Then France saved the day; her generals [81] assumed command and by June 11 had regained several points. However, the Hungarians still retained the valuable mineral and industrial areas, particularly the coal fields which they deemed vital for Hungary's existence.[82]

As Czechoslovakia's prestige continued to decline, Beneš sent three appeals to the Peace Conference for help.[83] By early June the Powers were disgusted with the situation; to them every Central European problem appeared as a menace to general peace and as a verification of the Balkanization of Europe. Since something had to be done, the Big Four, on June 9, sent Bela Kun an ultimatum demanding an immediate cessation of hostilities in Slovakia. To make the ultimatum more acceptable, they added a promise of " provisional recognition " in return. Bela Kun temporized, his hesitation being interpreted as a refusal both by the Powers and by the " White " Hungarian counter-revolutionists. Four days later, as Bela Kun was attempting another advance in Slovakia, he received a second ultimatum which ordered again a cessation of hostilities against the Czechs and a withdrawal within Hungary's own frontiers under a threat of a French

[81] Pelle, Mittelhauser and Hennocque.

[82] Temperley, *op. cit.*, vol. i, p. 355; Kaas and Lazarovics, *op. cit.*, p. 190.

[83] On March 8, 1919, a letter from Beneš requested the Allied and Associated Governments to send an energetic protest to Budapest and Vienna to cease military activities and propaganda hostile to Czechoslovakia (Miller, *op. cit.*, vol. xv, pp. 315-320). On March 24, 1919, Beneš requested the Inter-Allied War Council to hold Hungary to its decision of December 21, 1918, to evacuate Slovakia (Miller, *op. cit.*, vol. xvii, pp. 435-437). On April 9, 1919, Beneš requested Allied support to recover the locomotives the Hungarians had taken from Slovakia (Miller, *op. cit.*, vol. xvii, p. 435).

and Rumanian advance from Arad. This time Bela Kun yielded, as gracefully as circumstances permitted, since, in any event, a withdrawal would have been forced under the pressure of successful Czech counter-attacks and of counter-revolutionary uprisings in western Hungary. As a forlorn hope, the Hungarians, before withdrawing, set up a Slovakian Soviet Republic which endured only a few days.[84]

At this point the center of interest shifted to Rumania, which was disgusted by the indifference of the Supreme Council to Hungarian Bolshevism and by her own treatment by that august body. Rumania refused to abandon the line of the Theiss River before Hungary had demobilized according to Article 2 of the Convention of November 13, 1918. For once, her attitude met with the approval of the Allied military leaders, who admitted that Bela Kun had violated that agreement. Thereupon, the Supreme Council took the first active step for the suppression of Hungarian Bolshevism on July 17, 1919, when General Franchet d'Esperey threatened military intervention if the Soviet government did not resign and yield to a government freely elected by the people.[85] To render effective this Allied threat, Marshal Foch drew up a plan of campaign against Hungary whereby Rumania was to furnish 120,000 men; Yugoslavia, 50,000; and Czechoslovakia whatever she could spare, about 85,000.[86] On July 20, one day before these preparations were to be begun, Bela Kun succeeded in surprising the Rumanians and driving them across the Theiss with a loss of seventy-five field guns and thirty-six heavy guns. If the Hungarian reports were correct, the Rumanian line was broken on a

[84] *The Times* (London, henceforth referred to as *The Times*), July 2, 1919; *New York Times*, June 13, 14, 16, 18, 21, 25 and 26, 1919; Temperley, *op. cit.*, vol. i, p. 355.

[85] Temperley, *op. cit.*, vol. i, p. 356.

[86] Dillon, *op. cit.*, pp. 221-222.

front of from fifteen to thirty-five kilometers.[87]   Again the Supreme Council lost heart: instead of adopting actively Foch's plan, it sent agents to exhort the Hungarians to eliminate Bela Kun.   As might be expected, these efforts availed nothing.   More belligerent was the spirit of Rumania: vigorous counter-attacks were ordered, and the initial successes were followed by a general advance which did not halt until August 8, at which time all Hungary east of the Danube was in Rumanian hands.   Rumania dictated a new armistice whereby she recovered much of the property she had lost during the War.   Bela Kun did not await the end, but fled on August 1.   Bolshevism collapsed, the " reds ", after a brief interlude of Social Democrat rule under Peidl, being succeeded by " white " counter-revolutionists led by Horthy.   One reign of terror was succeeded by another.[88]   In all this, Rumania had learned to disregard the orders of the Powers, and, instead, confronted them with the fait accompli.[89]

Throughout this struggle, Czechoslovakia had not been at war with Hungary officially, but de facto.   Officially, the fiction of peace between the two countries had been maintained; the struggle had been regarded as a defense of Slovakia against the incursions of bands of irresponsible irregulars, of outlaws, whose attacks necessitated the employment of the armed forces of the Republic, but did not require a formal declaration of war against the country from whence they came.   The Czechoslovak government realized that final triumph had been attained by the aid of

[87] *The Times*, July 21, 1919.

[88] *Cf.* Graham, *op. cit.*, pp. 218-236 for further details of the régime of Bela Kun, and pp. 236-238 for the counter-revolutionary movements; also, Kaas and Lazarovics, *op. cit.*, pp. 294-315; Jaszi, *op. cit.*, pp. 110-152 (Bela Kun) and 177-211 (Horthy).

[89] *The Times*, August 4, 1919; Temperley, *op. cit.*, vol. i, pp. 356-357; vol. iv, pp. 487-490; Dillon, *op. cit.*, pp. 222-242.

friendly Powers, and that the struggle had revealed many defects in the military establishment that had to be remedied as soon as possible. An integral province of the Republic had been retained, and an external Bolshevik invasion had been repelled, yet the attendant circumstances had served to confirm the conviction of the Czechs that Bolshevism had been used by Hungary merely as the weapon of the moment. Although the sympathy of Russia for the success of Hungarian Bolshevism had been clearly manifested, Czechoslovakia still retained a suspicion that the war for Slovakia owed its inception to Budapest rather than to Moscow.[90]

While the issue of the armed struggle still hung in the balance, the Peace Conference had continued its efforts to determine the various frontiers of Hungary. On June 11, the foreign ministers listened to the final arguments of Bratianu for Rumania, Pašič for Yugoslavia, and Beneš for Czechoslovakia, and on the following day, drew a boundary favorable to Czechoslovakia. The question was difficult because of the absence of any clearly-defined linguistic frontier. In spite of the fact that the census of 1910 had given Bratislava 31,705 Magyars, 32,790 Germans and only 11,673 Slovaks, the city was granted to Czechoslovakia because the rural districts were solidly Slovak to its walls and because of the principle that a city should not be separated from its hinterland.[91]

To the east, as far as the mouth of the Ipel, practical considerations made the Danube the boundary. Much more debatable was the granting to Czechoslovakia of the Grosse

---

[90] Cf. Kadlec, K., "Magyars and the Czechoslovak Republic", The Czechoslovak Review, vol. iv, pp. 58-64. Cf. also, Miller, op. cit., vol. xviii, pp. 40-49, for Inter-Allied Investigation Commission's report on Austrian, German and Hungarian plotting within Czechoslovakia. One of the best accounts of the struggle is Chaloupecký, V., Zapas o Slovensko (Praha, 1930).

[91] Temperley, op. cit., vol. iv, p. 270.

Schütt, the extensive and fertile island extending almost from Bratislava to Komorno. Here again, in spite of a Magyar majority, because of economic dependence upon Slovakia and because the southern channel of the Danube would make almost an ideal frontier, the island was included with Slovakia. This decision was reached after a severe struggle. France desired to award the whole island to Czechoslovakia, whereas the United States believed that Hungary should retain it. Ultimately, the American delegates gave way when it was pointed out that a strictly ethnical line, as far as it could be determined, would create additional economic hardships by the manner in which it would cut across all the railways, and when Hungary was promised a more favorable frontier line further to the east.[92] In the course of the deliberations, it was stated also that Masaryk had promised the South African delegate, General Smuts, that he would not claim the Grosse Schütt if Czechoslovakia were conceded a bridge-head to protect Bratislava. The French delegate, Pichon, induced one of his colleagues, Laroche, to state that Beneš had informed him that Smuts had " completely misunderstood " Masaryk.[93] Miller points out that Laroche allegedly obtained, via Beneš, Masaryk's denial of ever having countenanced such a proposition.[94]

Eastward from the Ipel, Czechoslovakia received considerably less than she requested. Her extreme claims to the predominantly Magyar towns of Miskolcz, Sarospatak and Vacov, to the coal mines of Salgo-Tarjan and to the vineyards of Tokaj were disallowed, in spite of the fact that these areas did contain Slovak minorities. Similarly, Hungary was granted Satoralja-Ujhely, but the railway station, a mile distant, and the junction of the railways from Čap

---

[92] Nicolson, H., *Peacemaking* (New York, 1933), p. 275.

[93] *Ibid.*, p. 324.

[94] Miller, *op. cit.*, vol. xvi, p. 216.

and from Košice were left within Czechoslovakia for strategic reasons, in order to establish direct communications
with Rumania, via Subcarpathian Ruthenia.[95]

Beneš requested Ruthenia on the grounds of national self-
determination. His request was supported by a Ruthenian
delegation to which the Czechoslovak promise of the greatest
degree of autonomy compatible with the unity of the Republic appeared favorable. What were the alternatives?
Subcarpathian Ruthenian independence was out of the
question because of numerical weakness. A union with
kinsmen in either Poland or the Ukraine, on the opposite
side of the Carpathians, would be unnatural geographically.
The Supreme Council feared particularly a union with
Russia, that would not only add to the area controlled by
Bolsheviks, but which would expose the small states of
Central Europe to a serious strategic danger, if Russia ever
obtained a foothold to the west of the Carpathians. Most
of the Ruthenian leaders did not desire a union with alien
Rumania, and, above all, sought to escape from Hungary.
As Slavs, they had already expressed their desire to unite
with their Czech and Slovak kinsmen. Hence they not only
gladly accepted the liberal concessions promised by Czechoslovakia, but, of their own accord, came to the Peace Conference to add their plea to that of Beneš. On the other
hand, to Czechoslovakia, Ruthenia would be a welcome economic asset and would establish immediate territorial contact
with friendly Rumania.[96] In view of all these factors, the
Supreme Council agreed to the union on May 12, 1919.[97]

[95] Baker, op. cit., vol. ii, p. 312; Temperley, op. cit., vol. iv, p. 272;
Miller, op. cit., vol. xii, pp. 207-214; vol. xvi, pp. 215-217, 229-231, 274-
275; also cf. ibid., vol. xvii, p. 134, how Italy and the United States
stressed ethnology, and Great Britain and France, geography and military
strategy, in drawing the frontiers of Slovakia.

[96] Cf. Chmelár, J., Klíma, S. and Nečas, J., Podkarpatska Rus (Praha,
1923).

[97] Temperley, op. cit., vol. iv, pp. 272-273; Miller, op. cit., vol. xvi, pp.

There still remained the question of the boundary with Poland in the districts of Těšin, Orava and Spíš, the most difficult of all the boundary disputes and the one that required the longest time for final settlement. The Inter-Allied Commission created by the Peace Conference to solve the problem encountered many unexpected obstacles. For many years, until a compromise satisfactory to both parties could be attained, the friction engendered by this dispute threatened to cause war between Czechoslovakia and Poland.[98]

Czechoslovakia was successful in realizing her cardinal contentions on boundary questions. Even if some of her minor and more extreme demands had been disallowed, she had met with more than adequate recognition of her territorial needs. Henceforth, a satiated power territorially, she became one of the most ardent supporters of the maintenance of the status quo and of the inviolability of the Peace Treaties.[99]

Other Peace Conference Problems

Czechoslovakia had other problems at the Peace Conference besides those connected with her frontiers. In addition to trying to obtain war materials against Hungary, as has already been mentioned, Beneš, after the death of Štefánik,[100]

271-272. *Cf.* also, *ibid.*, vol. xvi, pp. 386-387 for drawing of Czechoslovak-Rumanian boundary on June 12, 1919.

[98] For full details, *cf. infra*, pp. 148 *et seq.*

[99] For the boundaries of Czechoslovakia, *cf.* Articles 27, 81, 82, 83 and 87 of the Treaty of Versailles; Articles 27, 53 and 91 of the Treaty of St. Germain; Articles 27, 48 and 75 of the Treaty of Trianon; and Articles 1-2 of the Frontiers Treaty of Sèvres; also *La Gazette de Prague*, August 4, 1920. Poland lost the Silesian plebiscite, hence Czechoslovakia failed to benefit as she had expected from Article 83 of the Treaty of Versailles.

[100] Milan Štefánik, Czechoslovakia's first Minister of War, was killed in an aeroplane accident on May 4, 1919, en route from Italy to Czechoslovakia.

negotiated with the Allies, particularly with the United States, for the return of the Czechoslovak forces from Siberia,[101] with France for the training of the Czechoslovak army, and with Hoover for provisions.[102] Then there were the questions of disarmament, minorities, the Anschluss, or union between Austria and Germany, reparations, and of obtaining for Czechoslovakia outlets by river and by rail across the territories of her neighbors.

The Great Powers feared lest the development of too much " individualism " by the new states injure their own prestige and interests. Thus, the initial plan on disarmament, prepared on May 23, 1919, by a commission of Inter-Allied generals, provided that all the Succession States would have to agree to armaments limited proportionally to those of the defeated states.[103] This plan was opposed by all the Succession States, on the grounds that such armaments would not be sufficient and because they believed a distinction should be drawn between vanquished and victor states. There followed the so-called American plan which met these objections in part. This new plan, which was negotiated partially by Beneš and Wilson in person and which allowed Poland 80,000 men and Czechoslovakia 50,000, also failed of general acceptance on June 5, 1919. One of the deplorable aspects of the failure of these initial attempts to limit armaments was the belief prevalent in Paris regarding the ease with which all the evils of the " Balkanization of Europe " were to be avoided. Acceptance of the principle of disarmament combined with demands for more arms for the time being, because of a general lack of faith in the

[101] For full details, *cf. infra*, pp. 114 *et seq.*

[102] *Cf.* Vochoč, *loc. cit.*, p. 99. Hoover was Food Relief Administrator.

[103] Baker, *op. cit.*, vol. i, pp. 403-404. Germany was allowed 100,000 men; Austria, 15,000; Hungary, 18,000; Bulgaria, 10,000; Greece, 12,000; Czechoslovakia, 22,000; Yugoslavia, 20,000; Rumania, 28,000; and Poland, 44,000.

immediate efficacy of the League of Nations, meant nothing of practical value.[104]

The minorities treaty for Czechoslovakia had been projected as early as May 22, 1919, but was not signed by Beneš and Kramář until September 10. Beneš signed without hesitation, for he realized that the treaty safeguarded the rights of the majority also, whereas Kramář required persuasion to sign, for he preferred to amend certain clauses so they would apply equally to all members of the League of Nations.[105] Article 14 of this treaty placed all the preceding Articles under the guarantee of the League, which was thereby made responsible for certain obligations, of which the most important were the following:

1. These Articles, not the minorities, were put under the guarantee of the League of Nations.

2. These Articles might not be modified without the consent of a majority of the Council.

3. The United States, Great Britain, France, Italy and Japan agreed not to withhold their assent to modifications approved by a majority of the Council.

4. Any member of the Council might set the machinery in motion by calling attention to an infraction or to danger of infraction, but a minority itself was unable to do so.[106]

Identical treaties were signed by Poland, Austria and Yugoslavia on the same day. Nevertheless, Yugoslavia and

[104] Temperley, op. cit., vol. iv, pp. 136-137; Vochoč, loc. cit., pp. 87-88; Baker, op. cit., vol. i, p. 406. Cf. also, ibid., vol. iii, pp. 218-224, the confidential report of April 11, 1919, of Major General F. J. Kernan to President Wilson on conditions in Central Europe and on the armies of Poland and Czechoslovakia.

[105] House and Seymour, op. cit., pp. 211-215; Miller, op. cit., vol. ix, pp. 256-260, 263; vol. xiii, pp. 23-25.

[106] Nouveau recueil général de traités et autres actes relatifs aux rapports de droit international (henceforth referred to as Nouveau recueil), iii série, vol. xiii, pp. 512 et seq.

Rumania, although signing, made almost identical protests against such limitations upon their sovereignty, particularly since Italy was not required to bind herself similarly.[107] Even Czechoslovakia was not entirely satisfied, and, in the Third Session of the Assembly, stressed the point that minorities disloyal to the state should lose all right of appeal for protection to the League, regardless of the fact that some other state, friendly to them, might make an appeal in their behalf. She argued that the act of signing a minorities treaty should not bind a state any further, but that any subsequent arrangements that might be adopted should be made to apply equally to all League members without any discrimination whatever.[108]   In conclusion, to demonstrate her good faith, Czechoslovakia, which had already been questioned in advance by the Peace Conference concerning the measures she intended to adopt towards the Bohemian Germans, submitted in detail a liberal program which conceded far more than had been demanded by the treaty, which, in the last analysis, had been intended merely as a minimum program.[109]

In most of the Succession States, the agitation on behalf of the Minorities Treaties had been led by the Jews. Within the Republic, they increased in importance from west to east, numbering 1.27 percent of the population in

[107] Temperley, *op. cit.*, vol. iv, p. 138.

[108] Beneš, *Problemy nové Evropy*, pp. 200-201; Hajn, A., " Ochrana národnostních menšin—otázkou mezinárodní ", *Zahraniční Politika*, vol. i, pp. 88-92; *cf.* also, Kellor, F. A., *Security against War* (New York, 1924), vol. i, pp. 70-79.

[109] Fouques-Duparc, J., *La Protection des Minorités* (Paris, 1922), p. 179; Pergler, C., " Minorities in Czechoslovakia ", *Current History*, vol. xvii, pp. 310-311; Miller, *op. cit.*, vol. xiii, pp. 403-407. *Cf.* also, Thompson, *op. cit.*, pp. 386-387, for joint protest of May 31, 1919, of Bratianu, Trumbič, Dmowski and Kramář, against minority clauses in the treaty with Austria, alleging unfair discriminations against their countries.

Bohemia, 1.57 per cent in Moravia, 1.78 per cent in Silesia, 5.3 per cent in Slovakia and 16.2 per cent in Ruthenia. Politically, the Jews were divided into three factions: Zionists, Nationalists and Assimilationists, who desired, respectively, an independent Palestine, autonomy and assimilation.[110] The Czechoslovaks, although much more tolerant and generous in their treatment of the Jews than the Poles or Russians, have, nevertheless, been unable to forget that in the past the Jews favored the dominant races. However, to Czechoslovakia the Jews were a secondary problem, not to be compared in importance with her German and Magyar minorities, a fact which was recognized when the Peace Conference did not require any pledge for them, for the minorities treaty would safeguard their rights also. The confidence in the tolerance of Czechoslovakia implied by the Peace Conference in this omission was duly appreciated by Beneš.[111] Subsequent events have amply justified this confidence. Most Jews have cooperated harmoniously with the Czechoslovaks.

Another problem of vital concern to Czechoslovakia was Anschluss. Czechoslovakia was opposed to such a union: should it be consummated, her fourteen million people would be surrounded on three sides by sixty-five or seventy million hostile Germans, and her existence would be threatened. The incorporation of Austria would more than make good Germany's losses in the World War, would re-establish direct contact with Hungary, would give Germany control of the Danubian area, would hamper to a still greater degree Czechoslovakia's already indirect access to France and Italy, and would foster irredentism among the Germans of Bohemia and the Magyars of Slovakia. There-

[110] Mercier, *op. cit.*, p. 180; House and Seymour, *op. cit.*, pp. 218-219.

[111] *Cf.* Beneš' speech of September 30, 1919, *Prager Abendblatt*, October 1, 1919.

fore, from the Czechoslovak viewpoint, an independent Austria had to be maintained at all costs.[112]

The Czechoslovak contentions concerning Anschluss, supported in toto by France, helped convince the Peace Conference, which, late in April, 1919, determined to prohibit the union of Austria and Germany. The Treaty of Versailles, approved in the plenary session of May 6 and signed on June 28, stated, in Article 80, that Germany recognized the independence of Austria as inalienable except by the consent of the League Council. Article 88 of the Treaty of St. Germain bound Austria to a similar pledge to abstain from any act, direct or indirect, which might compromise her own independence. It may be pointed out that, since the decision of the Council has to be unanimous and since France has permanent representation in that body, these Articles might as well have stated " with the consent of France ". One further obstacle had to be removed before Anschluss could be deemed absolutely prohibited. The new Weimar constitution was distrusted by Czechoslovakia and France inasmuch as Article 61 provided for the admission of Austrian Deputies to the Reich. The Allies applied pressure to Germany which was compelled to eliminate Article 61 as contrary to the Peace Treaty and to reaffirm her adherence

[112] *Cf.* Orbach, C. L., " Czechoslovakia's Place in the Sun ", *Current History*, vol. xiv, pp. 944-945; also Miller, *op. cit.*, vol. xvii, pp. 534-549, for correspondence from the Austrian government concerning the relations of German Austria and Czechoslovakia, March-April, 1919, as transmitted to the Peace Conference by the Swiss Legation at Paris. In contrast, *cf.* Kleinwaechter, F. F. G., *Self-Determination for Austria* (London, 1929), pp. 34-42. Austria deemed Anschluss justifiable politically as a question of life or death to her 6,500,000 people. Mutilated Austria, no longer a self-contained economic unit, did not believe herself capable of sustained independent existence. Vienna, a city of almost 2,000,000, resembled a head with no body to support it. The loss of statehood entailed by a union with Germany would be easier to endure than the economic misery of continued independence.

to Article 80 of the Treaty of Versailles.[113]   In this manner
were the dangers of Anschluss averted, permanently as
Czechoslovakia hoped, but only temporarily, as the sequel
was to show.[114]

Still another problem of the first magnitude was that of
reparations, an issue to which the Supreme Council turned
after drawing definitively the Austrian boundaries on May
13, 1919. The Czechoslovak desires were ably presented to
Clemenceau, the President of the Peace Conference, by a
letter of Beneš, of May 16, which requested decisions on
the questions of the pre-war and war debts of Austria-Hungary, on state property within Czechoslovakia, and on the
Austro-Hungarian banknotes, that had been rendered almost
worthless by reckless inflation.[115]   The agenda suggested by
Beneš was not adopted by the Peace Conference, with the
result that Czechoslovakia was compelled, later, to force a
solution of most of these problems on her own initiative.
The Great Powers considered the small states of Central
Europe as having been at war only with Austria-Hungary,
and, hence, as not entitled to share in German reparations.
The contention of these small states that bankrupt and ruined
Austria-Hungary could pay little, if anything, was not
heeded.[116]   In the belief that the question threatened to develop into a struggle more severe than the territorial one,
Czechoslovakia objected because no distinctions were being
made between Allied and enemy states.[117]

In order to enable Czechoslovakia to evade, juridically, the
reparations clauses of the Treaty of Versailles, the Com-

[113] Temperley, *op. cit.*, vol. iv, pp. 391-394; *The Times*, September 3, 1919.

[114] *Cf. infra*, pp. 173 *et seq.*

[115] Miller, *op. cit.*, vol. xviii, pp. 328-329.

[116] Baker, *op. cit.*, vol. ii, p. 386.

[117] *Československá Korespondence*, May 20 and 27, 1919; Vochoč, *loc. cit.*, pp. 113-114.

mission on Reparations decided that she became independent by her own efforts on October 28, 1918. On that date she was at war with Germany for the first time, and, accordingly, was a belligerent when the War terminated. Her independence had been recognized formally by identical Articles: by Germany in Article 81 of the Treaty of Versailles, by Austria in Article 53 of the Treaty of St. Germain and by Hungary in Article 48 of the Treaty of Trianon. Her status was above question. The Great Powers decided also that the enemy states should not pay for the entire cost of the War, but merely for the damages caused by it. This decision wrecked the plans of certain Czechoslovak circles, led by Dr. Rašín, the Finance Minister, who had understood that Czechoslovakia would assume her proportional share of the Austro-Hungarian pre-war debt, but who had also expected large reparations. In spite of Beneš' stressing of the point that the Czechoslovaks had been hostile to the Dual Monarchy throughout the War and had been granted an Allied status, neither Czechoslovakia nor Poland, which was in a similar situation, could obtain any reparations for war claims. The two states bitterly resented this discrimination, which they maintained was owing solely to the fact that they were both new states. On the other hand, Italy maintained that all the Succession States, and not merely the mutilated remnants of Austria and Hungary, should pay the war loans. Austria's entire debt was divided, a decision which made no substantial distinction between enemy and Succession States. The new states had expected to pay a share of the pre-war debt, but refused to be responsible for the war debts or for the notes issued by the Bank of Austria-Hungary, and objected to turning over to the Allies the crown property within their new boundaries.[118]

[118] Vochoč, *loc. cit.*, pp. 114-115.

Bankruptcy faced Austria and Hungary, which could never pay such enormous sums. In recognition of this obvious fact, the Allies pointed out that the Succession States would be better off than the Great Powers, if they were freed from these obligations, and stressed the fact that, since the War had been fought by all, its burdens should be shared by all. In reply, Beneš stated that Czechoslovakia should not be penalized for having aided the Allies, that she would pay her pre-war share, but no more. If the Great Powers feared that Austria and Hungary could not pay for both war debts and reparations, then, similarly, the new states could not pay for the war loans that had been floated in their territories. These war loans on Czech property were the greatest internal financial problem of the Republic. The crown property had belonged originally to the Kingdom of Bohemia. Austria, which had taken it, was not entitled to any payment for it. If Czechoslovakia could not collect war damages, she could not help pay Austria's war debts.[119] If this viewpoint of Beneš was to be regarded as radical, public opinion in Czechoslovakia was even more so: many of the leaders considered the problem cynically as void of principle, as merely a question of how much each small state could be made to contribute to the Allied international fund.[120]

In the midst of these differences of opinion, on June 16, 1919, Austria introduced a new and important point into the discussion, namely, that her Republic was new and consequently not responsible for the obligations of the former Dual Monarchy, nor had it ever waged war against the Allies. While Austria expressed her willingness to assume a share of her war debt, she declined to consider herself responsible

[119] Ibid., pp. 116-118; Peace Conference Delegation, 1919, Memoirs, no. 11, "La République Tchécoslovaque et son droit à la reparation des dommages de guerre".

[120] Československá Korespondence, May 27, 1919; Vochoč, loc. cit., pp. 116-118.

for it all. If her contention were accepted, she would be
the least heavily burdened of all the Succession States, since
her new Republic was the weakest of them all.[121]

Although the Allies had fought the whole Dual Monarchy,
they encountered, at this point, juridical difficulties in iden-
tifying it with the new Austrian Republic. The greatest
Allied fear was that, as long as any doubt remained regarding the conclusiveness of the abdication of Emperor Charles,
he might return to rule Austria. Since he would have no
rights over a new state, the new contention of Austria as
to her existing status would afford security to the new status
quo that the Allies were attempting to establish. Therefore,
they accepted in part the Austrian contention and regarded
her as a state with a new government, dating de facto recognition from May 22, when the credentials of the new Republic were accepted by the Peace Conference, and de jure
recognition from September 10, 1919, when the Treaty of
St. Germain was signed. To all appearances any waiting
for Austrian ratification of this treaty was deemed unnecessary.[122]

In the face of the common financial threat, Czechoslovakia,
Yugoslavia, Rumania and Poland decided on joint action,
but their fears failed to materialize. On May 29, 1919,
Le Temps announced unofficially that the Succession States
would not be compelled to pay the war debts of Austria-
Hungary. In the definitive treaty with Austria, they assumed merely their proportional shares of the pre-war debt,
and were not required to pay for crown property within
their borders. Czechoslovakia was permitted, in addition,
to recover certain historical articles which, in the past, had
been carried off to Vienna.[123]

[121] Temperley, *op. cit.*, vol. iv, pp. 395-397.
[122] *Ibid.*, vol. iv, pp. 398-400.
[123] Vochoč, *loc. cit.*, pp. 119-120.

The Austrian Reparations Commission was composed of two members each from the United States, Great Britain, France and Italy, and one representing the combined interests of Greece, Poland, Rumania, Yugoslavia and Czechoslovakia. The total amount of Austrian reparations was to be determined at some later date.[124] Italy was granted a special status. Her contribution was apportioned according to the revenues formerly collected in the Austro-Hungarian provinces she received. In addition, the other Succession States were compelled to pay " costs of liberation ", which were fixed at 1,500,000,000 gold francs. Of this amount, Czechoslovakia was not to pay more than half.[125] All payments were postponed to 1926, at which date the total amount of these costs, in bonds, was to be turned over to a commission that was to be designated by the four Great Powers. As these bond payments would mature, the states in question might liquidate them by surrendering equal amounts due them in reparations. All debts prior to July 28, 1914, were shared, but all subsequent indebtedness devolved upon Austria and Hungary alone. Similarly, all notes issued by the Bank of Austria-Hungary after October 27, 1918, were declared invalid.[126] In this manner the Great Powers solved some of the financial problems of the Danubian area and created others, particularly did they arouse the resentment of the smaller Succession States by their concession to Italy. The incomplete nature of the financial settlement left Central

[124] *League of Nations Treaty Series* (henceforth referred to as *Treaty Series*), vol. ii, pp. 22-47; vol. iii, pp. 261-262.

[125] The Austrian pre-war debt was finally divided 36 per cent for Austria, 22 percent between Yugoslavia and Italy, and 42 percent for Czechoslovakia. For additional details *cf* Piot, A., *La Couronne tchécoslovaque jusqu'au mort de Rašin, 1918-1923* (Paris, 1923), p. 236; Pasvolsky, L., *Economic Nationalism of the Danubian States* (New York, 1928), pp. 45-47; or *infra*, p. 341.

[126] Temperley, *op. cit.*, vol. v, pp. 14-24.

Europe open to the full play of selfish nationalism which was to retard greatly any return to " normalcy."

Distinct from these primarily financial problems was the final set of Czechoslovakia's Peace Conference questions, those essentially economic in nature. Of particular interest and importance was the establishment of economic outlets for the new state. The large surplus of manufactured goods which began to accumulate after the termination of the War had to be exported, yet Czechoslovakia's position rendered the problem difficult, since all outlets of any commercial significance lay across the territories of her former enemies. The problem required a series of special agreements. Since the question was of vital concern to all Central Europe, the Peace Conference, at its plenary session of January 25, 1919, created a Commission on the International Régime of Ports, Waterways and Railways, and granted to it the rights of investigation and recommendation.[127] Between February and the end of April, 1919, this Commission formulated a group of agreements, but its Polish and Czechoslovak delegates were not satisfied with the progress that was being made, and, on March 8, inquired with considerable indignation why their states " were not treated on the same moral footing as the other States ".[128] Following the bad precedent established by their colleagues who represented the Great Powers, they also refused to consider the advantages of reciprocity. Czechoslovakia demanded the internationalization of the Danube, Elbe, Oder and Vistula Rivers, and of the railroads that connected Bratislava with both Trieste and Fiume, and Praha with Strasbourg via Fürth and Nürnberg. In defense of these demands, Kramář argued, " When only two States were riparian, it might nevertheless be very desirable to bring about a wide internationaliza-

[127] *Ibid.*, vol. ii, p. 94.
[128] Baker, *op. cit.*, vol. ii, p. 309.

tion; for instance, in the case of the Elbe, Oder, or Vistula. If that were not done, newly formed States might find themselves forced to deal alone with a State like Germany." [129]

On the next day, March 9, in response to Polish and Czechoslovak complaints of having been ignored, France suggested to the Commission that the former enemy states be compelled to grant Allied traffic over their lines terms and service equal to those granted their own nationals.[130] Belgium and Czechoslovakia demanded that their former enemies be forbidden also to cut rates over lines in areas that were served by shorter lines within Allied territory.[131] No immediate action was taken on these requests. On April 26, Czechoslovakia and Yugoslavia proposed that any Allied states should be given the right, for twenty-five years, to build railways through the former enemy states.[132] This demand was not only unwarrantable, but failed to take into account many practical questions. For instance, how were the enemy states to be compelled to operate such railroads, and who would pay for their costs? The sponsors of the plan certainly did not intend to finance it themselves, but hoped to place the whole project under the supervision of the League. France, whose assistance to the Succession States might ordinarily be taken almost for granted, failed to show interest in this undertaking, which, in consequence, received no consideration because of a lack of adequate support. On August 13, Beneš who had succeeded Kramář on the Commission, was informed that Czechoslovakia was not to run her own trains across Austria and Hungary, because such humiliation of the vanquished states was both " unprecedented " and " unnecessary ".[133]

[129] *Ibid.*, vol. ii, p. 440.
[130] *Ibid.*, vol. ii, pp. 444-445.
[131] *Ibid.*, vol. ii, p. 445.
[132] Miller, *op. cit.*, vol. ix, pp. 212-213.
[133] *Ibid.*, vol. xi, p. 154.

In spite of this rebuff, Czechoslovakia, on the whole, was treated generously by the Commission. Though she was not granted any special privileges for her traffic across Germany to France, because this traffic was regulated by Article 356 of the Treaty of Versailles, she did receive, in Articles 322-324 of the Treaty of St. Germain and in Articles 305-306 of the Treaty of Trianon, respectively, free railway communications with the Adriatic via Budjovice-Linz-Klagenfurt-Trieste and Bratislava-Sopron-Fiume. The support of Italy was influential in obtaining for Czechoslovakia these privileges.[184]

Despite the objections of Poland, the Oder was internationalized from Opatovic. Czechoslovakia's plea for the Vistula was denied, on the ground that it would lie entirely within Poland after the Těšin decision that then appeared most probable. In July, 1919, the Morava and Dyje were also internationalized. By Article 339 of the Treaty of Versailles, to the great satisfaction of Czechoslovakia, the Elbe, together with the Vltava from Praha, was placed under the jurisdiction of an International Commission. Czechoslovakia received also, on a ninety-nine year lease, the use of certain so-called free zones within the ports of Hamburg and Stettin.[185]

There still remained the question of the most important river of Central Europe, the Danube. Prior to the War, there had been six riparian states—Germany, Austria-Hungary, Russia, Rumania, Bulgaria and Serbia—of which all, except the last, had had direct access to the sea. Hence,

---

[184] Temperley, *op. cit.*, vol. ii, p. 110; vol. iv, p. 274; Miller, *op. cit.*, vol. xi, pp. 40-41.

[185] Anon., "In the Matter of the Cessions by Germany to Czechoslovakia under Article 339 of the Treaty of Versailles", *American Journal of International Law*, vol. xviii, pp. 186-198; Baker, *op. cit.*, vol. ii, p. 446; Miller, *op. cit.*, vol. xi, pp. 71, 87, 97-98, 138, 147, 170-172, 177 and 193-198.

the authority of the European Commission of the Danube had been restricted to the delta below Galatz. The care of the Iron Gates, where the channel up to Braila is dangerous, was entrusted to Austria-Hungary by Article 57 of the Treaty of Berlin of July 13, 1878. During the War, the membership of the Commission, thanks to the expulsion of the Allies, had been restricted to Germany, Austria-Hungary, Bulgaria and Rumania, or, as stated in Article 24 of the Treaty of Bucharest of May 7, 1918, to " States situated on the Danube or the European coasts of the Black Sea ". After the Allied triumph in the War, the situation was reversed, and, by Article 346 of the Treaty of Versailles, membership was restricted to Great Britain, France, Italy and Rumania.

In the new Europe, there had been created seven riparian states, of which three—Austria, Hungary and Czechoslovakia—had no direct access to the sea. Since none of them was a Great Power, the Supreme Council had insisted upon international control from Galatz to Ulm, the upper limit of navigation, and, below Galatz, the authority of the European Commission of the Danube was reestablished by Articles 346-353 of the Treaty of Versailles. In spite of the fact that, because of the mutual hostility of the riparian states, international control had worked to their advantage, none of them were satisfied without actual membership in the Commission. However, patience had to be their lot; although the Danubian question was brought up during the Peace Conference, it was not settled definitely until much later; to be exact, on July 23, 1921. On that date the new statute was signed by all the Allied states except Poland and Portugal, and by all the former Central Powers except Turkey. Forty-three articles granted equal rights of navigation to all, apportioned duties, improvements and revenues proportionally, and sought to cover every possible contingency.[186] On June 30, 1922, when ratified by all, the new régime became effective.[187]

It appears also that the Great Powers were aware of the economic ills to which Central Europe would be exposed as a result of the " Balkanization " of that area by the Peace Treaties. In an effort to create an economic substitute for the Dual Monarchy, the Peace Conference paved the way for a Danubian Confederation.[188]   Article 222 of the Treaty of St. Germain specified that, for a five year period, Austria might conclude special accords with both Hungary and Czechoslovakia.   Because of mutual hostility, no immediate attempt was made to take advantage of this privilege.[139]

It was evident that Czechoslovakia had succeeded in winning her major contentions at the Peace Conference.   Such reverses as had been her lot were, on the whole, to be expected and were received on minor and extreme demands.   The

---

[186] *Convention Instituting the Definitive Statute of the Danube* (British White Paper) Cmd. 1754 of 1922.

[187] For detailed accounts of the Danubian question, *cf.* Chamberlain, J. P., *The Régime of the International Rivers: Danube and Rhine* (New York, 1923), or *The Danube* (Washington, 1918) ; Avennier, L., " Mezinárodní právo říční a režim na Dunaji", *Zahraniční Politika*, vol. i, pp. 106-110, 189-194, 294-300; or Pinon, R., " La Reconstruction de l'Europe danubienne", *Révue des deux mondes*, vi période, tome li, pp. 557-582. *Cf.* also, *League of Nations Official Journal* (henceforth referred to as *Official Journal*), February, 1927, pp. 138, 150-152, for the agreement of Great Britain, France, Italy and Rumania upon the competence of the European Commission of the Danube.   On September 8, 1924, Czechoslovakia ratified the convention and statute on the régime of navigable waterways of international concern, *cf. Official Journal*, November, 1927, p. 1510.

[188] *Cf. Svornost*, January 3, 1919, for rumors that Great Britain, France and the United States had agreed to create a Danubian Confederation led by Czechoslovakia.

[189] For full details of subsequent attempts to form a Danubian Confederation, *cf. infra*, pp. 278 *et scq.*

broad bases for her future well-being had been established; there remained to be decided the specific ways and means.[140] In common with the other Succession States, Czechoslovakia was to find her chief future obstacle in her own nationalistic attitude. Shortly after his return from the Peace Conference,[141] in his speech of September 30, 1919, before the Foreign Committee of the Senate, Beneš pointed out Czechoslovakia's victory, and showed how she had been left with fewer unsolved international problems than any of the other new states.[142] On November 3, 1919, when the Treaties of St. Germain with Austria and Versailles with Germany were submitted to the National Assembly for ratification, Beneš, in the discussions that followed, was asked to explain his actions. Four days later, at the plenary session, he explained the goal of his future foreign policy. His statement—that Czechoslovakia would strive to maintain the status quo as established by the Peace Treaties, and by an extensive system of new agreements would endeavor to establish friendly and cordial relations with all her neighbors—was heartily approved, as the first announcement of a new political system in Central Europe.[143]

[140] For further details, *cf.* Brož, A., *The First Year of the Czechoslovak Republic* (London, 1920) ; Butter, O., and Ruml, B., *La République tchécoslovaque* (Prague, 1921) ; Eisenmann, L., *La Tchécoslovaquie* (Paris, 1921) ; Dĕdeček, V., *La Tchécoslovaquie et les Tchécoslovaques* (Paris, 1919).

[141] *Cf. Národní Politika*, September 25, 1919, for the ovation received by Beneš upon his return to Praha after four years abroad.

[142] *Prager Abendblatt*, October 1, 1919.

[143] Beneš, *Problemy nové Evropy*, pp. 33-34.

CHAPTER II

Domestic Stabilization

INTERDEPENDENCE OF FOREIGN AND DOMESTIC POLICIES

THE post-war foreign policy of Czechoslovakia, as fore-shadowed by Beneš' speech of September 30, 1919,[1] was, of necessity, to rest upon two bases. As a prelude to a foreign policy of conciliation and peace, the new Republic would be compelled to set its own house in order; before any reconstruction could be hoped for throughout Central Europe, each state would have to complete first the solution of its own internal financial, economic, social and religious problems. Thus, while Czechoslovakia, during the first five years of her independent existence, 1918-1923, found that her chief foreign problems revolved around the reconstruction of Central Europe, she discovered also that her own future well-being would depend upon the thoroughness with which she solved her own domestic problems during the same period.[2]

Financial Policy

Czechoslovakia conceived her most vital domestic problem to be that of finance. In order to appreciate the difficulties of the situation, it should be remembered that the territories that comprised Czechoslovakia had formerly been dependent financially upon Vienna, and, to a lesser degree, upon Buda-

[1] *Cf. Prager Abendblatt,* October 1, 1919; or *supra,* p. 59.

[2] This chapter makes no pretense of an exhaustive treatment of Czechoslovakia's internal difficulties, but concerns itself only with those phases of the financial, economic, social and religious problems that concern, more or less directly, the foreign policy.

pest. In these two centers had been concentrated the financial and economic activities of the provinces. In view of such a development, it was only natural that the first bank in Praha, established in 1857, had been a branch of the Vienna Austrian Discount Bank and Credit Institute. In 1863 there was established, by German bankers and manufacturers, the first independent bank in Praha, the Bohemian Discount Bank. In 1867 there followed the Agricultural Credit Bank for Bohemia and Moravia. By the close of 1872, Praha had nineteen joint-stock banks, but the panic of the following year demonstrated their weakness, for only four survived. The next quarter century witnessed the establishment of several branches of Vienna banks throughout Bohemia, but no more joint-stock banks in Praha. However, the immediate pre-war period was marked by a great banking revival; between 1898 and 1914 about twenty new banks were started and the older institutions expanded their capital also. Patriotic Czechs may well have experienced satisfaction from the fact that most of these new banks were founded by Czechs, with the object of seeking to wrest financial supremacy from the Germans. In this financial struggle, the Czechs received no assistance whatever from the Slovaks, who were practically helpless in the grip of Budapest.[3]

It would, perhaps, have been questionable when, if ever, the Czechs, in the normal course of events, could have become dominant financially over the German minority, which received, directly and indirectly, assistance from the government. In view of this fact, as well as because of their own economic and financial weakness, the Czechs had faced a ser-

[3] For further details of this financial struggle, cf. Karasek, K., " Banking ", in Gruber, J. (ed.), *Czechoslovakia: A Survey of Economic and Social Conditions* (New York, 1924), pp. 166-169; Pasvolsky, *op. cit.*, pp. 7-32; or Brailsford, H. N., " Prague and Vienna ", *New Republic*, vol. xxxi, pp. 223-226.

ious struggle.   Although they had made marked gains in the decades just prior to 1914, they were still far short of their ultimate goal when the World War broke out.   Thus, for them, the War was a blessing in disguise.   It brought them independence and ended German financial and economic supremacy.   During the course of the War, the Czech banks lost little, and subscribed to the various war loans only under compulsion.   On the other hand, deposits continued to increase and the inflation brought about by the War enabled both banks and industries to realize enormous profits.   The securities of the various Czech industrial concerns increased rapidly in value and were bought up eagerly.[4]

In the midst of all this apparent prosperity, the Czechs realized keenly the dangers inherent in the situation because of the reckless inflation of Austrian currency.   The disproportion of Austrian revenues and expenditures, which had been notorious at different periods in the past,[5] became even greater during the War.   Beginning in 1892, Austria had attempted to attain financial stability and create a gold reserve by covering the circulation of her banknotes up to forty percent by gold which had been withdrawn from circulation and placed in the reserves of the Bank of Austria-Hungary.   This policy had been quite successful; on July 23, 1914, the gold reserve had been fifty-eight percent of the paper circulation.   During the course of the War, Austria found it impossible to maintain a sufficient gold reserve: her circulation, which had been, on July 23, 1914, 2,129,-000,000 paper crowns, had been increased, by October 26, 1918, to 30,679,000,000 paper crowns.[6]   In substance, this

[4] Rašin, A., *The Financial Policy of Czechoslovakia during the First Year of its History* (Oxford, 1923), pp. 16-17; Piot, *op. cit.*, p. 20.

[5] *Cf.* Piot, *op. cit.*, pp. 9-14, for a summary of Austrian finance from 1811 to 1914.

[6] Mildschuh, V., "Currency Conditions", in Gruber, *op. cit.*, p. 176.

paper money no longer represented notes of the Bank, but, instead, notes of the government of Austria-Hungary. Attempts of the government to maintain their value proved futile.[7] The sequel—an inevitable panic—was welcome to the " patriotic " Czechs, who contributed their bit towards making it worse by presenting for immediate payment their war loans.[8]

Vigorous steps were necessary if Czechoslovakia was to be protected from the evils of Austrian inflation. The earliest suggestion came from Dr. Alois Rašín, the first Minister of Finance.[9] Shortly after his appointment, Rašín, in November, 1918, proposed to the Supreme Council, by means of his country's spokesman, Beneš, that all the Succession States create International Commissions of Control, patterned on those for the Bank of Austria-Hungary or the German Reichsbank, to represent them until they could develop independent currencies of their own. This plan was a practical method of bridging over the necessary period of transition, while the financial separations from Austria were taking place, but was brought to nought because the Great Powers failed to appreciate adequately the financial dangers that threatened the Succession States.[10]

After this initial rebuff to his contemplated plan of financial cooperation with the Great Powers, Rašín proceeded on his own initiative, as he thought best. His chief immediate concern was to prevent any possibility that Czechoslovakia be compelled to guarantee a large portion of

---

[7] *Cf.* Piot, *op. cit.*, p. 14, for a chart of the fluctuations of Austrian exchange, 1914-18; Rašín, *op. cit.*, pp. 13-15; Chanal, E., *Monnaie et économie nationale en Tchécoslovaquie, 1918-1928* (Paris, 1929), pp. 67-71.

[8] Piot, *op. cit.*, p. 21. The writer means " patriotic " to the concept of the Czechoslovakia-to-be.

[9] For a brief biography of Rašín, *cf.* Chanal, *op. cit.*, pp. 63-66.

[10] Rašín, *op. cit.*, pp. 16-17; Piot, *op. cit.*, p. 29.

the Austro-Hungarian war bonds, which, at the termination of the War, amounted to 50,736,838,500 crowns. His fear was based upon the fact that the holders of these bonds were permitted to present them to the Bank of Austria-Hungary, which was compelled by law to advance seventy-five percent of their nominal value upon such collateral. In addition, the Bank was protected from all possible loss from this source by a guarantee of an indemnity by Austria-Hungary, should it ever become necessary. Rašín's first move was obvious— a request that the Bank discontinue the granting of loans based upon war bonds as a security, and, when this request was refused, his second move was to prohibit all branches of the bank in Czechoslovakia to honor war bonds. As a result of this prompt handling of the situation, the banks within Czechoslovakia became obligated only for the relatively small amount of 412,000,000 crowns of the war bonds.[11]

Thereupon, in December, 1918, while Austria was still following the pathway of inflation, Czechoslovakia resorted to a Liberty Loan of 500,000,000 crowns. This appeal to the patriotism of her people produced startling results: in the course of five days 1,072,000,000 crowns were subscribed; despite nine disastrous precedents of depreciated Austro-Hungarian war loans, the Czechoslovaks in this manner again demonstrated their faith in the future of their country. In contrast, regardless of the fact that Austria's request for a new loan had been rejected by the Bank Commission, the Bank of Austria-Hungary, which still continued to operate despite the dissolution of the Dual Monarchy, on December 31, 1918, loaned Austria 3,500,000,000 crowns and Hungary 1,500,000,000 crowns. The Bank also issued 200,000,000 crowns of new notes, printed only on one side, which Austria had authorized on the eve of the armistice.

[11] Rašín, *op. cit.*, p. 17; Piot, *op. cit.*, p. 30; Chanal, *op. cit.*, pp. 71-74.

In this emergency, before Czechoslovakia could be flooded with these new notes, Rašín refused to honor them, except for notes of one and two crowns, which were printed at the same time and which were needed especially in view of a temporary scarcity of small change. The resulting financial distress convinced many Czechoslovaks of the need of establishing a new currency as soon as possible.[12]

Since Czechoslovakia was the first of the Succession States to come to this conclusion, she had no precedent to follow, and had to work out her own method. There existed three principal views as to the best procedure. The first view, that of Dr. Jaroslav Preiss, the head of the Commercial Bank of Praha, was the most radical—that the currency issued by the Bank of Austria-Hungary be repudiated. The second view, that of Professors Brdlík and Koloušek, advocated that the old currency be retained as notes of Czechoslovakia, but that it be devaluated. Still more moderate was the third view, that of Rašín, who maintained that the Czechoslovak crown be established at a value equal to the pre-war parity of the Austro-Hungarian crown by a process of gradual deflation. Rašín did not pretend to be able to foresee the ultimate result of the measure he proposed, but he was convinced that it would involve the least economic dislocation, would attain financial stability in the safest way, and would avoid many obvious difficulties that would be present if either of the other two alternatives were adopted—in short, he felt his method was the sole means of averting immediate disaster.[13]

[12] Rašín, *op. cit.*, pp. 19-21; Piot, *op. cit.*, pp. 32-33; Mildschuh, *loc. cit.*, p. 177.

[13] For the details of the rival plans of Preiss, Koloušek and Brdlík, and Rašín, *cf.* Rašín, *op. cit.*, pp. 37-38; Piot, *op. cit.*, pp. 54-55; Chanal, *op. cit.*, pp. 74-83; Pasvolsky, *op. cit.*, pp. 205-206; or Koloušek, J., *Rašínová reforma měny* (Praha, 1921). For technical studies of the whole Czechoslovak currency problem, *cf.* Rašín, A., *Muj finanční plan* (Praha, 1921); *Inflace a deflace* (Praha, 1922); Schmidt-Friedlander, R., *Die Währungspolitik der Tschechoslowakei* (Reichenberg, 1929).

Before putting his project into effect, Rašín introduced a series of preliminary measures intended to curtail the transfer of crowns in either direction across the frontier, in order that the amount of capital within Czechoslovakia might be determined accurately. The branch banks were not permitted to withdraw their current accounts from the Bank of Austria-Hungary, nor to pay for the Bank's reserve bonds without a special permit from the Ministry of Finance. In addition, gold francs were required for the payment of customs duties, tourists could bring out with them only limited amounts of crowns and no capital in crowns might be exported.[14]

By February 25, 1919, Rašín had his plan completed. To ensure success, secrecy was maintained; the National Assembly held a secret session of half a day's duration in approving the project and all newspapers were censored. The essential provisions of Rašín's plan required that all notes circulating in Czechoslovakia be stamped, that half of the notes be retired and held as a forced loan bearing one percent interest for which non-transferable certificates were to be issued, and that, within three months, everyone who resided in Czechoslovakia as much as one month a year be compelled to declare all his property, personal or otherwise, at home or abroad. As the process of actual stamping was taking place, March 3-9, 1919, first in the banks, then in the rural communities and finally in the cities, troops guarded the frontiers, enforced the suspension of most business and closed the post-offices in order that no more notes be imported. Stamping was restricted to notes of 10, 20, 50, 100 and 1,000 crowns, whereas those of lesser denominations were retained, unstamped, in circulation temporarily. During the last half of 1919, 300,000,000 new notes which had been printed in the United States replaced the stamped ones which

[14] Piot, *op. cit.*, pp. 58-59.

were permitted to remain in circulation until June 20, 1920, and which lost all value on August 1, 1920. In this manner was the currency of Czechoslovakia separated from that of Austria.[15]

The secrecy and speed with which Rašín's plan had been carried out produced both at home and abroad reactions which demonstrated the timeliness of his measures. Within Czechoslovakia, after the initial feeling of stupor had passed, the peasants began to hoard the notes, particularly the small change, whereas the merchants proceeded to invest their money in valuable and easily salable merchandise whose price began to soar immediately. Abroad, Czechoslovakia's example proved contagious to the other Succession States which proceeded to stamp all Austro-Hungarian notes within their borders also.[16]

In the meantime, Austria blamed Czechoslovakia as the source of the evils which she, Austria, would be required to face as the result of having to bear alone the brunt of her wartime inflation. As soon as she ascertained the full import of Rašín's preliminary measures, Austria, on February 15, 1919, prohibited the importation of crowns from Czechoslovakia in order that the latter would be compelled to retain as many crowns as possible,[17] and, on February 26, protested formally against Rašín's measures of the day before as an unwarrantable attack upon the rights and privileges of the Bank of Austria-Hungary. The next day, Austria closed her own frontiers, stamped her own notes,

[15] Rašín, *The Financial Policy of Czechoslovakia during the First Year of its History*, pp. 26-28; Piot, *op. cit.*, pp. 66-71; Chanal, *op. cit.*, pp. 83-89; Pasvolsky, *op. cit.*, p. 206; Mildschuh, *loc. cit.*, p. 178.

[16] Yugoslavia, November 13, 1919; Poland, March 26, 1919; Rumania in April, 1919 (in Bessarabia), and between June and July, 1919, in the other provinces; and Hungary, March 17, 1920, the delay being caused by Bolshevism. Even Germany adopted the process during August, 1919.

[17] Piot, *op. cit.*, p. 59.

and by way of further retaliation, discriminated against her Czechoslovak creditors by paying claims that antedated February 26 in old crowns and claims of a later date in new Austrian crowns.[18]

Austria's objections were answered ably by a note [19] of Rašín's in which he pointed out that the Bank of Austria-Hungary, a mere agent of the Austrian government, had no right to complain against his measures, inasmuch as it had not observed Article 83 of its own statutes, with regard to issues of new notes. By granting loans to the other Succession States, it had violated its own specific promises to Czechoslovakia. It still maintained the practice of advancing seventy-five percent of the nominal value of the war bonds, whose actual value was but sixty percent. Moreover, it was subject to the caprices of the Austrian government, and had demonstrated its incompetence as a regulator of the economic life of the Succession States. Czechoslovakia had been willing to protect the common currency, but had received no cooperation, and therefore, in self-defense, had been compelled to adopt measures against a systematic depreciation of the currency.

In spite of the fact that Rašín's note had demolished the Austrian contention, Austria submitted her cause to the Peace Conference, where it was received with little consideration. In substance, Austria was condemned and Czechoslovakia vindicated by Article 206 of the Treaty of St. Germain, which ordered stamping in each Succession State within two months of ratification of the treaty and replacement by new money within a year of ratification. By the same article, the final step in the respective currency separations was to be the sending of the retired notes, within

---

[18] *Ibid.*, pp. 72-73; Rašín, *op. cit.*, pp. 29, 40.

[19] For the actual text of the note, *cf.* Rašín, *op. cit.*, p. 30; *cf.* also, Piot, *op. cit.*, pp. 73-74.

fourteen months of ratification, to the Reparations Commission, which, in return, would issue certificates that were to represent shares in the division of the resources of the Bank of Austria-Hungary.

Despite the approval of her financial program by the Peace Conference, Czechoslovakia, because of internal conditions, was unable to put it into full effect immediately. The process of deflation was retarded by many exceptions to the retirement of the notes: for instance, amounts below 250 crowns were entirely exempt, as were all public funds and one quarter of all salaries; moreover, Těšín and Ruthenia were not included because, as yet, their exact frontiers remained in doubt. Originally, Rašín had intended to withdraw from circulation eighty percent of the notes, but, in response to fears expressed in the National Assembly, declared himself satisfied with fifty percent.[20] Actually, of the total of 7,436,000,000 crowns, only 28.69 percent was withdrawn from circulation immediately, and on June 15, 1919, when the Kramář government fell, and after Rašín lost his post, eighty-five percent of the original amount was restored to circulation.[21] Rašín was not permitted to carry through his program personally because his brusqueness had gained him many foes, whereas his integrity and ability were not always appreciated.

The new government, a coalition of Agrarians [22] and

[20] For Rašín's speech of February 28, 1919, before the National Assembly, cf. Prager Presse, March 1, 1919, or Rist, C., La Deflation en pratique. (Paris, 1924), p. 107.

[21] Piot, op. cit., p. 79; Pasvolsky, op. cit., p. 207; Mildschuh, loc. cit., pp. 178-179. Cf. also, Piot, op. cit., pp. 86 and 106; Chanal, op. cit., pp. 89-97; or Rašín, op. cit., pp. 43-47 for the means whereby Czechoslovakia established a gold reserve.

[22] The Agrarian party, formed in 1906, became the most important numerically after 1925. Composed of agriculturists and peasants, it worked effectively for land reform and for the elimination of speculation

Socialists [28] headed by Tusar, was interested primarily ·in social questions rather than in finance. Rašín's immediate successors, Horáček and Sonntag, in power respectively for brief periods, failed to follow his policy of economy. On a deficit of 4,905,591,293 crowns in the budget of 1919, Rašín had brought about demobilization and the return of prisoners, the occupation of Slovakia, unemployment relief, a solution of the food shortage crisis and the renewal of operation of the mines and railroads.[24] In contrast with this excellent record, his successors had produced, in the 1920 budget, almost as great a deficit—4,851,926,238 crowns— while revenues had increased tremendously. In self-defense, they alleged the great costs of the war with Hungary and the occupation of Ruthenia, but failed to cite the main items of increase—salaries and equipment.[25] Nevertheless, they deserved credit for avoiding inflation. Instead, they resorted to new loans [26] which availed little, because both Slovaks and

in cereals. It is known also as the Republican party. Cf. Hoch, C., *The Political Parties of Czechoslovakia* (Prague, 1936), pp. 17-20.

[23] The Social Democratic party, formed in 1896, was the most important numerically until 1925, since which time it has held second place. Composed primarily of laborers, it agitated for social reform. Somewhat similar in composition and program is the National Socialist party which holds third place among Czechoslovak parties. *Ibid.*, pp. 20-27.

[24] Like his successors, Rašín had attempted to meet the deficit by negotiating loans. He had obtained from Hoover $54,000,000 for food supplies, but a second loan had been refused by the United States. On May 24, 1919, a day before the time set for signature, Italy had cancelled a treaty for a 60,000,000 lire loan for raw materials. Later negotiations of Rašín with Switzerland and of the Bank of Praha for a 25,000,000 franc loan in France also failed. Cf. Piot, *op. cit.*, p. 131; or Chanal, *op. cit.*, pp. 97-99.

[25] Excluding the army, salaries increased, between January, 1919, and January, 1920, from 1,939,000,000 crowns to 3,445,000,000 crowns and equipment from 1,147,000,000 crowns to 3,336,000,000 crowns. Cf. Rašín, *op. cit.*, p. 88; Piot, *op. cit.*, pp. 95-96.

[26] After the first Liberty Loan, they had attempted to meet the deficit by two subsequent loans, late in 1919 and early in 1920, which were only

Germans failed to subscribe. In the crisis that followed, public confidence could be restored only by a financial expert.

In the spring of 1920, a man of the hour was found in the person of Engliš, Professor of Economics at the University of Brno (Brünn), whose services in stabilizing the crown have never received the recognition they deserve. The financial situation was desperate: to all appearances both prices and the rates of exchange had failed to respond favorably to either the absence of inflation or the process of deflation, but had been influenced unfavorably by the many uncertainties that still existed in Czechoslovakia's financial situation. The chief difficulty lay in the fact that the total amount of Czechoslovakia's indebtedness had not been, and perhaps, at the time could not be, determined with exactitude. Its chief items included a foreign debt of 9,988,004,000 crowns, a domestic debt of 4,580,050,000 crowns, reparations costs of 9,750,000,000 crowns and 6,433,020,000 crowns which represented Czechoslovakia's share of the Austro-Hungarian pre-war debt. The Conference of Brussels, in October, 1920, estimated Czechoslovakia's debt at thirty-five billion crowns, but Engliš, early in 1921, thought forty billion crowns a closer estimate.[27]

At the time of the appointment of Engliš to the Ministry of Finance, the two chief financial problems concerned a fourth domestic loan and the war bonds. Public opinion was divided. Rašín opposed the honoring of the war bonds on the ground that the Treaty of St. Germain had absolved the Succession States from such burdens. On the other hand, Engliš felt that future domestic loans would obtain no support from the racial minorities, particularly from the wealthy Germans, as their indifference to the recent loan had

partially successful in that they produced about half of the total of the first loan.

[27] Rašín, *op. cit.*, p. 121; Piot, *op. cit.*, pp. 183-184.

indicated, unless some concessions were granted to the holders of the war bonds. He considered the two financial problems inextricably linked together, and the only adequate solution a compromise. His compromise measure, adopted on June 24, 1920, provided that, for each war bond of a nominal value of 100 crowns and an additional 75 crowns in cash, the bearer was to receive bonds worth 150 crowns in the new loan.[28]   Since the Austrian crown was being quoted at about one-fifth of the value of the Czechoslovak crown by the rates of exchange prevalent during the period assigned for this operation, August 2—December 15, 1920, this measure meant that Czechoslovakia was presenting the holders of the war bonds with a substantial gift.   The transaction also risked increasing materially the already enormous public indebtedness, since about 4,400,000,000 crowns of the approximately 6,000,000,000 crowns of war bonds that had been issued originally in Czechoslovak territories were still outstanding.   Regardless of the financial merits or demerits of Engliš' compromise, which produced a yield of approximately 500,000,000 crowns, a sum greatly needed to finance the Republic until the budget could be balanced, and which resulted in about 2,000,000,000 crowns of the war bonds being turned in, its success as a conciliatory measure was questionable: many of the Czechoslovaks resented the granting of concessions of such magnitude to their former foes,

[28] Republika Československá, Poslanecká Sněmovna, *Těsnopisecké zprávy o schůsích Poslanecké Sněmovny Národního Shromáždění Republiky Československé*, 10 meeting, June 19, 1920, pp. 490 *et seq.*, 1 session; Republika Československá, Senát, *Těsnopisecké zprávy o schůsích Senátu Národního Shromáždění Republiky Československé*, 10 meeting, June 24, 1920, pp. 394 *et seq.*, 1 session. Henceforth, these documents will be referred to as *Zprávy* (Poslanecká Sněmovna) and (Senát) respectively. Similarly, another set of documents will be referred to as *Tisky*.

whereas many Germans still remained dissatisfied and refused to consider the question of the war bonds solved.[29]

Czechoslovakia also had Engliš to thank for her budget of 1921, the first that was nearly balanced—at approximately eighteen billion crowns. In spite of the extraordinary expenses necessitated by the mobilization of October, 1921, against the attempted return to power in Hungary of the ex-King Charles,[30] this long-sought-for financial equilibrium had been brought about through an increase in taxation and by means of a new and drastic financial law whereby all expenditures of the various ministries above the original budget estimates were to be allowed only by special permission from parliament.[31]

The status of financial equilibrium was of brief duration. The budget of 1922 produced another deficit, totalling 988,-000,000 crowns, which was caused primarily by the inclusion in the budget of the hitherto uncovered deficits of the provincial administrations.[32] Still another loan became necessary if the printing of more paper money was to be again avoided. Engliš met the emergency, in the spring of 1922, by negotiating a foreign loan for 3,300,000 pounds sterling and $14,000,000 at Amsterdam, London and New York. The fact that a foreign loan could be negotiated was owing to the increased confidence felt abroad because of Czechoslovakia's efficient mobilization and favorable trade balance of 4,877,000,000 crowns in 1921. Nevertheless, the terms were severe: the interest rate was set at 8.3 percent;

[29] Engliš, K., "Government Finance", in Gruber, *op. cit.*, p. 195; Piot, *op. cit.*, pp. 185-186; Dumont-Wilden, L., "Les Difficultés intérieures de la Tchécoslovaquie", *Révue politique et littéraire*, vol. lix, pp. 156-159.

[30] For full details, *cf. infra*, pp. 184 *et seq.*

[31] For additional details, *cf.* Engliš, *loc. cit.*, p. 195 or Chanal, *op. cit.*, pp. 104-118.

[32] *Cf.* Engliš, *loc. cit.*, p. 196.

as security, Czechoslovakia was compelled to pledge the receipts from her customs and tobacco monopoly; and the League of Nations was entrusted with protecting the interests of her creditors.[33]

Meanwhile, the exigencies of domestic politics again changed the financial policy of the state. The Pětka (Quintumvirate), a coalition of five political parties which had been formed late in 1920 upon the basis of mutual concessions and which had become, subsequently, the dominant political bloc, gained actual power on October 5, 1922. By this move, Rašín became Minister of Finance for the second time, after an interval of more than three years. Immediately there arose rumors that the crown would rise to its par value. In view of Rašín's open hostility to the great industries, he was accused of seeking to bring about their ruin by a policy of speedy deflation.[34] While protesting against the veracity of such rumors, he refused the chief request of his critics, a reduction of the tariff, for the reason that the state could not afford to reduce radically its revenues. He admitted that Czechoslovakia could not thrive upon isolation and deplored the existence of an excessive economic nationalism. Constructively, he advocated a merging of the financial and economic foreign policies, particularly the negotiation of new commercial treaties abroad and the enforcement of strict economy at home. Of these suggestions, he was able to enforce immediately economy in domestic expenditures; but, despite an increase of 688 percent in

[33] *Official Journal*, August, 1922, pp. 1000-1001; *Zprávy* (Poslanecká Sněmovna), 131 meeting, March 29, 1922, pp. 25 *et seq.*, 5 session; Piot, *op. cit.*, pp. 200-202; *cf.* also, Pasvolsky, *op. cit.*, p. 264, for Engliš' own statement concerning foreign loans and how they should be spent.

[34] For full details, *cf.* the various Praha newspapers during October, 1922, particularly the attacks inspired, to all appearances, by the German industrialists in the German newspapers, such as the *Prager Abendblatt*, *Prager Presse* and *Prager Tagblatt*.

revenues since the first year of independence, and in spite of every economy, there still remained, for 1923, a deficit of 566,000,000 crowns. The chief items that contributed to this result were a reduction of 800,000,000 crowns of revenue because of a lower duty on coal and because of an ad valorem tariff reduction, concessions which he had granted despite his opposition to a general tariff reduction, and an increase of 711,000,000 crowns in interest payments because of the recent foreign loan. Finally, Rašín recognized the war bonds at the liberal rate of seventy-five percent, on condition that the holders subscribe to the fourth liberty loan which was being quoted at eighty-one at Amsterdam. In this last move, he was bound by the promises of Engliš, but, throughout his operations, he fostered a world-wide and ever growing confidence in the financial stability of Czechoslovakia.[35]

In the actual course of events, it was discovered that Rašín's original plans could not be followed in every detail. Though his successors had continued his policy for a graduated deflation and had avoided inflation, circumstances beyond their control had prevented any deflation sufficiently rapid to permit revaluation of the crown at its pre-war value. Consequently, the immediate restoration of parity had been abandoned tacitly in favor of definite stabilization at a lower figure. During the latter half of 1922, there developed a rapid increase in the value of the crown, owing largely to artificial circumstances, followed by rumors that stabilization could not be maintained. A " flight from the crown " produced abnormal speculation in foreign exchange, but this tendency was halted by drastic measures of the government, before the value of the crown was once more reduced. The

---

[35] Piot, *op. cit.*, pp. 229-236; Chanal, *op. cit.*, pp. 151-154; for summaries of the discussions in the Chamber of Deputies on October 31, 1922, on Rašín's projected financial measures, *cf. Národní Politika* or *Národní Listy*, of November 1, 1922 (each twice daily).

crown was stabilized at $.03 (.0296375). The time for permanent stabilization and for parity had not yet arrived. Such a step would necessitate first a " return to normalcy " in Central Europe and a settlement of the debt in notes that Czechoslovakia had inherited. Her claims against the Bank of Austria-Hungary for notes, bonds and current accounts totalled 10,097,000,000 crowns, the actual value of which was doubtful.[86]

Czechoslovakia acquired prestige because of her relative financial soundness amid general Central European instability. As the result of a severe business depression, her success seemed to be obtained at the cost of prosperity, yet even prosperity was destined to return when foreign trade recovered from its temporary decline. The chief credit for the inauguration and successful completion of the program of financial independence and stabilization was owing to Rašín, who, in his hour of triumph, was shot on January 5, 1923, by a young anarchist, Soupal, because he had reduced wages generally. At first hopes were held for his recovery, but he died on February 17.[87] Rašín's martyr's death enhanced his already great fame; patriotic Czechoslovaks felt convinced that other states, with equally able leadership, might also have attained financial stability as early as Czechoslovakia.[88]

Economic Policy

The second grand division of Czechoslovakia's extensive program of domestic stabilization revolved around the formulation and maintenance of constructive domestic and foreign economic policies. Primarily an industrial country,

---

[86] Pasvolsky, *op. cit.*, pp. 208-215; Piot, *op. cit.*, pp. 237-241; Engliš, *loc. cit.*, p. 198.

[87] Pasvolsky, *op. cit.*, pp. 215-217; Piot, *op. cit.*, pp. 249-253.

[88] For evaluations of Rašín, *cf. Le Temps*, January 11, 1923 and *Zprávy* (Senát), 150 meeting, February 21, 1923, pp. 1040 *et seq.*, 6 session.

she realized the vital significance, to her trade, of the economic changes created by the War. Although her territories, except for certain regions in the Carpathians and for Slovakia in 1919, had not been the scenes of actual warfare and had escaped more or less systematic devastation, they had, nevertheless, been greatly impoverished by the repeated requisitions of both Austrians and Magyars. As a result, the end of the War witnessed a great shortage of all raw materials—of leather, textiles, minerals, fuels, fats, foodstuffs, domestic animals and even of natural fertilizers. The scarcity of the last had caused her soil to lose much of its productivity.

Nevertheless, Czechoslovakia was fortunate both in the extent and in the diversity of her resources; within her borders there existed an abundance of the wealth necessary to establish and maintain a stable and prosperous state. Her territories had produced 16.1 percent of the wheat, 39 percent of the rye, 47.1 percent of the barley, 37.5 percent of the oats, 37.4 percent of the potatoes, 26 percent of the beef and 18 percent of the pork of the defunct Empire-Kingdom.[39] She had also inherited the lion's share of the Dual Monarchy's industries: 95 percent of the malt factories, 92 percent of the sugar factories, 90 percent of the glass industry, 80 percent of the building and ceramic industries, 75 percent of the chemical industry, 70 percent of the leather and paper industries, 65 percent of the breweries, 50 percent of the liquor industry and most of the textile industry.[40] Her forests (33.16 percent of her area),[41] her abundance of

[39] Piot, *op. cit.*, p. 38; Pasvolsky, *op. cit.*, p. 36; *cf.* also, Brdlík, V., "Agriculture", in Gruber, *op. cit.*, pp. 12-32.

[40] Piot, *op. cit.*, p. 38; Pasvolsky, *op. cit.*, p. 36; *cf.* also, Franzl, K., "Industries" in Gruber, *op. cit.*, pp. 89-109.

[41] *Cf.* Siman, K., "Forestry", in Gruber, *op. cit.*, pp. 33-42.

water power [42] and her mineral resources, particularly her coal,[43] represented other enormous sources of national wealth that awaited only further development.

While the Czechoslovaks were duly appreciative of the potential wealth of their country, they were also aware of the economic problems that confronted them because of the fact that their new state comprised only 140,485 square kilometers (54,241 square miles) and contained only 13,613,172 people, according to the census of February 15, 1921, or, respectively, 22 percent of the area and 26 percent of the population of the former Austria-Hungary.[44] Their whole foreign economic policy had to be based upon the fact that such a relatively small proportion of the area and population of the former Empire-Kingdom had inherited the great majority of the industrial plants. The excess of production over domestic consumption would insure an eventual favorable balance of trade and an influx of gold which would improve the financial situation, but such results could be accomplished only after all Central Europe had been stabilized and had established commercial contacts with Czechoslovakia. The new international boundaries that had been created by the War within the former Dual-Monarchy represented, to Czechoslovakia, just so many barriers that her trade would have to surmount. If she were to utilize the industrial equipment that the several preceding decades had created within her borders, she would have to become an importer of raw materials, an exporter of manufactured goods, and, primarily, an industrial state whose prosperity would be dependent upon foreign trade. Under the stimulus

[42] Cf. Zimmler, E., " Water Power ", in Gruber, op. cit., pp. 76-88.

[43] Cf. Peters, J., " Coal ", in Gruber, op. cit., pp. 67-75.

[44] Cf. Boháč, A., " Population ", in Gruber, op. cit., pp. 1-11; also, Résultats préliminaires du recensement de la population du 15 février, 1921 (Prague, 1921).

of such conditions, Czechoslovakia, whether motivated solely by clearly defined self-interest or also by a measure of altruism, felt herself destined to become the balance-wheel that was to stabilize Central Europe.

It was no easy task to put into effect so enlightened a foreign economic policy, one that would dove-tail so perfectly with Beneš' conception of what the scope of Czechoslovakia's entire foreign policy should be. Since the attainment of independence, many Czechoslovaks had aspired to realize their pre-war dream of a Republic that would be entirely independent in every respect, not only politically, but financially and economically. The same spirit that had won political, and later, financial independence, was introduced too far into the economic sphere; clear-cut economic facts were obscured by political and racial issues and prejudices. There arose, domestically, a struggle in which the politically dominant but economically weak Czechoslovaks sought to wrest economic supremacy from the Germans. This same struggle was carried over into the question of a foreign economic policy: fear of a restoration of the economic power of Vienna demanded a policy of economic nationalism that tended towards isolation. So bitter was the feeling that, as has already been indicated, Rašín himself had been accused, falsely, of deliberate plotting to ruin German industrialists by means of his monetary policy. To all appearances, the majority of the Czechoslovaks failed to appreciate clearly the contradiction between the internationalist policy apparently demanded by Czechoslovakia's economic position and the policy of isolation dictated by economic nationalism.[45]

The day of the attainment of independence, October 28, 1918, had witnessed the inauguration of a provisional system of strict control of all imports and exports, a step deemed

[45] *Cf.* Rist, *op. cit.*, p. 109; Chanal, *op. cit.*, pp. 132-138; Pasvolsky, *op. cit.*, pp. 265-266.

necessary because of the scarcity of all the necessities of life. On November 22, 1918, this function was assumed by the Czechoslovak Import and Export Commission, which, as a branch of the Ministry of Commerce, issued special permits regulating foreign trade. Precautions were taken to reduce exports temporarily; for instance, only limited amounts of coal and manufactured goods, and no foodstuffs nor raw materials, were allowed to leave the country. The motive for such drastic procedure was to assure the Czechoslovaks against any unnecessary hardships caused by insufficient supplies, but, regardless of its justification at the time, it served as a beginning for a policy of economic nationalism.[46]

Similarly, in order to create the smallest possible adverse trade balance, the Commission forbade the importation of all luxuries and goods that were obtainable in local markets. Further coordination between Czechoslovakia's financial and economic policies was assured by the creation of a Central Exchange Bureau which was to receive from the exporters all their foreign currency which was reassigned, by special permits, to the purchase of other necessities. In this manner not only was foreign trade regulated, but the financial status of the state was rendered more secure.[47]

The law of February 20, 1919, established independent customs duties for Czechoslovakia to replace the old Austro-Hungarian rates which had been effective until that date. In view of the indeterminate status of the frontiers at the time, tne former customs frontier was retained against Germany, and a new line, based upon the probable territorial decisions of the Peace Conference, was established gradually against Austria, Hungary and Poland. While new customs frontiers were drawn within the former Dual Monarchy, the old

[46] Pasvolsky, *op. cit.*, p. 275; *cf.* also, Peroutka, F., " The Commercial Policy and the Tariff ", in Gruber, *op. cit.*, p. 128.

[47] Peroutka, *loc. cit.*, p. 129.

organization and methods were preserved. The initial rates were based on the Austro-Hungarian tariff of 1906, but, in an emergency, the Minister of Finance, with the consent of the Ministers of Agriculture and Commerce, might temporarily reduce or abolish duties on certain necessities. Subsequently, animal products, cattle, fats, flour, grain, seeds and various raw materials were placed upon the free list, but pre-war rates were continued for semi-manufactured goods, whereas surtaxes of 200 and 220 percent were imposed, respectively, upon all other products and luxuries. Because of the fact that the currency was far below par, and because the duties were specific, the tariff was, in reality, lower than the pre-war one.[48]

Procedure was modified further by the law of February 26, 1919, whereby some of the powers of the Commission were assigned to industrial syndicates in order that domestic industry and trade might enjoy a measure of economic independence free from governmental paternalism. In practice, this step led to unfair discriminations. The law of June 24, 1920, deprived the syndicates of these powers which were granted to a Foreign Trade Bureau that resumed the earlier license system by revising the system of permits, by issuing lists of goods that might be exported freely, by liberalizing the regulations for imports and by continuing to cooperate in controlling foreign currency.[49]

Throughout the year 1919, Czechoslovakia encountered many obstacles to her foreign trade. Trieste was the sole outlet by sea until May, when Germany allowed transit privileges by way of the Elbe, according to Article 339 of the Treaty of Versailles. Until then, the proceeds of the liquidation of Czechoslovakia's war materials in France were applied to the

[48] *Ibid.*, pp. 127-128.

[49] *Ibid.*, pp. 129-130; *Zprávy* (Poslanecká Sněmovna), 8 meeting, June 16, 1920, pp. 372 *et seq.*, I session.

purchase, in Italy, of the first raw materials and semi-manufactured products that were imported into Czechoslovakia to relieve the needs of her textile industry. Throughout the Republic, trade was hampered by a shortage of freight cars. This shortage was relieved by a more efficient organization and by special privileges on Rumanian and Yugoslav railroads, which, after the ratification of the Treaty of St. Germain, became new outlets for goods that had formerly been exported via Hamburg. The best outlet—the Danube —required development of its facilities. The natural advantages of Czechoslovakia's leading port, Bratislava, could not be utilized until after July, 1920, when 228,500,000 crowns were allowed for the construction of a new harbor. Czechoslovakia's eagerness to develop new commercial contacts was again made manifest by her participation, in August, 1920, in the fair at Lyons. Subsequently, she held her own first fairs at Praha and Bratislava.[50]

As conditions within Czechoslovakia had begun to change, there evolved gradually a less extreme economic foreign policy. It came to be realized that the newly-won political and financial independence could be maintained without creating a state that was economically self-sufficient. Complete economic independence was an impossibility. Much more advantageous would be a condition of economic interdependence which would enable Czechoslovakia to reap the maximum advantage from her highly organized industrial system. In the course of this economic evolution, there came to light psychological as well as purely economic factors. A vital necessity of the political situation was a so-called " Western orientation ", if independence was to be safeguarded.[51] At the same time, the financial situation demanded a similar policy—Czechoslovakia felt herself com-

[50] Peroutka, F., "Foreign Trade", in Gruber, op. cit., p. 120.

[51] For full details, cf. infra, pp. 98, 100 et seq., 129 et seq.

pelled to seek markets whose purchasing power was based upon a more stable currency than was that of her own immediate neighbors. As a consequence, her trade had to adapt itself to world conditions and markets, and her competitive position in this trade became a matter of vital concern.[52]

Within Czechoslovakia there had developed two conflicting viewpoints concerning the question of industrialization: whether it would be best to curtail manufacturing and develop agriculture, or maintain and even expand her industrial activities.[53] The dense population, particularly in the western portions of the Republic, rendered any curtailment of manufacturing possible only at the cost of aggravating the already pressing problem of unemployment, whereas it was doubtful if agriculture could be expanded considerably. The problem was rendered more acute by the fact that Danubian areas, formerly within the Empire-Kingdom, were now world markets. Because of the great postwar growth of manufacturing in these formerly distinctly agricultural regions, the difficulty of retaining even her former domestic markets was enhanced for Czechoslovakia. Some reorganization of her industrial system became imperative. The ultimate solution was a compromise whereby she reduced those industries which encountered the strongest international rivalry and expanded those in which competition was less keen.[54]

Up to 1920, Czechoslovakia had followed a negative foreign economic policy: she had not attempted to increase her exports. Her supplies had been so depleted by the War that she desired no further drain upon her resources. The

[52] *Cf.* Chanal, *op. cit.*, pp. 138-146.
[53] *Cf.* Pasvolsky, *op. cit.*, pp. 268-269.
[54] *Ibid.*, pp. 271-273.

resulting near-balance between imports and exports might be maintained by a purely agricultural country, but not by a primarily industrial one; however wise such a policy might have been immediately after the attainment of independence, it could not be continued long without inviting economic disaster. This fact was appreciated by Hotowetz, the Minister of Foreign Trade, again one whose services have not been properly appreciated. Hotowetz wished to remove all restraints upon production and trade and encourage the greatest possible development of industry. To this end, he had helped to create the Foreign Trade Bureau and to publish a free list on July 27, 1920.[55] Thanks to his efforts, Czechoslovakia became converted to a more liberal foreign economic policy.

In her system of trade restrictions, Czechoslovakia's initial device—special import and export licenses—had been supplemented by a series of tariffs which became increasingly prohibitive. After several revisions during 1920 and 1921, the tariff law of May 21, 1921, the most drastic to date, created a system of surtaxes after the fashion of the post-war tariff of France. The basic or nominal rate was multiplied by varying coefficients that had been predetermined: for instance, the coefficients for luxuries and specially protected articles ranged from ten to sixteen; for manufactured goods and articles with lower protective rates, seven; and for goods whose importation was favored, one to five. Later in the year, because of the rapid depreciation of the German mark, even this tariff was deemed an insufficient protection against German competition. A new tariff, passed on December 18, 1921, and enforced from January 1, 1922, increased the

[55] Piot, *op. cit.*, pp. 168-174; *cf.* also, Cisař, J. and Pokorný, F. (Comps.), *The Czechoslovak Republic* (London, 1922), pp. 167-171; Caldwell, R. J., *The Economic Situation in Czechoslovakia in 1920* (Washington, 1921).

coefficients for manufactured goods between ten to fifteen and for specially protected goods between twenty to thirty. This revision, coupled with the rapid appreciation of the crown during the early part of 1922, doubled, and, in some instances, even trebled the pre-war rates.[56]

Although the initial motive for Czechoslovakia's elaborate trade restrictions had been the need for a temporary conservation of her essential commodities and for a temporary check upon the importation of non-essentials, later developments demonstrated other possible advantages that might be derived from this system. It became a powerful protector of the currency and was continued because of its valuable services in furthering financial stabilization. By 1921, its value became still more marked as a " bargaining " possibility in the negotiation of commercial treaties. In view of these advantages and because of the intense feeling of economic nationalism then prevalent, Hotowetz appreciated the difficulties that confronted any attempted abolition of such a system, but he realized that, surrounded by unstable currencies, Czechoslovakia dared not rely upon customs duties alone for sufficient economic and financial protection. He deemed a " Western orientation " abnormal economically and considered the Succession States Czechoslovakia's natural customers. To develop better commercial relations with these neighbors, he invited Austria, Hungary and the other four Succession States to a conference at Bratislava in December, 1920, but the project failed because of a lack of interest in the other states. In spite of this failure, Czechoslovakia, as she came to perfect her tariff system, abandoned gradually some of her restrictions on foreign trade. Although she still retained her license system on some commodities, a practice which caused her considerable

[56] Peroutka, "The Commercial Policy and the Tariff", *loc. cit.*, pp. 135-136; Pasvolsky, *op. cit.*, p. 277.

embarrassment in negotiating commercial treaties, by 1921 she had turned definitely towards ~~economic~~ freedom by abolishing the central controlling agencies for products such as alcohol, meat, sugar, etc.[57]

In the meantime, the post-war industrial boom had run its course in Czechoslovakia and was succeeded by a period of depression which enhanced the need for foreign markets.[58] The industrial situation that resulted was largely responsible for hastening the adoption of the new policy of industrial freedom. When the " Western orientation " failed to produce the anticipated economic results, Czechoslovakia was compelled to turn again to the markets of Central Europe. She could cover her domestic needs with from thirty to thirty-five per cent of her industrial output and the surplus had to be exported. At the same time, little provision had been made for hard times: financial deflation and the heavy taxes necessary to reduce the annual deficits of the early years had created an unhealthy economic situation. There were 329 bankruptcies in 1921 and 2698 in the following year. This lesson of the evils resulting from a lack of proper economic outlets was costly, but was well remembered, even amid great economic distress. Much consolation was derived from the fact that the larger agricultural industries, particularly sugar, thanks to cheap labor and to raw materials close at hand, continued to thrive.[59]

[57] *Zprávy* (Poslanecká Sněmovna), 30 meeting, December 3, 1920, pp. 1049 *et seq.*, 3 session; *cf.* also, Pasvolsky, *op. cit.*, p. 276; Piot, *op. cit.*, p. 180; Chanal, *op. cit.*, pp. 157-159.

[58] It is beyond the scope of this work to furnish statistics on the foreign trade of Czechoslovakia. The best source for such information is *Měsíční přehled zahraničního obchodu* (Monthly survey of foreign trade) published monthly at Praha by the Government Statistical Office.

[59] For detailed accounts of the economic trend within Czechoslovakia, 1920-1923, *cf.* Lockhart, R. H. B., " Central Europe and Czechoslovakia ", *Edinburgh Review*, vol. ccxxxviii, pp. 209-229; Mildschuh, *loc. cit.*, pp. 179-191; Chanal, *op. cit.*, pp. 182-216.

After her conversion to the doctrine of economic freedom through the influence of Hotowetz and of the depression, Czechoslovakia pursued ardently a policy of economic cooperation with her neighbors, and, despite the lack of adequate support for this ideal from the other Succession States,[60] continued independently along the course she had charted for herself. Although confronted by the conflicting necessities of protecting her domestic industries, of stimulating her exports, and of maintaining some system of trade control as long as it was maintained by her neighbors, she abolished the Foreign Trade Bureau on January 19, 1922, and transferred its powers, which were also greatly reduced, to the Ministry of Commerce. On September 9, 1922, there followed a tariff revision that reduced the coefficients, in many instances by as much as one-fourth. In this manner Czechoslovakia set the example for an economic foreign policy contrary to the highly nationalistic tendencies that were prevalent throughout Central Europe.[61]

There remained for Czechoslovakia the necessity of rendering effective her new foreign economic policy by the conclusion of a series of commercial treaties. By this means she hoped not only to recover Bohemia's pre-war position in world markets, but to establish upon a secure and permanent basis a still greater volume of foreign trade. Immediately after the armistice, the artificial barriers to trade seemed insurmountable. There arose on every hand mutual prohibitions and state control of commerce. The trade of Czechoslovakia suffered when Austria applied against her the tariff of 1906 and gave Germany a better rate, when Italy prohibited the importation of glass-ware, and Great

[60] For full details of Czechoslovakia's efforts to obtain the cooperation of the other Succession States in stabilizing Central Europe, *cf. infra*, pp. 189 *et seq.*

[61] Peroutka, *loc. cit.*, pp. 135-137.

Britain prohibited the importation of hops.   As a result of such restrictions and because of the unstable conditions that prevailed throughout Central Europe, the region where in normal times Czechoslovakia found her chief markets, no one desired any long-term commitments.   Therefore, Czechoslovakia's early commercial treaties, particularly those negotiated between 1919 and 1921, were not only temporary in character and binding for brief periods of time, but were characterized by more or less reciprocal " quotas ", based upon the transfer of stated amounts of specified commodities. Although such treaties soon proved inadequate, they only gradually assumed the form of ordinary commercial treaties. Czechoslovakia did not begin to negotiate treaties for the adjustment of tariffs until 1923, until which date her tariff remained autonomous and the most-favored-nation clauses of her early treaties inoperative.   The reasons why the negotiations for mutual adjustment of tariff rates were so long delayed were obvious.   The tariff rates of Germany, Austria, Hungary and Poland were even less stable than those of Czechoslovakia because of fluctuations in their currencies. France and Italy were interested primarily in import permits. Great Britain, Belgium, Denmark and Holland desired to retain their own respective tariffs, which they saw no reason for surrendering without equal advantages in return.[62]   The drive for tariff agreements, which was inaugurated during the struggle for domestic stabilization, 1918-1923, became involved also with so many non-economic Central European problems that, at first, it was relatively easier to reach agreements with more remote states.   Czechoslovakia realized that time was required to enlarge her commercial horizon and persevered in her efforts to create a comprehensive

[62] *Ibid.*, pp. 134-135; Chanal, *op. cit.*, pp. 159-164.

system of commercial treaties even after her economic stabilization had been attained.[63]

Social Reform

The third major aspect of the struggle for domestic stabilization concerned social reform. The abnormal conditions prevalent throughout Europe at the time of the establishment of the Czechoslovak Republic had been reflected in wages, prices, unemployment and general social distress. The ensuing misery had been aggravated by an inheritance of social evils and inequalities from the defunct Empire-Kingdom: of such questions, that of land reform was the most urgent. The general let-down which follows every post-war period became marked: the exhaustion and misery of the masses, the increase in materialism, and the weakening of moral ties had prepared the way for a favorable reception of the revolutionary doctrines emanating from Russia. To Czechoslovakia, the question of furthering her domestic stabilization through a comprehensive policy of social reform became merged with the more elusive problem of combating Bolshevism within her own borders.

The intense nationalism of Czechoslovak labor prevented the communist agitators from making much headway in trying to further their extreme demands. Nevertheless, the influence of the Russian social revolution was felt keenly, even if it did lack sufficient force to shatter the economic foundations of the Republic. The preaching of Bolshevism

[63] In a work of this scope it is impossible for the writer to analyze in detail every commercial treaty negotiated by Czechoslovakia. The most important ones, those that played conspicuous parts in Czechoslovakia's general foreign policy, will be discussed in detail subsequently in their proper setting. The best single collection of complete texts of these treaties, up to 1928, is *Obchodní smlouvy mezistátní*, 3 vols., edited by J. Dvořáček and Z. Konečný. A complete series of texts will be found, of course, in the *League of Nations Treaty Series*. Cf. also, *infra*, pp. 247-248.

complicated relations with Russia,[64] and, to some extent perhaps, weakened the spirit of domestic enterprise, but failed to check domestic consolidation. Czechoslovakia adopted a comprehensive scheme of social reform both as a form of domestic insurance against the outbreak of Bolshevism and as a solution for one major phase of her problem of domestic stabilization. Since this program concerned primarily Czechoslovakia's domestic rather than her foreign policy, the scope of this work permits merely a mention of the various laws, such as the eight-hour-day law for labor; state aid to demobilized soldiers, war invalids, unemployed, poor, widows and orphans; sickness and accident insurance; the housing reform; the creation of local miners' and of factory councils; the regulation of work in home industries; a property tax; public works; and agrarian reform.[65] The great majority of these laws were in effect by 1921, but the program they initiated is far from being completely realized even at this writing; however, it was a potent factor in helping bring about the stabilization of the Republic during the early years of its existence, and, added to from time to time, it continued to remain a weapon against the efforts of both Bolsheviks and Fascists.

Land reform, one of the major items of the new social policy, assumed an international aspect when it involved the break-up of large estates formerly belonging to the Crown. It became a factor in the general question of the post-war

[64] For full details of Czechoslovak-Russian relations, *cf. infra*, pp. 113 *et seq.*

[65] The best account, in English, of this labor and social legislation is to be found in a compilation of articles by leading Czechoslovak government ministers, professors and business men in Gruber, *op. cit.*, particularly "Land Reform", by A. Pavel, pp. 43-66; "Labor Legislation", by E. Stern, pp. 201-209; "Social Welfare Policy as Shown in the Assistance to the Unemployed, the Care of the War Sufferers and Social Insurance", by J. Brabec, pp. 210-219; "Child Welfare", by J. Janovský, pp. 220-226; "The Housing Question", by H. Kubišta, pp. 227-238; and "Crime", by A. Miřička, pp. 239-248.

financial settlement, which has already been discussed: but it also developed into a religious question when it concerned the property of the Catholic Church. Consequently, the question of land reform became involved in the fourth major phase of Czechoslovakia's domestic stabilization, the adoption of a definite religious policy.[66]

Religious Policy

Within Czechoslovak lands, the Protestant minority had regarded opposition to the Catholic Church as a national heritage from Hussite days. This feeling had been strengthened by the Concordat of 1855 between Emperor Francis Joseph and Pope Pius IX, whereby it had been decreed that the State should preserve the Roman Catholic religion, " with all its rights and prerogatives according to God's order and the Church's laws ". Thereby the Church had been granted control over all matters pertaining to marriage, morals and education. Such action on the part of the government, at a time when the Czechs were in the midst of their nationalistic revival, was considered by such leaders as Havliček, Rieger, Šafařík, and by the historians, Palacký and Tomek, as a State-Church conspiracy to destroy Czech nationalism.[67]

During the latter decades of the nineteenth century, the apparent alliance between the Catholic Church and the Austro-Hungarian government continued to grow more and more distasteful even to those Catholics who were also patriotic Czechs. Throughout the lands of the Bohemian Crown

---

[66] *Cf.* Křovák, R., *Věčný ukazovatel k zákonu a nařizením o pozemkové reformě* (Praha, 1922) ; *cf.* also, Kučera, B., " Československá pozemková reforma s hlediška mezinárodního práva", *Zahraniční Politika*, vol. iii, pp. 444-454.

[67] It was perhaps natural for the leaders of the nationalistic revival to hold such opinions, since they were Protestants, and since their movement was receiving practically no support from the Catholics. *Cf.* Liscová, Mrs. M., *The Religious Situation in Czechoslovakia* (Prague, 1925), p. 32.

there became more widespread the belief that the Catholic Church, in its desire to strengthen a loyal Great Power, opposed the various nationalistic movements that sought to disrupt the Dual Monarchy. Masaryk had come to hold such a belief early in life; although born of Catholic parents, he had soon left the Church, and, at one time, had considered seriously studying for the Protestant ministry. Throughout his whole career, his opposition to Catholicism had never wavered, a fact that had been attested by his consistent attitude in old Austria, and even by his inauguration of the campaign for Czechoslovak independence at Geneva on July 6, 1915, the semi-millennial anniversary of the death of John Hus.[68] During the course of the War, as the Czechoslovaks came to accept Masaryk's viewpoint on the question of independence, an increasingly influential minority also came to accept his religious conclusions. These facts explained Masaryk's lack of popularity with the Clericals even after he became President. Anti-Catholic sentiment became so violent that, in the course of the Czechoslovak revolution, a Praha mob, on November 3, 1918, destroyed many Catholic monuments and forced the prince bishop to take refuge abroad.[69] The attempted papal reconciliation of November 8 [70] had little effect upon the anti-Clericals.

[68] Masaryk, T. G., *The Making of a State* (New York, 1927), pp. 44-46; *Světová Revoluce*, pp. 66-67.

[69] *The New York Times,* November 4, 1918.

[70] For the Pope's letter of November 8, 1918, to the Nuncio in Vienna, which instructed the latter to enter into friendly relations with the Succession States, *cf. Arbeiter Zeitung*, November 8, 1918; Loiseau, C., "The Vatican and the New States of Central Europe", *New Europe*, September 25, 1919, pp. 241-247; or Buell, R. L., "The Vatican and the New World", *Current History*, vol. xvi, pp. 977-984. As a contrast to the Czechoslovak viewpoint concerning the attitude of the Vatican, *cf.* Ryan, J. H., "The Vatican's World Policy", *Current History*, vol. xvii, pp. 429-438, which states that the Pope was neutral and suspended judgment during the War; or Ausset, J., *La Question Vaticane* (Paris, 1928).

Since most of the inhabitants of the Republic were Catholic, and since many of the chief nationalist leaders were Protestant or anti-Clerical, the religious problem centered in the fact that the nationalistic intellectuals who had seized power through the revolution represented the nationalism but not the religion of the masses. After the attainment of independence, there developed in Czechoslovakia strong Catholic and anti-Catholic movements: the former demanding the establishment of formal relations with the Vatican; and the latter, the establishment of a new Czechoslovak National Church which would embody the reform measures advocated by the religious radicals. Friction was engendered between the two groups, but both appeared to hesitate before precipitating hostilities after the initial revolutionary ferment had once subsided. Matters came to a crisis on December 25, 1919, when the radicals insisted that mass be celebrated in Czech.[71] In anger, the radical clerics, who had already created a club of reforming priests, voted, on January 9, 1920, by 140 to 66 with 5 not voting, to effect a separation from Rome and to create a Czechoslovak National Church.[72] Thereupon, the Pope, on January 15, 1920, issued a bull of excommunication against the radicals, condemning in particular their proposal that Czechoslovak priests be released from the obligation of celibacy.[73]

The Papal Bull merely added fuel to the flames. For a time a Hussite revival appeared imminent as the radicals continued to gain ground. They called a national religious meeting at Praha during the week of February 13, for the purpose of either confirming the vote for separation from the Church or for continued adherence conditional upon the acceptance by the Church of specific reforms, such as a

[71] *Prager Abendblatt*, December 26, 1919.

[72] *Ibid.*, January 9, 1920; *Svornost*, January 10, 1920.

[73] *Prager Abendblatt*, January 16, 1920; *Svornost*, February 2, 1920.

national liturgy, the election of bishops by their own clergy-men, the abolition of celibacy and the reversal of the sentence upon Hus.[74] The action of the radicals received added impetus from the fact that the government was known to favor a division of the Church lands and the replacement of German and Hungarian bishops and other high Church officials by Czechoslovaks. Of the nearly fourteen million people in Czechoslovakia, over ten million were Catholics, but, it appeared, many of them only nominally so,[75] hence the radicals had high hopes of success. Although the result failed to justify their anticipations, separation was confirmed. The chief supporters of so radical a step were to be found among the parish priests who had left the Church to accept positions with the new government; from their number, there was selected a committee of twelve to organize the new Czechoslovak National Church. Throughout this agitation, the chief argument of the radicals had been that a separation from Rome would liberate Czechoslovakia from the bonds of a foreign culture.[76] The new Czechoslovak National Church, which thus began with about 250,000 adherents, decreed a separation of Church and State and approved both civil marriage and divorce. There remained the question of the status of the new clergy: since the Catholic Church refused to consecrate the new bishops, contacts were established with the Serbian Orthodox bishops, by whom the necessary ceremonies were performed, thus theoretically, according to the Catholic view, at least preserving intact the line of apostolic succession from St. Peter.[77]

[74] Seton-Watson, R. W., "The Czechoslovak Republic", *Contemporary Review*, vol. cxix, pp. 310-321.

[75] The census of 1921 listed 10,384,833 Catholics and 990,319 Protestants. *Cf.* also, Liscová, *op. cit.*, pp. 36-60, for statistics and descriptions of the various religious groups within Czechoslovakia. This work represents the viewpoint of a Protestant who attempts to be impartial.

[76] *Právo Lidu*, February 15, 1920.

[77] Stanoyevich, *op. cit.*, p. 291.

Regardless of whether any agreement upon a thorough-going reform would have been possible, the separation from Rome was precipitate. The Free Thinkers, perhaps the most influential of the radical religious groups, prevented any real compromise by alienating the extreme Clericals; and, whatever might have been said in defense of such a policy within Czech lands, its results in Slovakia were unfortunate. There, to the already great problems of administration and reconstruction,[78] was added that of religion. Even if the great majority of the Slovak intellectuals were Protestants, and if the verdict of history had been that the Catholic Slovaks had had a Magyar orientation, the Free Thinkers were still in error when they failed to recognize Father Andrew Hlinka,[79] whose loyalty, suffering and services on behalf of the cause of independence had merited high rewards. This neglect, added to Hlinka's almost fanatical loyalty to the Catholic Church and to the influence of Father Jehlička, an alleged agent of Hungary, so embittered Hlinka that he undertook a journey to Rome and Paris, under a forged Polish passport, to plead for absolute Slovak " autonomy " from Czech rule.[80] After the failure of this mission, Hlinka accepted his fate and reaffirmed his loyalty to the Czechoslovak Republic, but his ill-advised journey had cost him considerable prestige.[81]

Both the Free Thinkers and the Clericals realized that they had been too hasty: as a result, the moderates became more influential within each group. Nevertheless, after the Hlinka episode, friction between Church and State appeared to increase rather than decrease. The government was

[78] *Cf. Paličkář*, S. J. and Brož, A., " Czechs and Slovaks at Odds ", *Current History*, vol. xxii, pp. 784-788.

[79] *Cf.* also *supra*, p. 23.

[80] *Cf. Svornost*, October 25, 1919.

[81] Young, R. F., " Czechs and Slovaks ", *New Statesman*, vol. xiv, pp. 155-156.

anxious to sever and the Church to retain that intimate connection that had been their mutual heritage from pre-war days. Masaryk's opinion that a separation would strengthen both failed to convince the opponents of such a measure. The religious radicals were anxious to terminate religious instruction in the schools which were still under a large measure of Catholic influence. Similarly, they sought to purge the Church from what they deemed excessive German and Magyar influences. On the other hand the Clericals opposed strenuously the application of agrarian reform to the estates of the Church. Finally, after several minor concessions on the part of the Vatican failed to have any effect, the Pope, on September 11, 1920, consented to the separation of Church and State within Czechoslovakia, but requested that the matter be not discussed in the legislature.[82]

This move of the Pope was timely in averting an immediate religious crisis within Czechoslovakia, but was far from representing a permanent solution of the many issues that were at stake: it merely indicated the general conciliatory trend of papal policy, and the many details still remained to be determined. The government of the Republic was not, at this time, in the mood to meet concession with concession. During 1920, the various elements in the comprehensive scheme of domestic stabilization were making marked progress and the authorities had no intention of interfering with the general program, certainly not to the degree that would have been necessary to effect a definitive religious compromise. The main Catholic demand at the time—exemption of Church lands from the policy of land reform—would probably not have been granted. The government was aware of the dangers inherent in the religious situation—that it could ill-afford any undue friction with the Slovaks over religion at a time when stabilization was the key to both the

[82] *The New York Times*, September 11, 1920.

domestic and foreign policies of the state. Although the vital points of the policy of domestic stabilization were maintained, moderation became the keynote of the religious policy.[83] During the first five years of the Czechoslovak Republic, less was accomplished religiously than financially, economically and socially.[84] Nevertheless, in spite of the absence of any definitive religious settlement,[85] the success of the drive for domestic stabilization in other aspects was so successful that, certainly by 1923 if not earlier, Czechoslovakia came to be regarded generally as the most stable state in Central Europe.

[83] *Cf.* Rádl, E., *La Question religieuse en Tchécoslovaquie* (Prague, 1922).

[84] *Cf.* Anon., *Přehled činnosti za prve pětileti Republiky Československé* (Praha, 1923).

[85] For full details regarding the religious settlement, *cf. infra*, pp. 249 *et seq.*

CHAPTER III

THE GREAT POWERS, 1918-1923 [1]

OBJECTIVES OF FOREIGN POLICY

CZECHOSLOVAKIA'S policy of domestic stabilization during the first five years of independence, 1918-1923, went hand in hand with her foreign policy which aimed at the reconstruction of Central Europe and the maintenance of friendly relations with the Great Powers, particularly with the victors of the World War. Nevertheless, during these early years, Czechoslovakia hoped to remain free from their domination and their feuds. In other words, she hoped to preserve her diplomatic independence. At the same time, another cornerstone of her foreign policy was a " Western orientation ", which, because of Russian instability, she deemed vital to her continued independence. Thus, in her contacts with the victorious Western Powers she had to preserve a delicate balance if both friendship and freedom of diplomatic action were to be maintained.

Germany

Since Czechoslovakia's frontiers with Germany were the longest, and since the Elbe River furnished the best outlet by water for the new Republic, future relations between the two states became a matter of concern to the former. The latter also desired to avoid friction. With both accepting the results of the War, and in view of their close economic ties, it was almost inevitable that their first important

[1] The next chapter, "The Reconstruction of Central Europe, 1918-1923", will explain in detail additional aspects of Czechoslovakia's relations with the Western Powers.

question should have been that of trade. The traffic that had developed across their mutual frontier after the War had been hampered by many disputes and by the absence of any commercial treaty. This trade was stabilized by the treaty of June 29, 1920, which clarified the questions of customs duties, finance, transit, transportation, etc. A special clause provided for mutual termination of national control of the exportation and importation of certain specified commodities: by Germany, of chemicals, dyes, pharmaceutical products, iron, steel, toys, machinery, tools, agricultural implements, musical instruments, automobiles and photographic appliances; and by Czechoslovakia, of chemicals, beer, baskets, lumber, mineral waters, furniture, toys, leather-goods, musical instruments, pottery, porcelain, glassware, lace and semi-precious stones. Another clause specifically permitted the exchange of Bohemian lignite and Upper Silesian coal. The most important clause specified reciprocal most-favored-nation treatment. Any third Power might obtain similar advantages. Further clauses provided vaguely for mutual good will. The treaty was declared effective for three months after notice of its cancellation had been given by either state.[2] Even a casual perusal of Czechoslovak newspapers during late June and early July, 1920, would reveal the general satisfaction that resulted from this treaty, which was interpreted as indicating conclusively the absence of any immediate designs on the part of Germany against the integrity of Czechoslovakia.[3] Thus, the establishment of cordial relations with the most powerful neighbor proved surprisingly easy.

[2] *Treaty Series*, vol. xvii, pp. 69-137.

[3] It is interesting to note that the cordial note in Czechoslovak newspapers during the period in question was reflected generally in such German newspapers as *Vorwaerts, Vossische Zeitung, Prager Presse, Prager Tagblatt, Prager Abendblatt, Allgemeine Zeitung* and *Deutsche Allgemeine Zeitung.*

The Western Powers

Although the World War solved many questions and terminated several old feuds, it also created new problems. Among the post-war antagonisms, perhaps none was a greater potential threat to the maintenance of European peace than was French and Italian rivalry. This quarrel between the Latin rivals, which had been bridged temporarily because of common enemies before and during the War, in its revived post-war form had many aspects: psychological, colonial, naval and Continental. In its Continental phase, it threatened to divide Europe again into two armed camps.

Czechoslovakia desired to remain friendly with each of the three Western Powers and deplored any friction among them; nevertheless, should she ever be forced to make a definite choice, she probably would choose France. As will be shown subsequently, not only were the ties she had created with Paris closer than those with London or Rome, but almost every other reason would indicate the choice of France. For Continental purposes, France was not only the strongest in view of mere material force, but had shown the greatest interest in the welfare of the Slavs. There existed practically no friction between Slavic and French interests, whereas such was not the case between the Slavs and either Italy or Great Britain.[4] Moreover, France sought compensation for her pre-war Russian alliance in friendship with the lesser Slav states, whereas Italy deemed some of them potential rivals. Against Germany, Czechoslovakia would find France a powerful and a willing ally; Great Britain, relatively weak as a Central European force, even if she could be induced to enter into any such conflict; and Italy, a dubious military quantity.

Czechoslovakia felt grateful for French assistance in attaining independence; to Great Britain and Italy, both of

[4] For example, Italy *vs.* Yugoslavia, Great Britain *vs.* Russia.

which followed cautiously the trend of French policy, any such feeling of gratitude would be owing only in lesser degree. In view of Great Britain's insularity and traditional aloofness from Continental questions, Czechoslovakia felt correctly that London would have slight interest in and direct influence upon Central European problems. Similarly, while feeling gratitude for the assistance that the United States had so unselfishly granted, Czechoslovakia realized that future American direct interest or intervention in purely European affairs would be doubtful. Russia was Bolshevik. Therefore, the only Great Power that might rival France in the affections of Czechoslovakia would be Italy. Nevertheless, in spite of the fact that the feeling of friendship for Italy might be termed secondary, it was sincere, as even a casual examination of Czech newspapers from November, 1918, to April, 1919, would indicate. Strict censorship prevented the Czech press from criticizing Italy for her armistice of November 3, 1918, with Austria, an armistice which the Czechs deemed selfish, despite the fact that it was drafted by the Allied War Council, following an extensive correspondence between Austria-Hungary and Wilson, and that it was signed by the Allies, rather than by Italy alone.[5] During April and May, 1919, there ensued a change for the worse in Czech public opinion regarding Italy. Again the censorship prevented the feeling of hostility from assuming any open form other than the almost entire omission, in Czech newspapers, of any mention of Italy. Correctly or incorrectly, Czech public opinion considered Italian influence as thrown on the side of Hungary during the war over Slovakia. Tension was increased by the tragic death of Štefánik and the destruction of his papers as the result of an aeroplane crash on May 4, 1919, on the way home from Italy.

[5] *Cf.* Glaise-Horstenau, E. von, *The Collapse of the Austro-Hungarian Empire* (London, 1930), pp. 302-317.

The wisdom of the government in preventing any open criticism of Italy while the fate of Czechoslovakia's boundaries was being decided by the Peace Conference was obvious. In contrast, Czech gratitude for active French aid against the Hungarian Bolsheviks was all the more deep-seated.[6]

The agreement signed on November 4, 1920, between Czechoslovakia and France, Czechoslovakia's first general commercial treaty, marked a further advance in the friendship between the two countries. In contrast with the earlier limited commercial treaties negotiated by Czechoslovakia, this compact marked a new tendency. For mutual benefit, exceptions were made regarding respective monopolies: thus, France sent Czechoslovakia 30,000 tons of Algerian phosphates, in spite of a general prohibition of such an export, and received in exchange 50,000 tons of sugar. The most important single innovation was the division of imports into four categories, each of which received different privileges, the most favored group—raw materials, farm produce, metal and chemical products—being admitted free. France agreed either to reduce her general tariff rates or to apply her minimum tariffs against certain specified Czechoslovak goods.[7] This treaty, intended merely as a temporary measure, remained in force until the conclusion of a definitive commercial and tariff agreement on August 17, 1923.[8]

While France continued to support Czechoslovakia in every emergency, Czechoslovak relations with Italy continued

[6] As a result of the censorship and of a deliberate policy on the part of the Czechoslovak government, in its own obvious interest, to minimize the hostility felt against Italy, the writer has found it difficult to produce conclusive evidence for all these statements. His investigations and conversations with individuals near the scene of events have led him to the conviction that early Czech antagonism to Italy is a topic deserving of the attention of a later and perhaps more successful investigator.

[7] *Obchodní smlouvy mezistátní*, vol. i, pp. 24-157.

[8] *Treaty Series*, vol. xliv, pp. 21-125.

to remain strained. The Italian belief—that the bloc then in the process of formation, the Little Entente, was essentially a Pan-Slavic anti-Italian creation—was not correct; nevertheless, because of this misconception, no Italo-Czechoslovak rapprochement was possible until after the Italo-Yugoslav treaty of Rapallo, on November 12, 1920.[9]

In the spring of 1921, Italo-Czechoslovak relations improved when Beneš took advantage of the diminution of friction between Italy and Yugoslavia to make a visit to Rome and inaugurate negotiations for a definitive commercial treaty. The new treaty, concluded on March 23, 1921, met the Italian demand for privileges similar to those that had been granted France. It was to remain effective until December 31, 1925, and was renewable automatically, barring a year's advance notice of its cancellation by either party. For one year, both agreed partially to abolish restrictions upon imports and exports. While providing for reciprocal maximum advantages and for reciprocal protection of the liberties and interests of the respective citizens, neither country cared to bind itself to too definite a tariff policy. Each reserved the right to abolish the tariff clauses whenever either state should desire to abolish such clauses in its commercial treaties with all other states. In the last analysis, Italy was concerned primarily with exporting raw materials and foodstuffs, and Czechoslovakia with exporting manufactured goods. Italy annually was to export wine, fish, fruit, macaroni, early spring potatoes, vegetables, tangerines, figs, oranges, dried fruits, rice, cooking salt, soup, perfumes, raw silk, Venetian pearls, automobiles, motorcycles and electrical appliances in return for automobiles, motorized plows, furniture, toys, pianos, glassware, woolen carpets, lace, embroidered linen, coffee substitutes, 100

[9] For full details concerning the early relations of Italy and the Little Entente, cf, infra, pp. 167 et seq.

wagon-loads of paper, 20,000 tons of sugar and 50,000 bottles of liqueurs.[10]

On the same day, a second treaty conceded Czechoslovakia special transit privileges via Trieste, where there was established a Czechoslovak Customs Office to facilitate the required customs formalities in cooperation with Italian authorities. Henceforth, Czechoslovak imports landing in Trieste would be routed directly to their ultimate destination without requiring any customs inspection on the Czechoslovak frontier.[11]

A third treaty of the same date provided for the adjustment of claims debts and business relations between firms in the two countries. Italy also received payment from Czechoslovakia for foodstuffs and other goods already received.[12] Although these three treaties did represent satisfactory solutions of mutual economic, financial and juridical questions, renewed friction over rival plans for the reconstruction of Austria [13] prevented Czechoslovakia and Italy from exchanging ratifications until March 1, 1924.[14] Any true Italo-Czechoslovak rapprochement was delayed until after the signing of the Austrian Protocols on October 9, 1922, when Beneš journeyed to Venice to confer with Schanzer, the Italian Foreign Minister. The resulting pourparlers [15] produced a more tolerant attitude within both countries, as each came to realize that cooperation, rather than rivalry, in reconstructing Central Europe was to their mutual advantage.

[10] *Treaty Series*, vol. xxxii, pp. 183-239.

[11] *Ibid.*, vol. xxxii, pp. 241-259.

[12] *Ibid.*, vol. xxxii, pp. 261-279.

[13] For full details, *cf. infra*, pp. 193-195.

[14] *Zprávy* (Senát), 201 meeting, April 24, 1924, pp. 116 *et seq.*, 9 session.

[15] *Cf. The New York Times*, October 11 and 13, 1922; or Beneš, *Problemy nové Evropy*, p. 214. For full details, *cf. infra*, pp. 195-196.

While strengthening the ties with Italy, Beneš did not neglect the more vital question of relations with France. Although interested primarily in the maintenance of the status quo as established by the Peace Treaties, he wished to be prepared for any eventuality. France had introduced the question of security at the opening of the Peace Conference and had continued to urge, at every possible opportunity, a solution of this problem. After the withdrawal of the United States from direct participation in European affairs, France continued to importune Great Britain for some specific pledge in the event of another emergency. Repeated British refusals to become committed led to a series of exchanges of views between the two countries between 1919 and 1922,[16] after which date security became one of the principal questions confronting the League of Nations.[17]

The League of Nations

Beneš, in his desire to avoid having to make a choice between Great Britain and France, believed that their differences regarding the problem of security could best be adjusted by referring the question to what he regarded as the proper agency, the League. At the same time he hoped that membership in the League might also solve Czechoslovakia's own problem of security, further her policy of a " Western orientation " and prevent her from becoming a mere satellite of one of the Great Powers.[18] Beneš' faith in the League coin-

---

[16] *Cf. Papers respecting Negotiations for an Anglo-French Pact* (London, 1924); *Documents diplomatiques relatives aux negotiations concernant les garanties de securité contre une aggression de l'Allemagne* (Paris, 1924); Selsam, J. P., *The Attempts to Form an Anglo-French Alliance, 1919-1924* (Philadelphia, 1936), pp. 1-58.

[17] For full details, *cf. infra*, pp. 209 *et seq.*

[18] Beneš, E., *The Diplomatic Struggle for European Security and the Stabilization of Peace* (Speech of April 1, 1925, before the Foreign Committee of the Senate), pp. 7-9.

cided with the expectations of his people. Alarm was general over what might be termed international anarchy. The League was received with acclaim and its defects were deplored. With her composite population and her peculiar geographical position, Czechoslovakia eagerly welcomed this new promise of security. A satiated state, such as she, almost completely encompassed by hereditary enemies, needed every possible assurance of permanent international political stability and of a long-enduring peace during which she could develop internally and solve the more urgent of her domestic and foreign problems. As the result of such a viewpoint, it was almost inevitable that Czechoslovakia should become an active and enthusiastic member of the League.

Beneš regretted what were in his estimation several imperfections in the League of Nations as it had been constituted originally. Although realizing that the organization could not insure permanent peace, he deemed it a noteworthy step in the right direction and a fundamental part of his political conception of Europe. He wished to preserve whatever procedure might be necessary to give it a high prestige. At the same time, while he advocated certain reforms, he opposed any changes that might be sufficiently radical to vitiate its purposes. Beneš believed that the most beneficial reform would be the elimination of incompetence and inefficiency. To that end, he proposed that the Council be relieved of matters that did not require discussion by having such matters handled by its chairman and by the Secretary-General, and that other matters be voted by roll-call. To avoid the danger that reports of the Permanent Secretariat might be accepted without proper consideration, he suggested that each state on the Council divide the agenda among several experts. Beneš wished that disagreement on the part of one member of the Council might postpone any question to the next session, so that the session might be reserved for matters that required attention to details. He advocated that the Secretariat be urged to prepare its reports with greater speed, in order that the members of the Council might have better facilities for obtaining the necessary advance information upon the questions that they would have to consider. The principle behind all these proposals of Beneš was that it was more important for the Council to act well than to act speedily. If he had any ulterior motive, it was to render more difficult the adoption of a selfish or opportunist policy on the part of the Great Powers which had permanent representation in the League Council.[19]

Even though Czechoslovakia had accomplished little in the First Assembly of the League of Nations, she became active in the Second, where she was represented by Dr. Stephen Osuský. The chief issue involved Article 21 of the League Covenant, which concerned " regional understandings ". Beneš, as vice-chairman of the Revision Commission, grasped eagerly at the opportunity of effecting another reform by strengthening Article 21 and, at the same time, of furthering Czechoslovakia's problem of security by obtaining League recognition for the Little Entente. Since the League of Nations lacked sufficient means of coercion, he felt the need of supplementing Article 21 which stated that international agreements, such as arbitration treaties and regional understandings which furthered peace, would not be considered incompatible with any article of the Covenant. There followed a clash between China, which desired to delete " regional understandings " from the Article, and Czechoslovakia, whose amendment " would encourage regional conferences or conventions as an essential comple-

19 *Zprávy* (Poslanecká Sněmovna), 25 meeting, November 24, 1920, pp. 469 *et seq.*, 2 session; *cf.* also, Krčmář, J., " Dr. Beneš ve svazu národů ", *Dr. Edward Beneš*, pp. 159-169.

ment to universal agreements which must necessarily be very general and ill-defined in scope ".[20]

The Revision Commission finally decided to retain the original text of Article 21, but suggested also that all agreements among League members, concluded to clarify or supplement existing treaties or preserve peace, should not only be approved by the League of Nations but should be negotiated under its auspices.[21]   Although the Second Assembly failed to incorporate specifically in Article 21 the amendment proposed by Czechoslovakia, its principle was emphatically approved when the Second Assembly pointed out that all such supplementary agreements contributed toward the realization, by the League, of its practical objectives.[22]   The Little Entente was considered not only as a collaborator with the League, but as one means of rendering effective the principles of the latter.   League approval of the Little Entente became a source of gratification not only to Beneš, as furthering Czechoslovakia's security, but to another of its founders, Take Jonescu of Rumania, who had maintained that the Little Entente was a small League of Nations within a larger one, and that the same love of peace had inspired the creation of both organizations.[28]

Czechoslovakia found it impracticable to divorce her activities within the League of Nations from the problems of security and of her relations with the Great Powers.   She discovered that, from 1920 to 1923, her own security, as well as her friendly relations with Italy, were again threatened by a revival of agitation over the question of minorities which she had considered definitely settled by the treaty of

[20] *League of Nations Monthly Summary* (henceforth referred to as *Monthly Summary*), April, 1921, pp. 3-4.

[21] *Ibid.*, July, 1921, p. 30.

[22] *Ibid.*, October, 1921, p. 114.

[28] *Cf. Le Temps*, October 27, 1920, for Take Jonescu's speech at the Sorbonne two days earlier.

September 10, 1919.[24] The whole question of minorities was reopened by Tittoni, the Italian delegate to the League Council, whose report, which was adopted on October 22, 1920, led to a lengthy series of modifications of the original method of procedure. Henceforth, since the minorities question was considered international, no longer only members of the Council, but any member of the League of Nations, might invoke the aid of either the Council or the Permanent Court of International Justice in rendering effective the protection that had been guaranteed to minorities. Nevertheless, the privilege of calling attention to the infraction or threatened infraction of minority rights was reserved to members of the Council alone: the minorities themselves or states not represented in the Council were permitted merely to present a report or a petition, an act which would not force the Council to take legal cognizance of the matter and intervene. The resulting distinction between guaranteeing a clause in a treaty and actually protecting a minority was unfortunate, as was a further rule, adopted on October 25, 1920, to the effect that any petition or report concerning minorities, which had been brought before the Council, should be duly investigated by the president and two members appointed by him in order to determine whether the clauses of the minorities treaty had been violated or were in danger of being violated.[25]

As soon as the new method of minority procedure, as advocated by Tittoni, had been given an adequate trial, there resulted almost identical protests from Poland on June 3, 1921,[26] and from Czechoslovakia a day later.[27] Both states

[24] *Cf. supra*, p. 45.

[25] *Official Journal*, November, 1920, p. 8.

[26] Askenazy (The Polish Minister of Foreign Affairs) to Drummond (Secretary-General of the League of Nations), June 3, 1921, reprinted in *Official Journal*, September, 1921, p. 797.

[27] Beneš to Drummond, June 4, 1921, *ibid.*, September, 1921, p. 796.

based their objections upon the fact that the Permanent Secretariat of the League had injured their prestige by circulating numerous minority petitions inspired by questionable
sources. Even when such petitions had been dismissed as
baseless, the publicity and investigations that necessarily followed had subjected the two states to much annoyance. The
Czechoslovak note objected particularly to the publicity which
had been given by the Secretariat to the memorandum of
the President of the " Austrian Association for a League of
Nations ", in which a private organization had attacked
bitterly President Masaryk and the Czechoslovak Republic
for alleged disregard of the rights of the German minority.
The Czechoslovak government deemed it beneath its dignity
to enter into any controversy over a memorandum which it
considered inspired by "a hatred of everything not German "
Beneš admitted that the Secretariat had acted in strict conformity with Tittoni's resolution, and hence, if a repetition
of such occurrences was to be avoided, this report had to
be amended.

Tittoni's resolution was amended on June 27, 1921, by
the adoption of several Czechoslovak-Polish amendments
which specified that all minority petitions that did not orig-
inate with League members were to be communicated immediately to the state concerned; that the state concerned was
to have three weeks within which to inform the Secretary-
General whether it intended to make any comment upon the
subject; that Tittoni's procedure was to be followed if
neither answer nor comment was received from the state
concerned within three weeks; that two months' time was to
be granted a state which desired to comment upon the matter,
whereupon the Secretary-General would present both petition
and comment to the League members; that, in exceptional
and extremely urgent cases, the Secretary-General should
inform the state concerned of the petition before informing

other League members; that these amendments should become effective immediately upon all affairs that concerned Czechoslovakia and Poland; and that other states which had accepted the Minorities Treaties might have the same procedure applied to them if they so desired.[28]

In spite of a certain success attained by the Czechoslovak-Polish amendments, Beneš still harbored doubts whether annoyance had been eliminated. On April 5, 1923, he suggested further amendments regarding the procedure with minority petitions. He maintained that the right to address minority petitions or reports to the League was not restricted merely to the minorities themselves, but was held by everyone. He pointed out that the Minorities Treaties had not created organizations to act or speak on behalf of minorities, but had made the members of the Council responsible, and therefore that petitioners had no legal basis for claiming or referring to any authority allegedly derived from the minorities themselves. Minority petitions had been submitted frequently by professional propagandists, not for the benefit of the minority at all, but for the furtherance of political aims far removed from the alleged objective. Therefore, Beneš proposed that the Secretary-General be authorized to reject all petitions of a propagandist nature.[29]

Czechoslovakia had been particularly annoyed by receiving a large number of propagandist petitions, to all of which she had had to reply. After three years of such experiences, the Czechoslovak government reached the limit of its patience, and, again supported by Poland, succeeded, on September 5, 1923, in having the Council adopt a further amendment. Henceforth, it was decreed that the petitions must have in view the terms of the Minorities Treaties, must not

[28] *Ibid.*, September, 1921, pp. 749-750.
[29] *Ibid.*, July, 1923, pp. 717-718.

seek a severance of political relations with the state in which the minority existed, must emanate from an authentic source, must abstain from violent language, and must contain facts or information which had not been recently the subjects of a petition submitted to ordinary procedure. In addition, the President might extend the two months' period for comment if he deemed it reasonable or feasible, governmental communications should be restricted to members of the Council, a special Council resolution was required for communications to non-members, and the special Committee of Examination was granted merely the power to determine how many members were to call the attention of the Council to the matter in question.[80]

The various changes of minority procedure that had been adopted at the behest of Czechoslovakia and Poland were open to criticism, particularly to the charge of being reactionary. The new routine did not deprive the minorities of the right of effective appeal to the Council or of recourse to the public opinion of the world. Before one condemns Czechoslovakia for her action, one should remember that her motive was largely defensive. Because of the character of her minorities, some restriction of procedure was necessary in order to protect herself from annoyance. Then, too, the minorities within Czechoslovakia had relatively little basis for complaint, for the government, on the whole, did treat them fairly. The policy of tolerance which had been adopted prior to the Minorities Treaty had been confirmed again by the Czechoslovak Constitution. Articles 106-127 branded as a crime any act which discriminated against any nationality or which attempted forcible denationalization, and Articles 128-134, the Bill of Rights for National Minorities, guaranteed absolute equality before the law, and the same

[80] *Ibid.*, November, 1923, pp. 1290-1294.

civil and political rights to all Czechoslovak citizens regardless of language, race, or religion.[31]

It is always easier for criticism to be destructive than constructive. In view of the misuse to which the letter of Tittoni's proposals had been subjected, Czechoslovakia's amendments were perhaps more constructive than reactionary. Regardless of their characterization, what else remained to be done? In choosing what he regarded as the lesser of two evils, Beneš had demonstrated one of his cardinal virtues, an ability to compromise. Throughout his career, he has rarely been unbending; only in the gravest emergencies has he found it necessary to employ an outright negative; usually, even from the most adverse alternatives, he has managed to extract some benefit for his country. Czechoslovakia's election in 1923 to the League Council was a great triumph for Beneš personally. In the discussions that took place at Geneva in September, 1923, he deplored the pessimism prevalent as a result of the Greco-Italian crisis over the Corfu incident: he favored neither party, but was interested primarily in preventing the small states from losing faith in the League, whose basic principles he sought to save as the sole defense of the small states against fait accompli tactics and a return to the former system of alliances.[32]

The Russian Problem

The trend of events within Russia seemed to Beneš additional justification for a " Western orientation ". To Czechoslovakia, as to the rest of Europe, the rise of Bolshe-

[31] For detailed discussions of minorities procedure, cf. Macartney, C. A., *National States and National Minorities* (London, 1934) ; Stone, J., *International Guarantees of Minority Rights* (London, 1932) ; Kellor, *op. cit.*, vol. i, pp. 70-79. For further details regarding Czechoslovakia's treatment of her minorities, cf. Brož, A., *Three Years of the Czechoslovak Republic*, pp. 21-30; Graham, *op. cit.*, pp. 292-299.

[32] Beneš, *Problemy nové Evropy*, pp. 199, 265.

vism presented many new problems, the chief of which was the question of future relations with Russia. In Czechoslovakia the idea of intra-Slav cooperation was yet strong, and, in spite of the collapse of Russia, there still existed, after 1918, a strong minority that continued to regard her as the natural friend, protector and leader of the smaller Slav nations. The almost universal sympathy for Russia took many diverse forms: the rank and file, which deemed Bolshevism as just one more evil that Russia was compelled to endure,[38] advocated a " hands off " policy; a few extreme radicals sought to follow her into Bolshevism; whereas a larger minority, which sought to save Russia from herself, demanded armed intervention. Amidst these diverse opinions stood out the fact that the basic principles of Bolshevism were repugnant to most Czechoslovaks, who viewed communism with distaste. As the Bolsheviks sought to carry out their avowed purpose of overthrowing the established social order throughout Europe, Beneš found himself on the horns of a dilemma: how was he to combat the spread of Bolshevism within Czechoslovakia and yet remain friendly with Russia whom he still considered as a natural friend and ally, and what was perhaps of even greater importance, as one of the largest potential future markets for Czechoslovakia's surplus of manufactured goods?

The Siberian Campaign

Before Beneš dared even contemplate the future, he had to solve the immediate problem of extricating the Czechoslovak army in Russia, lest it become enmeshed and perhaps overwhelmed in the Russian domestic chaos. The friendship that had been engendered originally between the Czechoslovaks and the Bolsheviks because of mutual cooperation

[38] *Ibid.*, pp. 28, 123-126, 160-162; Gibbons, H. A., *Europe since 1918* (New York, 1923), p. 270.

against the Central Powers,[84] soon gave way to friction as
the agreements of March 26, 1918, whereby the Czechoslovaks had been guaranteed every assistance in their long
journey across Siberia in return for Masaryk's promise to
disarm, were not being carried out. Czechoslovak reluctance
to disarm, Bolshevik apathy, and the deterioration of the
railroads were perhaps equally to blame for the delay.
Seemingly endless halts were being made at station after
station, with the result that, by May, 1918, only three regiments had reached Vladivostok.[85]

At the same time, the official attitude of the Bolsheviks
also became less favorable; in fact, as early as March 30,
1918, the Czechoslovaks had intercepted a telegram from
the Omsk Soviet to Moscow which had requested their complete disarming and routing via Archangel.[86] After receiving many similar requests from other local Soviets, the
authorities at Moscow finally acquiesced. The Czechoslovaks, against their better judgment, agreed to disarm partially and to return the equipment they had received from the
Russians.[87] However, the Czechoslovaks distrusted the
Russians to the extent of hiding at least one rifle, and other
weapons, apiece, as the Bolsheviks, to their dismay, were to
discover later. At this time, the attitude of the Czechoslovaks was motivated largely by fear that they would be
expected to abide by Article 5 of the Treaty of Brest-Litovsk

[84] Cf. Kratochvil, J., Cesta revoluce (Praha, 1922), pp. 42-46, or
Baerlein, H., The March of the Seventy Thousand (London, 1926), pp.
99-103, for Czechoslovak-Bolshevik military cooperation against the
Central Powers at Kiev bridge, February 20, 1918, and at Bachmač,
March 2, 1918.

[85] Cf. Fischer, L., The Soviets in World Affairs (New York, 1930),
vol. i, p. 110.

[86] Baerlein, op. cit., p. 160; Stewart, G., The White Armies of Russia
(New York, 1933), p. 106.

[87] Československá Samostatnost, vol. iii, p. 5, February 27, 1918;
Fischer, op. cit., vol. i, p. 113.

of March 3, 1918, which had promised the Central Powers that " Russia will without delay carry out the complete demobilization of her army, inclusive of the forces newly formed by the present government ".[38]

Partial disarming was followed by a demand for complete disarming and for a surrender of control over part of the Trans-Siberian railroad.   In refusing this new demand of the Soviets, the Czechoslovaks became convinced of the wisdom of remaining armed on the eve of a five-thousand-mile-march through a region teeming with German and Hungarian prisoners of war and with possibly hostile Russians.[39] On April 21, the Bolsheviks promised the Germans that all German prisoners in Russia would be sent westward to be incorporated in the German army.[40]   In comparison, the eastward movement of the Czechoslovaks was regarded as unimportant, and the Germans were granted priority in the use of the railroad.   The former resented such treatment as fresh evidence of the powerful influence of Count Mirbach, the German Ambassador at Moscow.   The months of waiting had produced further tension between Czechoslovaks and Bolsheviks.   Although many of the former were Socialists, they were also nationalists.   On the other hand, the latter deemed them fools to wish to go to France to become involved again in a capitalistic war rather than demand peace at any price.   The Russians also distrusted the maintenance of discipline as an indication of counter-revolutionary tendencies, whereas the Czechoslovaks considered Russian desertion of the Allied cause treasonable.   Consequently, the outbreak of hostilities awaited merely some overt act.[41]

[38] Translation from the German, *The Times*, March 3, 1918.
[39] Kratochvil, *op. cit.*, p. 59.
[40] *Ibid.*, p. 60.
[41] Zmrhal, K., *Vlada Sovětu a Československi* (Praha, 1919) ; or Williams, M. O., " The Fighting Czechoslovaks ", *Asia*, vol. xviii, pp. 722-728. *Cf.* Fischer, *op. cit.*, vol. i, p. 111, for the statement that no documentary

As the Czechoslovak Legions proceeded eastward by detachments via Kursk, Tambov (where they were delayed a whole month), Penza and Samara, they became more convinced that the Bolsheviks were conspiring with the Germans to destroy their army.[42] The Legions eventually reached Čeljabinsk (Tcheliabinsk), where, on May 14, 1918, there ensued the celebrated incident that precipitated hostilities. At this station a Czechoslovak detachment met a trainload of Magyar ex-prisoners that was moving westward. A Czechoslovak was injured by a missile thrown from the train. In the riot that was precipitated, the offending Magyar was put to death. When the Czechoslovaks would not permit the local authorities to investigate, the Bolsheviks retorted three days later by imprisoning the Czechoslovak guard that should have intervened. After a Czechoslovak delegation that had been sent to protest was also imprisoned, the Legions seized the town, disarmed the Bolsheviks and freed their comrades.[43]

The attempt of the local Soviet to enforce its authority was supported by Trotsky, the Bolshevik Commissar of War, who, by a telegram relayed from station to station along the line of the railroad, ordered once more the complete disarming of the Czechoslovaks. On May 21, he ordered also the arrest of Maxa and Čermak, the leaders of the Russian branch of the Czechoslovak National Council at Moscow.[44] The Legions replied a week later at a congress held at Čeljabinsk, where they decided to surrender no more arms or ammunition, but to continue to Vladivostok,

proof exists regarding German pressure on the Bolsheviks to disarm the Czechoslovaks.

[42] Nosek, V., *Independent Bohemia* (London, 1918), pp. 97-98.

[43] *Ibid.*, p. 98; Kratochvil, *op. cit.*, p. 68.

[44] Masaryk, *Světová revoluce*, p. 317.

by force if necessary.[45]   They deemed such a course their only alternative, inasmuch as they were still determined to try to abide by the advice that Masaryk had given them at the time of his departure from Russia—that they abstain from all interference in Russia's internal affairs.[46]

Initially, the sole objective of the Czechoslovaks was to get out of Russia as soon as possible.   Because of the danger of further hostilities with the Reds, General Sokorov, the commander in the Volga region, went so far as to forbid specifically any aggressive (westward) movement.   The various detachments, often incompletely armed and equipped, and scattered over enormous distances, experienced difficulties in maintaining contact.   On May 25, the Czechoslovaks were diverted from this passive policy and committed to an entirely new course.   Captain Gajda seized Novonikolajevsk, thereby changing the war from a purely defensive journey out of the country to an active offensive-occupation and the holding of the region against the Bolsheviks.   In this manner, this hitherto unknown captain, on his own responsibility, caused international complications of a serious nature.[47]   As will be shown subsequently, Gajda played into the hands of Great Britain and France, with the result that

---

[45] Nosek, *op. cit.*, p. 98; for contrasting Czechoslovak and Bolshevik versions of the affair, *cf. Papers Relating to the Foreign Relations of the United States, 1917-1918*, 1918 (Russia), vol. ii, pp. 248-260, for letter of July 4, 1918, of Thompson (United States Consul at Omsk) to Lansing (Secretary of State).

[46] Masaryk, *op. cit.*, p. 216.

[47] Kratochvil, *op. cit.*, p. 82.   Radula Gäjda (Rudolf Geidl) had a spectacular career.   At the outbreak of war, he served in the Austrian army (for conflicting accounts of his career in the Austrian army, *cf.* Kratochvil, *op. cit.*, p. 82; Stewart, *op. cit.*, pp. 104-105; Baerlein, *op. cit.*, pp. 131-133).   After being taken prisoner by the Russians, he enlisted in the Czechoslovak forces where he attracted much attention and was rewarded by rapid promotion because of his ability, daring and love of the spectacular.   For his later career, *cf. infra*, pp. 257-258.

the Czechoslovak authorities at Paris were forced into acceptance of a situation entirely beyond their control.

The Legionaires numbered about 70,000 men,[48] the only disciplined force within Russia. Consequently, the seizure of much of the railroad, together with a wide area on both sides, became surprisingly easy. Before the end of May, they captured Penza after a three days' struggle, and then in turn seized Sysran, Kazan, where their efforts were rewarded by the arms within a well-stocked arsenal, and Simbirsk, important strategically as the junction of the railroads to Čeljabinsk and Petrograd. The Czechoslovaks were not content merely with control of the railroad, but occupied the best part of the Volga region, the granary of Russia. In Siberia, they seized Udinsk and won two victories, at Krasnojarsk and Omsk, over a large force of German-Magyar ex-prisoners. On June 25, General Diderichs, at the head of 15,000 men, seized Vladivostok after a perfunctory resistance. The eastern Legions, with the help of Allied troops, forced the Bolsheviks and German ex-prisoners to retreat to Charbarovsk, and, by September, completed the junction with other Legions from Irkutsk and western Siberia, thereby ensuring control over the whole railway.[49]

The Czechoslovak offensive threatened the existence of the Soviet government by wresting from its control the Volga

---

[48] Estimates vary from 50,000 to 70,000.

[49] Kratochvil, *op. cit.*, pp. 83-105; O'Higgins, H. J., *March of the Czechoslovaks across Siberia* (New York, 1918); Beneš, *My War Memoirs*, pp. 364-372; Chopin, J., "Les Tchécoslovaques en Russie", *Révue de Paris*, vol. xxv, pt. iv, pp. 777-796. *Cf.* also, Graves, W. S. (the officer commanding the Expeditionary Force of the United States in Siberia), *America's Siberian Adventure* (New York, 1931), p. 66, for his cable of September 8 to the War Department, "Practically all organized resistance, in Siberia, has disappeared". For further details of Czechoslovak-Bolshevik early clashes, *cf. Papers Relating to the Foreign Relations of the United States, 1917-1918*, 1918 (Russia), vol. ii, pp. 177-224 and 227-323.

region, the Urals and the whole of Siberia, areas which became the centers of various White or anti-Bolshevik movements. Germany was dealt a severe blow by being denied access to the raw materials and foodstuffs of Russia and to the thousands of her prisoners of war interned in Siberia. It remained to be seen whether the Czechoslovaks could maintain successfully the advantageous position that they had won.

Czechoslovak need of Allied assistance became increasingly apparent. An army of seventy thousand men, no matter how efficient, could not hope to control the Trans-Siberian railroad indefinitely. At best, such a force could remain in temporary possession until the Bolsheviks could muster an army sufficient to overwhelm it. The Allied Great Powers would have to decide whether they wished the Czechoslovak exodus to continue or if, in view of the recent developments, the Czechoslovaks were to be requested to remain as the backbone for an attempted Allied resurrection of the Eastern Front against both the Bolsheviks and the Central Powers. In either event, prompt Allied assistance was imperative if the Czechoslovaks were to extricate themselves from the toils of the Russian Revolution.

Initially, the United States opposed Allied intervention in Russia. Two notes of President Wilson to the Allied Ambassadors at Paris, of February 28[50] and March 5,[51] 1918, opposed Japanese intervention in Siberia, but expressed, diplomatically, confidence that Japan would act only for the best interests of Russia. On February 2 and March 3, Colonel House stated further his belief that Japanese intervention would throw Russia into the arms of Germany.[52] On

[50] Seymour, C. (ed.), *The Intimate Papers of Colonel House* (New York, 1926), vol. iii, p. 419.

[51] *Ibid.*, vol. iii, pp. 419-420.

[52] *Ibid.*, vol. iii, pp. 391 and 392.

March 11, Wilson expressed the sympathy of the United States with the misfortunes of Russia, and four days later received in return the appreciation of the Congress of Soviets,[53] but such amenities decided nothing. On March 26, Great Britain suggested a compromise which called for inter-Allied, rather than solely Japanese, intervention.[54] The British viewpoint was ably presented to Colonel House on May 1 by Sir William Wiseman, the Chief of the British Secret Service, who pointed out to the Allies four alternative lines of action: (1) to take no action, which would be almost unthinkable since it would leave the Germans free to act as they wished in Russia; (2) Allied intervention as the result of a Bolshevik invitation, which would be the best course, but which would be almost impossible to obtain; (3) an invitation to intervene from the exiled Kerensky; and (4) intervention without any invitation.[55]

Before the exchange of Anglo-American viewpoints had resulted in any definite decision, and before France and Italy, both of which were vitally interested in the crises on their own fronts during the 1918 German offensive, could join in any common line of action, these four Powers, on June 4, agreed, as an initial step, to protest to the Bolsheviks that the disarming of the Czechoslovaks would be considered by their governments as a hostile act, since the latter were Allied troops under the protection and care of the Entente.[56] In reply, Chicherin, the People's Commissar for Foreign Affairs, denied the right of the Entente thus to interpret the act, which he maintained was only what any neutral nation would do to armed foreign troops within her territories. He requested the Entente to censure the Czechoslovaks " for

[53] *Cf. ibid.*, vol. iii, p. 420, for both Wilson's note and the Soviet reply.
[54] *Ibid.*, vol. iii, p. 402.
[55] *Ibid.*, vol. iii, pp. 420-422.
[56] *Russian-American Relations, March, 1917–March, 1920*, pp. 224-226.

their brazen and unmistakable interference in the internal affairs of Russia ".[57]

When no satisfaction could be obtained from Moscow upon the question of the disarming of the Czechoslovaks, the United States concurred in active inter-Allied intervention in Siberia.[58] On August 3, the United States and Japan agreed to send troops to Siberia to help the Czechoslovaks. President Wilson granted them $7,000,000 credit, whereas France had already loaned them 11,000,000 rubles and Great Britain, 3,600,000 rubles.[59] The reason for the American attitude was stated, officially, to be the necessity for helping the Czechoslovaks extricate themselves from a dangerous situation which had been created as the result of a change in the attitude of the Russian government. Intervention for the purpose of interfering in Russian internal affairs was specifically disclaimed. Both Japan and the United States promised to withdraw their forces immediately upon the realization of the limited objectives of the intervention. When Chicherin protested that Russia never intended to deliver the Czechoslovaks to the Austrian and German prisoners of war or to their governments, but that the measures against the Czechoslovaks were legitimate measures of defense against the counter-revolutionary movements within Russia, and stated that the Czechoslovak conspiracy had been organized by France and supported by her financially, and that the United States failed to realize the gravity of its action upon

[57] *Izvestia*, June 13, 1918.

[58] *Cf.* Seymour, *op. cit.*, vol. iii, p. 408, for Masaryk's luncheon of June 12 with Colonel House to discuss Russian affairs; and *ibid.*, vol. iii, p. 415, for Wilson's letter of July 8 to Colonel House in which he stated his fears that the Japanese might not leave Siberia if allowed to intervene alone. *Cf.* also, *Papers relating to the Foreign Relations of the United States, 1917-1918*, 1918, (Russia), vol. ii, pp. 241 *et seq.* and 262 *et seq.* for proposal of Supreme War Council and United States' acceptance.

[59] Fischer, *op. cit.*, vol. i, p. 110.

its future relations with Russia, President Wilson remained unmoved.[60]

The Powers were delighted at the prospect of having created a new Eastern Front. Thanks to Czechoslovak distrust of the Bolsheviks and to Gajda, they now obtained easily what Masaryk had formerly refused—the use of the Czechoslovak army in Russia. Masaryk and Beneš seem to make out a good case that, except for a somewhat noisy minority led by Kramář, most Czechoslovaks were opposed to intervention in Russia at any time.[61]

However, the appeals of Kramář for intervention and the temporary enthusiasm of the Legionaires for Gajda, before they sobered sufficiently to realize how they had been dazzled and led to the brink of ruin, coupled with the more or less enforced silence on the part of the responsible Czechoslovak leaders, had led to many misunderstandings. The motives of Gajda were attributed erroneously to the Czechoslovaks as a whole, a general misapprehension that did Czechoslovakia much damage and which was perhaps encouraged by the stories that were sedulously but unofficially circulated

[60] Seymour, *op. cit.*, vol. iii, pp. 416-418; " Reply of President Wilson to a Senate Resolution concerning the American Troops in Siberia, June 26, 1919", *State Department*, Russian Series, number iv, p. 5; *United States Congress*, Senate, 65 Congress, 1919, "Hearings on Bolshevik Propaganda before a Sub-committee of the Judiciary", p. 24; *Russian-American Relations, March, 1917–March, 1920*, pp. 235-240, 258-270, 343-346; *Papers Relating to the Foreign Relations of the United States, 1917-1918*, 1918, vol. ii, pp. 67-68, Polk (Acting Secretary of State) to Morris (American Ambassador to Japan), March 5, against intervention; pp. 324-325, Ishii (Japanese Ambassador to the United States) to Polk, August 2, on the motives of Japanese intervention in Siberia; pp. 328-329, Polk to Morris, August 3, on American motives for intervention; Scott, J. B., *Official Statements of War Aims and Peace Proposals, December, 1916 to November, 1918* (Washington, 1921), pp. 359-362; Vinacke, H. M., *History of the Far East in Modern Times* (New York, 1928), pp. 411-414; Beneš, *My War Memoirs*, pp. 390-397.

[61] Beneš, *op. cit.*, pp. 352-364; Masaryk, *op. cit.*, pp. 215-218; Kratochvil, *op. cit.*, p. 109.

by the Allies throughout their newspapers during the months of June and July, 1918.[62] Even Masaryk was accused falsely of desiring a war against both the Germans and the Bolsheviks,[63] whereas, in reality, the Czechoslovaks were merely tools of Allied militarism, and, at first, unconscious tools at that.[64]

[62] For a summary of such stories, *cf.* Ross, E. A., *The Russian Soviet Republic* (New York, 1923), pp. 127-136.

[63] Fischer, *op. cit.*, vol. i, pp. 109-110, quotes Masaryk as having stated (October 9, 1917) that he had " explicitly agreed with Dukhonin that our army would be used only against the foreign enemy ", i. e. the Central Powers. After another quotation pointing out Czechoslovak financial dependence upon the Allies, Fischer again quotes Masaryk " I had thought of the war against the Bolsheviks and against Russia. I would have attached myself and our corps to an army which would have been strong enough for a struggle against the Bolsheviks and the Germans, and which would have defended democracy. . . . There was only one possibility for the fight against the Bolsheviks—the mobilization of the Japanese ".

[64] *Ibid.*, vol. i, p. 112. Fischer, vol. i, p. 111, also mentions the presence of Russian " White " officers in Czechoslovak ranks as an evidence of the counter-revolutionary tendencies of the latter. To prove that the motives of the Czechoslovaks were misinterpreted, the writer, in addition to referring to the actions and statements of Masaryk and Beneš, wishes also to call attention to the following statements: Ross, *op. cit.*, p. 126, states, " There is no question but that to get to France was the sincere desire of the Czechs and there was no suggestion that the force could be or desired to be used in Siberia ". *Cf.* Graves, *op. cit.*, p. 66, for the belated information contained in his cable of September 19, 1918, to the United States War Department, " The French and English are, undoubtedly, trying to get the Allied forces committed to some act which will result in the establishment of an Eastern Front ". The fact that the Czechoslovaks were not acting entirely upon their own initiative, but largely in response to orders received from the Powers that were financing them, was indicated by the cipher message received by Gray (American Consul at Omsk) on July 22, 1918, from the American Consulate at Samara. Gray was directed to inform the Czechoslovaks "confidentially" that " pending further notice, the Allies will be glad, from a political point of view, to have them hold their present position. On the other hand, they should not be hampered in meeting the military exigencies of the situation. It is desirable, first of all, that they should secure control

The Czechoslovak authorities at Paris, confronted with a fait accompli, were forced to acquiesce reluctantly to a condition of affairs beyond their control. For their own best interests, while the recognition of Czechoslovakia and its future boundaries hung in the balance, they were compelled to abstain from any adverse criticism of the use that the Great Powers contemplated for their eastern army. Being practical diplomats, they sought to wrest future advantages from their present distress by simulating acquiescence or even enthusiasm regarding recent Russian developments. Above all, the Czechoslovaks could not afford to leave, in the minds of influential Allied statesmen, any doubts whatever regarding the sincerity with which they entered into the Russian venture. Therefore Gajda was promoted and the seizure of the whole Trans-Siberian railroad was ordered. Speedy indeed was the reward of the Czechoslovaks. Their national objectives received the endorsement of the United States at the end of May,[65] and of Great Britain, France and Italy on June 3.[66] Thus, at a price, was Czechoslovakia's future assured, but the skill with which Czechoslovak

of the Trans-Siberian Railway, and second, if this is assured, at the same time possibly retain control over the territory which they now dominate. Inform the French representative that the French Consul-General joins in these instructions." *Cf.* Stewart, *op. cit.*, pp. 114-115. Stewart also points out, *ibid.*, p. 135, that "The Czechs whose whole future national existence depended upon an Allied victory were willing to perform any service for the Allies even to risking their lives in the Siberian mêlée". On p. 296 he states that the Czechoslovaks "rigorously abstained from all participation in Russian internal affairs, save to protect themselves". Finally, *cf.* *Papers Relation to the Foreign Relations of the United States, 1917-1918*, 1918 (Russia), vol. ii, pp. 265-267, for Caldwell (American Consul at Vladivostok) to Lansing, July 8, 1918, on Czechoslovak communication of June 25 as to their official motives.

[65] *Cf.* *Papers Relating to the Foreign Relations of the United States, 1918*, supplement i, vol. i, pp. 795-809, for the actual diplomatic correspondence on the subject between Lansing and American representatives abroad.

[66] *The New York Times*, June 6-7, 1918.

diplomats fell in with Allied wishes disguised their distaste for the whole Russian imbroglio to such an extent that their reluctance to participate has not been adequately appreciated. In view of his oft-repeated advice to abstain from interfering in the internal affairs of Russia, there can be no doubt that Masaryk deplored greatly the new turn of affairs. Although Beneš made no direct statement regarding the matter, there can be little doubt that he felt similarly, but could gain nothing by any outright condemnation of Allied objectives. However, it may safely be assumed that the object lession of being a cat's-paw was not lost upon Beneš and had a marked influence in causing him to advocate a policy whereby Czechoslovakia could maintain her diplomatic independence, free from the orbit of any of the Great Powers.

Meanwhile, in the regions held by the Czechoslovaks, there sprang up several counter-revolutionary movements, the most formidable of which was led by Admiral Kolchak in Siberia. In this movement, Japan saw an opportunity to further her own interests and occupied positions as far west as Lake Baikal. At first the Czechoslovaks fought well against the gradually increasing strength of the Bolsheviks, but soon awoke to the realization that they were being employed to fight the battles of others and that continued hostilities would profit them nothing. They became dissatisfied to remain mere pawns in the game of international politics, with the result that their discipline relaxed and mutinies took place. As soon as the news of the armistice reached Russia, the Legionaires demanded to be sent home as soon as possible, for they no longer had any reason for going to France. In their distress, they requested the guiding hand of some safe political leader.[67] Consequently, during the winter of 1918-1919, Štefánik visited Siberia together with General Janin,

[67] Kratochvil, *op. cit.*, p. 109.

whom France had sent to command all the Allied forces in Siberia, but his trip resulted in no improvement in the condition of the war-weary troops.[68]

The dangerous situation of the Legions did not escape the watchfulness of Beneš, who exerted himself to the best of his ability to try to extricate them without open friction with the Allies. As early as April 1, 1918, he had been the recipient of a memorandum from the British War Ministry, which had applied pressure to induce him to retain the troops in Russia. In response, as soon as he could leave temporarily his pressing duties in Paris, he made a flying trip to London, where, on May 10 he had a conference with Balfour and another, five days later, with Lord Robert Cecil, the British Minister of Blockade.[69] In all probability, Beneš agreed to let the Czechoslovaks fight the Bolsheviks, or at least remain in Russia. The results of two conferences have not, as yet, been made public. Judging from the fact that the question was left in abeyance for over a year by both Beneš and the British, there must have existed a wide divergence of viewpoints. On June 25, 1919 Great Britain reopened the discussion by suggesting that the Czechoslovaks cooperate with the right wing of Kolchak. Beneš agreed to order 30,000 men to advance via Viatka and Kotlas to Archangel, and that the remainder should go to Vladivostok. Both detachments were to be repatriated as soon as possible, by the fall of the year at the latest. The contemplated plan was deemed to produce a four-fold advantage: to effect a Czechoslovak junction with Kolchak and with the British in the north, to establish Kolchak's " Government of Northern

[68] For details of the remainder of the campaign, *cf.* Janin, General M., " Fragments de mon Journal Siberien ", *Le Monde slav*, December, 1924, pp. 221-240; March, 1925, pp. 339-355; April, 1925, pp. 19-24; "Au G. Q. G. Russe ", *Le Monde slav*, January, 1926, pp. 1-24; May, 1926, pp. 161-185.

[69] *Cf.* Fischer, *op. cit.*, vol. i, pp. 114-115.

Russia " upon a self-supporting basis after the Allied withdrawal, to relieve the dangerous situation in central Siberia which was caused by the presence of discontented Czechoslovaks, and to strengthen the Praha government by a return of the eastern army.[70] Thereupon, in August, Beneš ordered General Syrový to concentrate the Legions at Vladivostok, preparatory to evacuation, but nothing was done at the time. The Allies still continued to plead that the Czechoslovaks were needed as the core of the forces in Russia, but Czechoslovak discipline was lax, cooperation with Kolchak proved impossible because of divergent objectives, Bolshevik strength was increasing, and Allied transports failed to appear at either Archangel or Vladivostok.[71]

After all, the Czechoslovaks were a mere handful in comparison with the Bolsheviks, and it was a bitter realization that most of their heroic efforts had been in vain. The Legions did not desire to fight against the Reds; in fact, they sympathized with the peasants, who were brother Slavs, rather than with foreign Allies or with the counter-revolutionists who ravaged the country.[72] As the Reds continued to increase in strength and sweep eastward, Czechoslovak dissatisfaction mounted correspondingly. When the Reds captured Omsk,[73] thus threatening the whole position of the Czechoslovaks, there remained only evacuation or destruction. With the eastward retreat of the Czechoslovaks, the counter-revolutionary movement fell, in spite of all the

[70] *Cf.* Miller, *op. cit.*, vol. xvi, pp. 458 and 470-473 for letters exchanged between Lloyd George and Winston Churchill that relate the story of the pourparlers with Beneš.

[71] Kratochvil, *op. cit.*, p. 489; Chamberlin, W. H., *The Russian Revolution, 1917-1921* (New York, 1935), vol. ii, p. 182; *cf.* also, Graves, *op. cit.*, 277-278, for Czechoslovak announcement of November 16, 1919, of their desire to return home.

[72] *Cf.* Ross, *op. cit.*, pp. 210-211, how on November 24, 1919, five Czechoslovak regiments refused to obey Gajda's order to advance on Perm.

[73] *The Times*, November 18, 1919.

efforts of Kolchak and Gajda, for it had no real support from the Russian people. Kolchak was killed by the Reds at the capture of Irkutsk, February 7, 1920, soon after the Czechoslovak evacuation.[74] The trend of events convinced the United States that continued military intervention would lead to exactly the opposite result from what had been intended.[75] Beneš took advantage of this turn of sentiment to negotiate with the United States and Great Britain for the transports that the Legions needed.[76] On the day of Kolchak's death, February 7, 1920, at the small railway station at Kujtun, a definitive peace was signed by the Czechoslovaks and Bolsheviks, whereby prisoners were to be exchanged, evacuation was to proceed unhindered, and all equipment was to be returned by the Czechoslovaks, who promised to observe the strictest neutrality among the various Russian factions.[77] The first Czechoslovak transport left Vladivostok as early as December 9, 1919, the General Staff arrived in Praha on June 17, 1920, and the evacuation was completed on November 30, 1920.[78]

Intra-Slav Cooperation vs. a " Western Orientation "

While the Czechoslovak troops were still in Russia, Beneš' diplomatic ability was taxed severely as he attempted to maintain a happy balance between two policies that threatened to clash—intra-Slav cooperation and a " Western orientation ". After the armistice, French interest in the Czechoslovak

---

[74] Kratochvil, *op. cit.*, p. 657.

[75] *The New York Times*, January 17, 1920 (statement of Secretary of State regarding the withdrawal of American troops from Siberia, January 16, 1920).

[76] *Russian-American Relations, March, 1917–March, 1920*, pp. 356-357.

[77] Steidler, F. V., *Československé hnutí na Rusi* (Praha, 1921), pp. 107-108.

[78] *Ibid.*, pp. 96-99, 111. *Cf.* Cižmář, J., *Ruské a naše vojsko v revoluci* (Brno, 1926) ; Beaumont, A., *Heroic Story of the Czechoslovak Legions* (Prague, 1919) ; Hlinký, J., *Ruskem a Sibiři* (Praha, 1922).

Legions increased rather than decreased: France hoped to use them against the Bolsheviks after the War as much as against the Germans prior to the termination of that conflict. Furthermore, she desired to create in Central Europe a " cordon sanitaire " of small states to prevent the westward spread of Bolshevism. On March 28, 1919, Marshal Foch proposed armed intervention in Russia, which was to be carried out, under a French commander, by a general Central European mobilization, but his project, thanks to the efforts of President Wilson and Lloyd George, was rejected by the Peace Conference.[79]

Within Czechoslovakia, all the leaders of the various political parties were agreed upon the necessity of insuring the state against domestic Bolshevism by the adoption of a comprehensive policy of social reform [80] prior to the adoption of a definite foreign policy concerning Russia, and as the Republic grew more and more stable, with one exception, took a definite stand against a policy of armed intervention. Kramář alone continued to importune Beneš to become an active member of the contemplated " cordon sanitaire " by continued intervention in Russia, if for no other reason than to prevent Poland, which was posing as the guardian in the East, from obtaining an advantage at the Peace Conference over Czechoslovakia in the boundary disputes [81] then rife between the two countries. However, war-weariness was so acute within Czechoslovakia that Kramář could muster little support for his project.[82]

[79] Baker, R. S., *What Wilson Did at Paris* (New York, 1920), p. 47; Thompson, C. T., *The Peace Conference Day by Day* (New York, 1920), pp. 272-273; *cf.* also, *Svornost*, June 20, 1919.

[80] *Cf. supra*, pp. 89-91.

[81] For a detailed account of the boundary disputes between Czechoslovakia and Poland, *cf. infra*, pp. 148 *et seq.*

[82] Hrušovský, *loc. cit.*, p. 126. For Kramář on Russia, *cf.* Kramář, K., *Die russische Krisis; Geschichte und Kritik des Bolschewismus* (München, 1925).

The Russian question was vital to Czechoslovakia, which, because of Russia's unsettled internal condition, had to adopt a policy of reserve. The internal affairs were no concern of Czechoslovakia, but the general trend of Russian policy had to be ascertained and established before she could adopt any decided attitude. Czechoslovakia asked nothing better than to remain on good terms with the Russian people, for the time being she preferred a united democratic federated Russia with Slavophil ideals. Praha, as another Slav center, hoped above all that it would never be necessary to take up arms against Russia,[83] and it was regrettable that Bolshevik Russia failed to understand Czechoslovak desires any better than Czarist Russia had done earlier.[84] Because of this fact, the Russian question tended to occupy in Czechoslovakia a position similar to that of Pan-Slavism before the War, and, just as the course of the War had destroyed the pre-war Slav policy and had demonstrated that Pan-Slavism was a premature ideal, so was any new policy threatened similarly with destruction by Russian intransigeance because of a lack of understanding.[85] The official attitude of the Czechoslovak government was perhaps best enunciated in a book of Masaryk's, *O Bolševictví*,[86] wherein he regarded Bolshevism, and particularly the program of Lenin, as trade unionism in a form which violated Karl Marx's basic principles, inasmuch as the latter had sought a high de-

[83] *Cf.* Mowrer, P. S., *Balkanized Europe* (New York, 1921), pp. 204-205.

[84] *Cf.* Anon., "La Russie tsariste et la question tchécoslovaque", *Le Monde slav*, November, 1924, pp. 124-138.

[85] Beneš, *Problemy nové Evropy*, p. 28.

[86] Masaryk, T. G., *O Bolševictví* (Praha, 1921), is perhaps best known in its French translation, *Sur le Bolchevisme*, Geneva, Sonor, 1921. Masaryk expressed the same beliefs in an address commemorating the first anniversary of the Czechoslovak Republic, *cf. Národní Listy*, October 29, 1919.

gree of economic and social development, whereas the former envisaged a primitive development upon the level of the illiterate Russian peasant. Masaryk held that Russia should help herself and that Bolshevism could not be overthrown by military intervention, but only by a comprehensive system of social reform and political education. He felt convinced that Bolshevism was a temporary condition in the evolution of Russia, but warned against using such a belief as a justification for reaction. To him, Bolshevism represented merely an abortive form of socialism.

Thus, Czechoslovakia's foreign policy, after November 30, 1920, eschewed intervention in Russia. Beneš personally had a strong conviction that armed intervention would have meant a continuation of the World War and another subversion of the status quo, rather than the reconstruction of Europe upon which his heart was set. An invasion of Russia would be a greater undertaking than the Allies cared to attempt, and history had shown repeatedly the difficulty of carrying out successfully such a project. The expeditions to Archangel, Siberia and the Caucasus had given an indication of the vast expenditure of effort that would be necessary. To Beneš, therefore, it was not a problem of Kolchak, Wrangel, Denikin, Yudenich or any other "White" reactionary: he had no faith in any of them, whom he considered all as militarists of the old régime, incapable of creating a new state. Consequently, he adopted a distinctly negative foreign policy with regard to Russia, and became more concerned in what Czechoslovakia would not do, rather than in what she would do.[87]

Although Beneš sought to prove conclusively that Czechoslovakia would not intervene in Russia, he wished also to leave no doubt as to his fervent hope that conditions there

[87] Beneš, E., *Problemy nové Evropy*, p. 292; *Five Years of Czechoslovak Foreign Policy*, p. 21.

would soon become stabilized sufficiently to permit the re-establishment of normal relations with the rest of the world. Without Russia, he deemed European peace and politics alike impossible, and maintained that a blockade and the ensuing prohibition of all intercourse would tend to prolong hard times within Russia, to aggravate the suffering of her people, postpone her participation in European politics, and result in further injury to all concerned. He hoped to prevent war between Russia and any other Slav state. Apart from its own merits, this policy of Beneš was also motivated in part by his desire to save the lives of the prisoners of war, which included not only the Legions, but also many others scattered throughout Siberia who had been unable to join this force. As a result, nearly all were eventually repatriated. In fact, Beneš went so far as to state that, initially, his Russian policy was guided more by his desire to rescue these prisoners than by Czechoslovakia's economic interests, which, at the time, were limited as far as Russia was concerned.[88]

Since severe fighting during the later phases of the Russian campaign had led to the capture of many Czechoslovaks, this problem of repatriation became important and led to discussions of other problems. As early as January, 1919, there took place, between Moscow and Praha, an exchange of notes whereby Czechoslovakia's independence was recognized by Russia, but, at the same time, the latter protested against the arrest of certain of her agents within the territories of the former.[89] A Russian Red Cross mission, in charge of Hillerson, was sent to Praha to cope with the problem of repatriation, but, from the moment of its arrival,

[88] Beneš, *Five Years of Czechoslovak Foreign Policy*, p. 22; *Problemy nové Evropy*, pp. 292-293.

[89] *Cf.* Dennis, A. L. P., *The Foreign Policies of Soviet Russia* (New York, 1924), p. 398.

propaganda among local communists became so violent as greatly to alarm Czechoslovak leaders.[90]

On January 31, 1920, Beneš announced formally his Russian policy to the foreign committee of the Senate. He deplored the fact that there still remained two marked instances of friction between Slav states: Bulgaria-Yugoslavia and Russia-Poland. Czechoslovakia hoped to draw all the Slav states into friendship with one another and with herself, but did not seek to be involved in their internal affairs. She did not concern herself with Magyar propaganda regarding eastern Galicia, and felt that Poland should similarly disregard Hungarian agitation over Slovakia. Likewise, she did not wish to intervene in Russia, and asked merely that Russia cease agitation within Czechoslovakia. Beneš promised to continue his policy of non-intervention even if there should be any truth in current rumors of Russian designs upon Estonia and Latvia.[91] Having all faith in Russia's future, he believed that Russia should be left to the Russians. Nevertheless, Russia would have to terminate her reign of terror, cease her threats of foreign intervention and of a world-wide social revolution, and establish economic contacts with the Western Powers before she could hope for recognition.[92]

The salient feature of this new Slav policy of Beneš was its restraint. In spite of Czechoslovak-Polish friction over boundaries,[93] Beneš refused to increase the existing intra-Slav tension by taking advantage of Poland's distress

[90] For the fears expressed by Masaryk, cf. *Národní Listy* and *Národní Politika*, October 13, 1920.

[91] Beneš, E., *The Foreign Policy of Czechoslovakia* (speech of January 27, 1921, before the Czechoslovak Chamber of Deputies), p. 29.

[92] *Národní Listy*, February 1, 1920; Beneš, *Problemy nové Evropy*, pp. 43-51, 123-126; cf. also, Beneš, E., "Les Slaves et l'idée slave pendant et après la guerre", *Le Monde slav*, March, 1926, pp. 321-381.

[93] Cf. infra, pp. 148 et seq.

during the summer of 1920, when the Russian armies were at the gates of Warsaw. He continued to remain neutral despite pressure exerted by an Allied military mission which visited Praha on July 22, 1920, on its way from Paris to Warsaw. His policy received the support of President Masaryk, who also sympathized with Russia, but who likewise agreed to decline France's request to aid Poland.[94] Perhaps Beneš could best be interpreted as a middleman who desired to bridge the gap between Russia and the Western Powers, but whose services were desired by neither.[95]

Nothing came of an appeal, on December 24, 1919, of the Czechoslovak Social Democratic Women to the " Women of all Nations " against the blockade which was bringing misery and starvation to millions of Russian women and children.[96] None the less, Beneš' statement of policy of January 31, 1920, helped bring about a renewal of negotiations with Russia. On February 8, the Social Democrats in the Czechoslovak National Assembly drafted a resolution which called for political and commercial recognition of Soviet Russia,[97] but again no rapprochement resulted.

Chicherin hoped to utilize these advances by a note of February 25, 1920, to Beneš, of which extracts are as follows:

. . . Deceived by worthless intriguers, the Czech soldiers turned their swords against their Russian brothers ; they did not know that the Russia of the workman and the peasant is the only state that desires to be a true friend of small nations— nations who until now were subservient to the leadership and supervision of the mighty . . . The war with the Czecho-

---

[94] D'Abernon, E. V., *The Diary of an Ambassador* (New York, 1929), vol. i, p. 74; *cf.* also, any Praha newspaper of July 28, 1920.

[95] *Cf.* Fischer, *op. cit.*, vol. ii, p. 505.

[96] *Soviet Russia*, vol. ii, p. 181.

[97] *The New York Times, Svornost*, February 9, 1920.

Slovaks was a murderous tragedy. After untold sacrifices and sufferings the Czecho-Slovak soldiers, those who were fortunate enough to escape death in Siberia, recognized the great error of which they had been victims, and closed an agreement [98] with the Soviets, which guaranteed them a free passage—a thing they, of course, could have had long before.

. . . The Russian Government is fully convinced that there exists no serious obstacle in the way of renewing peaceable and friendly relations with both Republics, and send, therefore, today to the Government of all the nations of the Czechoslovak Republic a formal proposal to begin negotiations for the purpose of establishing peaceable relations and a peace agreement between both countries. We are convinced that commercial relations between the two countries would result in the greatest mutual benefit for both States, and that permanent friendship will come to life, beneficial to both countries. We would request the Czechoslovak Government to inform us regarding their wishes as to the place where our delegates could meet the delegates of Czecho-Slovakia.[99]

A second note from Chicherin two days later expressed the hope that the working masses of Czechoslovakia would prevent a war with Russia.[100]

On March 11, in reply to a parliamentary interpellation before the Foreign Affairs Committee of the National Assembly, Beneš stated the goal of his subsequent Russian policy. It appears that an explanation was demanded of Beneš because the governments of France and Italy had requested a clarification of his intentions. Beneš expressed a conviction that Czechoslovakia must neither anticipate events nor lag behind other Powers. His policy regarding Russia must await the action of the Great Powers with whose

[98] The Treaty of Kujtun, February 7, 1920, already discussed.
[99] *Soviet Russia*, vol. ii, pp. 615-616.
[100] *Ibid.*, vol. ii, p. 422.

foreign policies his own was associated.[101]   On April 2, he
stated, further, that the Czechoslovak government was ready
to open negotiations with Russia " along with other Allied
Powers ".[102]   In this manner, while expressing a willingness
to subordinate his Russian policy to a " Western orientation ", Beneš made clear to the Great Powers the fact that
Czechoslovakia's cooperation did not mean subservience or
the loss of diplomatic independence.

Beneš replied to Chicherin by a note of April 14 that he
was ready to negotiate, and that only the resumption of
normal relations between Western and Eastern Europe could
relieve the unbearable situation in which Europe found itself.
He was delighted because of the safe return of the Legions
and because of the prospects for future friendship.[103]   Beneš'
optimism was premature, for no advantage was taken of
Chicherin's offer; in fact, direct negotiations were abruptly
discontinued.   Except for Beneš' statements of March 11
and April 2, there is no direct evidence that Beneš was
compelled to make a choice between his eastern and western policies; however, if such were the case, it would be to
the best interests of Czechoslovakia to attempt to conceal
the fact.   There were many anti-Russian influences that
might have brought pressure on Beneš.   In Czechoslovakia
public opinion in general, as well as the Kramář and Agrarian blocs, opposed too hasty a rapprochement with Russia,
particularly after the Legionaires arrived to relate their
experiences.   Then, too, there should be remembered, in addition to the ever-powerful influence of France, the fact that
Czechoslovakia was on the eve of the formation of the Little

101 *Národní Politika, Národní Listy*, March 11, 1920; *Svornost*, March
15, 1920.

102 *Národní Politika, Národní Listy*, April 2, 1920; *Svornost*, April
3, 1920.

103 *Soviet Russia*, vol. iii, pp. 52-53; *Právo Lidu*, May 11, 1920.

Entente,[104] the other members of which, Yugoslavia and Rumania, particularly the latter, were on bad terms with Russia, and that, in view of this fact, Czechoslovakia could hardly afford to risk their distrust by appearing too friendly with the Bolsheviks.[105]

Nevertheless, certain Czechoslovak individuals and organizations still attempted to draw the two countries closer together. Representatives of the Czech Consumers' League left for Russia in order to open relations with the Russian economic organizations.[106] On March 22, 1920, an official Czechoslovak mission had a long session with Lenin regarding prisoners of war and the establishment of agricultural relations, but, although the immediate objectives of the mission were attained and although mutual expressions of good will were plentiful, the incident did little to better relations generally.[107] Another futile gesture of Czechoslovak good-will was the telegram of greeting from committees of the Social Democrat party and from the trade unions of Praha to a mass meeting of English workers, scheduled for August 22, which declared their solidarity with the latter in their refusal to participate in any act hostile to Soviet Russia.[108] This act was followed by a Czechoslovak delegation of trade unionists which visited Petrograd and Moscow October 15 and 17.[109] In response, a delegation of Russian laborers visited Brno to examine Czech methods of

[104] *Cf. infra,* pp. 162 *et seq.*

[105] The writer is aware that the inference that Beneš was faced with a choice is more or less speculative; but in view of the general methods of Beneš, and particularly the unusual generalities in his speech of January 27, 1921, to the Czechoslovak Chamber of Deputies, *The Foreign Policy of Czechoslovakia* (pp. 28-32 on Russia), the theory of a choice appears the best explanation for the abrupt termination of negotiations.

[106] *Prager Tagblatt,* February 29, 1920; *Soviet Russia,* vol. ii, p. 342.

[107] *Soviet Russia,* vol. ii, p. 622.

[108] *Právo Lidu,* August 20, 1920.

[109] *Soviet Russia,* vol. iii, p. 493.

organization and welfare of the working classes.[110] Yet, relations between the two countries grew more and more strained, for, as soon as Russia realized that a rapprochement was impossible, she resumed her former tactics of spreading propaganda by accusing Beneš falsely of favoring reaction in Russia and by urging the Czechoslovak proletariat to attack him.[111]

In spite of this renewal of agitation within Czechoslovakia, the Bolsheviks came to realize gradually that such tactics were doing their cause more harm than good. During 1920 and 1921, they turned gradually to a policy which they hoped would terminate their isolation. Czechoslovakia felt some of its effects. Despite the allotment of large sums of money to Hillerson, the campaign for world revolution fell off rapidly within the Republic, a fact which could not be accounted for solely by the effect of the Russian famine upon the minds of Czechoslovak radicals. In July, telegraphic communication was opened with Soviet Russia, but, during the summer, there followed also an exchange of unofficial missions between Czechoslovakia and the Ukraine.[112]

The Genoa Conference

As early as the latter part of 1919 there had been indications of a change in European viewpoints and policies towards Russia. The successive collapses of the various counter-revolutionary movements had demonstrated that the Bolsheviks could neither be beaten nor starved; yet, on the other hand, how was trade to be resumed? Could the world continue to remain part communist and part capitalist? Could the Bolsheviks be trusted? The French policy of the "cordon sanitaire", except for Poland, was weakening gradually, and the British were averse to the continuation of

[110] *Ibid.*, vol. iii, p. 606.

[111] "Burtsev and Beneš", *ibid.*, vol. iii, pp. 482-483.

[112] Dennis, *op. cit.*, p. 399.

expensive and useless armed intervention. By 1920 all concerned were seeking some other solution of the problem.[113] The Russian leaders, realizing the necessity of relieving the famine and general distress that was then prevalent in Russia, proclaimed the New Economic Policy. The resulting abandonment of strict communistic practices was confirmed by the trade agreement of March 16, 1921, with Great Britain, the first of the Allies to recognize Russia de facto.[114]

The general economic crisis of 1921 gave birth to the idea of an international economic conference to settle definitively the problems of Europe as a whole. At the reparations conference of December 10, 1921, Briand and Lloyd George discussed the project and the conference of the Supreme Council at Cannes on January 6, 1922, was called primarily with this object in view. At this latter meeting, Lloyd George succeeded in arranging for a conference at Genoa, which was to meet from April 10 to May 16, 1922, to attempt to solve in particular the problem of Russia. There arose marked differences of opinion as to the provisional agenda, and Poincaré, who had succeeded Briand as the spokesman of France, insisted that the Peace Treaties and the question of reparations be excluded specifically from any discussion. Consequently, the agenda was composed of the questions of peace, prosperity, order, credit, exchange and transportation for all Europe, Russia included.[115]

Although the Little Entente and Poland were directly concerned in the questions that were to be discussed at Genoa, the problem of Russia was regarded quite differently by

[113] *Ibid.*, pp. 377-378; Buell, R. L., *Europe: a History of Ten Years* (New York, 1929), pp. 272-275; Temperley, *op. cit.*, vol. vi, pp. 311-324.

[114] Temperley, *op. cit.*, vol. vi, p. 325.

[115] *Resolutions Adopted by the Supreme Council at Cannes, January 1922, as the Basis of the Genoa Conference* (London, 1922) ; Temperley, *op. cit.*, vol. vi, p. 326-328; Cosma, A., Jr., *La Petite Entente* (Paris, 1926), pp. 84-86.

Praha, Belgrade, Bucharest and Warsaw.[116]   Since all four
states were interested in preventing the reopening of the question of reparations and any revision of the Peace Treaties,
they eagerly adopted the French thesis of the inviolability of
the latter.   They wished to remain in accord with the Great
Entente and with one another.   To collaborate in a common
policy, they held their own Conference at Bucharest,[117] February 20-24, and a later Conference at Belgrade,[118] March
9-12, in which they prepared a specific program for Genoa.

Beneš, in the realization that it was merely a question of
time before his negative Russian policy would become positive, welcomed every opportunity for European cooperation
in a common policy towards Russia; in fact, he was one of
the pioneers in advocating a European conference regarding
her.[119]   To this end, before the Genoa Conference met, he
visited London [120] and Paris [121] to present the viewpoints of
the Little Entente and to ascertain those of the Western
Powers.   At the same time he became the intermediary
through whom a compromise was reached upon the points
still at issue between Great Britain and France,[122] for he realized how important to Czechoslovakia was the solidarity of
the Western Powers.   He obtained the support of France
regarding the inviolability of the Peace Treaties and also that
of Great Britain regarding de facto recognition of Russia.
In the estimation of Beneš, the Genoa Conference should

[116] For full details, *cf. infra*, pp. 197 *et seq.*

[117] *Le Temps*, February 28, 1922; Cosma, *op. cit.*, p. 87; Mousset, A.,
La Petite Entente (Paris, 1923), pp. 82-83.

[118] Mousset, *op. cit.*, pp. 83-85; Cosma, *op. cit.*, pp. 91-93.

[119] *Cf. Prager Presse*, December 25, 1921, for Beneš' statement on
behalf of Russia.

[120] *Cf. The Times*, February 16, 1922.

[121] *Cf. Le Temps*, February 23, 1922; also Danubius, *La Petite Entente
et l'Orient, Un Cri d'Alarme* (Paris, 1922).

[122] *Cf. Correspondence Between His Majesty's Government and the
French Government Respecting the Genoa Conference* (London, 1922).

have three main objectives: the reconstruction of Russia and the renewal of economic contacts with her; the stabilization of economic relations among other states by individual internal reforms; and the abolition of the distinction between victor and vanquished states, whereby the latter were to be granted, for the first time since the War, a voice in the deliberations. He realized that the first objective might be the most difficult to realize, but he hoped to effect its consummation by supplementing it with a series of acts aimed specifically at the reconstruction of Russia, particularly by providing relief for Russian refugees,[123] by some concessions regarding Russia's repudiated debts, and by leaving open the possibility that the Western Powers, should they still distrust Russia, might exact further special guarantees from her.[124] The last two objectives of the Conference—a general stabilization of economic relations and the reintroduction into the " Concert of Europe " of the former enemy states—had been championed by Czechoslovakia for three years.[125]

The Genoa Conference opened optimistically on April 10, 1922, and, at its first plenary session, the twenty-nine states present, in addition to those within the British Empire, decided to appoint four Commissions: on politics, finance, economics and transportation. Since the burning issue was the renewal of relations with Russia, the first, or Political Commission, dominated the entire Conference. It was perhaps an error to stake the success of the entire Conference upon this question.[126] On April 16, the world was stunned by the announcement of the Treaty of Rapallo, whereby Russia and Germany agreed to cancel all debts unless Russia paid other creditors and to make a separate trade agreement. This new

[123] *Official Journal*, March, 1922, p. 274; April, 1922, pp. 338-340.

[124] Beneš, *Problemy nové Evropy*, pp. 165-170; Cosma, *op. cit.*, p. 87.

[125] *Cf.* Šrom, J. E., " Sovětské Rusko a Jánov ", *Zahraniční Politika*, vol. i, pp. 429-434.

[126] *Cf.* D'Abernon, *op. cit.*, vol. i, p. 331.

alignment aroused the fears of the Western Powers and of Poland.[127] It was declared to have vitiated the efforts of the Political Commission and rendered futile its comprehensive agenda, which included such questions as the recognition of the Russian pre-war debt, Bolshevistic propaganda in foreign countries, and the repayment of the Rumanian gold which had been sent by the Rumanian National Bank to Moscow in 1916, under Allied guarantee during the German occupation of Rumania, and which had been confiscated by the Soviet. No general improvement seemed possible without a comprehensive debt agreement, which was a concession that Russia refused to grant. The Russian proposal regarding a comprehensive anti-war pact, and the question of disarmament, despite the support of the states of the Little Entente, were similarly doomed because of the opposition of the Western Powers. Consequently, in view of the solidarity between Germany and Russia, although the life of the Conference was prolonged until May 19, three days beyond the time which had been allocated originally, it failed to solve the problem of Russia,[128] which was relegated to a new Conference at the Hague [129] on June 26. This fresh attempt failed again because of a lack of agreement between the Powers and Russia, which was expected to make all the concessions.

[127] For the Treaty of Rapallo and the subsequent exchange of notes between Russia and Poland (April 25–May 3, 1922), cf. *L'Europe nouvelle,* May 13, 1922. Cf. also, D'Abernon, *op. cit.,* vol. i, pp. 309-319 and 333-335.

[128] For the details of the Genoa Conference, cf. Giannini, A., *Les Documents de la Conférence de Gênes* (Rome, 1922) ; Mills, J. S., *The Genoa Conference* (New York, 1922) ; *Memorandum of the Russian Delegation to the Genoa Conference* (Genoa, 1922) ; *Reply of the Russian Delegation to the Memorandum of May 2, 1922* (Genoa, 1922) ; *Les Reclamations de la Russie aux États responsables de l'intervention et du blocus* (Genoa, 1922) ; *Conférence économique internationale de Gênes 9 avril–19 mai, 1922* (Paris, 1922).

[129] Cf. *Papers Relating to the Hague Conference, June–July, 1922* (London, 1922).

Even though the problem of Russia continued unsolved, the Genoa Conference remained a source of gratification to the Little Entente because of the strengthening of its ties with France and because of the recognition it had obtained from the Powers. Together with Poland, it had been invited to send to the Supreme Council one delegate to represent the bloc, which was included in this manner in all the Commissions and which was considered by Great Britain, France and Italy, for all practical purposes, as a fourth Great Power.[130]

Beneš had been particularly gratified by the activity of the Little Entente at Genoa, and regarded the recognition that had been attained as the reward of solidarity among the three little Powers and Poland. This solidarity had been enhanced by a well-prepared program, which had been aided by daily meetings of the representatives of the four states at Beneš' headquarters at the Hotel Bristol, where the topics for discussion had been elaborated in advance of each meeting of the Conference.[131]

The Rapprochement with Russia

After the Genoa Conference, Czechoslovakia would have been little nearer a solution of her Russian problem than before had it not been for her own efforts. In view of the differences of opinion concerning Russia that existed among the Great Powers and even among the members of the Little Entente, Beneš turned to the alternative of a separate commercial treaty between Czechoslovakia and Russia: he would not have been himself had he let slip such an opportunity.

---

[130] Cosma, *op. cit.*, pp. 95-98; Codresco, *op. cit.*, vol. i, pp. 253-262; Mousset, *op. cit.*, pp. 92-95; Dvořáček, J., "Jánovská Konference", *Zahraniční Politika*, vol. i, pp. 165-170.

[131] For Beneš' speech of May 23, 1922, before the Czechoslovak parliament, summarizing his actions at Genoa, *cf.* Beneš, *Problemy nové Evropy*, pp. 175-192; *L'Europe nouvelle*, June 3, 1922; or *Zprávy* (Poslanecká Sněmovna), 130 meeting, May 23, 1922, pp. 423 *et seq.*, 5 session; 142 meeting, May 30, 1922, pp. 591 *et seq.*, 5 session.

During the course of the Conference, he sounded Chicherin upon the subject. The approach was difficult, for the latter was suspicious of a Little Entente that was dominated by France. Chicherin, in the belief that Czechoslovakia and Yugoslavia owed racial allegiance to Slavic Russia rather than to Latin France, regarded Beneš as a Slav renegade.[132] At Genoa, Beneš had advocated merely de facto recognition of Russia, and had vigorously opposed de jure recognition, on the ground that the time for such a move was not ripe, lest it be followed by evil consequences in Europe in general and among the labor parties in particular, which in turn might result in even greater reaction from the Right. In spite of these sources of friction, Beneš' approach was welcomed by Chicherin, who agreed readily to a treaty, which was concluded at Genoa, but signed later.[133]

The provisional treaty, which was signed at Praha on June 5, 1922, was a compromise in which both countries abandoned their extreme demands in order to effect a rapprochement, Russia in particular giving up de jure recognition and credits, demands which she had regarded hitherto as vital portions of any treaty that she would negotiate. The text indicated that Russia desired to retain a monopoly of foreign trade, since it condemned in advance any business arrangements that might be drawn up with private individuals or groups in Russia that did not either represent the Bolshevik government directly or have special permission from it to engage in foreign trade. Czechoslovakia was unable to obtain any better terms on the problem of the restoration of the property of her own citizens in Russia than the mere statement that the question would be reserved for future discussion. Russia agreed similarly to reserve for

---

[132] *Cf.* D'Abernon, *op. cit.*, vol. ii, p. 88. *Cf.* also, *ibid.*, vol. i, p. 316, for the report that, on April 26, 1922, Russia had proposed that Czechoslovakia prohibit the export of arms to the Russian borderlands.

[133] Beneš, *Problemy nové Evropy*, p. 293; *Five Years of Czechoslovak Foreign Policy*, pp. 23-24.

future discussion the problem of de jure recognition, and, for the time being, to remain satisfied with the de facto recognition that the mere negotiation of a commercial treaty would entail. Other agreements that were generally the more favorable to Czechoslovakia were: the guarantee of security of the property and of unrestricted travel to the citizens of the other country, a cessation of propaganda against one another, a diplomatic and consular agreement, and a pledge of neutrality in the event of an attack on either by some third Power.[134] On the whole, the tone of the treaty was cordial. In view of the intimate relations that had been established between Russia and the Ukraine,[135] Czechoslovakia negotiated also, on the same day, a similar treaty with the latter.[136]

In this manner, Czechoslovakia solved temporarily her Russian problem and placed relations between the two countries upon a workable basis. After the conclusion of the commercial treaty, communist agitation, although still present, declined even more noticeably than during 1921. As the sequel was to show, in the opinion of Beneš, the five years of tortuous negotiations with the Great Powers had not been in vain. The result was a happy compromise between his eastern and western policies which had helped Czechoslovakia, and Central Europe as well, to work out its own particular problems of reconstruction with a minimum of interference from the Great Powers. The latter had been permitted to assist in the process of reconstruction, but had not been allowed to attract within their individual orbits the small states of this region.[137]

[134] For the text, cf. *Obchodní smlouvy mezistátní*, vol. i, pp. 386-391.

[135] For the Russo-Ukrainian Treaty of Alliance of December 28, 1920, cf. *Prager Presse*, July 16, 1922 (German text).

[136] For the text, cf. *Obchodní smlouvy mezistátní*, vol. i, pp. 392-397.

[137] Cf. Beneš, *Five Years of Czechoslovak Foreign Policy* (Speech of February 6, 1924, before the Foreign Committee of the Senate), pp. 20-29.

CHAPTER IV

The Reconstruction of Central Europe, 1918-1923
Beneš' Central European Objectives

DURING 1918-1923 Beneš considered the reconstruction of Central Europe the most important of his many problems. Within this region the World War had brought about changes that would require the best efforts of all concerned, if stability was to be restored. Central Europe had its own peculiar problems and viewpoints; it could not follow blindly the policies of any of the Great Powers or rely upon either East or West alone. With Russia beset by her own internal troubles and with Germany relegated temporarily to a position of relative impotence, the Central European stage appeared set as the scene for French and Italian rivalry. The foreign policy of Czechoslovakia envisaged the diplomatic independence of Central Europe, certainly that of its small victor states at least. Beneš sought to create in this area a political and economic structure that would be both constructive and permanent.[1]

Beneš, a thorough realist, appreciated the difficulties that would have to be surmounted if his objective was not to remain a theoretical ideal. He feared the inevitable interference of interested Great Powers. Then, too, he was by no means certain of the cooperation of even the victorious small states of Central Europe, to say nothing of the vanquished. Besides Czechoslovakia, victorious Rumania, Yugoslavia and Poland, and vanquished Austria and Hun-

---

[1] *Cf.* Beneš, E., "Problème des petites nations après la guerre mondiale", *Le Monde slav*, December, 1925, pp. 413-435.

gary formed integral parts of the new Central Europe. Would it be possible to arrive at any common understanding that would be mutually satisfactory to all six states, or even to the four victorious ones, who might then impose it upon the defeated two?

Czechoslovakia regarded her small neighbors with varying degrees of friendship or antipathy. She felt most hostile towards Hungary, the only one of the defeated states that failed to resign itself, even temporarily, to the results of the World War. Towards Austria, the feeling of antipathy was relatively mild, partly because of Austria's conciliatory policy, partly because of Czechoslovakia's desire to prevent Anschluss, and partly because Austria was expected to become, after Germany, her best customer. On the other hand, the highest degree of friendship was felt towards Yugoslavia, partly because of the close Slavic kinship and partly because the two countries were almost entirely free from clashing interests. Similarly, relations with Rumania were cordial, since no major interests came into conflict. Only with Poland, Czechoslovakia's nearest Slav neighbor, were relations uncertain immediately after the attainment of independence.[2]

Boundary Disputes with Poland

The analogies between Poland and Czechoslovakia were marked. Both were new Slavic states; in both some leaders had looked to Russia and some to Germany or Austria-Hungary for salvation, but, in the end, both had won independence with the aid of the West, especially of France; both were exposed to Russian Bolshevism and a resurrection of German militarism; and both had obtained such large minorities that they needed assistance in maintaining the status quo established by the Peace Treaties. Consequently, co-

[2] *Cf.* Masaryk, T. G., *Les Slaves après la guerre* (Prague, 1923).

operation against the former enemy states might almost have been taken for granted as a necessity for their continued independent existence. However, since the oppression that Poland had been forced to endure at the hands of Russia caused her to have little faith in the ideals of intra-Slav co-operation, racial appeals from Praha evoked little response in Warsaw. Moreover, Beneš, while advocating warm friendship for Poland, advised against any hasty relationship which might lead to an entangling alliance, particularly since Poland, apparently secure because of the backing of France, was pursuing an aggressive territorial policy, an attitude well calculated to develop antagonisms with all her neighbors. In the estimation of Beneš, Poland apparently failed to appreciate the dangers involved in her exposed geographical position and forward policy. Therefore, he considered it wise for Czechoslovakia to avoid a course that might commit her to some cause foreign to her own interests.[3]

The land hunger of both countries, moreover, dissipated any hopes of immediate friendship between them. In their desire for more territory, the two states engaged in a series of boundary disputes which, for approximately five years, overshadowed all other contacts and threatened both their mutual friendship and Poland's cooperation in Czechoslovakia's plans for the reconstruction of Central Europe. The frontier areas in question were Těšin, Orava and Spíš, of which the first was the most important.

The Duchy of Těšin, which contained an area of 877 square miles and, according to the census of 1910, 426,370 inhabitants, of whom fifty-five per cent were Polish, twenty-seven per cent Czech and eighteen per cent German, lies between Bohemia and Upper Silesia. Before the Peace Conference met, and even before either Czechoslovakia or Poland had established permanent governments, the respective

[3] Beneš, *Problemy nové Evropy*, p. 29.

National Councils, as early as November 5, 1918, had divided the Duchy, and had granted to Poland Tĕšin, Bílsko (Bielitz) and the Polish-speaking portions of Frystat. For the time being, the Duchy was to be governed by a central committee of seven Czechs, seven Poles and five Germans.[4]

In spite of this amicable settlement, which was understood by both parties to be merely temporary until such a time as the Peace Conference would apportion the territory in question, Poland, on December 10, 1918, attempted to draft men from the Duchy into her army and announced that, in January, 1919, the Duchy would hold elections for deputies to be sent to the Diet at Warsaw. After a Czech representative had been arrested for protesting against such procedure, Czechoslovakia, on January 22, 1919, demanded Polish evacuation of the Duchy.[5] A week later, in defense of this move, Beneš stressed the danger of basing hasty conclusions upon Austrian statistics which were notoriously inaccurate.[6] Meanwhile, after the demand for evacuation had been rejected by Poland, frontier skirmishing ensued for a few days.

Tĕšin was claimed at the Peace Conference by both Czechoslovakia and Poland. Since the Duchy was an economic unit and had not been divided in the past, Czechoslovakia claimed it in its entirety for the following reasons: (1) Tĕšin had formed part of the Kingdom of Bohemia; (2) most of the Poles were either Silesians or other immigrants; (3) the coal fields should not be separated from the industries outside the Duchy 'hat were dependent upon them; (4) the railway from Oderburg to Jablunka was indispensable both economically and strategically because, on the main line from Berlin to Budapest, it connected Slovakia with

[4] Temperley, *op. cit.*, vol. iv, p. 356.

[5] *Prager Presse*, January 23, 1919.

[6] Miller, *op. cit.*, vol. iv, pp. 68-70.

Bohemia and Moravia; (5) since a portion of the undeveloped Karvin basin lay within Poland, the latter would not be deprived entirely of the coal of the region; and (6) Czechoslovakia had to obtain complete possession of the railways and mines in order to maintain the economic unity of the Duchy, which she felt could not be guaranteed adequately otherwise, not even by subsequent special treaties.[7]

Poland, on the other hand, though she conceded to Czechoslovakia the one district to Frydek, which contained the best coal deposits, continued to insist upon retaining the other three—Těšin, Frystat and Bilsko—for linguistic reasons. She demanded, further, the Oderburg-Jablunka railway. Poland contended that the economic considerations advanced by Czechoslovakia did not justify the latter's demands for ownership. In the estimation of Poland, Czechoslovakia's major difficulty—a shortage of coal—could be easily surmounted by special conventions permitting coal imports from the Karvin mines.[8]

On January 27, the Peace Conference opened its deliberations upon the question of Těšin, and, on February 3, reached a decision whereby both disputants were warned against attempting to create any fait accompli within a territory that was to be assigned by the Conference. It then relegated the dispute to an Inter-Allied Commission which recommended that Czechoslovakia hold provisionally the northern, and Poland the southern part of the Duchy. In the interim, the local administration which had been created during the preceding November was to remain in control.[9]

---

[7] *Peace Conference Delegation, 1919. Memoirs*, no. 4, " Le problème de la Silesie de Teschen "; *cf.* also, Kellor, *op. cit.*, vol. i, pp. 343-346; Temperley, *op. cit.*, vol. iv, pp. 349, 353-354.

[8] Temperley, *op. cit.*, vol. iv, pp. 354-355.

[9] *Ibid.*, p. 357 ; Miller, *op. cit.*, vol. iv, pp. 423-424; vol. xiv, pp. 155-157.

Beneš accepted this temporary arrangement on the same day, but wrote also to Clemenceau, invoking anew the doctrine of historical boundaries, a plea that received no response. Beneš was aware that France remained in doubt as to which of her two friends she should favor, and that Poland, because of her greater population might easily carry more weight. Paris felt that Poland must not be weakened in any way, not only in view of a possible conflict with Germany, but because, with Rumania, she formed a bulwark against Russia.[10]

At this stage of the controversy, Beneš' hand seemed to be forced by the clamor of Czechoslovak public opinion, which demanded action.[11] The Czechoslovaks apparently failed to appreciate that the friendship of Poland was more valuable than the small area in dispute, and, elated by the relatively easy territorial victories that were being won on the other frontiers at the Peace Conference, could not understand the delay over Těšin. They did not realize that the good impression which Czechoslovakia had created with her reserve and moderation might be jeopardized if too forward a policy regarding Těšin should be adopted. In this dispute, however, neither country had the unreserved support of France, which deemed the friendship of both essential to her. France toyed temporarily with the idea of replacing Austria-Hungary by Poland and Czechoslovakia. She sought to evade the necessity of making a choice by suggesting either arbitration or a plebiscite.[12]

To prevent another outbreak of hostilities and avert the possibility that the Peace Conference might award the entire

[10] Beneš, *op. cit.*, pp. 62-64; Vochoč, *loc. cit.*, pp. 108-109.

[11] Beneš and Kramář made a private agreement that the latter would defend the demand for Těšin obstinately, while Beneš would remain amenable to compromise. *Cf.* Beneš, *op. cit.*, p. 66. However, this move, which was originally considered good tactics, became a boomerang.

[12] Beneš, *op. cit.*, pp. 64-65; House and Seymour, *op. cit.*, p. 70.

Duchy to Poland, Beneš felt it necessary to end the dispute, even at the cost of concessions. Consequently, he suggested that Bílsko be awarded to Poland, and the remainder of the Duchy to Czechoslovakia, a proposal which was accepted by the territorial commission on April 14, 1919, but which was rejected by Poland. At the request of the United States, Beneš opened direct negotiations with Paderewski, the Polish Foreign Minister, but could reach no agreement except to continue negotiations.[18] On April 20, the Těšin Commission presented a new plan whereby Poland would receive Bohumín, Karvin and Těšin, and Czechoslovakia the remaining regions in which she might construct new connections from Frydek to Jablunka, but this project was ruined also by delays in agreement between the two states.[14] Three days later Czechoslovakia refused to yield Orava for strategic reasons, lest Poland obtain a footing in the upper valleys on the Czechoslovak side of the Carpathians.[15] As a sign of moderation, Beneš offered to cede Těšin up to the Vistula, but refused to yield further. The deadlock was apparently broken by a Czechoslovak-Polish Conference at Cracow at the end of July, but, after an auspicious opening, differences once more arose when Czechoslovakia again offered the area up to the Vistula, whereas Poland insisted upon a plebiscite which she hoped would be more favorable to her.[16]

When no decision had been reached by August 5, 1919, the last day which had been set by the Powers, the whole dispute was referred to the Supreme Council. On August 22 Czechoslovakia rejected the territorial commission's proposal to divide the Karvin coal fields. Early in the following month, Beneš and Dmowski presented their final argu-

[18] *Cf.* Miller, *op. cit.*, vol. xvii, pp. 35-39, for the telegraphic correspondence among Beneš, Švehla and Paderewski concerning Těšin.

[14] Beneš, *op. cit.*, pp. 66-67.

[15] Miller, *op. cit.*, vol. xvi, pp. 107-115.

[16] Vochoč, *loc cit.*, p. 110.

ments to the Supreme Council, which, from all indications, was moved primarily by the plea that the coal of Těšín was vital to Czechoslovakia.   At the same time the representatives from Těšín agreed with Beneš and Kramář that the Olsa River represented the limit of Czechoslovakia's vital needs.   France attempted to save Karvin and the railroad from Košice to Bohumín for Czechoslovakia, but, when the Powers failed to agree, accepted the plebiscite on September 27, 1919.[17]   All men and women over the age of twenty and residents since August 1, 1914, might vote.   The Plebiscite Commission finally arrived on January 30, 1920, to encounter propaganda and racial friction which culminated in riots in May when 11,600 Těšín miners struck in the Karvin area. Consequently, a fair plebiscite was deemed hopeless by the Commission itself.[18]

By the summer of 1920, it seemed as if Poland would be ruined by the Bolshevik invasion.   Her war with Russia had been the direct result of her policy of expansion.   In spite of the advice of the Allies and of offers of peace from Chicherin, Poland had sought to revive her frontiers of 1772. For a time she was successful, even to the capture of Kiev, but her ambition proved superior to her resources.   A Russian counter-offensive reached the gates of Warsaw by July, 1920.   Poland was saved only after desperate efforts on her part, and because of the help of France, which sent munitions and a staff of officers, led by General Weygand, who assumed supreme command.[19]   Subsequently, the Russians were driven to the east.   The Treaty of Riga,[20]

[17] *Ibid.*, p. 111.

[18] Temperley, *op. cit.*, vol. iv, pp. 358-360.

[19] *Cf.* D'Abernon, *op cit.*, vol. i, p. 75.

[20] *Treaty Series*, vol. iv, p. 32; for full details of Poland's boundary struggles, 1918-20, *cf.* Przybylski, A., *La Pologne en lutte pour ses frontières* (Paris, 1929).

of October 12, 1920, which terminated the war, resulted in ethnographically unwarrantable Polish gains.

In the hour of Poland's greatest distress, Beneš had to make one of the major decisions of his diplomatic career. Public opinion in Czechoslovakia demanded a strong stand against Poland, or even military cooperation with Russia against her. Beneš, with the support of President Masaryk, determined to be strictly neutral: he wisely refused to heed either the domestic clamor or the rumor of a French request to help Poland. Allegedly, French pressure was exerted upon Czechoslovakia by the Allied military mission, which visited Praha on July 22, 1920, on its way from Paris to Warsaw.[21] According to another rumor emanating from Warsaw,[22] even the State Department of the United States was reported to have informed Czechoslovakia that the route must be kept open for ammunition and supplies to Poland! Without exception, the Praha newspapers of July 28 discussed at length what the action of the government should be if the Allies should actually make such a demand. Czechoslovak labor organizations were particularly active in demanding a prohibition of arms shipments to Poland across Czechoslovak territories. There can be no doubt that the action of Germany, which, on July 25, proclaimed neutrality and forbade transportation of all war materials to either belligerent,[23] had great influence upon the actions of Czechoslovakia, which on August 7, issued a similar declaration of neutrality.[24] Apart from the dislike of becoming involved in a foreign quarrel, Beneš' policy was dictated by his desire to promote intra-Slavic solidarity, an ideal which had already

[21] *Čas, Národní Listy, Národní Politika,* July 23, 1920.

[22] *Gazeta Warszawska,* July 24, 1920; *Svornost,* July 26, 1920.

[23] *Deutscher Reichsanzeiger und Preussischer Staatsanzeiger,* July 28, 1920.

[24] *Právo Lidu,* August 8, 1920; *Svornost,* August 9, 1920.

been dealt a cruel blow by the Russo-Polish war and which he felt would be further injured by Czechoslovakia's participation on either side. He hoped that Russia would recover her former position as a Great Power, whereas Poland feared that such an event might subvert the new status quo which had been established by the Treaty of Riga.[25]

Beneš' moderation became more praiseworthy in view of the fact that Czechoslovakia and Poland had other sources of friction besides boundary disputes. They differed also in their policies concerning their Ukrainian minorities. Poland ruled sternly in Galicia which she had seized by force in 1919, and which, except for a temporary Russian occupation during the summer of 1920, remained hers de facto until March 15, 1923, when the Allies awarded it to her de jure. In contrast, Czechoslovakia had promised Ruthenia concessions almost tantamount to national autonomy. Then, too, Poland flirted with Hungary, with which she had no quarrel, and which, according to generally prevalent rumors, offered during July, 1920, her aid against Russia, in return for Polish support in recovering territory from Czechoslovakia, Rumania and Yugoslavia. In any event, such rumors retarded the rapprochement between Czechoslovakia and Poland.[26]

Czechoslovak-Polish relations became still further complicated by an apparent attempt on the part of Germany to fish in troubled waters. Poland resented bitterly German sympathy with Czechoslovakia during the Těšin dispute. Beneš was far from having, as rumors intimated, any understanding with Germany at Poland's expense. On the contrary, he believed that Germany desired Poland to obtain both

---

[25] Beneš, *op. cit.*, pp. 92-94.

[26] Jeden Svědek, "Beneš a Mala Dohoda", *Dr. Edvard Beneš*, pp. 234-235; Mousset, *op. cit.*, p. 18; Toynbee, A. J., *Survey of International Affairs, 1920-23*, p. 282; Beneš, *op. cit.*, pp. 120-122.

Galicia and a large portion of Russia, but not Posen and Silesia, not, as Germany maintained, in order to strengthen Poland, but in order to antagonize her and Russia, and force Czechoslovakia to become unfriendly to one of them. Beneš deemed Germany's action a further justification for his policy of intra-Slav cooperation, and felt that her future course could be checked only by the united action of the three Slav states. In the Upper Silesian dispute, he supported Poland, rather than Germany, in spite of the existing friction, and gave the lie to the then current rumor that the Allies would compensate Poland with Těšin for the expense of her recent war with Russia.[27]

In the meantime, the Těšin dispute continued to drag along. The Czechoslovak Committee on Foreign Affairs still preferred a plebiscite to arbitration, despite the failure of one attempt to hold an impartial vote. This fact was distorted by the press until the Czechoslovak public came to delude itself with the belief that a majority vote in a plebiscite would award Czechoslovakia the whole Duchy. It was considered good tactics to claim all and bargain later. Beneš realized that, even if Czechoslovakia did obtain most of the coal-producing areas, it would still be an economic disaster, whereas Poland had other valuable mines in Upper Silesia. In a conference with Millerand at Spa, he was informed that Poland would be granted every area in which she would poll a majority, a decision which he felt would involve the loss of Karvin. Not wishing to bear the sole responsibility for accepting or refusing the Allied offer, and preferring an agreement dividing the Duchy to a plebiscite, he sought to ascertain the attitude of the Senate Committee on Foreign Affairs, but could get no response in time. Compelled to act independently, Beneš signed with Paderewski the agreement of July 28, 1920, whereby Czechoslovakia obtained the whole

[27] Beneš, *op. cit.*, pp. 69-71, 152-153; Hrušovský, *loc. cit.*, pp. 130-131.

Karvin area, the entire strategic railway, and the suburbs of Těšin on the western bank of the Olsa River, whereas Poland received the eastern part of the Duchy together with most of the city of Těšin except for the railway line and station.[28]

In seeking parliamentary approval for his agreement with Paderewski, Beneš encountered the most intense opposition that he had met thus far in his career. Both the National Democrats and Bohemian Germans denounced a decision which neither they nor the Poles would consider final.[29] The *Prager Tagblatt* in particular " protested against 50,000 Germans being given to ' insatiable Poland ' "[30] . . . The *Národní Listy* stated that " Czechoslovakia will never desert the minority lost in the decision ".[31] The *České Slovo* was almost alone " in being happy that a decision had been reached ".[32] A crisis developed on August 4 when Beneš addressed to the Foreign Affairs Committees of the Senate and the Chamber of Deputies an exposé in which he explained the necessity for dividing Těšin after the Conference of Ambassadors[33] had ignored Czechoslovakia's historic

[28] For full details, cf. Beneš, *op. cit.*, pp. 71-81; Temperley, *op. cit.*, vol. iv, pp. 361-363. On November 29, 1920, at Brno, the two countries signed a treaty which provided for a " Mixed Commission" to protect the respective minorities, but the treaty was never ratified. *Cf.* Fouques-Duparc, *op. cit.*, pp. 318-319. *Cf.* also, *Papers Relating to the Foreign Relations of the United States, 1920* (Washington, 1935), vol. i, pp. 36-73, for the correspondence of the American Government regarding Těšin. Apparently, President Wilson desired to have a voice in the final settlement, but had no intention of signing the agreement of July 28, 1920.

[29] *Právo Lidu*, July 31, 1920.

[30] *Prager Tagblatt*, July 31, 1920.

[31] *Národní Listy*, July 31, 1920.

[32] *České Slovo*, July 31, 1920.

[33] After the Supreme Council ceased to exist (January 21, 1920), a new agency, the Conference of Ambassadors, composed of the Ambassadors of the United States, Great Britain, Italy and Japan to Paris, and of a representative of France, assumed responsibility for the execution of the Peace Treaties.

rights to the Duchy. Although his report was approved by the narrowest margin—eleven votes (Social Democrats, National Socialists and Agrarians) to ten (Germans, National Democrats and Clericals)—the Committees as a whole commended his conduct of the negotiations. It appears that a favorable reception had been assured by Beneš' driving home the points that he had considered a plebiscite cowardly because it evaded direct negotiations with Poland, and that, by the division of the Duchy, Czechoslovakia's gains had exceeded her losses. According to Beneš' figures, Czechoslovakia had obtained 292,000 inhabitants, including 37,000 Poles, whereas Poland had received 143,000 inhabitants, only 2,000 of whom were Czechs.[34] The approval of the Committees having been won, ratification followed almost as a matter of course on January 28, 1921.[35]

Closely connected with the Těšin question were similar disputes in Orava and Spíš, particularly over Javorina. Javorina, a small region on the northern slope of the Tatra Mountains in the district of Spíš, contained a pass of great strategic value that was coveted by both countries. Czechoslovakia claimed Orava and Spíš on economic and strategic grounds, whereas Poland's claims were historic and ethnic. On July 28, 1920, the Conference of Ambassadors defined the boundaries of Těšin, Orava and Spíš and appointed a Delimitation Commission, composed of one representative of each of the Principal Allied Powers and of Poland and Czechoslovakia, to draw the actual frontiers on the ground.[36] Although both Beneš and Paderewski signed the agreement, the latter, two days later, raised an objection because the principle of nationality had not been heeded in accordance

[34] *Národní Politika*, August 5, 1920; *Svornost*, August 11, 25-26, 1920.
[35] *Zprávy* (Poslanecká Sněmovna), 49 meeting, January 28, 1921, pp. 1988 et seq., 2 session.
[36] Beneš, *op. cit.*, pp. 117-119; *Treaty Series*, vol. ii, pp. 49-58.

with Point 13 of President Wilson's Fourteen Points, in-asmuch as 25,000 Poles in Spíš and Orava had been awarded to Poland and 45,000 to Czechoslovakia.[37]

Nevertheless, on August 10, Poland and Czechoslovakia concluded the Frontiers Treaty of Sèvres[38] which confirmed the boundaries that had been established on July 28 except for some frontier modifications in Spíš. In general, the old frontier line between Galicia and Hungary was retained, but the treaty never became effective because it was not rati-fied. Meanwhile, the Delimitation Commission began its labors, and on April 23, 1921, adopted certain modifications of the line in Těšin and Orava which were approved by the Conference on May 25. On that occasion, the representative of Poland voted, as a conciliatory gesture, in favor of these changes in the hope that, in return, Poland might obtain Javorina.[39] When the two disputants still failed to reach any agreement, the Commission, on July 5, was forced to report to the Conference that it was unable to make any satisfactory recommendation.[40] It explained its failure to act by the fact that the modifications that had been proposed were beyond the scope of its discretionary powers.[41] The Conference temporized by referring the matter to the con-testants, who on November 6, 1921, signed an agreement whereby, in mutual good will, they undertook to reach an agreement in six months. On December 22 the Conference suspended the execution of the decision of July 28, 1920, to August 16, 1922. When no agreement was reached by that time, the Allied members of the Commission, on September 12, proposed, and on September 25 accepted, by a vote of

[37] *Permanent Court of International Justice*, series C, no. 4, pp. 138-140.
[38] *Treaty Series*, vol. viii, p. 39.
[39] *Permanent Court of International Justice*, series B, no. 8, p. 52.
[40] *Ibid.*, series B, no. 8, p. 44.
[41] *Ibid.*, series B, no. 8, p. 45.

five out of six, a new line somewhat more favorable to Poland, but which still retained for Czechoslovakia the crests of the Tatras.[42] In spite of the fact that the repeated delays were increasing the unrest in Javorina, where the inhabitants appeared generally indifferent as to whether they should become Poles or Czechoslovaks as long as their villages and grazing lands were not separated, the Conference of Ambassadors, on November 13, 1922, refused to approve the new solution without further investigation.[43]

At last, after four years of bickering, the Conference of Ambassadors, on July 27, 1923, confessed its own inability to agree and referred the dispute to the League Council, a move that was opposed by Poland as involving further delay.[44] Such, however, was not the case. The Council referred the dispute to Senor Quinones de Leon, of Spain, and requested also an advisory opinion from the Permanent Court of International Justice regarding the delimitation of the frontier between Poland and Czechoslovakia.[45] The Court met, on November 13, 1923, in extraordinary session,[46] and held that the decision of July 28, 1920, was final,[47] but withheld an opinion on the question whether the Delimitation Commission had exceeded its authority in its recommenda-

[42] *Ibid.*, series C, no. 4, pp. 245-247; *Zprávy* (Poslanecká Sněmovna), 161 meeting, October 26, 1922, pp. 194 *et seq.*, 6 session.

[43] *Permanent Court of International Justice*, series C., no. 4, pp. 183, 260-263.

[44] *Cf.* Vochoč, V., "Javorina", *Zahraniční Politika*, vol. ii, pp. 793-808; Krčmář, J., "Československopolská hranice v území spišskem před Stalým Dvorem v Haagu a před Radou Společnosti Národu", *Zahraniční Politika*, vol. iii, pp. 7-20, 102-118, 186-196, 600-603.

[45] *Official Journal*, November, 1923, pp. 1316-1317, 1332-1333.

[46] *Cf. Permanent Court of International Justice*, Fourth Session (Extraordinary, November 13–December 6, 1923), Documents relating to Advisory Opinion no. 8 (Jaworzina), series C, no. 4, p. 438.

[47] *Ibid.*, series B, no. 8, p. 30.

tion of September 25, 1922.[48] The Council, after accepting Czechoslovakia's contention that the Commission had exceeded its powers, requested this last to obtain fresh proposals in agreement with more recent deliberations.[49] In conformity with these instructions, the Commission proposed a new frontier line on March 12, 1924. Two weeks later, the Conference approved the proposal, which was embodied in the protocols drawn up at Warsaw in May by a mixed Czechoslovak-Polish Commission.[50] The signing of these protocols on May 6, 1924, terminated the dispute.[51] In itself, the Javorina dispute had been a minor matter, but it had become extremely important in exacerbating the relations between the two countries.[52] With its solution, Czechoslovakia not only completed the delimitation of her frontiers, but removed the main obstacle to a rapprochement with Poland that was to result in a relatively high degree of cooperation in the reconstruction of Central Europe.

The Formation of the Little Entente

Beneš had not allowed the Czechoslovak-Polish quarrel to distract his attention from his main objective, the reconstruction of Central Europe. He believed that, in this area, his country would derive the greatest advantages from a continuation of the embryonic Little Entente policy that he had inaugurated even before Czechoslovakia had attained independence.[53] As early as October and November, 1918, he had entered into tentative negotiations with Jonescu of

[48] *Ibid.*, series B, no. 8, pp. 39-40.

[49] *Official Journal*, February, 1924, pp. 345-348, 357-364.

[50] *Monthly Summary*, June, 1924, p. 828.

[51] *Permanent Court of International Justice*, series E, no. 1, p. 220.

[52] *Cf.* Kellor, *op. cit.*, vol. i, pp. 346-347, for the details of several characteristic frontier "incidents".

[53] *Cf.* Codresco, F., *La Petite Entente* (Paris, 1931), vol. i, pp. 133-155, for a discussion of precedents for the Little Entente.

Rumania, and with Pašič and Trumbič of Yugoslavia, with regard to cooperation among their respective countries.[54] These attempts proved to be premature. Amid their mutual worries in obtaining satisfactory peace settlements, the three small Powers dropped the project temporarily. Beneš, who had welcomed the departure of the Emperor-King Charles into exile in Switzerland after the termination of the World War [55] and the separation of Austria and Hungary, began to be worried anew during 1919 by the symptoms of reactionary tendencies, particularly in Hungary. After the termination of the war over Slovakia and the resulting overthrow of the Soviet government of Bela Kun,[56] Archduke Joseph came into power at Budapest. In the estimation of Beneš, this move might foreshadow an attempted Habsburg restoration which would threaten anew the peace of Central Europe. He protested to the Supreme Council, which, by a note of August 21, 1919, made clear to Budapest that no Habsburg could have a place in any Hungarian government.[57] As a result, Joseph's tenure was extremely brief,[58] but the menace that he typified rendered almost inevitable the formation of some opposing combination of the small victor states.

[54] *Cf.* Jonescu, T., " The Future of the Little Entente ", *The Living Age*, vol. cccxi, p. 699; Toynbee, *op. cit.*, p. 287; Cosma, *op. cit.*, p. 17.

[55] *Cf. Arbeiter Zeitung*, November 12 and 14, 1918, for Emperor Charles'- proclamations of withdrawal from the affairs of Austria and Hungary respectively. *Cf.* also, *ibid.*, November 17, 1918, for article " The Dynasty Must Go ".

[56] *Cf. supra*, p. 39.

[57] *Documents diplomatiques concernant les tentatives de restauration des Hapsbourg au trône de Hongrie* (henceforth referred to as *Documents, Hapsbourg*), no. 1.

[58] Bela Kun was overthrown on August 1, 1919, and was succeeded by Peidl. *Cf. The Times*, August 9 or *Le Temps*, August 10, for Joseph's proclamation on assuming power. He resigned in less than three weeks (*cf. The Times*, August 26 for his proclamation on leaving power).

Czechoslovakia reopened negotiations with her two prospective partners when Beneš offered alliances to Trumbič in Paris on December 30, 1919,[59] and to Vaida-Voëvod at Bucharest on January 5, 1920.[60] Since Yugoslavia welcomed the advance the more enthusiastically, direct negotiations between the two countries were inaugurated during February. The Kapp Putsch in March and the flirtation of France and Hungary during July made the need for haste apparent.[61]

The latter of these two threats aroused particular fear. After Czechoslovakia had refused to assist Poland against Russia during the summer of 1920, France considered the offer of Hungary to send four divisions to aid Poland, but refused primarily because Hungarian intervention would have taken place only at the cost of territorial compensations that would have necessitated a revision of the Peace Treaties to the detriment of Czechoslovakia, Rumania and Yugoslavia. Realizing that Hungarian friendship at such a price would have been too costly, France herself helped Poland. However, before France made her choice, Paris and Budapest had exchanged many communications, more or less secret in nature, that had been alarming to Hungary's neighbors. Beneš was aware that such negotiations were taking place,

[59] *Documents diplomatiques relatives aux conventions d'alliance conclus par la République Tchécoslovaque avec le Royaume des Serbes, Croates et Slovenes et le Royaume de Roumanie* (henceforth referred to as *Documents, alliance*), no. 1.

[60] *Documents, alliance*, no. 2.

[61] *Ibid.*, nos. 6 and 19. On January 22, 1920, Jan Slaviček, a member of the Czechoslovak parliament, threatened Hungary with an alliance between Czechoslovakia and Yugoslavia (*cf.* Hrušovský, *loc. cit.*, p. 180). During the course of the negotiations for the Treaty of Trianon, there was cooperation between Osuský of Czechoslovakia, Zolger of Yugoslavia, and Ghika of Rumania against Count Apponyi of Hungary, *cf. Zprávy* (Senát), 27 meeting, December 21, 1920, pp. 643 *et seq.*, 2 session; 28 meeting, December 22, 1920, pp. 678 *et seq.*, 2 session.

but was almost alone in trying to dispell alarm, for he felt that France could be trusted to do nothing inimical to Czechoslovakia.[62] Nevertheless, Czechoslovakia continued to fear particularly that, should Hungarian troops cross Slovakia on their way to the east, they would do their best to increase irredentism. About 2,500,000 Magyars resided in the four neighboring states. These minorities were responsive to nationalist appeals from Budapest.[63] During September, further alarms were spread by the Vienna *Arbeiter Zeitung* and the Praha *Právo Lidu,* both of which published repeated " revelations " of Magyar machinations, allegedly directed from bases at Vienna and Szombathely against Austria; from Vienna, Miskolcz and Gyor against Czechoslovakia; and from Kaposvar, Pecs and Szeged against Yugoslavia.[64] Although such " revelations " were perhaps inspired as much by anti-Hungarian sentiment as by Magyar provocation, they were effective in hastening the cooperation of Hungary's neighbors.

Beneš appreciated the difficulties that confronted him: in view of the divergent interests of his prospective partners, he believed that it would be necessary to negotiate step by step, by a series of bilateral treaties. On August 14, 1920, at Belgrade, Beneš and Nincic signed a defensive treaty of alliance. Article 1 specified that each state was to aid the other against an unprovoked attack by Hungary. According to Article 2, the method of assistance would be determined by a later agreement between the competent technical authorities, i. e. by a military convention. Article 3 stated that neither country might conclude an alliance with a third Power without informing the partner in advance. Article 4 provided that the treaty was to endure for two years, and

---

[62] *Documents, alliance*, nos. 19, 28-30.

[63] *Cf.* Crane, J. O., *The Little Entente* (New York, 1931), p. 176.

[64] *Cf.* Mousset, *op. cit.*, pp. 13-14.

would be renewable. If denounced upon expiration, it was to remain effective for another six months. Article 5 required registration of the treaty with the League of Nations, and Article 6 arranged for an exchange of ratifications at Belgrade as soon as possible.[65]

Beneš, always an opponent of secret diplomacy, desired publicity for the alliance, lest its objectives be misunderstood. At Belgrade, on August 15, he granted a lengthy interview to a correspondent of the *Journal des débats*, and, on September 1, presented a lengthy exposé to the Czechoslovak parliament. Beneš' first reason for the formation of what he himself styled " the so-called Little Entente " [66] was the unrest prevalent throughout Europe, as a result of which the small states in particular felt insecure as to their future as long as each remained isolated. His second reason was economic: he believed that political contacts would lead ultimately to economic cooperation. His third motive was the domestic stabilization of the states concerned so that each might work out without interference its own political and social reforms. He felt that the realization of these first three objectives would remove from the minds of some of his people any lingering regrets over the destruction of Austria-Hungary, whose main justification for existence, in recent times, had been the law and order which she had provided for the diverse peoples of Central Europe, a service which, in his estimation, could be rendered equally well by the new organization. Fourthly, the concrete and immediate reason for the formation of the Little Entente was the attitude of Hungary, which sought to contest the verdict of the World War, retain her former aristocratic social order, and regain her lost territories. Beneš' fifth and final reason

[65] *Documents, alliance*, no. 25; *Treaty Series*, vol. vi, pp. 209-213.

[66] *Cf*. Machray, R., *The Little Entente* (London, 1929), pp. 105-106, on how the Little Entente was named.

was to be found in the general European situation: although continuing to profess faith in both the League and the Great Entente of Great Britain and France, he felt that the policies of both should be reinforced and rendered more effective by special " regional understandings ".[67]

The second link in Beneš' chain, an alliance with Rumania, required more careful preparation. Except for Masaryk's visit late in 1917 and for cooperation at Paris in Beneš' embryonic Little Entente policy,[68] the two peoples had had practically no contacts with one another. Predominantly Latin, Rumania had little sympathy with the Slavophil tendencies of her two prospective partners. Take Jonescu, who deserves to rank with Beneš as a co-founder of the Little Entente, had, since 1919, advocated closer ties among the late Allies. After becoming Minister of Foreign Affairs in June, 1920, he had secured in the Rumanian parliament a majority which favored his policies. When Beneš, en route from Belgrade, reached Bucharest on August 17, Jonescu had already drafted a treaty analogous to that between Czechoslovakia and Yugoslavia.[69]

The inclusion of Rumania would give territorial contiguity to the Little Entente, but would also present many new problems. On October 30, at Praha, Czechoslovakia and Rumania appointed two mixed commissions: one to delimit their frontier in Ruthenia, and the other to make recommendations upon economic questions.[70] Italian objections to

[67] Beneš, *Problemy nové Evropy*, pp. 284-285; *Five Years of Czechoslovak Foreign Policy*, pp. 12-14; *The Foreign Policy of Czechoslovakia*, pp. 32-33; *Právo Lidu*, August 16, September 1, 1920; *cf.* also, Machray, *op. cit.*, pp. 126-134; Mousset, *op. cit.*, pp. 23-26; Cosma, *op. cit.*, pp. 20-22; Codresco, *op. cit.*, vol. i, pp. 157-165, 183-186.

[68] *Cf.* Rouček, J. S., *Contemporary Rumania and Her Problems* (Palo Alto, 1932), pp. 136-140.

[69] *Documents, alliance*, nos. 26-27.

[70] *Ibid.*, no. 32.

the new alignment were removed by the defensive agreement[71] of November 12, 1920, between Italy and Yugoslavia, and by an exchange of notes, of February 8, 1921, between Beneš and Sforza regarding their common interests.[72] Beneš and Jonescu had different conceptions of the scope of the Little Entente. Jonescu feared not only Hungary, but Bulgaria and Russia, whereas Beneš desired a treaty that would apply merely to the first. This essential weakness in the Little Entente—the divergent policies concerning Russia between Rumania on the one hand and Czechoslovakia and Yugoslavia on the other—was appreciated by each state, and hence was kept carefully in the background. Jonescu desired particularly a guarantee of retaining Bessarabia, to which Beneš would not agree. Jonescu envisaged a belt of small states from the Aegean to the Baltic, on the order of France's contemplated " cordon sanitaire ", which would cooperate on all international questions and have the force of a Great Power. To this end, he desired to include Greece, and, particularly, Poland.[73] On the other hand, Beneš believed that Poland's geographic position and peculiar problems, particularly her hostility to Russia, which was shared by the other Baltic states, should exclude this whole group from anything more than cooperation with the Little Entente. Similarly, he was not concerned with Rumania's and Yugoslavia's relations with Bulgaria and Greece, whose inclusion he believed would give too Balkan a character to the organization. He maintained that an attempt to include too many questions would weaken any

[71] *Ibid.*, no. 34 (The Treaty of Rapallo).

[72] *Ibid.*, nos. 39-40. In the negotiations of Italy, both with Yugoslavia and Czechoslovakia, the first agreed to insist upon the enforcement of the Treaties of St. Germain and Trianon, and upon the exclusion of the Habsburgs.

[73] Jonescu, *loc. cit.*, vol. cccxi, pp. 699-703; *cf.* also, Mousset, *op. cit.*, pp. 26-29.

bloc that might be created, and won his point. As a result, the Little Entente became more limited in scope, but decidedly more effective.[74]

Before the Czechoslovak-Rumanian negotiations had been embodied in a treaty, the exiled ex-Emperor-King Charles of Austria-Hungary made his first attempt to regain the Hungarian throne. Perhaps in the erroneous belief that the Great Powers would not interfere [75] and that Austria and Hungary might welcome some form of union under his rule, Charles attempted his first coup d'état on March 27, 1921. After the withdrawal of the Rumanian army of occupation from Budapest on November 14, 1919, there had come into power the " White " government of Admiral Horthy, from whom Charles expected every assistance; however, in the hour of need, Horthy gave Charles no aid. The representatives of Great Britain, France, Italy, Rumania, Yugoslavia and Czechoslovakia at once protested against the presence of Charles in Hungary.[76] Czechoslovakia and Yugoslavia in particular considered it a casus belli and proceeded to invoke the clauses of their treaty that provided for such an emergency.[77] The Hungarian National Assembly met in special session and approved Horthy's attitude and remonstrances to Charles as strictly constitutional. On March 31 it answered

[74] Le Temps, August 26, 1920; Beneš, Problemy nové Evropy, pp. 83-87; Jonescu, T., " How the Little Entente Began ", The Living Age, vol. cccxi, pp. 627-632; Cosma, op. cit., pp. 25-29.

[75] For full details concerning Charles' first attempt cf. Werkmann, Baron K. von (Private Secretary to the Emperor), The Tragedy of Charles of Habsburg (London, 1924), pp. 127-144; or Ashmead-Bartlett, E., The Tragedy of Central Europe (London, 1923), pp. 252-257 (account of A. Boroviczeny, Charles' aide-de-camp). Ashmead-Bartlett maintains that Charles had absolute guarantees from Briand that France would not interfere. Cf. also, Cosma, op. cit., pp. 40-49; Mousset, op. cit., pp. 29-34.

[76] Documents, Hapsbourg, nos. 8-12.

[77] Zprávy (Poslanecká Sněmovna), 66 meeting, March 31, 1921, pp. 30 et seq., 3 session.

the Allied protests by promising to enforce the departure of the ex-King.[78]   Beneš, who had deemed the Hungarian government suspiciously passive in the crisis, still remained unconvinced of its good faith, and, on April 3, sent to Budapest an ultimatum in which he threatened to take immediate measures if Charles were still on Hungarian soil by six P. M. of April 7.[79]   The measures contemplated a declaration of blockade, which was to be followed, if necessary, by a military demonstration.   Beneš had planned to have friendly Powers cooperate, but believed that the need for haste justified his independent action.   On April 4 the joint ultimatum that had apparently been planned became a fact when Yugoslavia suggested that Charles be granted three days of grace, a suggestion that both Czechoslovakia and Rumania accepted.[80]   On the same day, the Conference of Ambassadors presented its note to Hungary.[81]   In spite of the fact that Charles was already preparing his departure, Beneš instructed the Czechoslovak Minister at Budapest to present the text of the ultimatum to the Hungarian government,[82] an act which, technically, was independent, since the Ministers of Rumania and Yugoslavia, in the absence of instructions, failed to protest jointly.[83]

Charles' first attempt hastened the negotiations necessary to complete the Little Entente.   On April 23, 1921, Czechoslovakia and Rumania concluded their alliance on essentially the same terms as the Czechoslovak-Yugoslav treaty, except for an additional Article (4) whereby the two states agreed that, " in order to coordinate their efforts on behalf of peace, they would consult with one another upon all ques-

[78] *Documents, Hapsbourg*, no. 13.
[79] *Ibid.*, nos. 16-18.
[80] *Ibid.*, nos. 19-21.
[81] *Ibid.*, no. 12.
[82] *Ibid.*, no. 24.
[83] *Ibid.*, no. 25.

tions of foreign policy that concerned their relations with Hungary ".[84]

Side by side with her political negotiations, Czechoslovakia inaugurated with her prospective partners economic discussions which made relatively equal progress. After extensive preliminary negotiations, a commercial treaty was signed with Yugoslavia on October 18, 1920, whereby fixed amounts of goods were to be exchanged. This agreement was to endure until June 30, 1921, at which time new clauses might become effective or the old agreement might be renewed. The original agreement drew a distinction between annual contingents and special permits. It allowed free mutual exports of agricultural and industrial products only to the extent of the domestic requirements of both states. Yugoslavia guaranteed to deliver 100 truckloads of preserved meat, 300 of lard, 1,000 of bacon, 6,000 of wheat, 10,000 of iron ore, 100 of manganese ore, and lesser amounts of hoop-iron, lead, hemp, soda, pyrites, etc., whereas Czechoslovakia promised to furnish 300 truckloads of coal for river navigation, 1,200 of pit coal, 1,500 of railway coal, 3,000 of coke, 2,500 each of sugar, tin plate, crude iron, machine parts, and farm machinery, 500 of plate glass, 220 of paper, and 400 of other industrial products. In addition, trade was to be facilitated by the mutual granting of most-favored-nation advantages, a reduction of customs formalities, freedom of transit, rapid transportation facilities, fixed import duties, and the permission for the nationals of each to establish branches of industrial concerns in the territories of the other.[85] Nevertheless, in 1920, transportation difficulties

[84] *Zprávy* (Poslanecká Sněmovna), 86 meeting, October 18, 1921, pp. 25 *et seq.*, 4 session (announcement of the governmental program by Beneš, then Prime Minister also) ; *Treaty Series*, vol. vi, pp. 215-219; *Documents, alliance*, no. 65.

[85] *Treaty Series*, vol. xvii, pp. 9-29; *Zprávy* (Senát), 65 meeting, August 5, 1921, pp. 319 *et seq.*, 3 session.

and currency fluctuations were so great that it was cheaper for Czechoslovakia to import flour and grain from the United States.

In like vein, Czechoslovakia and Rumania signed, at Bucharest, on April 23, 1921, the day of their political treaty, a commercial agreement embodying reciprocity and most-favored-nation treatment. Special clauses concerned postage, telephones, telegraphs, and other methods of communication and transportation both by railroad and via the Danube. In general, Czechoslovakia exchanged industrial products, particularly machinery and other metallic goods, for raw materials, especially for cereals, naphtha, and crude and refined oils.[86] Both countries derived considerable economic advantages from this treaty.

There still remained to be concluded the third connecting link, the treaty between Rumania and Yugoslavia. Direct negotiations were begun on June 7, 1921, and concluded ten days later. At the time of the negotiations, both states were harassed by bands of Macedonian comitadjis, whose raids Bulgaria was unable to prevent. Both were dissatisfied over the reluctance with which Sofia was carrying out the disarmament and reparations clauses of the Treaty of Neuilly. Consequently, the new treaty, which in other respects was a counterpart of its two predecessors, included clauses against Bulgaria as well as against Hungary.[87]

The three links in the Little Entente chain were supplemented by military conventions: Czechoslovakia-Rumania, July 2, 1921; Czechoslovakia-Yugoslavia, August 1, 1921; and Rumania-Yugoslavia, January 23, 1922. These treaties defined the signatories' mutual obligations against unprovoked attacks from Hungary or Bulgaria, the military preparations that would be made in defense of their territorial in-

[86] *Treaty Series*, vol. xv, pp. 235-257.

[87] *Documents, alliance*, no. 72.

tegrity, and the mutual guarantee of the Treaties of Trianon and of Neuilly.[88]

The Problem of Austria

Beneš felt that, with the formation of the Little Entente, his work was merely begun. If the constructive value of the new organization was to be enhanced, it would be necessary to attract within its orbit such other small states of Central Europe as would be willing to cooperate with its policies. Austria was the most promising of such prospective additions. In fact, if any of the new states needed assistance, it was Austria, whose survival as an independent entity hung in the balance.[89]

In despair, the Austrians looked upon Anschluss as their sole hope of salvation,[90] but it was not to be.[91] Austria was compelled to embark upon a desperate struggle for an independent existence. Attempts either to unite with Germany or to recover her German minorities failed, and the new government suppressed energetically incipient Bolshevik tendencies. Impotent militarily and almost surrounded by hostile neighbors, Austria accepted her fate. The Peace Conference, aware of her desperate plight, sought to aid by allowing wide discretionary powers to the Reparations Commission, which was entrusted with supervising the enforcement of the economic and financial clauses of the Treaty of St. Germain. On March 1, 1919, Great Britain, France and Italy took equal shares in a loan to Austria of $30,000,000, which was increased eventually to $48,000,000, in order that she might purchase foodstuffs for her starv-

---

[88] Mousset, *op. cit.*, pp. 22-23; Cosma, *op. cit.*, pp. 30-34; Codresco, *op. cit.*, vol. i, pp. 176-182; Machray, *op. cit.*, pp. 153-156.

[89] *Cf.* Toynbee, *op. cit.*, pp. 314-316.

[90] *Cf.* Graham, *op. cit.*, pp. 154-156.

[91] For full details as to how France and Czechoslovakia prevented Anschluss, *cf. supra*. pp. 47-49.

ing population.[92]   This measure proved to be a mere
palliative.   In April, 1920, the Reparations Commission was
aided by the newly created International Relief Credits
Committee, which, from Paris, attempted to take charge of
Austrian relief.   One of its first acts was to authorize
Austria to issue bonds which were secured by specific national
assets and monopolies and which became a sort of first mort-
gage upon all Austrian revenues.[93]

The Little Entente saw in the Austrian situation not only
an opportunity for service, but a grave political and economic
menace to its own security.   In Czechoslovakia, which was
the most concerned, public opinion still remained hostile to
Austria because of the friction that had been engendered
during the process of separation.   Most Czechoslovaks failed
to appreciate that assistance to Austria would be the best
method of averting Anschluss and might also enable her
to become their best customer among the small states of
Central Europe.   Beneš received considerable domestic criticism for expressing the opinion that Czechoslovakia, because
of her peculiar position, was best able and should be most
eager to extend economic, financial, and perhaps even political
aid to Austria.   Beneš' further opinion that Austria would
be enabled to stand on her own feet if immediate assistance
were forthcoming caused much speculation as to what he
might have promised her.[94]

Direct negotiations between Austria and Czechoslovakia
were inaugurated during January, 1920, when the Austrian
Chancellor, Dr. Renner, accompanied by several technical
experts, visited Beneš in Praha.   The pourparlers concerned

[92] *Rapport sur les travaux de la commission des réparations,* vol. i
(1920-1922), p. 281.

[93] *Ibid.,* vol. i, p. 287.

[94] *Cf.* Hrušovský, *loc. cit.,* pp. 134-135.   Beneš adopted practically the
same viewpoint in his speech of January 27, 1921, in the Chamber of
Deputies, *The Foreign Policy of Czechoslovakia,* pp. 8-16.

two major questions: economic relations and problems arising from the enforcement of the Peace Treaties. Beneš'
domestic opponents took advantage of the unfavorable condition of public opinion to stress the needs of Czechoslovakia
herself, then in the midst of the process of domestic stabilization, and to point out what they considered the folly of
attempting to aid a rival when in so great need herself.[95]
On the other hand, the Great Entente, as well as Czechoslovakia's prospective partners in the as-yet-unformed
Little Entente, favored Beneš' policy out of fear lest
Austria's desperate plight drive her into a union with Germany.[96] Yet even Beneš apparently lost patience when he
stated, on February 13, that " Austria must help herself if
she does not desire to prolong her own agony ".[97]

On June 17, 1920, the Treaty of Brno [98] provided for
mutual protection for the respective minorities and for the
clarification of the respective definitions of citizenship.
Since several minor points still remained in doubt, the Treaty
was amplified by a supplementary protocol [99] of August 3.
The chief constructive virtue of these two treaties was perhaps the provision for a special Court of Arbitration which
was to try all disputes that might arise either from the rights
of citizenship or from questions concerning the educational
facilities that were provided for minorities.

Between November, 1920, and June, 1921, Great Britain,
France.and Italy toyed with several sporadic suggestions for
aiding Austria,[100] but few of them produced any results.
Czechoslovakia preferred to do her own negotiating with

[95] *Právo Lidu*, January 22 and 24, 1920.

[96] *The Times*, January 22, 1920.

[97] *Svornost*, February 14, 1920.

[98] *Zprávy* (Senát), 11 meeting, July 13, 1920, pp. 497 *et seq.*, 1 session;
Treaty Series, vol. iii, pp. 183-229.

[99] *Treaty Series*, vol. iii, pp. 230-232.

[100] *Cf.* Toynbee, *op. cit.*, pp. 44-45, 320.

Austria.[101] A new commercial treaty was signed at Praha on May 4, 1921. The first of the two major divisions contained general provisions based upon most-favored-nation clauses. It included also the additional items of facilitation of frontier traffic and cooperation in levying customs, in preventing infringement of customs regulations, in prosecuting violators, in inspecting cattle suspected of disease, and in the honoring of goods which had been tested properly prior to shipment. The second part of the treaty, which was to become effective on June 1, 1921, involved modifications of the existing system of import and export licenses. Finally, both countries granted concessions upon many individual items.[102] This treaty became the entering wedge for the mutual reduction of control over foreign trade.

This new commercial treaty had been consummated largely as the result of a distinct change in Czechoslovak public opinion regarding Austria. Whereas in 1919 Beneš had been subjected to severe criticism for pleading for the adoption of a generous Austrian policy, less than two years later his people had accepted his viewpoint. On May 25, 1921, in answer to an interpellation of the Foreign Affairs Committee of the National Assembly, Beneš announced that he had really intervened in order to preserve the Peace Treaties and to prevent a plebiscite whereby Austria might unite with Germany. He stated that he had made his views clear to both the Austrian minister at Praha and to the Czechoslovak representative at Vienna.[103] The changed sentiment had been a direct outgrowth of Czechoslovakia's industrial situation. As soon as it was realized that Austria could no

---

[101] *Cf. Prager Tagblatt*, March 18, April 5, June 4-5, 1921, for Czechoslovak sentiments concerning the various abortive Allied projects for the aid of Austria.

[102] *Treaty Series*, vol. xv, pp. 13-157.

[103] *Národní Politika*, May 26, 1921; *Svornost*, June 1, 1921.

longer afford to purchase Czechoslovakia's coal or industrial products, aid became imperative if the two alternatives of Anschluss or anarchy were to be avoided. It was regrettable that Czechoslovakia as a whole had failed to appreciate the true condition of affairs before 1921, for many unpleasant incidents might have been avoided, but even that date was not too late for the adoption of a new policy.[104]

Czechoslovakia's desire to aid Austria was shared by her two Little Entente partners. Before the War, about seventy per cent of Serbia's exports had been absorbed by Austria. The trend of this trade had been changed by the War. In consequence, on June 27, 1920, Austria and Yugoslavia concluded a provisional treaty of commerce which, after four different renewals, became a definitive treaty. By its terms, Austria agreed to purchase most of Yugoslavia's exports of wheat, meat, prunes, live-stock, etc. Rumania was also well disposed towards Austria, for, although economic contacts were on a lesser scale, the two countries had few interests that clashed.[105]

In view of such generally amicable sentiments, it became relatively easy for Czechoslovakia partially to associate Austria with the policy of the Little Entente. President Masaryk, whose views on Austria coincided with those of Beneš, negotiated with President Hainisch of Austria, at Hallstatt on August 10, 1921, a loan of 500,000,000 Czechoslovak crowns.[106] The rapprochement was cemented at Praha on December 16, 1921, when the Presidents and Prime Ministers of the two states—Masaryk, Hainisch, Beneš and

[104] Cf. Hejn, E. T., "The Czechoslovak Viewpoint", The American Review of Reviews, vol. lxv, pp. 490-491.

[105] Cf. Mousset, op. cit., pp. 117-125; Codresco, op. cit., vol. ii, pp. 183-203.

[106] Cf. Papoušek, J., "Základy Masarykový koncepce zahraniční politiky", Zahraniční Politika, vol. i, pp. 349-350.

Schober—signed the treaty of Lány which provided for general cooperation and for the arbitration of any disputes.[107]

The Attempted Rapprochement with Poland

Just as Beneš had hoped to attract Austria within the orbit of the Little Entente, so had he hoped similarly to associate Poland with its policies. To this end, he had inaugurated with the latter a series of negotiations entirely separate from those relating to boundary disputes. The approach was economic. The first agreement of August 21, 1919,[108] sought to regulate temporarily the exchange of Czechoslovak coal and Polish naphtha, but was denounced by Poland, which deemed it disadvantageous. Similarly, the second agreement of March 12, 1920,[109] was also of a temporary character, but remained in force. Both treaties were inadequate in that they concerned merely limited aspects of mutual commercial questions. A new and more general treaty was signed at Praha on September 24, 1920, in regard to problems of transportation and customs and passport procedure.[110] Three days later another agreement specified that Czechoslovakia should export to Poland 37,000 tons of coal and 15,000 tons of coke every month. In addition, provided that Poland made the necessary application, a further 10,000 tons of coal and a proportional tonnage of coke might be added to the monthly quotas. In return, Czechoslovakia was to receive 7,083 tons of raw naphtha and 1,250 tons of naphtha derivatives per month. Payments would have to be made in advance at the prices then current in the exporting states. This agreement did not change earlier agreements and was to be of temporary duration, until

[107] *Treaty Series*, vol. ix, pp. 247-251; *Documents, alliance*, annex 2.
[108] *Národní Listy*, August 21, 1919.
[109] *Prager Presse*, March 12, 1920.
[110] *České Slovo*, September 24-25, 1920.

the German-Polish dispute over Upper Silesia should be terminated.[111] On October 20, 1921, the two states signed their first general commercial treaty.[112]

In the meantime, France, realizing that both Czechoslovakia and Poland were essential to her for possible future aid against Germany, bent her best efforts to effect a rapprochement between them. The first step was the Franco-Polish political agreement, which was signed at Paris on February 19, 1921.[113] It was followed rapidly by a similar agreement between Poland and Rumania which was signed at Bucharest on March 4, 1921,[114] by Sapieha and Take Jonescu. The core of this latter agreement, which had been negotiated with the approval of the military leaders of both countries, provided for mutual assistance against an unprovoked attack from the East and for consultation prior to the drafting of any new alliances.

After these preliminaries, the next step, a Czechoslovak-Polish treaty, proved much more difficult. There was little diminution of friction until after Poland had accepted the decision of the Supreme Council in regard to Těšin. Poland was not especially interested in the primary objectives of the Little Entente; to her the Russian and Baltic problems seemed much more important.[115] Only gradually was the mutual antipathy overcome.[116] A change for the better took place during the summer of 1921 when Prince Sapieha was succeeded as Foreign Minister of Poland by Skirmunt. The new Foreign Minister desired to renew, with both Take

[111] *Ibid.*, September 27-28, 1920.

[112] *Obchodní smlouvy mezistátní*, vol. i, pp. 264-294; *Zprávy* (Senát), 123 meeting, June 30, 1922, pp. 441 *et seq.*, 5 session.

[113] *Treaty Series*, vol.`xviii, pp. 12-13.

[114] *Ibid.*, vol. vii, pp. 77-79.

[115] Mousset, *op. cit.*, p. 39.

[116] *Cf. Národní Politika, Národní Listy* and *Čas*, July 24, 1921; *Gazeta Warszawska*, August 23-24, 1921.

Jonescu and Beneš, the policy of collaboration that had been inaugurated during the 1918 Congress of Oppressed Nationalities at Rome.[117] As a result of Skirmunt's visit to Praha, he and Beneš, on November 6, 1921, signed a defensive treaty which was intended to seal the rapprochement between the two states and the collaboration of Poland with the Little Entente. The new agreement provided that the two Slav states respect one another's territorial integrity, maintain a benevolent neutrality in the event of an attack on either by a third state, permit the free passage of war materials, proclaim disinterestedness in Slovakia (Poland) and Galicia (Czechoslovakia), respectively, conclude a new commercial treaty, arbitrate points in dispute, communicate to one another treaties negotiated with a third state, recognize mutually treaties already concluded, suppress propaganda directed against one another, and conclude the present treaty for five years.[118] However, Poland never ratified this treaty, much to the regret of Beneš.[119] Poland cooperated with the Little Entente to some extent, but her rapprochement with Czechoslovakia remained to be consummated at a later date.[120]

The objective of Beneš' various Central European manoeuvres was not to recreate Austria-Hungary in any form: at this time he and his Little Entente partners were opposed to the formation of any Danubian Confederation, which they feared might be dominated by Vienna and Budapest.[121]

[117] Cf. Beneš, *My War Memoirs*, 316-318.

[118] *Documents, alliance*, annex 1.

[119] Beneš, *Five Years of Czechoslovak Foreign Policy*, pp. 18-19 (speech of February 6, 1924).

[120] For full details, cf. infra, pp. 242 et seq.

[121] Beneš, *The Foreign Policy of Czechoslovakia*, p. 17; cf. also, Hodža, M., "Mala Dohoda, jej tradicie a jej dnešný úkol", *Zahraniční Politika*, vol. i, pp. 610; Seton-Watson, R. W., "The Psychology of the Succession States", *New Europe*, vol. xvii, pp. 62-64.

His policy of intra-Slav cooperation was intended to enable the Slavs to occupy in European affairs the place of influence to which he believed them entitled and which they had not hitherto enjoyed. This objective had been clearly brought out on January 24, 1921, in Beneš' inaugural lecture as Professor of Sociology at Charles University in Praha.[122] He hoped that his new policy would result in Praha, and Warsaw also, taking its "true" position in Central Europe, at the expense, perhaps, of Vienna and Budapest.

Beneš desired also to impress upon the minds of Allied statesmen the fact that his policy of intra-Slav cooperation was not militaristic. He replied cordially to a letter of the League Council of March 8, 1921, which requested his viewpoints regarding disarmament. By a note of August 28, 1921, Beneš welcomed a limitation of military, naval and air expenditures during the two fiscal years following the next year, and stated that his government was "prepared to participate in negotiations regarding concrete proposals for limitation."[123] When other states refused to cooperate in the project, the matter was dropped.

Friction with Hungary

In spite of the apparent hopelessness of any reconciliation with Hungary, Beneš resolved to make the attempt, which he hoped might avert any attempted coup on the part of ex-King Charles. After serving notice on his own people of his project,[124] Beneš met Teleki, the Hungarian Premier, and Gratz, the Foreign Minister, on March 14, 1921, at Most nad Litava (Brück) where it was decided to appoint four commissions that were to apply gradually, to economic matters

[122] *Cf.* Beneš, *Problemy nové Evropy*, pp. 233, 240-246 for his lecture, "The Idea of a Czechoslovak State".

[123] *Official Journal*, November, 1921, p. 960.

[124] Beneš, *The Foreign Policy of Czechoslovakia* (January 27, 1921), pp. 17-22.

common to both countries, the principles of the Treaty of Trianon.[125] Nothing could be accomplished until after the situation had quieted down as a result of the first attempted coup of Charles. In this crisis, Beneš' vigorous action had been motivated in large measure by the suspicion that the Hungarian ejection of Charles had not been sincere. After Charles' first failure, Teleki was succeeded by Bethlen, and Gratz by Banffy. Beneš, still optimistic, resumed negotiations with Hungary at Mariánské Lázně (Marienbad) late in June, [126] but again nothing resulted beyond a joint anti-Habsburg agreement, because further negotiations were once more postponed by the Burgenland crisis.

By the Peace Treaties, Burgenland had been transferred from Hungary to Austria without a plebiscite, a procedure which had been resented by the Hungarians, especially those in Ödenburg (Sopron). When the time for the cession arrived, August 29, 1921, the Hungarians, instead of evacuating the area, drove out the Austrians who had come to take possession. To Allied remonstrances, Hungary replied by requesting direct negotiations between Vienna and Budapest, but was informed by the Conference of Ambassadors that an immediate evacuation of the region would be a necessary prerequisite to any agreement with Austria.[127]

Beneš, in response to a Hungarian request for mediation, asked the Conference of Ambassadors, on September 10, for a speedy solution of the controversy,[128] and, in interviews with Banffy and Schober, attempted to arrange a compromise whereby Austria would yield a portion of the disputed

---

[125] *Cf.* Machray, *op. cit.*, p. 157.

[126] *Cf. The New York Times*, June 26, 1921, or Machray, *op. cit.*, pp. 157-158 for the elaborate agenda that had been planned for this conference.

[127] Machray, *op. cit.*, p. 160; Cosma, *op. cit.*, pp. 50-55; Codresco, *op. cit.*, vol. i, pp. 201-208; Mousset, *op. cit.*, pp. 50-53.

[128] Mousset, *op. cit.*, p. 53.

area. On September 26, at the Conference of Brno, he reopened negotiations with Hungary for the third time.[129] Although Czechoslovak mediation was welcome to Rumania, it was not to Yugoslavia, which feared lest Beneš' suggestion regarding Austria's cession of Ödenburg lead to further attempts to modify the Treaty of Trianon.[130] Similarly, Czechoslovakia's action aroused the jealousy of Italy, which arranged that Hungary should ask for her mediation in preference to that of Czechoslovakia. Italy's initiative produced results, for the Conference of Ambassadors, which followed its usual questionable policy of considering the small states as Powers with merely limited interests, and of yielding to her as to a Great Power, ratified the Protocol of Venice of October 13 which ordered a plebiscite for Ödenburg.[131] The plebiscite of December 14-15 resulted in 15,334 votes for Hungary, and 8,227 for Austria, whereupon the latter yielded Ödenburg.[132]

Beneš' objections to undue interference in Central Europe on the part of the Great Powers acquired still more force as the consequence of the manner in which the latter handled a similar dispute over Baranya, a region at the confluence of the Danube and Drave Rivers. When Serbia occupied it in 1918, she did not proceed as in other areas of whose possession she was certain, but appointed merely the chief officials and left the details of local government to the natives. The Treaty of Trianon awarded her merely the southern part, two communes in the region of Darda. At the suggestion of Hungary, the Conference of Ambassadors linked together the two disputes and demanded that Yugoslavia evacuate Baranya before Hungary evacuate Burgenland.

[129] Cf. Machray, op. cit., p. 158.

[130] Mousset, op. cit., pp. 53-55; Von Werkmann, op. cit., pp. 300-306.

[131] Official Journal, August, 1922, annex 377, pp. 907-913.

[132] Toynbee, op. cit., pp. 304-307.

Since the note to this effect was addressed to Belgrade, the uproar over the apparent favoring of Hungary was not surprising. Despite public opinion, Yugoslavia obeyed the order.[183]

Any lack of harmony that might have existed within the Little Entente over the Burgenland and Baranya questions was instantly hushed as a result of the second attempted coup of Charles, who had spent the time since his first venture in Switzerland.[184] On October 20, 1921, Charles arrived via aeroplane near Sopron. He attempted to justify his breach of faith to Switzerland, whose neutrality he had violated in spite of specific promises to the contrary, by maintaining that the obligations placed upon him by foreigners were inferior to those of his own country, which, in its troubled condition, needed his guidance.[185] This time the Little Entente was fully prepared for the emergency. On October 22, both Ententes, through their representatives at Budapest, demanded the departure of the ex-King.[186]

The course of events within Hungary had been too much for Beneš, who stated that the return of Charles was a casus belli.[187] Beneš presented to Hungary five specific demands: (1) strict execution of the territorial and military clauses of the Treaty of Trianon, (2) disarmament, (3) definitive solution of the Habsburg question, (4) indemnity for the costs of Czechoslovak mobilization, and (5) annulment of the Austro-Hungarian agreement of Venice regarding Burgenland.[188] On October 23 he warned the Great

[183] *Cf.* Mousset, *op. cit.*, pp. 56-58; Machray, *op. cit.*, pp. 159-161; *Official Journal*, August, 1922, annex 378, pp. 915-917.

[184] Werkmann, *op. cit.*, pp. 157-184.

[185] *Documents, Hapsbourg*, no. 35.

[186] *Ibid.*, nos. 30-32.

[187] *Zprávy* (Poslanecká Sněmovna), 90 meeting, October 26, 1921, pp. 217 *et seq.*, 4 session; *Documents, Hapsbourg*, no. 32.

[188] Toynbee, *op. cit.*, p. 293.

Powers that the Little Entente would intervene militarily, and alone if necessary.[139] Immediately both Czechoslovakia and Yugoslavia issued orders for mobilization, which was begun by the former four days later. It proceeded smoothly, thus demonstrating that the defects in the Czechoslovak military system which had come to light two years earlier during the war with Hungary over Slovakia had been corrected.[140] Compelled to acquiesce in the situation, the Hungarian government captured Charles on the same day,[141] and, on October 26, opened with him negotiations for his renunciation of the throne, a step which he refused to take.[142] The Little Entente appealed to the Conference of Ambassadors,[143] which responded with an ultimatum warning Hungary that she alone would have to bear the full responsibility for the results of any rejection of the demands of the Little Entente.[144] This warning was reiterated to Count Banffy on October 26 by Beneš, who pointed out that military intervention could be avoided only if Hungary agreed in writing to execute the Treaty of Trianon and deprive the Habsburgs of their rights to her throne.[145] At the same time Beneš requested that the Powers grant the Little Entente representation on the special sub-committee of the Disarmament Commission for Hungary and that the latter pay at least a nominal indemnity to cover the costs of mobilization.[146] On

[139] *Documents, Hapsbourg*, no. 37.

[140] Beneš, *Problemy nové Evropy*, p. 144; *The New York Times*, October 29, 1921. *Cf.* also, *The New York Times*, November 9, 1921, or *La Gazette de Prague*, November 12, 1921, for Masaryk's order for demobilization, to be completed by the end of the month.

[141] *Documents, Hapsbourg*, nos. 33-34.

[142] *Cf.* Ashmead-Bartlett, *op. cit.*, pp. 261-285.

[143] *Documents, Hapsbourg*, no. 42.

[144] *Ibid.*, no. 43.

[145] *Ibid.*, no. 48.

[146] *Ibid.*, no. 49. The mobilization had cost Czechoslovakia 450,867,935 crowns, or almost $10,000,000; *cf.* Machray, *op. cit.*, p. 179.

the next day the Conference of Ambassadors demanded that Hungary proclaim the deposition of Charles and surrender him to the commander of the British Danubian fleet for removal to some other place of residence which was to be determined by the Powers.[147]   When Hungary agreed to these terms, the *Glowworm* took Charles to his new place of exile, Madeira, where he died on April 1, 1922.[148]

Beneš remained dissatisfied after Charles had been removed from the scene, because the questions of the dynasty and of the indemnity still awaited solution. He continued to demand the immediate compliance of Hungary upon these points, if military intervention was to be avoided,[149] but he denied having addressed an ultimatum to Hungary directly.[150] Hungary decided to risk the clemency of the Great Powers rather than that of the Little Entente. On October 30, the Conference of Ambassadors, by note, warned Beneš against any hasty action without consulting in advance the Great Powers, denied his claim for an indemnity on the ground that the Hungarian government had overthrown Charles by its own unaided efforts, but agreed to insist upon the deposition of the Habsburgs.[151]   With no recourse left, Hungary agreed to pass the required deposition law within eight days,[152] but Beneš continued to doubt her good faith.[153]

The projected act of deposition, which contained all Beneš' points except the indemnity, was presented to the Hungarian

[147] *Documents, Hapsbourg*, no. 50.

[148] Toynbee, *op. cit.*, p. 294.

[149] *Documents, Hapsbourg*, nos. 51 and 54.

[150] *Cf. ibid.*, no. 63 for Beneš' statement that rumors of an ultimatum (such as reported, for instance, in Toynbee, *op. cit.*, p. 295) were of Hungarian origin. Beneš points out that the Hungarian Minister at Praha, Tahy, admitted having misinformed his own government.

[151] *Ibid.*, no. 55.

[152] *Ibid.*, no. 59.

[153] *Ibid.*, no. 58.

parliament on November 3.[154] Beneš raised a still further objection, namely, that the document merely mentioned Charles specifically, but permitted the possibility that some other Habsburg might regain the throne by means of a subsequent free election.[155] At his insistence, the Conference of Ambassadors took the same viewpoint,[156] and, on November 10, exacted from Hungary a subsequent declaration that no Habsburg could ever become a candidate for the Hungarian throne, and that no candidate could be selected without a prior agreement with the Great Powers.[157] In this manner was the Conference of Ambassadors at last satisfied.[158] To clinch the matter and to satisfy Beneš, it proclaimed the law an " International Act ",[159] thereby, in its estimation, providing a guarantee superior to that of an act which might be revised at some subsequent date.[160]

In addition to the previously announced objectives of the Little Entente, Beneš' unbending insistence upon guaranteeing the deposition of the Habsburgs with every conceivable legal safeguard had been motivated by his desire to prevent Hungary from falling back upon the so-called juridical argument in order to annoy her neighbors. When Charles had gone into exile late in 1918, he had not abdicated,[161] but had merely suspended his royal power and had left Hungary the right to act as her interests might dictate. Since he had not signed the Peace Treaties, his own rights and those of his

[154] *Ibid.*, no. 64.

[155] *Ibid.*, nos. 65-66.

[156] *Ibid.*, no. 67.

[157] *Ibid.*, no. 71.

[158] *Ibid.*, no. 72.

[159] *Ibid.*, no. 73.

[160] *Cf.* Machray, *op. cit.*, p. 179.

[161] His abdication was of questionable legality because it had not been counter-signed by a parliamentary minister.

heirs as well, by the juridical argument, still extended over the territories that had belonged to Hungary in 1914, even though large portions of this area had been "occupied" later by members of the Little Entente. Beneš feared lest, in the eyes of the Hungarian Legitimists, a Habsburg restoration would automatically abrogate the Treaties of St. Germain and Trianon and legally justify Hungary's claims to the areas that had been torn away as a result of the World War. In the light of this argument, the members of the Little Entente felt that their existence as independent entities would be menaced by a Habsburg restoration.[162]

Charles' second attempt had been the first severe test of the Little Entente's efficiency and of the progress that had been made by Beneš' system of collaboration. Hungary had yielded apparently to the Great Powers, yet, in the last analysis, her compliance had been forced by the pressure of the Little Entente. Czechoslovakia and Yugoslavia had adopted identical policies, whereas that of Rumania had been unique. Rumania's sincerity had been above question, for, not only had she proclaimed her solidarity with her two partners by a note of October 26,[163] but had proceeded to mobilize six divisions of infantry and two of cavalry. After the intervention of the Great Entente, she had agreed to demobilize before the termination of the crisis. Although she had supported the demands of her two partners for compensation for the costs of mobilization, she had made no similar demand of her own. Italy, on October 24, had also promised to support the Little Entente in a vigorous policy against

---

[162] *Cf.* Temperley, *op. cit.*, vol. iv, pp. 118-119; Mousset, *op. cit.*, pp. 14-15; Codresco, *op. cit.*, vol. i, pp. 209-231; Beneš, *Problemy nové Evropy*, pp. 141-148. For Beneš' explanations to parliament, *cf. Zprávy* (Poslanecká Sněmovna), 90 meeting, October 26, 1921, pp. 217 *et seq.*, 4 session; *ibid.*, 91 meeting, November 16, 1921, pp. 265 *et seq.*, 4 session.

[163] *Documents, Hapsbourg*, no. 46.

Hungary,[164] yet advised a resort to diplomatic methods of terminating the dispute.[165] Even Poland had cooperated with the Little Entente and had, in substance, warned Hungary not to depend upon former friendship.[166]

Central European Economic Cooperation

The crises to which the Little Entente had been subjected had demonstrated both its vitality and its necessity, and had resulted in a consolidation of the viewpoints of the three allies. The new alignment was not imperialistic; on the contrary, it was satiated and had nothing further to conquer. Above all, it sought to preserve the new political status quo which had been established by the Peace Treaties. Regardless of the alleged political necessity for retaining the discrimination between victors and vanquished, there existed no economic basis for the continuation of such a policy. Even the vanquished states welcomed to some degree the economic aspects of Beneš' plans for the reconstruction of Central Europe, whereas the victors realized equally that Central Europe could not be reconstructed economically without the assistance of their former enemies. All the Succession States would have to cooperate if there was to be restored, in the existing six fragments, the economic well-being of the former Empire-Kingdom.[167] Beneš hoped also that economic cooperation would further his policy of reconstruction by drawing both Austria and Hungary from their political isolation.[168]

[164] *Ibid.*, no. 38.

[165] *Ibid.*, no. 44.

[166] *Cf.* Mousset, *op. cit.*, p. 43. For the attitudes of the various countries during this crisis, *cf.* also, Beneš, E., "The Little Entente", *Foreign Affairs*, vol. i, pp. 66-72; Jeden Svědek, "Beneš a Mala Dohoda", *La Révue de France*, année 2, tome v, pp. 595-623; *L'Europe nouvelle*, November 5, 1921.

[167] *Cf.* Cosma, *op. cit.*, pp. 73-76; Codresco, *op. cit.*, vol. i, pp. 235-237.

[168] *Zprávy* (Poslanecká Sněmovna), 91 meeting, November 16, 1921, pp. 265 *et seq.*, 4 session.

Early in December, 1920,[169] Beneš had invited the other five Succession States to an economic conference at Bratislava, but the project failed because of a general lack of interest. Nevertheless, Beneš refused to lose hope that a future " Bratislava Conference ", as he termed it, regardless of the time or place of meeting, would " lead to some positive result ". In his speech, *The Foreign Policy of Czechoslovakia,* delivered in the Chamber of Deputies on January 27, 1921, he pointed out that, at such a conference, Czechoslovakia would strive to solve the problems of transit, communication, navigation, apportionment of rolling stock and of shipping, and of obstacles in the way of transport and exchange of goods. Beneš termed these problems European in scope, and, despite his optimism, warned his listeners that any effective solution would have to go to the root of the evils and would require international cooperation, patience and a long period of time.[170]

In the interval between the two attempts of Charles, the Succession States had called, for economic purposes, the Conference of Rome, from April 6 to June 15, 1921, but nothing of general constructive value could be accomplished, for neither Austria nor Hungary attended.[171] Another Conference at Portorose from October 15 to November 25, 1921, was attended by all six states. Hitherto, the trade of all had been hampered by the inability of any state to regain possession of freight cars when they had once passed its frontiers. To remedy this situation, the various delegates, upon their own responsibility, agreed that, after January 1, 1922, each state should mark its own rolling-stock, which should then be allowed to circulate freely within all the other states, but without prejudicing the right of ownership of the original owner until a final distribution should be made

[169] *Ibid.,* 30 meeting, December 3, 1920, pp. 1049 *et seq.,* 3 session.
[170] Beneš, *The Foreign Policy of Czechoslovakia,* p. 14.
[171] *Cf.* Mousset, *op. cit.,* pp. 98-99; Machray, *op. cit.,* pp. 156-157.

by the Reparations Commission: Austria alone was authorized to retain all the rolling-stock within her territories. In addition, the delegates sought to prepare a series of commercial treaties and a general tariff agreement, to facilitate foreign trade within each state by lessening or abolishing import and export prohibitions, to reduce postal tariffs from twenty to twenty-five per cent and to plan new telegraph and telephone lines, particularly between the various capitals.[172] It became difficult to enforce these recommendations, except for the one concerning Austria's rolling-stock. The several states put into effect voluntarily much of this ambitious program, enough to save the Conference from total failure and to restore in some measure the economic cooperation that had been destroyed by the World War.[173] According to Beneš, of the twenty protocols approved at Portorose,[174] eleven wènt into partial effect very shortly, eight others were put in partial effect within a year, and only one, referring to a general tariff union of all the Succession States, was dropped.[175] By subsequent individual negotiations, the members of the Little Entente in particular proceeded to strengthen the economic ties with one another.[176]

[172] *Cf. Úmluva o poštovních stycích mezi Rakouskem, Madarskem, Italii, Rumunskem, Kralovstvím Srbů, Charvátuv a Slovincú a Československem, sjednana v Portorose 23 Listopadu, 1921*; *cf.* also, *International Conciliation*, July, 1922, pp. 5-9, for Shotwell, J. T., "The Portorose Conference"; and pp. 10-23, for Smith, C. B., "An Account of the Portorose Conference". Colonel Smith, the American representative on the Reparations Commission in Vienna, and subsequently observer for the American Government at Portorose, did more than perhaps any other individual to bring about the Portorose Conference. He has also an interesting editorial in *The Independent*, December 3, 1921, pp. 226-227.

[173] *Cf.* Machray, *op. cit.*, pp. 187-189.

[174] *Cf. International Conciliation*, July, 1922, pp. 24-84.

[175] *Cf.* Beneš, *Problemy nové Evropy*, p. 210, regarding the progress that had been made.

[176] *Cf.* Mousset, *op. cit.*, pp. 99-116; Codresco, *op. cit.*, vol. ii, pp. 243-251.

The partial success of the Conference of Portorose caused Beneš to state that the desperate domestic situations within both Austria and Hungary represented the greatest retarding influences for his plans in Central Europe and that both of these former enemy states would have to be thoroughly reconstructed before normal conditions could be restored.[177] In this manner he sought to conceal his discomfiture over the fact that Czechoslovakia had refused to ratify the Portorose protocols,[178] although Hungary had signed and was willing to ratify them if the other states did likewise.[179] One obstacle to Czechoslovakia's ratification was Yugoslavia's refusal to ratify.[180] But of even greater influence perhaps, was the fact that Czechoslovak public opinion had not been completely converted, as yet, to a policy of economic cooperation with the former enemy states.[181]

The Reconstruction of Austria

Although having little faith in the palliative measures that the Powers were proposing for Austria, Beneš united with them in the Austrian loan of February, 1922, whereby Great Britain agreed to loan Austria 2,250,000 pounds sterling, France, 55,000,000 francs, Italy 70,000,000 lire, and Czechoslovakia 500,000,000 crowns, a measure that relieved only temporarily the needs of Austria. Most of the Czech loan was used to pay earlier debts for coal.[182]

Conditions within Austria became more desperate during the summer of 1922. In May, Schober resigned as Chancellor and was succeeded by a Jesuit, Ignaz Seipel, who

---

[177] *Cf.* Beneš, *Problemy nové Evropy*, pp. 108-112 and 205-215.
[178] Pasvolsky, *op. cit.*, p. 276.
[179] *Ibid.*, p. 369.
[180] *Ibid.*, p. 533.
[181] *Cf. supra*, pp. 79 *et seq.*
[182] Toynbee, *op. cit.*, p. 321 ; Pasvolsky, *op. cit.*, p. 114.

adopted a double policy—curtailment of expenditures and attainment of foreign aid. To this latter end, Seipel undertook, late in August, a pilgrimage to Praha. He asked the opinion of Beneš upon three points: should Austria appeal to the League, would such an appeal produce results, and, if such an appeal should fail, what would be the attitude of Czechoslovakia regarding an Austrian appeal for the assistance of her immediate neighbors? Beneš replied that he would regard any regional grouping of states to aid Austria as dangerous to the peace of Europe, but that he believed that the League would help Austria effectively, and that, in any event, Czechoslovakia would use all her influence to help bring about such a possibility. Thereupon, Beneš informed the other victorious Powers of his pourparlers with Seipel and requested their aid to help avert an Austrian crisis.[183]

Beneš' cautious reply to Seipel had been motivated in part by a fear of the reaction of Italy. As he had anticipated, Italy became threatening and, while Seipel was conferring in Praha and Berlin, sent a circular warning Germany, Austria and all three members of the Little Entente that a union between Austria and any neighbor would be regarded as a casus belli.[184] At once, Seipel hastened to meet Schanzer, the Italian Foreign Minister, at Verona, in order to disclaim any intention of uniting either with Germany or with the Little Entente, and, at the same time, to deny current rumors that Italy had desired, by means of an economic union, to rule Austria with the Duke of Aosta as viceroy.[185]

Austria appealed once more to the Powers during the London Conference, August 7-14, 1922, and, on the 15, was

---

[183] Beneš, *Problemy nové Evropy*, pp. 205-206; *cf.* also, pp. 205-215 for his exposé of October 24, 1922, on the Austrian question. For further details *cf.* Bauer, *op. cit.*, pp. 262-264.

[184] *Národní Politika*, August 24, 1922.

[185] *Neue Freie Presse*, August 25, 1922; *Prager Presse*, August 26, 1922.

referred by the Supreme Council to the Financial Committee of the League. After an investigation, the latter reported that economic reconstruction, as well as financial reform, would be necessary for a permanent solution of the Austrian problem.[186] This report confirmed the contentions of Beneš, who, speaking for the Little Entente and Poland, stressed the belief that the political aspects of the question were the most important factors in the reestablishment of general confidence in the future of an independent Austria. To that end, he advocated the formation of a special group of guarantors for Austria, but, to meet the objections of Italy, this group of interested states should operate under the auspices of the League. Beneš believed also that such procedure would lessen the rivalry of Italy and the Little Entente in the affairs of Central Europe, and might prevent the recurrence of unfounded rumors on the order of one then prevalent, namely, that Czechoslovakia and Yugoslavia were on the verge of attacking Austria.[187] In all these manoeuvres, Beneš sought to abate international friction and further international cooperation, for he was aware that his opponents, particularly the Magyars, were seeking to fix the responsibility for a large measure of the distress of Central Europe upon Czechoslovakia's series of international agreements; whereas the contrary was perhaps true: to cite just one instance, the commercial treaty that Czechoslovakia had granted to Austria on May 4, 1921,[188] according to Beneš,[189] had been far more liberal than the Conference of Portorose had demanded. All Czechoslovakia's economic agreements had been dictated by immediate necessity, but were only tem-

---

[186] *Official Journal*, November, 1922, pp. 1464-1479.

[187] Beneš, *op. cit.*, pp. 207-209.

[188] *Cf. supra*, p. 176.

[189] Beneš, *op. cit.*, p. 210.

porary, and hence were open to revision whenever conditions should become stabilized.[190]

Beneš pleaded that Austria should not be compelled to undertake any reforms that might be impracticable because of her internal situation.[191]   On October 4, 1922, there were signed at Geneva three protocols for the reconstruction of Austria. The first stated that the five signatories—Great Britain, France, Italy, Czechoslovakia and Austria— would respect the political independence and territorial integrity of Austria, would not compromise her sovereignty by requesting any unusual economic or financial privileges, and would submit all disputes to the Council and abide by its decisions; the second stipulated the terms of the loan, the securities that guaranteed it, the powers of the Committee of Control, and the obligations of the creditors; the third specified the obligations of Austria and the powers of the Commissioner-General. The sums that Czechoslovakia had advanced previously were deducted from her share.[192]

Beneš seized the opportunity that presented itself during the joint negotiations over the Austrian protocols to try to clarify relations with Italy. In this connection he made a trip to Venice, where, on October 9, he held with Schanzer a conference at which the effects of the Austrian crisis upon the two countries were discussed. The two statesmen realized the necessity of ending rumors of their political rivalry with one another and with other Allied states, and both desired to maintain the status quo regarding Austria. The conference ended with an understanding that the reconstruc-

---

[190] *Ibid.*, pp. 209-211; *Zprávy* (Senát), 120 meeting, June 27, 1922, pp. 380 *et seq.*, 5 session.

[191] Beneš, *op. cit.*, pp. 211-212; Toynbee, *op. cit.*, p. 323.

[192] *Treaty Series*, vol. xii, pp. 385-411; *Monthly Summary*, vol. ii, pp. 1-33, supplement, October, 1922; *Agreement for Guaranteeing a Loan to Austria.*

tion of Austria would be hastened by a rapprochement between Italy and the Little Entente.[193]

In the meantime, the League plans for the reconstruction of Austria were progressing favorably. On November 14, 1922, the Austrian parliament established a new bank of issue, and, four days later put an end to inflation. On December 12, Dr. Zimmerman, the Burgomaster of Rotterdam became Commissioner-General, a post he assumed on the 16. By January 23, 1923, Austria had floated successfully in Amsterdam, Brussels, London, Paris, Stockholm and in Switzerland a short-term loan of 50,000,000 gold crowns, which was secured by Austrian customs and a tobacco monopoly, and which was expected to cover merely the interim until a long-term loan could be floated. A new twenty-year loan of 650,000,000 gold crowns was authorized on April 16, 1923, was guaranteed by Great Britain, France, Italy, Belgium, Sweden, Denmark, Holland and Czechoslovakia,[194] and was oversubscribed several fold, a financial triumph that indicated widespread faith in the measures that were being taken for the reconstruction of Austria.[195]

The three protocols ended Austria's four years of currency depreciation and improved her economic position.[196] Czecho-

[193] *Zprávy* (Poslanecká Sněmovna), 159 meeting, October 24, 1922, pp. 14 *et seq.*, 6 session.

[194] Great Britain, France and Czechoslovakia each guaranteed twenty-four and a half percent of the loan; Italy, twenty and a half percent; Belgium and Sweden, two percent each; and Denmark and Holland, one percent each. *Cf.* Winkler, M., "The Investor and League Loans", *Foreign Policy Association*, vol. iv, supplement 2, p. 16. The writer prefers the figure of 650,000,000 gold Austrian crowns given in *Treaty Series*, vol. xii, Protocol no. 2, rather than the figure of 630,000,000 gold crowns given by Winkler.

[195] *Monthly Summary*, vol. iii, pp. 1-35, supplement, March, 1923; *Official Journal*, March, 1923, pp. 307-343; April, 1923, pp. 435-466.

[196] *Cf.* Basch, A. and Dvořáček, J., *Austria and Its Economic Existence* (Prague, 1925), pp. 39-40.

slovakia ratified the loan guarantee on December 21, 1922.[197] In his desire to appear entirely impartial, Beneš deprecated the infusion of national antipathies into the question. He was particularly insistent that selfish national interests be eliminated. He denied vehemently that he had ever desired to dictate the sending of a comptroller to Vienna or any other interference with Austrian sovereignty, but maintained that the League should have exclusive control over operations and should receive full credit for their success.[198] Beneš had a well-defined motive behind his apparent impartiality. The best interests of Czechoslovakia demanded an independent Austria, a state sufficiently strong to maintain its identity apart from the orbit of any Great Power. When foreign assistance for Austria became imperative, the League represented, to Beneš, the ideal agency by means of which Austrian reconstruction would be effected, and the fact that the protocol took the form that it did (i. e. an ironclad pledge of Austria's independence) was largely owing to Beneš' own efforts.[199]

Early Little Entente Conferences

The members of the Little Entente realized that the success enjoyed in 1921 had been the result of cooperation. Therefore, for 1922, they resolved to make their constructive policy felt even beyond Central Europe; if possible, they hoped to create something more than a mere defensive organization. Not only Central Europe, but the whole Continent was then in the process of reconstruction. The main issues involved —the recognition of Russia, the economic reconstruction of Europe, and the relations between Great Britain and France

---

[197] *Monthly Summary*, supplement, March, 1923, p. 36.

[198] Beneš, *op. cit.*, p. 213; *cf.* also, *The Financial Reconstruction of Austria*, Agreement approved by the League of Nations on September 16, 1924.

[199] *Cf.* Krčmář, *loc. cit.*, p. 171.

—were vital to the Little Entente, whose members resolved to hold a series of preliminary conferences in order to arrive at a general understanding and present a united front at the Genoa Conference. Each of the three states viewed the Russian problem in a different light: Rumania, and Poland as well, had serious disputes with her; whereas both Czechoslovakia and Yugoslavia had the Slavophil idea of friendship, although the former would have preferred a Russian republic, and the latter a monarchy.[200] Then, too, the Little Entente hoped to avoid being faced with a choice between Great Britain and France, who showed a wide divergence of views regarding both Russia and Germany.[201]

The first of the preliminary conferences was held at Bucharest, February 20-24, 1922, when Pašič and Ninčič, Bratiano and Duca, the Premiers and Foreign Ministers of Yugoslavia and Rumania, respectively, took advantage of the betrothal of King Alexander and Princess Marie of Rumania to bind the two states still more closely together. Beneš, who at the time was on a trip to Paris and London to ascertain the viewpoints of these Powers towards the Little Entente,[202] was represented by Veverka, the Czechoslovak Minister to Rumania. The chief results of the conference were the solution of the dispute between Rumania and Yugoslavia over the boundary in the Banat of Temesvar and an agreement upon a common line of action for Genoa.[203] Upon Beneš' return from the West, he conferred, at Bratislava on March 2, with Ninčič, and approved the results of the Conference of Bucharest. The two partners decided to amplify the program of the Little Entente for the coming

[200] Codresco, *op. cit.*, vol. ii, pp. 161-172.

[201] Mousset, *op. cit.*, pp. 76-78; Machray, *op. cit.*, pp. 189-190.

[202] Cf. *supra*, p. 141.

[203] *Le Temps*, February 28, 1922; Cosma, *op. cit.*, pp. 88-89; Mousset, *op. cit.*, pp. 80-82; Codresco, *op. cit.*, vol. i, pp. 239-244.

Genoa Conference. They were particularly interested in recommending the participation of the League of Nations in the ensuing deliberations, in opposing any discussion regarding the revision of the Peace Treaties, and in reopening commercial and economic relations with Russia, regardless of the question of Russian recognition.[204]

The final preliminary conference of experts was held at Belgrade, March 9-12. Yugoslavia submitted a memoir that was adopted as the basis for the work of the various Commissions, which, at Genoa, would seek to improve economic conditions by a general reestablishment of international communications and transportation, by financial stabilization and by balancing budgets. Another important point was the decision of the three partners to hold, in the future, regular periodic conferences at which to discuss such new problems as might arise.[205]

The Conference of Belgrade was of interest also because Poland, who had sent merely an observer to the Conference of Bucharest in February,[206] now participated in the deliberations, despite the fact that her representative was still, technically, an observer. To avoid isolation, Poland appeared willing to collaborate with the Little Entente upon questions of common interest, yet seemed to fear too intimate a connection. Poland had many interests foreign to those of the Little Entente. She had no fear of Hungary, but was afraid that both Czechoslovakia and Yugoslavia might welcome a Russian hegemony in Central Europe. She was convinced that no solution of the Russian problem would be possible unless her own territory was used as a

---

[204] Codresco, *op. cit.*, vol. i, pp. 245-246; Machray, *op. cit.*, pp. 192-193; Cosma, *op. cit.*, pp. 90-91; Mousset, *op. cit.*, pp. 82-83.

[205] Mousset, *op. cit.*, pp. 83-85; Cosma, *op. cit.*, pp. 91-93; Machray, *op. cit.*, p. 193; Codresco, *op. cit.*, vol. i, pp. 247-251.

[206] *Cf.* Cosma, *op. cit.*, p. 88.

means of transit whereby Russian isolation would be terminated. In this connection, Poland dreaded lest Germany decide to help Russia as the result of a new " Drang nach Osten " of which she herself might be the first victim. In order to draw to her side the Baltic states, Poland, on March 17, 1922, called the Conference of Warsaw. Finland, Estonia and Latvia sent delegates. The Conference agreed to aid mutual commerce, and to recognize the peace treaties that ended the war with Russia, but all these resolutions proved futile when Poland disavowed her plenipotentiaries. Thereupon, the Baltic states held another Conference at Riga, where, on March 30, they agreed on a common line of action for Genoa.[207]

At the Genoa Conference, the recognition that the bloc of the Little Entente and Poland received [208] was owing again to their solidarity upon that occasion, a result which blinded many observers to the fact that such close collaboration was temporary. Beneš was disappointed because Poland had sent merely an observer to the Conference of Belgrade which she refused to consider as a quadruple affair, for he deemed her relations with the Little Entente sufficiently intimate for a closer connection,[209] whereas Ninčič even spoke of a " Quadruple Entente ".[210] However, Poland remained consistent in her attitude, and, from time to time, continued to send observers to some of the Little Entente Conferences, but remained aloof from any closer contacts. For Central Europe, the primary significance of both the Genoa Conference and of the series of preliminary conferences that had

[207] Mousset, *op. cit.*, pp. 87-88.

[208] *Cf. supra*, p. 144.

[209] Beneš, *op. cit.*, p. 290; *Five Years of Czechoslovak Foreign Policy*, pp. 18-19.

[210] Mousset, *op. cit.*, pp. 132-133, 147-149; Cosma, *op. cit.*, pp. 156-181 (*passim*) ; *The Times*, August 23, 1923.

preceded it was perhaps the fact that the little Powers admitted the possibility of renewing relations with Russia while still adhering to the French thesis of the inviolability of treaties.[211]

Since Bucharest and Belgrade had been the sites of the preliminary conferences, it was logical that the first of the regular periodic meetings of the Little Entente be held at Praha. At this Conference, which met on August 25, 1922, there were present Beneš, Duca, Pašič and Piltz, the Polish Minister to Praha. The negotiations centered on two topics: the attitude the four states should adopt at the Third League Assembly which was to open on September 4 and the renewal of the Czechoslovak-Yugoslav treaty of alliance. In the discussions of the 27 and 28, there were introduced also the questions of the reconstruction of Austria, the admission of Hungary to the League, the treatment of minorities, the delimitation of the Austro-Hungarian and Austro-Yugoslav frontiers, the danger of having to make a choice between Great Britain and France, and the rumors of a Bavarian Wittelsbach restoration in Germany. After due deliberation, the Conference agreed to endorse Beneš' policies regarding Austria and the Western Powers, to proclaim against the Wittelsbach possibility as less favorable than the status quo, and to permit Hungary to enter the League provided that she accept definitely the situation that had been created by the Treaty of Trianon.[212]

On August 31, at Mariánské Lázně to whose waters Pašič had again resorted for his annual cure, the Czechoslovak-Yugoslav treaty of alliance was renewed and amplified by a more exact definition of their respective obligations. The

[211] Mousset, *op. cit.*, p. 88.

[212] Mousset, *op. cit.*, pp. 149-156; Cosma, *op. cit.*, pp. 101-108; Codresco, *op. cit.*, vol. i, pp. 273-278; Machray, *op. cit.*, pp. 200-201. No published minutes of Little Entente conferences exist.

original treaty of August 14, 1920, was extended again, not for two, but for five years; all the other treaties that each state had negotiated (Czechoslovakia with Rumania, Austria and Poland; Yugoslavia with Rumania and Italy) were approved; a mutual basis was to be found for economic, financial and transportational collaboration; mutual political and diplomatic assistance was to be given in international relations; and consultation was to take place upon all questions that might affect common interests.[213]

The Praha-Mariánské Lázně Conference marked an important phase in the evolution of the Little Entente. It changed the new bloc into a Power that had to be considered in all European questions. Nevertheless, the Little Entente had marked defects: on only limited questions would its action become automatic, and the Czechoslovak-Yugoslav link was far stronger than the other portions of the chain.

To Beneš, the latter defect appeared less important than the fact that the interests of the three partners coincided; yet, even though he stressed the point that the manner of union was of secondary importance, he did admit that the existing system of fragmentary bilateral treaties could be improved, for instance, by further treaties upon the model of that of Mariánské Lázně.[214]

At the Lausanne Conference, which opened on November 20, 1922, to attempt to settle the affairs of Southeastern Europe, the Little Entente was found in the background. Beneš, who did not arrive to confer with his partners until the 28 because of the exigencies of domestic politics,[215]

---

[213] *Documents, alliance*, annex 5; *Treaty Series*, vol. xiii, pp. 231-235.

[214] *Zprávy* (Senát), 195 meeting, March 18, 1924, pp. 58 *et seq.*, 9 session; 196 meeting, March 19, 1924, pp. 65 *et seq.*, 9 session.

[215] On October 7, 1922, Beneš resigned the Premiership which he had assumed on September 26, 1921, but retained his portfolio as Minister of Foreign Affairs. His decision was made, not because of any ministerial crisis, but because he could not do justice to both positions.

was not interested in the Greco-Turk question, with regard to which he left his two colleagues a free hand; his sole interest lay in a rapprochement of Bulgaria and Greece with the Little Entente, perhaps on the order of the Balkan League of 1912. Nevertheless, Beneš remained true to his earlier policy. Out of deference to his colleagues he was willing to consider the inclusion of Greece and Bulgaria within the Little Entente even though he would have preferred merely collaboration with them. The inclusion of Greece within the Little Entente had been the dream of Take Jonescu to the day of his death, June 21, 1922, but could not be consummated in spite of the various dynastic ties among Greece, Rumania and Yugoslavia.[216] The treaty of May 19, 1913, which was to last ten years, still bound Greece and Yugoslavia by a military and political alliance, a treaty which Greece desired to renew. Yugoslavia could not forget Greece's interpretation of the document during October, 1915, in Serbia's hour of greatest need. When General Dousmanis arrived in Belgrade in early February, 1922, to negotiate a renewal, he encountered a reserved reception, for, although a signer of the treaty, he had opposed aid to Serbia against the Central Powers. As a result, in spite of Greece's offer of special commercial rights to Yugoslavia via Salonika, the treaty of alliance failed of renewal. Rumania's request for reciprocal economic advantages from Greece, the granting of which might nullify the special advantages of trade via Salonika, was perhaps another factor that led Yugoslavia to reject the advances of Greece.[217] Similarly, a rapprochement with Bulgaria failed to materialize beyond an

[216] Elizabeth of Rumania married King George of Greece; Marie of Rumania, King Alexander of Yugoslavia; and Helen of Greece, Carol of Rumania.

[217] Yugoslavia denounced the old treaty definitively on November 15, 1924. *Cf. The Times*, November 20, 1924; Codresco, *op. cit.*, vol. ii, pp. 229-240.

amicable exchange of views, largely because bands of Macedonian comitadjis still continued their raids across both the Greek and Yugoslav frontiers.[218]   Thus, although the year 1922 had resulted in a strengthening of the Little Entente, the closing months left much uncertainty as to the future: for even the treaties of October 23, 1922,[219] whereby Yugoslavia and Italy agreed to execute certain disputed details of the earlier Treaty of Rapallo, represented a rapprochement of questionable duration, inasmuch as a few days after their signature a new régime, in the person of Mussolini, seized power in Italy.

The Czechoslovak-Rumanian treaty was renewed on May 7, 1923.[220]   Although this new treaty was to last three years, it had not been strengthened as had been the one between Czechoslovakia and Yugoslavia.   The second regular annual Conference took place on July 26 at Sinaia, the Rumanian royal summer palace.   After an exchange of views, it was decided to do nothing about Russia for the time being, and to exclude both Greece and Bulgaria from active membership. The Conference agreed with Beneš that Hungary remained the chief problem of Central Europe and, despite her intransigeance, should be reconstructed after the fashion of Austria. The greatest permanent result of Sinaia was perhaps the strengthening of the bilateral system of treaties on September 14, 1923, by a tripartite military convention which provided for mutual cooperation in the event of a casus foederis, for which the three military staffs were to begin to work out solutions immediately.[221]

[218] Bulgaria was refused a port on the Aegean Sea, which she requested in accord with Article 48 of the Treaty of Neuilly. *Cf.* Mousset, *op. cit.,* pp. 133-141, 159-162; Cosma, *op. cit.,* pp. 108-110; Machray, *op. cit.,* pp. 207-209; Codresco, *op. cit.,* vol. i, pp. 279-282; vol. ii, pp. 151-159.

[219] *Treaty Series,* vol. xviii, pp. 387-523.

[220] *Ibid.,* vol. xviii, pp. 81-83.

[221] Beneš, *Problemy nové Evropy,* p. 263; Cosma, *op. cit.,* pp. 110-115;

The Reconstruction of Hungary

Beneš felt that assistance to Hungary would be the last step that would be required for the reconstruction of the small states of Central Europe. Although willing to rehabilitate Hungary after the fashion of Austria, he believed that additional safeguards would be required. While willing that Hungary's national revenues should be released from the terms of the Treaty of Trianon as collateral for a new loan, Beneš desired to assure himself that the new funds would not be devoted to either military or propaganda purposes: to that end, he suggested that the Little Entente safeguard itself through a commission of control. Since his own direct negotiations with Hungary during 1922 had produced only a commercial treaty of November 22,[222] which neither country had ratified, he believed that the problem of Hungary should be submitted to the League which had functioned so well in the case of Austria.[223]

Even though the condition of Hungary was by no means as desperate as that of Austria had been, her rapidly depreciating currency, unbalanced budgets, unemployment and general economic distress were sufficiently marked to render improbable any great improvement solely through her own unaided efforts. In fact, Hungary confessed her inability to save herself on April 22, 1923, on which date she requested that the Reparations Commission release, as security for a new loan, the national resources that had been impounded by

Machray, op. cit., pp. 220-221; Toynbee, op. cit., p. 302; Codresco, op. cit., vol. i, pp. 291-294; Le Temps, July 27, 30, 31, August 2 and 12, 1923; The Central European Observer, July 28 and August 4, 1923. The treaty of May 7 renewed for three years both the Czechoslovak-Rumanian defensive alliance of April 3, 1921, and the military accord of July 2, 1921. Similarly, on July 7, 1923, the Rumanian-Yugoslav military convention of June 7, 1921, was renewed for three years.

[222] Prager Presse, November 23, 1922.

[223] Beneš, Five Years of Czechoslovak Foreign Policy, pp. 16-17.

Article 180 of the Treaty of Trianon. The Little Entente, which held considerable Reparations Claims against Hungary, agreed not to oppose this measure, provided that none of the new fund was " misapplied ", that it be granted " most-favored-nation treatment " by Hungary in Reparations, that Hungary give guarantees of her good faith, that she disarm definitely and agree to a protocol on the Austrian model.[224]

Before the question of Hungarian reconstruction had made much progress, Hungary and Czechoslovakia became involved in a boundary dispute over Salgo-Tarjan, a region valuable for its coal deposits and stone quarries. The two communes involved, Samoskö and Samosujfalu, which contained 20.5 square miles and a predominantly Magyar population of about 1,900, were claimed by both states: by Hungary, for economic and ethnic reasons, and by Czechoslovakia upon a legal technicality, namely, because the Treaty of Trianon had authorized frontier rectifications only by unanimous consent of the members of the Delimitation Commission, which, in the instance of Salgo-Tarjan, had been deadlocked three to three until the chairman had voted in favor of Hungary. After both states had agreed to accept arbitration, the dispute was submitted to the League Council, which, on February 15, 1923, drew a new frontier. Hungary was awarded both communes proper, whereas Czechoslovakia received the coal mines, most of the stone quarries, and an unasked-for slice of northern Hungary. The compromise was regarded with mixed feelings by Hungary, which had gained a part of the disputed area only at the cost of other territory which had been hers indisputably.[225]

[224] Official Journal, February, 1924, pp. 413-414; Monthly Summary, May, 1923, supplement, pp. 1-59.

[225] Monthly Summary, January, 1923, p. 14; February, 1923, pp. 21-22; March, 1923, p. 60; April, 1923, p. 88; Official Journal, March, 1923, pp. 282-293; June, 1923, pp. 556-558, 559, 601-602, 632-634; Treaty Series, vol. lvii, pp. 87-113.

At the Fourth Session of the Assembly of the League, on September 29, 1923, the Little Entente, with the understanding that it should be represented on the Council during the deliberations concerning Hungary, proposed that that body authorize the Financial Committee and the Secretariat to inaugurate the procedure necessary to begin the reconstruction of Hungary, a proposal that the Council approved immediately. The Reparations Commission acquiesced on October 17, but only upon condition that the states with individual claims against Hungary be associated with the League in the process of reconstruction. After several further investigations and conferences, the plans for the reconstruction of Hungary were embodied in two protocols of March 14, 1924.[226] The first, signed by both Ententes (Great Britain, France, Italy, Czechoslovakia, Yugoslavia, Rumania) and Hungary, obligated Hungary to fulfill voluntarily the clauses of the Treaty of Trianon.[227] Beneš had worked hard to obtain such a pledge from Hungary, particularly regarding the military clauses of the Treaty of Trianon. In fact, despite Italian displeasure, he had insisted, throughout these negotiations, upon a favorable treatment of Czechoslovakia's financial obligations before he would consent to the scheme for Hungary.[228] He won his point. The second protocol, which was signed solely by Hungary, listed her financial obligations as a good neighbor.[229] On May 1, Jeremiah Smith, Jr., a prominent Boston financier, became the Commissioner-General. During June, a loan of 11,-000,000 pounds sterling was floated successfully in the same manner, and under the same auspices as that of Austria, with

---

[226] *Monthly Summary*, May, 1924, supplement, documents 2-8; *Official Journal*, February, 1924, pp. 414-429.

[227] *Treaty Series*, vol. xxv, pp. 423-425.

[228] *Cf.* Toynbee, *op. cit.*, 1924, p. 453.

[229] *Treaty Series*, vol. xxv, pp. 427-440.

the marked difference that Hungary's own national resources were deemed sufficient security, and, hence, no foreign guarantee was necessary.[280]

Czechoslovakia took advantage of the general improvement of relations with Hungary to settle certain other issues. On February 9, 1924, the two states signed the two protocols concerning Salgo-Tarjan,[231] and on March 8 agreed upon the question of mortgages.[232] Finally, on May 1, 1924, Czechoslovakia ratified a convention regarding archives, which had been signed on April 6, 1922.[233] In spite of these amicable gestures, no real friendship resulted, as the sequal was to show.[234] None the less, Benes' more than five years of efforts for the reconstruction of Central Europe had been partially successful: his masterpiece, the Little Entente, was a vital force, both politically and economically. It had managed to exert considerable influence upon the decisions of even the Great Powers regarding Central Europe, and had had some influence upon other affairs beyond that region.[235]

[280] *Monthly Summary*, April, 1925, p. 112; *Official Journal*, June, 1924, pp. 872-877.

[231] *Treaty Series*, vol. xxx, pp. 325-345.

[232] *Ibid.*, vol. xxxvi, pp. 61-73. Mortgages and capital invested in financial establishments (deposit books and current account claims) were assigned to the state in which the establishments were situated.

[233] *Ibid.*, vol. xx, pp. 11-17.

[234] For the renewal of Czechoslovak-Hungarian friction, *cf. infra*, pp. 271 *et seq.*

[235] *Cf.* Benes' own summary of his work, *Five Years of Czechoslovak Foreign Policy* (speech of February 6, 1924, before the Foreign Affairs Committee of the Senate); *Problemy nové Evropy*, pp. 279-306; or *Boj o mir a bezpečnost státu* (Praha, 1934, henceforth referred to as *Boj o mír*), pp. 233-267.

CHAPTER V

The Search for Security, 1924-1926

" the treaty of mutual assistance "

Just as Beneš had deemed the reconstruction of Central Europe [1] the major problem of his first five years as Foreign Minister, so did he envisage security as the major problem during the next phase of the foreign policy of Czechoslovakia.[2] By the latter part of 1923, the problem of security, with which there had become inextricably linked the question of disarmament, had become one of the chief concerns of the Great Powers. France, which had strongly advocated the inclusion of Article 8 in the League Covenant, now submitted it for solution. Meanwhile, the series of unsuccessful negotiations with Great Britain, whereby France had hoped to achieve security,[3] had produced a " Treaty of Mutual Assistance ", technically under League auspices, which represented the joint projects of Lord Robert Cecil and Colonel Requin. It provided for restriction and permanent control of armaments, assistance by the signatories for any state attacked, recognition of regional treaties as the

---

[1] Beneš, E., *Boj o mír*, pp. 233-267; *Five Years of Czechoslovak Foreign Policy*, pp. 12-19.

[2] Beneš, *Five Years of Czechoslovak Foreign Policy*, p. 5; " The Foreign Policy of Czechoslovakia ", *Nineteenth Century*, vol. xcv, pp. 483-490; " European Security ", *International Conciliation*, no. 212.

[3] *Papers respecting Negotiations for an Anglo-French Pact*; *Documents diplomatiques relatives aux negociations concernant les garanties de securité contre une aggression de l'Allemagne*; Beneš, *Boj o mír*, pp. 301-324; *The Diplomatic Struggle for European Security and the Stabilization of Peace* (speech of April 1, 1925, before the Foreign Affairs Committee of the Senate), pp. 7-9; Selsam, *op. cit.*, pp. 1-58; *cf.* also, *supra*, p. 105.

best means of rendering such assistance, differentiation between various parts of the world in order to permit greater freedom in enforcing the treaty, and control over its functioning to be vested in the League.

The " Treaty of Mutual Assistance " aroused the interest of Beneš, not only because he was the representative for the Little Entente, but because of his official capacity as rapporteur for the Third Committee of the General Assembly, the Committee which had been entrusted with the problems of security and the reduction of armaments. To Beneš this treaty appeared as an almost ideal supplement to the League Covenant, as thus far the best suggestion that had been made for furthering security and general disarmament. Until a better solution should be proposed, he believed it his duty to support and attempt to improve this project. Nevertheless, Beneš supported the treaty with many reservations. He preferred a majority, rather than a unanimous, vote of the Council to determine which state should be regarded as the aggressor in any dispute. Czechoslovakia, a small country which might easily be ruined by a single military thrust, objected to having her limited defensive areas reduced further by demilitarized zones. She desired to revise Articles 13 and 18 of the projected treaty so as to permit individual states to revise their scale of armaments whenever the factors involved in their security should change. Beneš believed that armaments could be reduced only in proportion to the security attained, but objected to the mutual interdependence of the problems of security and of progressive reduction of armaments. He felt convinced that better results could be obtained by a separation of these two questions. Hence, he demanded a corresponding supplement for Article 8 of the League Covenant. In voicing this demand, Beneš stated his belief that the proposed treaty was an extension of the Covenant, particularly a restatement in concrete

form, of Articles 10 and 16. As a final plea, he pointed out
that Czechoslovakia, as well as other small states, regarded
the treaty as one which could be rejected only at the risk
of arousing a conviction that even comparative security could
be attained only through the patronage of some Great Power.
Therefore, he suggested that two procedures should be
followed simultaneously—negotiations regarding both the
" Treaty of Mutual Assistance " and special treaties referring
to demilitarized zones.[4]

The French Alliance

Beneš was too astute a diplomat not to have prepared the
way for the alternative policy he here foreshadowed—an
alliance with France. During the latter half of 1923 he
made several visits to the western capitals. Between July 6
and 20, he visited Paris, London and Brussels, to get their
viewpoints upon the question of the reconstruction of Hungary and to take soundings regarding his coming alliance
with France. After attending the Little Entente Conference of Sinaia from July 26 to August 1,[5] where it seems
safe to infer he took further soundings, he wished to clarify
the attitude of Italy towards the Little Entente. On August
26, Beneš visited Rome to ascertain Mussolini's attitude regarding Hungarian reconstruction and other special Italo-
Czechoslovak questions. He found Il Duce cordial. Plans

[4] Beneš, E., " O sniženi zbrojeni " (speech of September 29, 1923, the
day of Czechoslovakia's election to the League Council, during the plenary
session as rapporteur for the Third Commission of the Fourth Assembly),
reprinted in *Zahranični Politika*, vol. ii, pp. 1257-1264; *cf. Official Journal*,
special supplement, 1922-1923, annex 34, pt. 2, pp. 2-100 (record of
seventeen Council meetings during September, 1923) ; *ibid.*, September,
1924, pp. 1172-1176 (Beneš' reply of August 17, 1924, to League Secretariat) ; *ibid.*, special supplement no. 23, 1924, pp. 61-65 (Beneš' defense
of " Treaty of Mutual Assistance " before Fifth Assembly, September
5, 1924).

[5] For details, *cf. supra*, p. 204.

were made speedily for a tariff agreement and for a debt settlement which was to become a part of the general inter-Allied debt question. Italy agreed to treat Czechoslovak war debts in the same manner as her own debts would be treated by Great Britain. These pourparlers, Czechoslovakia's first official contact with Mussolini, defined their relations more clearly than had ever been the case before and convinced Beneš that Mussolini intended to continue the policy regarding the Little Entente that he had proclaimed in his first speech regarding foreign affairs, on November 16, 1922, when he stated that Italy's attitude towards the Little Entente would remain " correct ".[6] Beneš failed to indicate [7] whether he had discussed with Mussolini his projected alliance with France, and perhaps he did not.

Beneš' advances were more than welcome to France, which hoped, through Czechoslovakia, to attract the Little Entente within its sphere of influence. After prolonged wrangling,[8] the French Senate, on December 17, 1923, approved loans of 400,000,000 francs to Poland, 300,000,000 to Yugoslavia, and 100,000,000 to Rumania,[9] loans which Rumania alone refused.[10] Czechoslovakia inaugurated direct negotiations for an alliance with France on October 16, 1923, as the result of a visit which Masaryk and Beneš made to Paris, whither they had been invited by the French President, Millerand. After an enthusiastic reception,[11] they went on to Brussels and London. In response to questions as to the

[6] Cf. Currey, M., Italian Foreign Policy, 1918-1932 (London, 1932), pp. 78-80.

[7] Cf. Beneš, Problemy nové Evropy, pp. 261-265, for this series of visits which prepared the way for the French alliance.

[8] Cf. The Times, November 20, 1923.

[9] Le Temps, December 18, 1923.

[10] Cf. Toynbee, op. cit., pp. 440-444; Codresco, op. cit., vol. ii, pp. 119-132.

[11] Le Temps, October 17-18, 1923.

reasons for the trip, Masaryk, on October 23, replied that
he desired to reduce the tension between Great Britain and
France, whose continued Entente he deemed vital.   Czechoslovakia would not negotiate any treaty hostile to either.[12]

Beneš was anxious lest a French alliance give umbrage to
Great Britain,[13] and, in order to avert so unfortunate a possibility, returned again to London on January 13, 1924.   At
this time he sought to prove that the projected alliance was
not militaristic in nature and contained no military convention, although he did confess that the French General Staff
had desired such an agreement.   Above all, he denied that
his country would become a vassal of France.   In conclusion,
Beneš stated that he would have preferred a joint Anglo-
French guarantee, but when this became impossible, he had
no alternative, for Czechoslovakia's insecurity necessitated a
military guarantee by some Great Power, a commitment
which France alone was willing to assume.[14]   Thereupon,
Beneš returned to Paris.   Here the treaty of alliance, whose
exact terms were drafted early in January,[15] was signed on
January 25.[16]   It was ratified by Czechoslovakia on February 14 [17] and by France on February 29.[18]   Ratifications
were exchanged in Paris on March 4.[19]

[12] *Ibid., The Times*, October 24, 1923; Codresco, *op. cit.*, vol. i, pp.
295-298; Machray, *op. cit.*, pp. 228-229; *cf.* also, Anon., *President
Masaryk in Paris, Brussels and London in October, 1923.*

[13] *Zprávy* (Poslanecká Sněmovna), 219 meeting, October 30, 1923, pp.
24 *et seq.*, 8 session; *ibid.* (Senát), 173, 174 and 175 meetings, October
30, November 8 and 9, 1923, pp. 11 *et seq.*, 24 *et seq.* and 92 *et seq.*,
respectively, 8 session.

[14] *Cf.* D'Abernon, *op. cit.*, vol. iii, p. 34.

[15] *Le Temps*, January 8, 1924.

[16] *Cf.* Toynbee, *op. cit.*, p. 444.

[17] *The Central European Observer*, February 15, 1924.

[18] *Le Temps*, March 1, 1924.

[19] *Ibid.*, March 5, 1924.

By Article 1 the two countries agreed to cooperate on all foreign questions that might threaten their security or the status quo that had been established by the Peace Treaties of which they were signatories.   By Article 2 they promised to agree in whatever specific measures they might deem necessary to protect themselves whenever their common interests might be menaced, a promise that went beyond the purely diplomatic support that had been envisaged in Article 1. Article 3 contained a declaration against Anschluss and in favor of maintaining the Geneva Protocols of October 4, 1922, as the basic solution for the problem of the reconstruction of Austria.   Article 4 vetoed the restoration of the Habsburgs in Hungary, and Article 5 the Hohenzollerns in Germany.   The method of enforcing Articles 3, 4 and 5 would be determined by consultation between the two allies. Article 6 specified that all disputes, not otherwise decided, be arbitrated either by the Permanent Court of International Justice or by other arbiters selected by the two states.   By Article 7 both promised to inform each other of the treaties that they had already negotiated and to consult one another before concluding any new ones: moreover, the present treaty contained nothing contrary to the spirit of the French alliance with Poland or with Czechoslovakia's treaties with Austria, Italy, or her Little Entente partners.   Finally, Article 8 required the registration of the treaty with the League of Nations according to Article 18 of the Covenant.[20]

Although this treaty of alliance, which henceforth might be regarded as next in importance only to the Little Entente treaties, represented in one sense merely the culmination of a long friendship between the two states, in another sense it represented a radical departure in Czechoslovak foreign policy.   Heretofore, Czechoslovakia had concentrated her attention upon obtaining immediate security against Hun-

[20] *Treaty Series*, vol. xxiii, pp. 163-169.

gary, and had shunned too intimate contacts with any of the Great Powers. By midsummer, 1923, Beneš' plans for the reconstruction of Central Europe were practically consummated and a wider horizon came into view. He began to scan the distant future and to seek more adequate protection against Germany than was offered by the League. The danger of losing a measure of diplomatic independence by appearing as the satellite of a Great Power seemed less acute than that of insecurity. In fact, in a later exposé, Beneš confessed that " from the very beginning of our policy it had always been our intention to arrive at a treaty of this kind ".[21] Thus, although Beneš took care lest he voice any criticism of the League of Nations, in which he proclaimed publicly, upon every possible occasion, the utmost faith, his actions indicated much less faith in that organization than did his words: perhaps, his alliance with France was intended merely as a supplementary guarantee, but it did represent a return to a system of alliances.[22]

The Czechoslovak alliance with France was negotiated essentially to defend the status quo (Articles 1, 3, 4, 5), but also included safeguarding " common interests " (Article 2), an elastic term. Although the treaty provided patently for diplomatic consultation, some of its phrases (i. e. " agree . . . as to the measures ", " measures to be taken ", " common action ") might mean consultation regarding military action. In the absence of any specific mention of a plan for concerted military action or any outline of military cooperation, it appeared that the two governments took the view that the agreement imposed no military obligations beyond mere " understandings between the General Staffs of the two

[21] Beneš, *Five Years of Czechoslovak Foreign Policy*, p. 25.

[22] *Cf.* Vochoč, V., " Naš spolek s Francií ", *Zahraniční Politika*, vol. iii, pp. 1-6; Aubert, L., " Security: Key to French Policy ", *Foreign Affairs*, vol. ii, pp. 122-136.

nations ".[23]   It seemed that even this interpretation had been agreed upon only after considerable pressure from France, which regarded Poland as militarily unreliable.   Foch himself conceded that Beneš was correct in rejecting any military convention which would provoke almost inevitably a similar opposing combination in reply.[24]   Beneš stated that

> The only purpose of this treaty is the pacification of Central Europe and the rapprochement of all European States.   European States must all realize that they must cooperate and cannot exist to themselves within their own frontiers.   Our treaty with France is a continuation of the policy begun by our treaties with Poland and Austria.[25]

In eulogy of the solidarity between Czechoslovakia and France, he declared in parliament, " Never has France's friendship ,and aid failed us during the four years' strife or since the Armistice.   None of the Allies has done more politically for the independence of Czechoslovakia than France ".[26]

As might have been expected, the treaty encountered much criticism in foreign countries.   The chorus of disapproval seemed so widespread that as early as January 1, 1924, Mr. Mastný, the Czechoslovak Minister to Great Britain, was impelled to deny categorically that any military alliance was contemplated.[27]   In view of the tension between Great Britain and France over the Ruhr question and over the Separatist Movement within Germany, a section of British public opinion resented the alliance as expressing a definite preference of Czechoslovakia for France and as the latest French

[23] *The New York Times*, March 5, 1924.

[24] *Cf.* D'Abernon, *op. cit.*, vol. iii, p. 35.

[25] *The New York Times*, January 27, 1929.

[26] *Národni Politika*, February 6, 1924; *L'Europe nouvelle*, February 2, 1924.

[27] *The Times*, January 2, 1924.

attempt to encircle and crush Germany.[28] To Italy it signified impending French domination of Central Europe,[29] an
opinion which drew from the *Národní Listy* the retort that
Italian ill-feeling was inspired by inability to rival France
successfully in Central Europe.[30] Austrian and German
public opinion agreed that the treaty represented fresh evidence of French oppression and encirclement.[31] Poland felt
slighted because the agreement referred only to the treaties
that had been signed by both France and Czechoslovakia, and
failed to call attention to France's other allies.[32]

Among all the foreign comments upon the alliance of
France and Czechoslovakia, one German attack stood out as
the most vicious. The *Berliner Tageblatt* published several
documents which it asserted to be the texts of secret military
appendices to the treaty. These documents represented an
alleged attempt to revive a policy of German " encirclement " similar to that of Edward VII in forming the Triple
Entente. It was also " revealed " that Beneš had been
rebuffed by Yugoslavia when he had sought to have her join
the French alliance; that, instead, she had seized the initiative among the Little Entente states and inaugurated a rival
policy of rapprochement with Italy, as had been evinced by
the " Pact of Rome ". Thus, allegedly, Beneš had not been
able to force the hands of his Little Entente partners so as
to compel them to accept the hegemony of France, and, as a
result of the action of Yugoslavia, France came to fear
possible Italian domination of the Mediterranean. Of the

[28] *Ibid.*, December 28-29, 1923; *The Manchester Guardian*, January 1,
3, 5 and 6, 1924.

[29] *Corriere della Sera*, January 1, 4, 6, 7 and 8, 1924.

[30] *Národní Listy*, January 9-10, 1924.

[31] *Neue Freie Presse*, January 2, 1924; *Berliner Tageblatt*, March 4
and 11, 1924.

[32] *Le Temps*, January 5, 1924; *Gazeta Warszawska*, January 6 and
8, 1924.

ten clauses of the alleged "secret" treaty, three were substantially the same as in the true party: prohibitions of Anschluss, and of the restoration of the Habsburgs and the Hohenzollerns. Four other clauses were perhaps inferred from Article 1 of the true treaty as possible violations of the status quo: war by Germany against either France or Czechoslovakia or against both; war between Germany and Poland; between Czechoslovakia and Hungary; and German aid to the Soviet Union in any future war. The three final clauses represented contingencies not contemplated in the authentic treaty: neutrality in the event of a war between the U. S. S. R. and Poland, aid to Rumania against the Soviet Union, and opposition to Italian domination of the Mediterranean.[33]

This attack on the treaty of alliance was reinforced by the Vienna *Neue Freie Presse,* which commented upon the fact that, in view of the Geneva Protocols and the disarmed condition of both Austria and Germany an alliance between France and Czechoslovakia could hardly be considered either "heroic" or "contributory to general European peace", and that, if authentic, these revelations demonstrated that secret diplomacy was still very active.[34]

Both the French and Czechoslovak legations in Vienna repudiated all knowledge of the secret treaty.[35] Beneš pronounced the documents "foolish and false" and "without foundation".[36] Nevertheless, he was requested to make an explanation to the Parliamentary Committee on Foreign Affairs, which, after a heated session, kept its proceedings secret.[37]

[33] *Berliner Tageblatt,* March 18, 1924; *cf.* also, Toynbee, *op. cit.,* p. 445.

[34] *Neue Freie Presse,* March 19, 1924.

[35] *Ibid.,* March 20, 1924; *cf.* also, *Le Temps,* March 23, 1924.

[36] *Národní Listy, The Times* and *The New York Times,* March 20, 1924.

[37] *Národní Politika,* March 21, 1924.

Disbelief in the authenticity of the secret clauses was soon justified. The Czechoslovak government ascertained that, except for the names and dates, many clauses were exact duplicates of earlier authentic treaties which had been published in Professor Přibram's *The Secret Treaties of Austria-Hungary*, and that the alleged French treaty with Yugoslavia, supposedly negotiated after the initial rebuff to Beneš, reproduced the Austra-German Protocol of September 24, 1879, Bismarck's treaty with Andrassy.[38]

Despite this exposé, the *Berliner Tageblatt* still continued to defend the authenticity of its documents,[39] even against other members of the German press which generally conceded their falsity. The *Frankfurter Zeitung* pronounced them " apochryphal ".[40] The Socialist *Vorwaerts*, which, generously, expressed an opinion that the publishers acted in good faith, nevertheless proclaimed the secret treaty a " forgery ".[41] The *Vossische Zeitung* took pains to cite certain textual peculiarities as the basis for its doubts.[42] The general consensus of German public opinion was that the " revelations " constituted an international hoax which had been inspired by forgers.[43]

As a matter of fact, military consultations between Czechoslovakia and France had ensued prior to the drafting of the treaty of alliance. On May 14, 1923, Foch was feted in Praha on his homeward trip from Warsaw. An inspection of the Czechoslovak army was followed by military con-

[38] Pinon, R., " The Franco-Slovakian Treaty of Alliance ", *Current History*, vol. xx, pp. 748-753; *cf.* also, Přibram, A. F., *The Secret Treaties of Austria-Hungary* (Cambridge, 1920), vol. i, pp. 18-31, for the Austro-German alliance of 1879.

[39] *Berliner Tageblatt*, March 25, 1924.

[40] *Frankfurter Zeitung*, March 21, 1924.

[41] *Vorwaerts*, March 23, 1924.

[42] *Vossische Zeitung*, March 23, 1924.

[43] *The New York Times*, March 25, 1924.

versations similar to those that had taken place between Foch and Polish military authorities. Although the Marshal praised the armies of both allies of France, he marveled particularly at the military achievements of Czechoslovakia during the first five years of independence.[44] Thus, even if the specific implications of Foch's visit did remain a mystery, German suspicions were not unfounded.

France, Italy and the Little Entente

Beneš' initiative was apparently welcome to his Little Entente partners, which, during 1924, also sought to enhance their security by creating closer ties with the Great Powers of the west. Yugoslavia and Rumania were negotiating French loans, and hence were already somewhat in the French orbit. The three small states felt that they could establish such relationships without becoming mere tools. The prestige that they had attained through their mutual cooperation and because of the moderating influence that they had exerted upon the various Central European crises had given them hopes of attaining one of their fondest dreams—of becoming one of the four major European blocs, along with the U.S.S.R., Germany and the Western Powers. New issues were needed, particularly to combat current rumors that the Little Entente was on the verge of dissolution because the reconstruction of Hungary had removed the menace that had been its chief raison d'être. Hence, Czechoslovakia's alliance with France, which had always supported the Little Entente, met with the approval of both Yugoslavia and Rumania.[45]

In order again to discuss the various aspects of their respective problems regarding security, the members of the

[44] *Svornost*, April 25, May 23 and 30, 1923; *Právo Lidu, Prager Tagblatt*, May 15, 1923; *Le Temps*, May 23, 1923.

[45] *Cf.* Chmelář, J., "Československá zahraniční politika v roce 1924", *Zahraniční Politika*, vol. iv, pp. 1-6; Rankovitch, J., "France and the Little Entente", *The Living Age*, vol. cccxvii, pp. 7-13.

Little Entente held the Conference of Belgrade, January 10-
12, 1924. Even before the delegates met, rumor exaggerated the extent of the rapprochement with France. Although
Beneš was alleged to have prepared Franco-Yugoslav and
Franco-Rumanian treaties analogous to the Franco-Czechoslovak alliance,[46] he failed to present such projects, regardless how desirable he may have deemed them.[47] When the
Conference actually opened, it approved the action that had
been taken regarding reconstruction of Hungary, from
which satisfactory guarantees were exacted,[48] and then
turned to the problem of relations with the Great Powers.
In view of the impending recognition of the Soviet Union
de jure by the Western Powers,[49] Beneš felt it necessary to
clarify the attitude of the Little Entente regarding the
U.S.S.R., a question which he believed could no longer be
kept in the background lest it disrupt the unity of the three
partners. Although opposed personally to the immediate
recognition of the U. S. S. R. de jure, not because of principle, but because of a belief that such a step would be premature, Beneš was prepared to do so if Moscow would
renounce foreign propaganda, whereas Yugoslavia considered Soviet conditions a purely internal affair, and Rumania
demanded Bolshevik recognition of her title to Bessarabia.[50]
When Rumania remained firm in her opposition to Soviet
recognition, Beneš refused to press the matter further, even
after Ninčić stressed the joint Czechoslovak and Yugoslav

[46] *The Times*, January 7, 1924.

[47] *Ibid.*, January 12, 1924.

[48] *Cf. supra*, p. 206.

[49] This step was actually initiated by Great Britain on February 1, 1924,
and imitated by France, Italy and many other Powers. *Cf.* Toynbee,
op. cit., pp. 228-262.

[50] Beneš, *Five Years of Czechoslovak Foreign Policy*, p. 36; *Problemy
nové Evropy*, p. 304; D'Abernon, *op. cit.*, vol. ii, p. 275.

interests in a strong Soviet Union: [51] to have done so might have alienated Rumania, which was resentful of the fact that, in the event of a war with the Soviets, the support of her partners would be problematic. In such a conflict, Rumania's only ally would be Poland. However, Poland, in fear of being asked to commit herself still further, refused to attend the Conference of Belgrade. As a result, the decision of the Conference that each member of the Little Entente should retain freedom of action regarding a Soviet policy was the only basis upon which continued cooperation could be guaranteed.[52]

Mussolini's apprehensions regarding the activities of France in Central Europe were evident.[53] In order to counteract the threat of French preponderance, through control of the Little Entente, he had recourse to the same methods. As a result, there developed, between France and Italy, keen competition for the favor of the members of the Little Entente and of Poland. Through negotiations begun at the time of the Conference of Belgrade, Mussolini also drew closer to the Little Entente when he signed with Yugoslavia, on January 27, 1924, the " Pact of Rome " which minimized friction between the two countries. This treaty included: first a " Pact of Friendship and Cordial Cooperation "; secondly, a protocol which stated that the new agreement contained nothing that did not agree with Yugoslavia's earlier treaties with her Little Entente partners, that it was non-aggressive in that it guaranteed the Peace Treaties and promised mutual neutrality in the event of an unprovoked

[51] The New York Times, July 16, 1924.

[52] Ibid., January 10, 12, 13 and 14, 1924; The Times, January 14 and February 8, 1924; Le Temps, January 16, 1924; cf. also, Codresco, op. cit., vol. i, pp. 299-304; Toynbee, op. cit., pp. 449-450; Cosma, op. cit., pp. 115-118; Machray, op. cit., pp. 230-233; L'Europe nouvelle, January 19, 1924.

[53] Cf. Corriere della Sera, January 3-4, 1924.

attack by a Third Power, that it promised mutual cooperation and diplomatic support against external threats of violence, and that it would last for five years; and, thirdly, a supplement which recognized the annexation of Fiume by Italy and ceded to Yugoslavia Port Baros and the delta immediately adjacent.[54] In the words of Beneš, this treaty was " joyfully welcomed " by the Little Entente: he and Ninčič had kept one another informed of their respective negotiations with France and Italy,[55] and both took pains to explain that they had not intended to commit the Little Entente to friendship to France alone.[56] Nevertheless, Yugoslavia's alliance with Italy was both fragile and unnatural;[57] in any great emergency she would have preferred one with either Paris or Moscow, whose military strength was greater and whose friendship she considered more sincere.[58]

Rumania appeared dissatisfied over her relative insecurity, and, although she did rebuff France by rejecting, on January 22, 1924, the proffered loan of 100,000,000 francs,[59] she reopened negotiations with her the following April. Rumania desired particularly a French guarantee of Bessarabia, a commitment that France was apparently willing to assume, provided that Yugoslavia would undertake a similar responsibility. However, Yugoslavia, on April 23, refused to assume such a guarantee.[60] Similarly, Beneš declared

[54] *Treaty Series*, vol. xxiv, pp. 31-89.

[55] Machray, *op. cit.*, pp. 233-235.

[56] *Cf.* Currey, *op. cit.*, pp. 123-125; *The Times*, January 18, 1924.

[57] Friction still existed regarding land-owning quarrels and minority rights.

[58] *Cf.* Toynbee, *op. cit.*, pp. 448-449; Codresco, *op. cit.*, vol. i, pp. 305-308; vol. ii, pp. 133-149.

[59] Toynbee, *op. cit.*, p. 444. Apparently, Rumania resented the fact that France had been more willing to grant loans to Poland and Yugoslavia.

[60] *The Times*, April 26 and May 10, 1924.

that, in the event of a war over Bessarabia between the U. S. S. R. and Rumania, he would assist the latter only in the event that Hungary should aid the former.[61]

Beneš and Ninčić met at Bled from May 13 to 15, 1924, to discuss the project of a four-Power treaty, whereby Yugoslavia was to adhere to the Franco-Czechoslovak alliance and Czechoslovakia to that between Italy and Yugoslavia. Although such a treaty would have rendered more secure the position of each Power concerned, it failed to be consummated because Beneš, true to his principle of avoiding strictly Balkan commitments, refused to guarantee the Treaty of Neuilly in addition to those of St. Germain and Trianon.[62]

The Italo-Czechoslovak Treaty

The failure of the pourparlers at Bled did not deter Beneš from continuing his search for Czechoslovak security, for there remained one other alternative—independent negotiations with Italy. An alliance with Italy would confirm Beneš' contentions that he wished to remain equally friendly with Great Britain, France and Italy, and that no Great Power would be permitted to exercise domination over the Little Entente.[63] While Masaryk went to Taormina, Sicily, for his vacation, Beneš went to Rome, where, on May 15, he stated publicly that his objective was to negotiate with Mussolini an agreement that would guarantee the preservation of the status quo, promote the maintenance of order in Central Europe, assure Italo-Czechoslovak cooperation in time of war and enable both states to use the port of Fiume to their mutual economic advantage.[64] The text of the new

[61] *Ibid.*, May 19, 1924; *Národní Listy*, May 18, 1924; Machray, *op. cit.*, p. 241.

[62] *The Times*, May 10, 15, and 17, 1924.

[63] *Corriere della Sera*, May 18, 1924.

[64] *Ibid.*, May 16, 1924; *cf.* also, Currey, *op. cit.*, pp. 129-130.

treaty was drafted [65] on May 18 and approved by Masaryk two days later.[66]   It was signed on July 5,[67] ratified by Italy on July 10 [68] and by Czechoslovakia on July 17.[69]   Ratifications were exchanged in Rome on August 21.[70]

The treaty was brief: in Article 1 the signatories promised to cooperate in safeguarding their common interests; in Article 2, to maintain the Treaties of St. Germain, Trianon, and Neuilly; in Article 3, to limit the treaty to five years, with the mutual right of either denunciation or renewal one year prior to expiration; and, in Article 4, to register the document with the League of Nations.[71]   Of these terms, Article 2 is of particular interest in that Beneš conceded Mussolini a guarantee of the Treaty of Neuilly, a commitment which he had refused Yugoslavia.   Although Beneš has not expressed himself publicly upon this point, he may have felt that the friendship of Yugoslavia was assured sufficiently without any such guarantee, whereas that of Italy, which, with that of France, he regarded as the absolute minimum requirement for the adequate security of Czechoslovakia, would not be assured without such a commitment. Moreover, the Treaty of Neuilly was only of secondary importance to Italy, whereas an Italian guarantee of the three Peace Treaties, particularly those of St. Germain and Trianon, was most important to Czechoslovakia.   Beneš' own comments were as follows:

Our country is rich and prosperous and we therefore have everything to lose and nothing to gain by any change.   The

[65] *The New York Times*, May 18, 1924.

[66] *Ibid.*, May 20, 21, 1924.

[67] *Prager Presse*, July 6, 1924.

[68] *Corriere della Sera*, July 11, 1924.

[69] *Prager Presse*, July 18, 1924.

[70] *Corriere della Sera*, August 22, 1924.

[71] *Treaty Series*, vol. xxvi, pp. 21-25.

object of my policy, therefore, has been to consolidate our present position by working hard to create a network of treaties around Czechoslovakia to guarantee her against any setting aside of the existing Peace Treaties which lay down her independence and status.

With our membership in the Little Entente on the one hand and our treaties with France and Italy we now feel safe, as we consider that peace in Central Europe is assured.[72]

In view of the rivalry between Italy and France, the Italo-Czechoslovak treaty was perhaps even more welcome to Mussolini than to Beneš, for it reestablished within Central Europe a sort of equilibrium between the two rival Great Powers. When Mussolini had come to power, the Little Entente had been friendly to France and distinctly hostile to Italy. Italian distrust of its ultimate objectives had been aggravated by the conclusion of the Franco-Czechoslovak alliance. In response, Mussolini had concluded with Yugoslavia the " Pact of Rome " which had eased the main sources of friction between the two states, and had followed this initial diplomatic triumph with a loan to Poland and the Italo-Czechoslovak alliance. Italian influence in Central Europe had been strengthened to an extent where it almost counter-balanced that of France, and, not yet content, Mussolini proceeded to sound out Rumania also.[73] Nevertheless, Czechoslovakia's alliance with Italy was not as close as that with France.

The Praha and Ljubljana Conferences

Beneš continued to welcome suggestions that might provide additional safeguards for the preservation of the status quo. At the Little Entente Conference of Praha, July 11-

[72] *The New York Times*, May 18, 1924; *cf.* also, *Prager Presse*, June 23, 1925, for Beneš' general statement on foreign policy concerning the French and Italian alliances.

[73] *The New York Times*, May 18, 1924.

12, 1924, he not only discussed with his colleagues, Ninčič and Duca, current problems, such as a unified attitude regarding debts, reparations and cooperation with the League of Nations, but advocated the eventual admission to the League of Germany, whose absence, together with that of the Soviet Union, he believed a menace to general security and disarmament. At the same time he deplored the ignorance or ill-will of those who were engaged in disseminating rumors that predicted an impending dissolution of the Little Entente.[74]

As the result of a political upheaval in Yugoslavia, Pašič was succeeded as Prime Minister by Davidovič, and Ninčič as Foreign Minister by Marinkovič. Beneš took advantage of his journey to Geneva to attend the meeting of the League Council on August 27, 1924, to tarry for a few hours at Ljubljana to confer with Marinkovič. On the next day, Duca also arrived at Ljubljana. The two sets of conversations concerned primarily the U.S.S.R., with regard to which the three partners again agreed to disagree: Rumania opposed Soviet recognition de jure until the question of Bessarabia should be solved; Yugoslavia failed to express any decided opinion; and Beneš alone was willing to grant recognition, which even he conceded to be premature in view of the existing state of public opinion within the three countries.[75]

The Geneva Protocol

The Treaty of Mutual Assistance failed of adoption, primarily because of the opposition of Great Britain to a universal agreement. Beneš was entrusted by the Third Com-

[74] *The Times*, July 4, 11 and 14, 1924; *Le Temps*, July 13-14, 1924; *Deutsche Allgemeine Zeitung*, July 15, 1924; Cosma, *op. cit.*, pp. 118-123; Machray, *op. cit.*, pp. 242-247; Codresco, *op. cit.*, vol. i, pp. 309-313.

[75] Toynbee, *op. cit.*, pp. 452-453; Machray, *op. cit.*, pp. 248-250; Codresco, *op. cit.*, vol. i, pp. 315-318; *cf.* also, Miller, D. H., *The Geneva Protocol* (New York, 1925).

mittee of the League Assembly with the formulation of a project which would meet the objections of London. The result of the labors of many statesmen, particularly of Beneš, Politis (Greece), Herriot and MacDonald, was a resolution of September 6, 1924, which developed into the Geneva Protocol that sought to facilitate both the limitation and the reduction of armaments as provided by Article 8 of the League Covenant by ensuring the security of each state through a peaceful solution of every international dispute. By means of compulsory arbitration, clear definition of an aggressor in future conflicts, and of provisions for sanctions and alliances, all aggressive wars were to be prevented.[76]

On October 28, 1924, Czechoslovakia became the first state to ratify the Geneva Protocol.[77]   This procedure was in conformity with two principles of foreign policy which Beneš had steadfastly pursued: to ensure the security of the state by Czechoslovakia's power and by means of defensive treaties which had been negotiated under the auspices of the League, and to seize every possible opportunity to further universal guarantees of peace, also preferably under the same auspices.   He regarded the new negotiations as a confirmation of the correctness of the general trend of his own foreign policy, for now even the policy of regional agreements, which had been the object of marked criticism, met with approval.   Beneš promised that his foreign policy would continue to follow these principles not only because they were ethically just and expressive of mankind's highest moral ideals, but because, from the viewpoint of practical politics, they had been, and would always continue to be, the best source of security for a state like Czechoslovakia.[78]

[76] *Monthly Summary*, October, 1924, supplement, pp. 1-35.

[77] *Official Journal*, November, 1924, pp. 1662-1663.

[78] *Zprávy* (Poslanecká Sněmovna), 294 meeting, October 30, 1924, pp. 16 *et seq.*, 10 session; *ibid.*, Senát, 231 meeting, November 4, 1924,

Nevertheless, the Geneva Protocol was also doomed by the action of Great Britain, which, both at the meetings of the League Council at Rome in December, 1924, and at Geneva in March, 1925, was the first in rejecting its principles.[79] Without the adherence of Great Britain, no general protocol would be worth while, hence her rejection was fatal.

Locarno

Although Beneš was profoundly disappointed because of the failure of the Geneva Protocol,[80] in the framing of which he had played an important part, he did not indulge in any vain regrets; rather, he sought to utilize the regular Conference of the Little Entente during 1925 for the purpose of sounding his partners regarding their attitudes towards the security negotiations then taking place between the Western Powers and Germany.[81]   The regular annual meeting of the Little Entente had been planned at Bucharest originally for March 15-20, 1925,[82] but was postponed at the request

pp. 26 et seq., 10 session; 232 meeting, November 5, 1924, pp. 95 et seq., 10 session; Beneš, The Diplomatic Struggle for European Security and the Stabilization of Peace, pp. 24-27; Five Years of Czechoslovak Foreign Policy, pp. 30-34; Problemy nové Evropy, pp. 299-303; Boj o mír (speech of October 30, 1924), pp. 268-300; cf. also, International Conciliation, September, 1925, pp. 19-21; Arbitration, Security and Reduction of Armaments (extracts from the debates of the Fifth Assembly, reports and resolutions of the Assembly and Council), pp. 210-216 for Beneš' report and the ensuing discussion; Arbitration and Security.

[79] Cf. The Times, March 13, 1925, for the speech of Sir Austen Chamberlain, the British Foreign Secretary, against the Protocol. This speech is reprinted also in International Conciliation, September, 1925, pp. 25-35. Cf. also, ibid., pp. 36-43, for the reply of MacDonald, the former British Prime Minister, April 10, 1925. For further details, cf. also, Toynbee, op. cit., pp. 36-64.

[80] Official Journal, April, 1925, p. 454.

[81] Cf. Chmelář, J., " Československá zahraniční politika v roce 1925 ", Zahraniční Politika, vol. v, pp. 1-7.

[82] Deutsche Allgemeine Zeitung, February 22, 1925.

of Yugoslavia,[83] and did not actually meet until May 9-11. At that time, the three Foreign Ministers discussed the problems of the day. By mutual agreement, the Russian question was omitted. Czechoslovakia did not share the interest of her partners in Bulgarian outrages. All three states favored a continuation of the existing method of Austrian reconstruction, and, as a result of a statement of Premier Bethlen of Hungary regarding the injustice of the Treaty of Trianon, a statement which the Little Entente considered deliberately provocative, united in a protest against any change in the status quo.[84] Beneš was particularly pleased that his colleagues regretted the failure of the Geneva Protocol and approved his various security negotiations;[85] confident of their support, he could deal with the Great Powers with much more assurance.

Germany s Foreign Minister, Stresemann, wished to collaborate in the negotiations, for the problem of security concerned his country as much as it did the victor states.[86] This opinion was embodied in the German memoire of February 9, 1925, which suggested a special guaranty pact for the West, that was to be coupled, simultaneously, with a series of arbitration treaties with Germany's neighbors to the East.[87]

[83] *Corriere della Sera*, March 19, 1925.

[84] *The Central European Observer*, May 15, 1925.

[85] *Cf.* Machray, *op. cit.*, pp. 259-265; Codresco, *op. cit.*, vol. i, pp. 319-331; Cosma, *op. cit.*, pp. 123-142; Toynbee, *op. cit.*, 1925, pp. 250-255; *L'Europe nouvelle*, May 23, 1925.

[86] *Cf.* Beneš, *The Diplomatic Struggle for European Security and the Stabilisation of Peace*, pp. 14-19, for a summary of earlier German proposals.

[87] *Papers respecting the Proposals for a Pact of Security made by the German Government on February 9, 1925*, Miscellaneous no. 7 (His Majesty's Stationery Office) ; *Neuf pièces relatives à la proposition faite le 9 février, 1925, par le Gouvernement allemand et la réponse du Gouvernement française* (République Française, Ministère des Affaires Étrangères).

Few diplomatic secrets were ever preserved more faithfully than were these German proposals, which became eventually the Locarno agreements. Had they been disclosed prematurely, the general reaction might have been so violent within every state concerned that the chances for ultimate success might have been severely jeopardized. The six weeks of uncertainty to which the press was subjected produced many false rumors that were of service in warning the public that general security negotiations were under way, so that, when the facts were published, the ground had been prepared for their favorable reception.[88]

France and Great Britain, followed by Belgium, Italy, Poland and Czechoslovakia, announced their adherence to the general principles of the German proposals. On April 1, 1925, Beneš informed Chamberlain, the British Foreign Secretary, of the viewpoint of Czechoslovakia, which still continued to regard the Geneva Protocol as the best solution of the problem of security. However, Czechoslovakia agreed " to examine the German proposals and arbitration treaties as a certain advance in the universal work of peace ". Before assuming any definite stand, she wished to satisfy herself as to the exact meaning of the memoire and its attendant arbitration treaties. She considered it essential that the proposed guaranty pact must not encroach upon the Peace Treaties in any way, that it should inaugurate a new period of peace which was to be supplemented by the admission of Germany into the League, and that it must lead eventually " to a guaranty pact which would be universal, or at least European, in scope ". Except for such reservations, Czechoslovakia accepted the German offer, particularly since she could lose nothing by such action. According to Beneš, Herriot, the French Prime Minister, approved these reservations in toto. This reserved attitude on the part of Czechoslovakia was

[88] *Cf.* D'Abernon, *op. cit.*, vol. i, pp. 5-6.

motivated in part by the election of Von Hindenburg as President of the German Reich on April 26, 1925, an event which was interpreted by many Czechoslovaks as a part of a general undercurrent of reaction against the status quo within the vanquished states.[89]   Thereupon, at Geneva, Beneš, Briand, Hymans of Belgium and Skrzynski of Poland agreed to examine the German proposals.[90]

As soon as Great Britain, France, Belgium, Italy, Poland and Czechoslovakia had agreed upon a common policy, they sent Germany two notes of June 16 and August 24 which laid down as essential to any agreement the following principles:

(1) Germany and France agreed to respect the territorial status quo and the Treaty of Versailles, and also the agreements made to secure its application, as well as to repudiate all recourse to force or to war against one another.

(2) Both parties recognize the demilitarization and inviolability of the Rhine frontier.   Exceptional cases whereby it would be possible for military forces to violate this frontier will be determined in a definite manner.

(3) Great Britain, and eventually Italy, will guarantee the arrangements made.

(4) Germany will enter the League of Nations and assume the rights and obligations of a Member.

(5) Germany will draw up arbitration treaties with her neighbors; France will guarantee those with Poland and Czechoslovakia.[91]

---

[89] *Ibid.*, vol. iii, pp. 160-161.

[90] Beneš, *op. cit.*, pp. 21-23.

[91] *Reply of the German Government to the note handed to Herr Stresemann by the French Ambassador at Berlin on June 16, 1925, respecting the Proposals for a Pact of Security*, Miscellaneous, no. 9 (His Majesty's Stationery Office).

The negotiations lasted eight months.[92] Czechoslovakia and Poland objected to Article 15, paragraph 7 of the Covenant, which left them with inadequate security whenever the League Council failed to reach a unanimous verdict in any dispute. The Conference of Locarno, held October 5-16, 1925, attempted to meet these objections by separate treaties between France and Poland, and France and Czechoslovakia, whereby mutual aid was to be given immediately in all cases of unprovoked attack. Although Poland regarded this arrangement still inadequate, Czechoslovakia approved it as the best compromise that could be obtained. On the other hand, Germany abandoned her initial opposition to a French guarantee of her arbitration treaties with Poland and Czechoslovakia, and consented that they be identical with those with France and Belgium. Germany's views, together with her entry into the League and a com-

[92] The following newspaper references cover the most important of the negotiations prior to Locarno: French note of June 16 replying to the German note of February 9, *Le Temps*, June 18, *The New York Times*, June 19; Chamberlain's speech in the House of Commons, *The Times*, *The New York Times*, June 25; German acceptance of the note as a basis for negotiations, *Vossische Zeitung*, *Le Temps*, June 28; House of Lords' debate, *The Times*, *The New York Times*, July 7; the German reply to the French note of June 16, *The New York Times*, July 20 and 22; Stresemann's speech to the Reichstag, *Vorwaerts*, *Vossische Zeitung*, *Deutsche Allgemeine Zeitung*, *The Times*, *The New York Times*, July 23; the German note of July 20, *The Times*, July 22, *Le Temps*, July 23, *L'Europe nouvelle*, September 12; the French reply of August 24, *The Times*, *The New York Times*, August 27, *Le Temps*, August 28, *L'Europe nouvelle*, September 12; the German reply of August 27, *The Times*, *The New York Times*, August 29, *Le Temps*, August 30, *L'Europe nouvelle*, September 12; Briand-Chamberlain pourparlers, *The New York Times*, August 13; London meeting of experts, *The Times*, September 1, 2, 5 and 7; French invitation to a conference, *Le Temps*, September 18; German acceptance, *The Times*, September 25; German note of September 26, *Le Temps*, September 30; British note of September 29, *The Times*, *The New York Times*, September 30, *Le Temps*, October 1; the French note of September 29, *Le Temps*, October 1.

promise on Article 16 of the Covenant, were to be stipulated in the Rhine pact in a manner more agreeable to Germany.[93]

On October 16, 1925, the Locarno Protocol was initialed: [94]

(1) The Rhine Guaranty Pact, among Germany, France, Great Britain, Italy and Belgium; [95]

(2) Four Arbitration Treaties between Germany and Belgium,[96] France,[97] Poland,[98] and Czechoslovakia; [99] and

(3) French treaties of guaranty with Poland [100] and Czechoslovakia.[101]

By the terms of the Germano-Czechoslovak Arbitration Treaty, for which negotiations had begun as early as Sep-

[93] Disarmed Germany sought to safeguard herself from becoming a battle-field in the event of the League taking action against some other state. Similarly, she tried to avert the possibility of French troops using her territory as a means of transit to aid Poland in case of a war with the U. S. S. R. *Cf.* Langsam, W. C., *The World since 1914* (3 ed., New York, 1936), p. 482, note.

[94] *Documents signés ou paraphés à Locarno le 16 octobre, 1925, précédés de six pièces relatives aux négociations préliminaires* (République Française, Ministère des Affaires Étrangères); *Monthly Summary*, vol. v, pp. 1-24, supplement, December, 1925; *Final Protocol of the Locarno Conference* (London, His Majesty's Stationery Office, 1925); *Final Protocol of the Locarno Conference, 1925, and treaties between France and Poland and France and Czechoslovakia* (New York, Carnegie Endowment for International Peace).

[95] The signatories "collectively and severally" guaranteed the territorial and military *status quo* in the Rhineland as determined by the Treaty of Versailles. They also agreed to settle all questions peaceably and not to resort to war against each other except in a few clearly-defined possibilities where such action would meet with the approval of the League of Nations. *Cf. Treaty Series*, vol. liv, pp. 289-301.

[96] *Ibid.*, vol. liv, pp. 303-313.

[97] *Ibid.*, vol. liv, pp. 315-325.

[98] *Ibid.*, vol. liv, pp. 327-339.

[99] *Ibid.*, vol. liv, pp. 341-351.

[100] *Ibid.*, vol. liv, pp. 353-357.

[101] *Ibid.*, vol. liv, pp. 359-363.

tember 21, 1925,[102] the way was prepared for a policy of conciliation before recourse was to be had to judiciary procedure, should the two states so desire. Questions of the first category (juridical) were obliged to be submitted to an especially created Permanent Conciliation Commission of five members, of which each state would appoint one and consult regarding the other three, who were to be from three different states. If the two parties could not agree upon this agency, the question might be submitted to the Permanent Court of International Justice or to a special arbitral tribunal, under the Hague Convention.

For questions of the second category (political), negotiations of conciliation were also obligatory. By Article 17, such questions devolved upon the Permanent Conciliation Commission. If not settled within one month after the completion of the work of this Commission, they would be presented for solution to the League Council according to Article 15 of the Covenant. However, these two methods of conciliation and judgment were not applicable:

(1) To questions provided for by other Agreements (i. e. minorities, etc., which were already provided for by the League).

(2) To questions which originated from events which antedated the present Treaty and which were covered by the Covenant (i. e. old disputes could not be revived).

(3) To questions in which the subject of dispute, after internal legislation in one country, was released from the jurisdiction of its national tribunals, so that the competent juridical authority had not rendered a decision upon it.

Article 19 of the Arbitration Treaties conferred upon the agencies mentioned (Arbitral Tribunal, League Council and Commission of Conciliation) the right to take provisional

[102] *The Times*, September 22, 1925.

measures to hinder any modification of the status quo. Much importance was attached to this point. Parties in a dispute were offered substitutes for hasty procedure which ordinarily made matters worse. The fact that old disputes alone were excluded from peaceful settlement gave some assurance that the disputants would not resort to war. Nevertheless, as Beneš has pointed out, it should be noted that, for one frontier, Germany had concluded a guaranty pact, and, for the others, merely arbitration treaties. This action was due to the fact that, except for France, no Great Power was willing to assume the guarantee of any except the western frontier.[103] Also, according to Beneš' interpretation, by Article 21 of the Germano-Czechoslovak Arbitration Treaty, each state retained the rights and privileges of a Member of the League, a provision which supplemented Article 10 of the Covenant, whereby each had agreed to respect the political independence and territorial integrity of the other. In the event of war, Czechoslovakia would invoke against Germany Articles 15 (paragraph 7) and 16 of the Covenant.[104]

France's reciprocal guarantees with Poland and Czechoslovakia were motivated also by the desire to approach as closely as possible the Rhine Guaranty Pact in the matter of the German frontiers to the East. In the case of Czechoslovakia, the new treaty was designed to revise and supplement the Franco-Czechoslovak Treaty of Alliance and the new Arbitration Treaties. Beneš assumed that if a dispute would come up between Czechoslovakia and Germany, in which Czechoslovakia accepted the arbitral decision but Germany did not and began hostilities, or if the League

---

[103] Beneš, *Les Accords de Locarno* (exposé of October 30, 1925), pp. 15-16.

[104] *Ibid.*, p. 16. These parts of the Covenant specified the sanctions that League members were to apply against any aggressor.

Council could not decide unanimously a question submitted to it for settlement, war would be permissible. Beneš felt that both possibilities were met by Article 1 of the Czecho-slovak Guaranty Treaty with France, wherein each party became the sole judge of whether a casus foederis had arisen. Since by Article 2 of the Rhine Guaranty Pact, the passage of the Rhine was permitted in certain specially cited cases only (thereby rendering more difficult the extension of French aid to Poland and Czechoslovakia) and since those cases were the only ones, after the signing of the Treaty of Locarno, in which Czechoslovakia would be in any danger of war, his inference was that the Guaranty Treaty with France was intended only for such special cases.[105]

In the estimation of Beneš, the acts of Locarno constituted an indivisible whole, materially as well as juridically; they were based on the same ideas and pursued the same ends. All entered into effect at the same time, and were to end simultaneously under the same conditions (Articles 8 and 10 of the Rhine Guaranty Pact, Article 22 of the Germano-Czechoslovak Arbitration Treaty and Article 4 of the Czechoslovak Guaranty Treaty with France). Becoming valid when Germany entered the League, they were not lim-ited as to duration, but might be abrogated one year after the League Council, by a two-thirds vote, would decide that the League assured the contracting parties sufficient guar-antees. They could not be denounced by any one of the contracting parties.[106]

Of greater significance than the mere terms of the pact was the spirit evinced at Locarno—a cooperative feeling that all must unite to safeguard the peace of Western Europe. Its importance lay in the fact that the basic principles of the Geneva Protocol were applied successfully in the Rhineland

[105] *Ibid.*, pp. 18-20.
[106] *Ibid.*, pp. 21-22.

area to allay whatever future danger might develop from resentment in Germany over the Treaty of Versailles, which had deprived her of approximately twelve per cent of her European territory and which had left her with unsatisfactory frontiers. The victor states realized that German military impotence was temporary, and sought to ensure themselves against a renewal of German strength. To this end, Locarno seemed a favorable adjustment. To Germany it signified that, rather than continue to consider her a permanent outcast, the Allies welcomed her again within the Concert of Europe; she would enter the League, and, as a token of recognition as a Great Power, would receive a permanent seat on the Council. France would attain her long-sought-for security, but in a manner which promised to promote a rapprochement with Germany rather than perpetuate a coalition against her. Locarno embodied the British principle of seeking to ensure Franco-German peace without assuming dangerous commitments, such as an anti-German alliance or a guarantee of the frontiers of the small Allied states of Central and Eastern Europe, whereas it still afforded adequate security for Poland and Czechoslovakia. Despite the obvious fact that such an agreement did not mean necessarily the end of war, it was indubitably a step of great moral significance. As such, it was one happy result of the long search for security, in that it greatly enhanced both the prestige and the power of the League by arranging for the future admission of Germany, and by providing for the extension of some of the League's major principles to one of the most dangerous threats to the peace and security of the whole Continent.[107]

[107] Cf. ibid., pp. 22-28; also, Fenwick, C. G., " The Legal Significance of the Locarno Agreements ", *The American Journal of International Law*, vol. xx, pp. 108-111, 1926; Krčmář, J., " Přispěvky k výkladu o ocenění locarnských smluv ", *Zahraniční Politika*, vol. iv, pp. 1334-1355.

Upon the termination of the Conference of Locarno, Beneš sent Masaryk a telegram to the effect that all Czechoslovakia's security objectives had been attained.[108]   A week later, in a speech of October 30, 1925, before the Parliamentary Permanent Committee, Beneš explained in great detail how the Locarno agreements embodied the ideals for which the foreign policy of Czechoslovakia had been striving for seven years, how the Rhine Guaranty Pact constituted an indirect guarantee for Czechoslovakia also, and predicted that Czechoslovakia's relations with Germany would enter a more cordial phase.   He also ventured the incorrect prediction that Locarno would hasten the solution of the Russian question by the conclusion of a series of treaties between the U.S.S.R. and the rest of Europe on the same model.   Of greatest interest, perhaps, was his stress upon the word " immediate " in paragraphs 1 and 2 of Article 1 of the French Treaty of Guaranty, whereby neither party had to wait any procedure, but could and would proceed without delay with measures for mutual assistance in any emergency that might arise under Article 15, paragraph 7, or Article 16 of the League Covenant.   To quote Beneš, " Our former Treaty with France thus acquires an entirely new character without losing any of its old effectiveness ".   To clinch his point, he brought out the fact that Article 2 of the Guaranty Treaty permitted France to cross the Rhine in all cases wherein Czechoslovakia would be in danger of being attacked by Germany.[109]

The 1925 Guaranty Treaty did go further than the 1924 Franco-Czechoslovak alliance in pledging aid—" immediate " assistance was more effective than agreement as to " common action " or to " measures to be taken ".   The new agreement

---

[108] *The Central European Observer*, October 23, 1925.

[109] *La Gazette de Prague*, October 31, 1925; *The Central European Observer*, November 6, 1925; Beneš, E., *Les Accords de Locarno*.

did not pretend to cover as many possibilities as the earlier treaty. Its specific nature against Germany—the one probable threat that the Little Entente was not sufficiently strong to meet—more than compensated Czechoslovakia for any objections that might be made.

Except for the German minority, Beneš encountered little parliamentary opposition to his security negotiations with the Western Powers. The German deputies denounced as insincere Beneš' statement that the alliance with France was a necessary prelude to a genuine understanding in the West and that a Franco-German rapprochement must precede one between Germany and Czechoslovakia,[110] but the various Czech and Slovak parties renewed their expressions of confidence in Beneš. Thus supported, he carried the security negotiations to a successful conclusion. On October 16, at Locarno, Beneš signed the Treaty of Arbitration with Germany and the Treaty of Guaranty with France.[111] These two treaties were ratified by Czechoslovakia on February 28, 1926,[112] and the ratifications were registered with the League of Nations on September 14, 1926.[113]

Beneš took advantage of his homeward journey from Locarno to confer at Bled with Nincic who had again become Yugoslavia's Foreign Minister. The latter expressed satisfaction with the results of Locarno and agreed that Rumania should be informed of their point of view.[114] As a result, the attitude of Czechoslovakia was adopted by both of her partners.[115]

---

[110] *Zprávy* (Poslanecká Sněmovna), 284 meeting, October 7, 1925, pp. 551-552 and 557-559, 11 session; *ibid.*, 287 meeting, October 13, 1925, pp. 620-629, 11 session.

[111] *Prager Presse*, October 17, 1925.

[112] *Ibid.*, March 1, 1926.   [113] *Ibid.*, September 15, 1926.

[114] *Le Temps*, October 22, 1925.

[115] *Cf. Prager Presse*, December 19, 1925, for the official statement of the policy of the Švehla government; also, D'Abernon, *op. cit.*, vol. iii, p. 194.

Security to the East

Although the Locarno agreements and membership in the Little Entente provided apparently an adequate guarantee for the immediate safety of Czechoslovakia, Beneš did not remain content, but attempted to maintain a parallel line of negotiations regarding security to the East. Ever an optimist with regard to the future of relations with Moscow, Beneš welcomed the suggestion of the Soviet representative at Praha, in October, 1924, for a newer and more satisfactory Soviet-Czechoslovak commercial treaty. This initial sounding produced no immediate results, for the question of commercial relations between the two countries soon became subordinated to that of de jure recognition.[116] Approximately two months later Beneš, in the Congress of the Czechoslovak Social Democratic Party, stated his belief that the time had arrived for according the U.S.S.R. de jure recognition.[117] This announcement aroused immediate protests from army circles, from the Agrarian Party, and from Kramář, who staged with Beneš a heated debate before the Foreign Affairs Committee of the Chamber of Deputies. Beneš attempted to defend his stand by stating his belief that the Soviet government was not supporting the propaganda of the Third International. He pointed out that the establishment of diplomatic " normalcy " would not only be opportune, but would prove to be no hindrance in counteracting domestic communist propaganda.[118] In spite of this plea, a majority still continued to oppose immediate recognition, a fact which went far in explaining Beneš' later cautious Soviet policy.[119]

[116] Toynbee, *op. cit.*, 1924, p. 259.

[117] *Prager Presse*, December 16, 1924.

[118] *Ibid.*, *Národní Listy* and *Národní Politika*, December 15-21, 1924.

[119] For full details of the political situation within Czechoslovakia and its influence upon foreign policy, *cf.* Chmelář, J., *Political Parties in Czechoslovakia* (Prague, 1926). For Kramář vs. communism, *cf. Zprávy*

Undeterred by his failure to arrive at a better understanding with the Soviet Union, Beneš continued his search for security to the East by persevering in his hitherto unsuccessful attempts to effect a rapprochement with Poland. As has already been narrated,[120] the numerous interests that Czechoslovakia and Poland had in common had been overshadowed by their disputes over boundaries and their divergent policies regarding the Soviet Union. As a result, in spite of the common tie of mutual treaties with France, the cooperation between Poland on the one hand, and Czechoslovakia and the Little Entente as a whole on the other, had been spasmodic and uncertain. It remained for the year 1924 to furnish renewed indications of a bettering of relations.[121] The last boundary dispute, that of Javorina, was finally decided on May 6 by a conference at Cracow, which also drew up a protocol permitting freedom of movement for the local population, for tourists and for foodstuffs.[122] In October, at Geneva, the two Foreign Ministers, Beneš and Skrzynski, prepared a comprehensive program for a general understanding upon all questions in dispute,[123] as a result of which direct negotiations for a new commercial treaty were inaugurated in Warsaw during November.[124]

Prior to the German proposals of February 9, 1925, which resulted ultimately in the Locarno agreements, Poland had apparently underestimated the dangers to which she might be exposed at the hands of a revived Germany, which would,

(Poslanecká Sněmovna), 5 meeting, December 19, 1925, pp. 136-142, 1 session.

[120] *Cf. supra*, pp. 148 *et seq.*

[121] *Cf. Gazeta Warszawska* article of March 17, 1924, denouncing "those who desired to continue Czechoslovak-Polish friction".

[122] *Treaty Series*, vol. xlviii, pp. 397-423.

[123] *Le Temps*, October 17, 1924.

[124] *Ibid.*, November 27, 1924.

in all probability, seek to abolish the Corridor and regain her lost areas in Upper Silesia and in Posen. Poland's unfortunate position between the two millstones, Germany and the Soviet Union, combined with her own land-hunger which had antagonized both, had placed her in a quandary. In view of her relatively greater feeling of hostility towards the U.S.S.R., she had hitherto stressed the differences rather than the similarities between her own foreign policy and that of Czechoslovakia. To Poland, both Moscow and Berlin represented menaces of the first magnitude, whereas to Czechoslovakia, Germany alone was a threat, but one which represented a danger that was much less imminent. On the other hand, Czechoslovakia's fears regarding Hungary were of no concern to Poland, which had been traditionally on good terms with the Magyars. Before 1925, Poland had felt secure in her French and Rumanian alliances, and had even attempted to play the Soviets and Germany against one another to her own advantage. However, the Locarno negotiations opened the eyes of Poland to a new possibility: what if the Soviets offered France an alliance? Might not France prefer the stronger ally and leave Poland isolated? Would not ordinary prudence dictate closer ties with both France and Czechoslovakia, and indicate an inclusion in the Locarno agreements of some further guarantee of Germany's eastern frontiers in order to counteract any changes in France's eastern treaty obligations which might develop from a Western European Security Pact? [125] As a result, the Polish negotiations for a rapprochement with Czechoslovakia received a fresh impetus, and a special conference for railway problems was arranged. [126]

The satisfactory progress that was being made in the negotiations with Poland was announced to the Senate Foreign

[125] *Cf.* D'Abernon, *op. cit.*, vol. iii, p. 45.

[126] *Le Temps*, March 2, 1925.

Affairs Committee on April 1, 1925, by Beneš who considered the imminent rapprochement most important " in view of the fact that it means the definite liquidation of all the disputes which have existed between the two countries and the opening of a new period of friendly relations between the two states ".[127] Six days later a provisional commercial and tariff agreement became effective.[128] To conclude the negotiations, Beneš undertook a journey to Warsaw, where he arrived on April 20, and where, three days later, he signed three treaties that confirmed the rapprochement.[129]

The first treaty, which was termed a " liquidation convention ", specified detailed regulations regarding the financial, juridical and minority questions that were still outstanding as a result of the partitions of Těšin, Spíš and Orava,[130] and was relatively easy to negotiate.

Similarly, the third treaty, a lengthy commercial agreement, was easily consummated. It conceded a reciprocal most-favored-nation status, comprehensive reciprocal tariff reductions, and mutually favorable railroad rates. Poland could export freely, across Czechoslovakia, coal to the rest of Central Europe, a region wherein lay several of her best customers, and Czechoslovakia could export her manufactured goods across Poland to the U.S.S.R. There was appended, as an annex, a veterinary convention which was intended to protect Czechoslovakia from the importation of diseased cattle.[131]

It proved more difficult to reach an agreement upon the second and most important treaty, that of conciliation and

[127] *Prager Tagblatt*, April 2, 1925; *The Central European Observer, Svornost*, April 3, 1925.

[128] *Treaty Series*, vol. lvi, pp. 285-289.

[129] *Cf.* Toynbee, *op. cit.*, 1925, vol. ii, pp. 247-250; *L'Europe nouvelle*, May 2, 1925.

[130] *Treaty Series*, vol. xlviii, pp. 287-381.

[131] *Ibid.*, vol. lviii, pp. 9-95.

arbitration. Except for problems arising from territorial disputes or for those for which another procedure had already been prescribed, all other questions which could not be settled by the ordinary diplomatic methods within a reasonable time were to be submitted to conciliation first and then to arbitration, unless, according to Article 1, the latter method was preferred initially. Article 3 specified that, within six months after ratification, the two states agreed to create a permanent Conciliation Commission of five members, one from each state, one selected by each state from a third state, and the president being a neutral nominated by mutual consent. If no agreement could be reached, the President of the Swiss Federal Council was to name the president. Articles 12 and 13 laid down respectively six and three months as the periods within which the Commission was to report its findings and the disputants were to indicate whether they accepted its decision. If conciliation failed, Article 15 provided for a special arbitral tribunal. As an alternative, Article 17 permitted a resort to the Permanent Court of International Justice. In either event, Article 21 specified that the decision would be binding for both disputants. Of interest also was Article 23 which stated specifically that the treaty did not modify in any respect the Geneva Protocol, assuming that the latter would ever become effective. Article 25 fixed the duration of the treaty at five years, beginning thirty days after the exchange of ratifications. A supplementary protocol stated that it was not necessary to create any body competent to cope with territorial differences, since such differences could be terminated only by mutual agreement.[132]

[132] *Zprávy* (Senát), 282 meeting, October 1, 1925, pp. 522-528, 11 session; *ibid.* (Poslanecká Sněmovna), 365 meeting, September 29, 1925, pp. 712-717, 11 session; *Treaty Series*, vol. xlviii, pp. 383-395.

Before the treaty of conciliation and arbitration was ratified, Czechoslovakia and Poland signed two additional treaties to cement further their rapprochement. The treaty of May 30, 1925, eliminated many obstacles that had heretofore retarded tourist traffic,[133] and, similarly, the sanitary convention of September 5, 1925, terminated much of the frontier friction between the respective medical authorities.[134]

The treaty of conciliation and arbitration was finally ratified on April 14, 1926, when Skrzynski visited Praha to return the visit that Beneš had paid Warsaw the year before. The former took pains to be unusually cordial and stated publicly their "absolute agreement" upon all political problems.[135] Apparently, the substitution of friendship for friction was welcome to both Slav states.[136] Nevertheless, Polish foreign policy remained unchanged in other respects. Poland still held aloof from too intimate contacts with the Little Entente by preserving neutrality regarding Hungary in response to a "correct" Little Entente attitude towards the Soviet Union.[137] Upon the vital questions of security and a common policy regarding the eastern frontiers of Germany—Poland and Czechoslovakia cooperated to the fullest extent. Beneš was particularly happy over the rapprochement, which in his estimation gave the finishing touch to his search for security by extending after a fashion the spirit of Locarno to the East and ensuring for Czechoslovakia a more secure all-around defense in any future emergency.[138]

[133] *Treaty Series*, vol. l, pp. 243-251.

[134] *Ibid.*, vol. lviii, pp. 143-177.

[135] *Cf. Prager Presse* and *The Times*, April 15, 1926.

[136] *Cf. Le Temps*, February 15, April 7 and May 16, 1925; *Gazeta Warszawska*, February 15 and May 16, 1925; *The New York Times*, April 24, 1925; *Právo Lidu*, April 24, 1925, April 15 and 16, 1926.

[137] *Cf.* Toynbee, *op. cit.*, 1926, p. 153; Machray, *op. cit.*, pp. 257-259; Codresco, *op. cit.*, vol. ii, pp. 215-228.

[138] Beneš, *The Diplomatic Struggle for European Security and the Stabilization of Peace*, pp. 28-29.

CHAPTER VI

Efforts to Maintain the New Status Quo

Commercial Treaties

The optimism generally prevalent as a result of the successful culmination of the Locarno negotiations found its reflection also within Czechoslovakia. With the apparent solution of the major problems of reconstruction and security, Beneš turned to the next phase of his foreign policy— the safeguarding of the new status quo. In the process of readjustment, there yet remained to be made many adaptations to the new environment. Beneš, always an ardent advocate of peace, was eager to do his part.

As soon as a fair degree of domestic stability had been attained, Czechoslovakia inaugurated a drive to obtain favorable commercial treaties from all her neighbors,[1] a policy that was ultimately successful, despite many obstacles. By the end of 1925, about forty commercial treaties had been negotiated. Attempts were made also to stimulate overseas trade. For a long time no treaties could be made with Latin American states because of mutual distrust, poor contacts, and tariff policies, hence the process of regaining the important pre-war traffic as middleman for coffee and colonial products was retarded. Nevertheless, during the middle 1920's Czechoslovakia's foreign trade continued to show marked gains.[2] Except for the commercial treaties

---

[1] Cf. supra, pp. 87-89.

[2] For the years 1923, 1925 and 1927, respectively, Czechoslovakia's imports amounted to 10,222,000, 17,618,000 and 17,962,000 crowns, respectively; her exports, 12,573,000, 18,821,000 and 20,135,000 crowns, respectively. Cf. Publications of the League of Nations (henceforth referred to as Publications), Economic and Financial, 1930, ii, x, p. 142.

considered in detail elsewhere, the following are the most important negotiated by Czechoslovakia: with Latvia, October 7, 1922;[3] Greece, December 28, 1922,[4] and April 8, 1925;[5] the Netherlands, January 30, 1923;[6] Great Britain, July 14, 1923;[7] Norway, October 2, 1923;[8] the United States, October 29, 1923;[9] Denmark, January 31, 1924;[10] the Irish Free State, May 8, 1924;[11] Sweden, April 18, 1925;[12] Spain, July 29, 1925,[13] and December 13, 1928;[14] Bulgaria, October 16, 1925;[15] Japan, October 30, 1925;[16] Albania, January 19, 1926;[17] Switzerland, February 16, 1927;[18] Finland, March 2, 1927;[19] Turkey, May 31, 1927;[20] Estonia, June 20, 1927;[21] and Canada, March 15, 1928.[22]

The Debt Settlement with the United States

Another important question was the settlement of Czechoslovakia's debt to the United States. Because of the economic dislocation and of a desire to obtain more lenient terms, Czechoslovakia, in common with other debtors of the United States, was in no great haste to come to a definite understanding immediately after the termination of the War. No agreement was reached until October 13, 1925. Upon that date, Czechoslovakia agreed to pay $115,000,000 in

[3] *Treaty Series*, vol. xx, pp. 379-393.

[4] *Ibid.*, vol. xxi, pp. 217-219.

[5] *Ibid.*, vol. xxxviii, pp. 291-299.   [6] *Ibid.*, vol. xxxi, pp. 85-91.

[7] *Ibid.*, vol. xxix, pp. 377-387.   [8] *Ibid.*, vol. xx, pp. 355-361.

[9] *Ibid.*, vol. lvi, pp. 271-278.   [10] *Ibid.*, vol. xxiii, pp. 139-147.

[11] *Ibid.*, vol. xlvi, pp. 419-425.   [12] *Ibid.*, vol. xxxvi, pp. 289-297.

[13] *Ibid.*, vol. lx, pp. 329-351.   [14] *Ibid.*, vol. xcviii, pp. 65-79.

[15] *Ibid.*, vol. lvi, pp. 260-269.   [16] *Ibid.*, vol. lviii, pp. 263-277.

[17] *Ibid.*, vol. lxiv, pp. 349-353.   [18] *Ibid.*, vol. lxiv, pp. 7-75.

[19] *Ibid.*, vol. lxvi, pp. 385-401.   [20] *Ibid.*, vol. lxxi, pp. 335-359.

[21] *Ibid.*, vol. lxxvii, pp. 341-357.   [22] *Ibid.*, vol. lxxxii, pp. 147-151.

principal (amount actually borrowed $91,800,000, the rest unpaid interest) and $197,811,433.88 in interest. Interest was fixed at three per cent for the first ten years and at three and one-half per cent for the next fifty-two years. For the first eighteen years the annual payments would range from $4,022,700 to $4,565,425. It was agreed also that, during this period, Czechoslovakia would pay annually only $3,000,000 and defer the rest to the nineteenth year and later. On the deferred amount, interest payments would be the same as upon the principal, three per cent for the first ten years, and three and one-half per cent thereafter. On June 15, 1943, the deferred amount was to be added to the principal and paid off in forty-four annual payments ranging from $5,879,225 to $5,884,725. This settlement, as of June 15, 1925, which spread payments over a sixty-two year period, which reduced interest payments from an original rate of five per cent, and which represented a considerable cancellation, was apparently satisfactory to both countries.[23]

The Catholic Question

If Czechoslovakia was to attain stability, it was also vitally important that she solve in some satisfactory manner the Catholic question that had vexed her since the attainment of independence. Of all the major aspects of the comprehensive policy of domestic stabilization,[24] the question of relations with the Catholic Church had made the least progress. The passage of time had increased the feeling of hostility between the Catholics and the religious radicals. The Slovak bishops went so far as to issue, on Christmas Day, 1924, a

[23] Moulton, H. G. and Pasvolsky, L., *War Debts and World Prosperity* (Washington, 1932), pp. 86-95 (*cf.* pp. 434-435 for detailed schedule of payments) ; *World War Debt Settlements* (New York, 1926), pp. 82-95; *The New York Times*, October 13, 1925 ; *Prager Presse, Národní Politika, Národní Listy*, October 14, 1925.

[24] *Cf. supra*, pp. 91 *et seq.*

pastoral letter which banned membership in anti-church organizations, a decree which was interpreted to include even the quintumvirate [25] which then maintained in power the Švehla government.[26] Masaryk delivered on New Year's Day, 1925, an address in which he stated his belief that the proposed separation of Church and State was not an indication of anti-clerical tendencies, but would result in an intensified spiritual life.[27] However, ardent Catholics remained unconvinced of the advisability of a separation.

The actual severance of diplomatic relations between Czechoslovakia and the Vatican resulted from the events of July 6, 1925. July 6, the anniversary of Hus' martyrdom at Constance, had recently been selected by the Czechoslovak parliament, without any marked political opposition, as one of the new national holidays that were to replace several old religious ones. This particular date had long been popular, for most of the Czechoslovaks, regardless of religious denomination, revered the memory of John Hus as an early anti-German patriot, and as one of the creators of the national language. Beneš was greatly surprised when the Papal Nuncio to Praha, Monsignor Marmaggi, informed him that the presence of the high officials of the Czechoslovak government at the festivities of July 6 would be interpreted as an intentional offense to the Holy See.[28]

In spite of this protest, July 6, 1925, was observed throughout the Republic with great enthusiasm. In Praha, where the Hussite flag was flown over the presidential palace, the government was represented officially by the President, the Prime Minister and other cabinet members. To Catholic protests, the government answered in a conciliatory

[25] *Cf. supra*, p. 74.
[26] *Národní Politika*, December 26, 1924.
[27] *Ibid.*, January 2, 1925.
[28] *Ibid.*, *Národní Listy*, July 3, 1925.

manner that no offense had been intended, but that the whole affair had been a purely national demonstration. It was also pointed out that its intention to participate in 1928 in the celebration of the millennial anniversary of St. Václav (Wenceslaus), the Catholic patron saint of Bohemia, should prove a sufficient indication of impartiality and of an absence of anti-Catholic tendencies.[29]

Regardless of all explanations, Marmaggi informed Beneš on July 6 that he was leaving Praha the next day in response to an order to that effect. Czechoslovakia felt compelled to recall its representative at the Vatican.[30]

The break with Rome profoundly affected the political situation within Czechoslovakia. The religious radicals, with the Socialists in the van, held several meetings whose object was to demand the abolition of the Legation at the Vatican and the immediate separation of Church and State. After the National Socialists staged a violent interpellation in parliament,[31] even the quintumvirate, hitherto almost all-powerful politically, became concerned whether it could maintain its bloc. The government, on July 19, published an official communiqué, which, while attempting to remain conciliatory, pointed out that any interference on the part of the Vatican with the internal affairs of Czechoslovakia would be inadmissible. The government denied all responsibility for the recent rupture of relations and announced that its future policy would be the maintenance of a " correct " attitude religiously. The differences between the Vatican and Czechoslovakia centered in five grievances: (1) Negotiations for a Concordat made no progress; (2) the new administrative methods sought to destroy local autonomy; (3) the policy of agrarian reform was breaking up Church prop-

29 *Národní Listy*, July 6, 1925.

30 *Ibid.*, July 6, 1925; *Prager Presse*, July 6, 7 and 9, 1925.

31 *Tisky* (Senát), no. 2211, July 8, 1925, 11 session.

erties; (4) the law for national holidays disregarded well-established Catholic anniversaries; and (5) the Nationalists and Socialists sought to control education.[32]

Even the Clerical cabinet ministers, who were personally opposed to the religious policy of the government, acquiesced, lest their withdrawal enable the radical Liberal, Socialist and Agrarian parties to enact their anti-Clerical program.[33] To avert an immediate crisis, parliament adjourned until September. Fresh fuel was added to the flames when the government, on August 12, proclaimed formally that Mariánské Lázně, famous as a spa, would henceforth be state property. The land in question had been owned by the Tepl Abbey, whose abbot, Dr. Helmer, was a prominent German nationalist; hence the action was conceived as a joint attack upon both German nationalists and supporters of the Papacy.[34] Despite the contention of the Czechoslovak government that the whole religious controversy was strictly an internal affair of the Republic, the pope, on September 23, 1925, issued a communiqué stating that he could not concede to the government of a state whose population was two-thirds Catholic a reservation of the right to offend the Holy See indefinitely.[35] The dispute led to the calling of new elections, although, normally, the Chamber of Deputies would have continued into 1926, and the Senate for another two years and a half.[36] The ensuing elections of November 15 and 22 were generally favorable to the quin-

[32] Ibid., no. 2212, September 14, 1925, 11 session, points out that the text of the communiqué was issued to all Praha newspapers on July 19 and that these are to be regarded as official sources. The communiqué is also reprinted in Bernus, P., "Le Gouvernement tchèque et le Vatican", Le Journal des débats, vol. xxxii, pt. 2, pp. 130-131.

[33] Národní Listy, July 19, 1925.

[34] Prager Presse, August 12, 1925.

[35] Národní Politika, September 24, 1925.

[36] Cf. The New York Times, October 18, 1925.

tumvirate, even though the latter's majority in the Chamber was decreased. The coalition included Agrarians, Social Democrats, National Socialists, National Democrats and Clericals. Before the elections, this bloc had mustered 173 votes against 121 in the opposition; after the election, the totals were 159 and 141. Because of the scanty majority, Premier Švehla offered his resignation, which President Masaryk refused to accept.[37]

For a period of over two years after the rupture of relations, no rapprochement was reached despite gestures of friendship from both sides. In 1927, the government showed its goodwill by abstaining from any official participation in the festivities of July 6, an attitude greatly appreciated by the Church, which, in turn, returned the compliment by recognizing the celebration of Hus' anniversary as a national holiday, non-provocative in itself, and as an event at which the attendance of the ministry was understood.[38]

The Clericals, particularly the followers of Father Hlinka, refused to believe that Beneš, a religious liberal, really desired to reestablish friendly relations, and sought to place upon him the responsibility for the failure to reach any understanding.[39] In attempting to discredit such allegations, Beneš informed the Parliamentary Committee for Foreign Affairs that

the Czechoslovak Government is anxious to avoid useless social conflicts and desires a solution of the problem of relations with the Vatican that will be acceptable to all parties. There can be no complete separation of Church and State in Czechoslovakia, but neither can there be a permanent, indisputable Concordat.

[37] *Národní Politika*, November 16 and 23, 1925.

[38] *Svornost*, September 10, 1927.

[39] For interpellation, cf. *Tisky* (Poslanecká Sněmovna), no. 776, v, December 15, 1926, 4 session.

A satisfactory outcome of the present negotiations is expected shortly.[40]

On December 20, 1927, Pope Pius met Dr. Krofta, the Czechoslovak plenipotentiary sent specially to the Vatican, in a private audience, and, later in the day, Dr. Krofta and Cardinal Gasparri, the Papal Secretary of State, agreed upon the exact terms of a compromise. While Dr. Krofta was on his return to Praha to present the new agreement for ratification, Monsignor Marmaggi began his preparations to resume his duties as Nuncio at Praha in January, 1928.[41]

In order to come to an agreement, the Vatican had decided to change its existing policy regarding Czechoslovakia—to abandon attempts for a Concordat and to establish instead a modus vivendi. The text, which was not made public until after an exchange of notes, was ratified by Czechoslovakia on January 20, 1928,[42] and by the Pope on February 2, 1928.[43] A day earlier, before the Foreign Affairs Committee of the Senate, Beneš made clear the seven points that formed the basis of the agreement:

(1) No Czechoslovak diocese had any authority beyond its boundaries, and no foreign diocese was to have any influence in Czechoslovakia. A mixed committee would draw anew the boundaries of each diocese.

(2) State control of Church lands, inaugurated during the land reforms, was to end, and the Church authorities were to resume control over unexpropriated Church holdings.

(3) Monasteries and orders having cloisters in Czechoslovakia could have no seats outside of Czechoslovakia.

[40] *Zprávy* (Poslanecká Sněmovna), 102 meeting, October 25, 1927, p. 14, 5 session.

[41] *Prager Presse, Svornost*, December 21, 1927.

[42] *Právo Lidu*, January 21, 1928; *Svornost*, January 25, 1928.

[43] *Svornost*, February 3, 1928.

(4) Bishops had to be citizens of Czechoslovakia and could be installed only with the consent of the Czechoslovak government. The government could refuse to endorse any high Church official connected with irredentist or separatist movements against Czechoslovakia.

(5) Church officials must take an oath of allegiance to Czechoslovakia.

(6) The Czechoslovak government guaranteed freedom of public worship to all religious creeds.

(7) The Czechoslovak government would pay the salaries of the Catholic Clergy, just as it was paying the ministers of other religious denominations recognized by the state.[44]

Delicate indeed had been the problem of the appointment of bishops. Czechoslovakia had acquired large areas, formerly Hungarian, which were still under the religious control of bishops residing in Hungary. The government desired that the religious and political boundaries coincide, particularly since the major portions of several Hungarian dioceses were now within the boundaries of Slovakia. The strength of Magyar influence in Slovakia explained also Czechoslovakia's insistence on the fourth point in the modus vivendi.[45] On the other hand, the Church desired primarily to regain control of the holdings lost by Czechoslovakia's policy of

[44] *Národní Listy, Prager Presse*, February 1, 1928; *Svornost*, February 2 and 17, 1928; *L'Europe nouvelle*, February 18, 1928; Anon., "Modus vivendi mezi Československem a Vatikánem", *Zahraniční Politika*, vol. vii, pp. 97-98 (Beneš to Gasparri, text of Czechoslovak note of January 29, 1928); Beneš, E., "Exposé Ministra Dra. Edvarda Beneše o modu vivendi mezi Československem a Vatikánem", *Zahraniční Politika*, vol. vii, pp. 200-203 (text of Beneš' speech of February 1, 1928). *Tisky* (Poslanecká Sněmovna), nos. 1465 and 1467, February 6, 1928, 5 session, point out that the text of the modus vivendi was given by the government on January 31, 1928, to all Praha newspapers, which are to be regarded as official sources.

[45] *Svornost*, April 23, 1928; *Národní Listy*, April 4, 1928.

land reform. Here was a substantial grievance, whereas the concessions granted to Czechoslovakia were all theoretical, involving prerogatives that had already been lost. This fact was seized upon by the religious radicals, who accused the Church of materialistic and mercenary motives, of having given up all the principles for which it had long stood in order to regain its lands. In spite of the cordiality with which the modus vivendi was received by the Czechoslovaks, the radical minority still persisted in its agitation against the Church.[46]

The modus vivendi had been made possible only by the moderation and conciliatory attitude displayed by both parties. Czechoslovakia, although firmly determined to retain July 6 as a national holiday, still tried to eliminate such aspects of the ceremony as might be considered deliberately provocative by the Catholic Church. With such friendship evinced by both sides, there was no need for a definite stipulation in the modus vivendi on the question of national holidays.

As another gesture of friendship towards Czechoslovakia, Monsignor Marmaggi was succeeded as Nuncio to Praha by Monsignor Ciriaci, who was *persona gratissima* to the Republic because of his long negotiations, from September to December, 1927, with Dr. Krofta.[47] The rapprochement between the Vatican and Czechoslovakia was confirmed by the decoration of President Masaryk, on September 28, 1929, with the grand cross of the Papal order of the Holy Sepulcher, a distinction granted hitherto only to a few reign-

[46] As typical samples, cf. *Právo Lidu*, January 9, 1929, and *Svornost*, January 26, 1929, for articles purporting to show the great disappointment of the Vatican at the fact that Czechoslovakia had attained independence; or *Prager Presse*, January 26, 1930, and *Svornost*, March 13, 1929, and February 15, 1930, for charges of unwarrantable dabbling of the Church in the internal affairs of Czechoslovakia.

[47] *Svornost*, February 20, 1928.

ing sovereigns.[48] It appeared as if Beneš' explanation of the modus vivendi, as a victory for neither side but as a thoroughly satisfactory agreement which promised a permanent religious settlement, would be justified.[49]

Fascism

As the middle 1920's wore on, Bolshevism became less of a menace, because of better relations with the U.S.S.R. and because of reviving domestic prosperity. By 1926, Fascism also raised its head. The leader of the Czechoslovak Fascisti was Radula Gajda, the hero of the Siberian campaign[50] and now Chief-of-Staff of the Czechoslovak army. Immediately before the opening of the great Sokol Congress at Praha, he received a compulsory leave of absence (September 1, 1926)[51] owing to rumors that he was contemplating an imitation of Mussolini's "march on Rome" with the aid of the Sokol athletes.[52] Well-informed men pointed out that the Sokols were a unit for the Republic and that Gajda could have no reasonable hope of success, but the government refused to assume any unnecessary risk. Gajda was punished

[48] *Ibid.*, October 12 and 24, 1929; *Berliner Tageblatt, Národní Listy,* September 28, 1929; *cf.* also, *Národní Listy,* May 18, 1929, or *Svornost,* June 4, 1929, for President Masaryk's viewpoint on the celebration of the anniversary of St. Václav and on Catholicism in general.

[49] Beneš, *Boj o mír* (speech of February 2, 1928), pp. 388-396.

[50] *Cf. supra*, pp. 118 *et seq.*

[51] Republika Československá, Ministerstvo Národní Obrany, *Osobní Věstník*, vol. ix, p. 233.

[52] The famous Sokol (falcon) Gymnastic society, founded in 1862, had cleverly utilized the externals of physical drill as a cloak to cover a well-planned democratic and nationalistic program. Austria was slow to realize its menace, not trying to suppress it until during the winter of 1915, at which time the Sokols had 953 branches and 110,000 members in Austria alone, as well as other units in all parts of the world where there existed large Czech settlements. *Cf.* Fisher, L. K., "What the Sokols Stand for", *The Bohemian Review*, vol. i, pp. 1-4; Temperley, *op. cit.,* vol. iii, p. 251; Mercier, *op. cit.,* p. 58.

by degradation in rank to that of a private in the reserves. He was allowed three-fourths of his pension because of physical disability and because the government did not wish to make him a martyr. This sentence, passed by the Supreme Disciplinary Commission of the Ministry of National Defense, was approved by the Senate on October 26, 1926, after a spirited interpellation.[53] Gajda's drastic punishment seemed to deprive the Fascisti of any strength they might have possessed. In general, Czechoslovak public opinion welcomed the verdict, which made the cause of the Fascists appear ridiculous. Both Masaryk and Beneš considered the movement within Czechoslovakia a comic opera gesture.[54]

Minority Reconciliations

The German minority within the Republic, which had hitherto refused to cooperate politically with the Czechoslovaks, became reconciled and apparently surrendered any immediate hopes for a union with Germany. On October 12, 1926, the two most prominent German parties, the German Agrarian and the Christian Social, entered the Švehla Cabinet. Their leaders, Spina and Mayr-Harting, received, respectively, the portfolios of Public Works and of Justice.[55] This event marked the acceptance of the post-Locarno status quo by the German minority.[56] Similarly, the consolidation of the state was again furthered on January 15, 1927, when the Slovak Popular (Catholic) party, led by Father Hlinka, also joined the Švehla coalition by accepting two posts in the Cabinet: Tiso, the portfolio of Public Health; and Gažik, that of the

[53] *Zprávy* (Senát), 46 meeting, October 26, 1926, pp. 252-262, 3 session.

[54] *The New York Times*, February 12, 1928. It might be noted also that the two chief Fascist demands were an anti-Jewish governmental policy and a new constitution with a stronger executive.

[55] *Prager Presse*, October 12, 1926.

[56] *Cf.* Borovička, *op. cit.*, p. 123.

Unification of Laws.[57]   By this move, the Magyar irreden-
tists were dealt a severe blow.   These successive reconciliations of the Germans and discontented Slovaks with the
Czechs presented one of the best guarantees for the permanence of the state.[58]

Better Relations with the Soviet Union

One of the chief disappointments that Beneš was destined
to encounter in his desire to safeguard the new status quo
was the lack of fulfillment of his optimistic prediction [59] that
an Eastern Locarno with the Soviet Union would follow the
conclusion of the agreement with the Western Powers.   In
fact, Locarno and its sequel, the rapprochement between
Czechoslovakia and the U.S.S.R's enemy, Poland, rendered
more remote the possibility of a Czechoslovak-Soviet
rapprochement.   Regardless of the reaction of Moscow to
such actions on the part of Czechoslovakia, Beneš had never
intended them as evidences of hostility to her, but merely as
necessary moves in the solution of the problem of security.
He went so far as to admit that his hands were tied, that his
delay in recognizing the Soviets had been forced by repeated
protests from high Czechoslovak military authorities.[60]
Despite such pressure, Beneš again advocated publicly the
recognition of the U.S.S.R. on May 1, 1926.[61]   At Little

[57] *Ibid.*, pp. 124-125; *Prager Presse*, January 15, 1927.

[58] *Cf.* Mirkine-Guetzevich, B., and Tibal, A., *La Tchécoslovaquie*
(Paris, 1929), pp. 49-50.   One of the best pleas for a greater degree of
cooperation between the Czechoslovaks and the German minority is contained in the book by E. Rádl, *Der Kampf zwischen Tschechen und
Deutschen* (Reichenberg, 1928).   For Czech and Slovak reconciliation,
cf. Seton-Watson, R. W., *Slovakia, Then and Now* (London, 1931).

[59] *Cf. supra*, p. 239.

[60] *Cf. Zprávy* (Senát), 8 meeting, February 23, 1926, pp. 155-156,
1 session, for the Senate's statement of political reasons for its refusal
to recognize the U. S. S. R. de jure.

[61] *The New York Times*, May 1, 1926.

Entente Conferences, particularly at Jachymov (Joach-
imsthal), he risked antagonizing Rumania by his insistence
that each member retain freedom of action concerning the
Soviet Union, and by his repeated refusals to participate in
any hostile gesture against her, a policy that was supported
generally by Yugoslavia also.[62]   Yet, it is doubtful if even
diplomatic consideration for the feelings of Rumania would
have been sufficiently influential to have restrained Beneš.
Czechoslovakia, a Slav state with professed Slavophil sentiments, could have been expected normally to have lost no
time in recognizing Russia after Great Britain and France
had done so.   Beneš had stated (March 11, 1920)[63] that
Czechoslovakia would neither anticipate nor lag behind the
Western Powers in the matter of Russian recognition.   The
fact that he did lag behind against his own volition was owing
primarily to the composition of the Czechoslovak governmental coalition, which, because of its political antipathy to
Communism, prevented de jure recognition of the Russian
Soviet.[64]

The provisional commercial treaty, signed by Russia and
Czechoslovakia on June 5, 1922,[65] had resulted in an improvement of business relations, yet had not been entirely
satisfactory to either.   From 1922 to 1925, the amount of
intercourse continued to increase annually, but, after that
date, there ensued a period of decline, caused perhaps by the
fact that both countries, through numerous commercial
treaties, had found better markets elsewhere.   By 1928, the
decline of Soviet-Czechoslovak trade had become so marked
as to attract the attention of statesmen in both countries.
Soviet imports from Czechoslovakia fell from over 100,-

[62] *Ibid.*, May 14, 1927.
[63] *Cf. supra*, pp. 136-137.
[64] *Cf. Národní Politika*, February 27, 1927; *Svornost*, March 17, 1927.
[65] *Cf. supra*, pp. 145-146.

000,000 crowns in 1925 to 31,000,000 crowns in 1928, and Czechoslovak exporters began to complain that their products were being overlooked by the Bolsheviks.[66]

In order to restore lost contacts, Moscow took the initiative in the negotiations for a new Soviet-Czechoslovak commercial treaty. Early in 1928, Stein, the secretary of the Soviet delegation at the disarmament conference at Geneva, held preliminary discussions with Veverka, the Czechoslovak representative. On March 9, 1928, Stein and Dr. Niederle, councillor at the legation and acting commissioner for Litvinov, the leader of the Soviet delegation at Geneva, conferred with Beneš. No great disagreement existed between the viewpoints of the two countries.[67] The Soviet Union agreed to withdraw the demand formerly considered indispensable—de jure recognition, but sought to do so, if possible, without giving the matter any domestic publicity.[68] Every assistance in loading goods, in consolidating rates, and in granting notable reductions for products in which both countries had a particular interest, was offered by the Soviet Union. The time and place of the final negotiations were to be settled by mutual agreement. Official Czechoslovak circles considered the chances for a successful conclusion of the negotiations favorable.[69]

Czechoslovakia requested the inclusion in any new treaty of the following points: (1) a most-favored-nation clause for herself; (2) reciprocal facilitation of traffic; (3) a tariff agreement with mutually autonomous rates; (4) strict import and export quotas; (5) a consular convention; and (6) indefinite postponement of the question of de jure recogni-

66 Ceské Slovo, Arbeiter Zeitung, May 15, 1928; Svornost, May 16, 1928.
67 Svornost, March 24-25, 1928.
68 The New York Times, April 2, 1928.
69 Prager Presse, March 22, 1928.

tion of the U.S.S.R., which question was not to be raised during the negotiations.[70]

These proposals were submitted by Beneš to Litvinov, who forwarded them to Moscow. The first three points were conceded immediately, but the fourth encountered violent objections because the Soviet government hesitated to commit itself to the purchase of as large a quantity of Czechoslovak goods as Czechoslovakia did of Soviet products. On the other hand, Czechoslovakia objected to certain Soviet tariff regulations. Then, too, mutual difficulties were raised with regard to the details of powers of the consuls in residence and of a satisfactory visa arrangement.[71]

Although the negotiations were spun out for weeks, no definite agreement on the various points in dispute could be reached. However, the economic contacts between the two countries became more intimate than ever before. Before the negotiations came to an end, nearly two hundred of the leading manufacturing and exporting concerns of Czechoslovakia had entered into business relations with the Soviet Union.[72] Great impetus had been given this trade by the establishment in Praha, late in 1927, of a foundation whose object was the creation of economic ties between the two countries, and under whose auspices there was opened on September 26, 1928, an exposition of Soviet goods.[73] Statistics issued by Basil Sacharov, the Commissar of Foreign Trade, showed that Soviet imports from Czechoslovakia rose from 31,000,000 crowns for 1928 to 298,000,000 crowns for 1929.[74] It was also hoped that, in the future,

---

[70] *Ibid.*, March 20, 1928.

[71] *Svornost*, April 4, 1928.

[72] *České Slovo*, June 2, 1928; *The New York Times*, June 24, 1928.

[73] *Svornost*, October 14, 1928.

[74] *Ibid.*, December 29, 1929. For further details, *cf. ibid.*, November 3, 1928, and June 6, 1929.

still better use would be made of the Danube River as the main artery of trade between the U.S.S.R. and Central Europe.[75]

Friendship with Poland

Similarly, Czechoslovakia and Poland, states which had their " frontiers hardly solidified " [76] and which had almost as much to gain from Locarno as had France and Germany, drew even closer together.   The two Slavic friends sought to strengthen the new status quo by concluding a series of additional treaties which attempted to regulate ordinary international activities.

Much was expected from the treaty of aerial navigation, which had been signed at Praha on April 15, 1926, in the midst of the enthusiasm engendered by the visit of Skrzynski.[77]   Regular air mail service was to be provided between Brno and Lwow, where customs airdomes were to be erected.   There was to be no duty on parts or tools needed for aircraft.   Czechoslovakia agreed to grant to one Polish air navigation company, to be designated specifically by Poland, the right to fly Polish aircraft over Czechoslovakia at regular intervals from Cracow or Katowice to Vienna, but such aircraft must land en route at the customs airdome at Brno.   Poland agreed to grant similarly to one Czechoslovak company the right to fly over Poland to Užhorod, Moravská Ostrava, or Podwoloczyska.   However, each country reserved the right to revoke without advance notice the special privileges given to the favored company and to grant them to others.[78]

[75] *Ibid.*, July 29, 1928, and April 10, 1929.

[76] *Cf.* D'Abernon, *op. cit.*, vol. iii, pp. 183-184.

[77] *Cf. supra*, p. 246.

[78] *Treaty Series*, vol. lxvii, pp. 305-331.

The high expectations raised by the treaty of aerial navigation were never realized. The volume of business was much less than had been anticipated, and there were many objections to the monopoly and customs features of the agreement. Many wild and unfavorable, even if false, rumors circulated regarding the menace to neighboring states that might be embodied in allegedly secret military clauses of the treaty. In view of the fact that objections to the treaty seemed to outweigh any possible advantages that might be derived from its continuation, it was denounced by mutual consent as of December 31, 1930.[79]

Four treaties of February 8, 1927, granted access to the authorities of each country to certain archives of the other and provided for the free exchange of documentary information. The first treaty dealt with the exchange of documents of the former Austrian, Hungarian, and Austro-Hungarian military authorities;[80] the second treaty regulated the disposal of documents still remaining with the Austrian military authorities and provided for independent requests on the part of both Poland and Czechoslovakia to Austria for records still in Austrian hands;[81] the third treaty concerned the disposal of railway records and archives;[82] and the fourth treaty arranged for the mutual loan of documents, prior to those mentioned in Article 23 of the " liquidation convention " of April 23, 1925.[83] Similar in scope was the treaty of April 14, 1927, which provided for the exchange of judicial archives.[84] A treaty of May 30, 1927, facilitated railway traffic across the frontiers,[85] and one of February

[79] *Prager Presse*, January 1, 1931.

[80] *Treaty Series*, vol. lxx, pp. 261-273.

[81] *Ibid.*, vol. lxx, pp. 275-287. [82] *Ibid.*, vol. lxx, pp. 289-297.

[83] *Ibid.*, vol. lxx, pp. 299-303. [84] *Ibid.*, vol. lxxxii, pp. 157-169.

[85] *Ibid.*, vol. xcviii, pp. 233-295.

18, 1928, regulated fishing and the preservation of fish in frontier waters.[86]

The denunciation of the treaty of aerial navigation and protests in certain Polish circles about the alleged favors granted by Czechoslovakia to Ukrainian radicals hostile to Poland,[87] were minor exceptions to the generally cordial tenor of relations between Poland and Czechoslovakia. For the time being, their rapprochement appeared to guarantee friendship by the adoption of tolerant and far-sighted foreign policies whereby they gave one another consistent support in all negotiations concerning security, disarmament and world peace. They agreed to keep in the background the point of their greatest divergence—their respective policies regarding the Soviet Union.

Franco-Italian Rivalry

In the West, the spirit of Locarno had failed to mitigate the rivalry that existed between France and Italy. By 1926 this conflict of interests had become so obvious, particularly in Central Europe, that the small states of that area faced the possibility of having to forget their post-war division into victors and vanquished in favor of a new alignment under one or the other of the Latin rivals. Such an eventuality would threaten both Beneš' hope for the maintenance of the new status quo and one main objective of the Little Entente, that of seeking to preserve its diplomatic independence from any one of the Great Powers. While contracting friendly ties with both France and Italy, the members of the Little Entente were determined not to become satellites of either.[88]

France's relatively greater measure of success in concluding treaties with the victor states was again clearly marked.

---

[86] *Ibid.*, vol. cxix, pp. 385-401.

[87] *Gazeta Warszawska*, May 22, 1929; *Svornost*, May 23, 1929.

[88] *Cf.* Toynbee, *op. cit.*, 1926, pp. 146-147.

On June 10, 1926, she signed two treaties with Rumania: a treaty of friendship [89] and a convention for the pacific settlement of disputes.[90] On November 11, 1927, France and Yugoslavia signed two similar treaties of friendship [91] and arbitration.[92] Both treaties of friendship were to last five years. In each case the contracting parties agreed to examine jointly all questions that might endanger the status quo which had been established by the Peace Treaties. If either were attacked without provocation, both governments would agree without delay upon the action each should take within the terms of the League Covenant. However, the treaties were discreetly vague upon the subject of furnishing military aid in an emergency, and were drawn with care in order to contain no definite obligations with regard to such a possibility.

The most that Italy could obtain from the Little Entente was a treaty of friendship with Rumania on September 16, 1926,[93] a treaty which was unpopular within the latter.[94] A renewal of friction between Yugoslavia and Italy over Balkan and Adriatic questions caused Mussolini to seek support elsewhere. By 1927, Italy had established friendly contacts with Albania, Bulgaria, Greece, Hungary, Poland and Turkey.[95] Mussolini could feel that he had made some progress in his efforts to counteract French preponderance

[89] *Treaty Series*, vol. lviii, pp. 225-231.

[90] *Ibid.*, vol. lviii, pp. 233-243.   [91] *Ibid.*, vol. lxviii, pp. 373-379.

[92] *Ibid.*, vol. lxviii, pp. 381-391.   [93] *Ibid.*, vol. lxvii, pp. 393-397.

[94] *The New York Times*, September 16, 21 and 26, 1926.

[95] It is beyond the scope of this work to attempt to present in detail French or Italian foreign policy. For further information, *cf.* Toynbee, *op. cit.*, 1928, pp. 147-161; Machray, *op. cit.*, pp. 303-308, 328-330, 332-334, 340-342; Codresco, *op. cit.*, vol. ii, pp. 119-149; Currey, *op. cit.*, pp. 211-233; Schuman, F. L., *War and Diplomacy in the French Republic* (New York, 1931), pp. 253-301 and 401-409; Cippico, Count A., *Italy the Central Problem of the Mediterranean* (New Haven, 1926), pp. 85-101.

in Central Europe. However, these new friendships were destined to cause him gradually to emerge as the leader of the revisionist bloc. The uneasiness within the Little Entente was not dispelled by Mussolini's denial that this response to France was " cause and effect ".[96]

During the quest for foreign support, Franco-Italian relations remained tense. Early in 1928, the arrival of a new French Ambassador to Italy, Count Maurice de Beaumarchais, was welcomed as the beginning of a rapprochement. The wild rumors then current of an Italian demand for the cession of Corsica and Tunis did not materialize, but there did result an abatement of friction and a restoration of better conditions when France agreed to Italian requests for a share in the international régime at Tangier, for a recognition of her dominant interests in the Adriatic, and for measures against anti-Fascist plotters within France.[97] The situation was further clarified on June 5, 1928, when Mussolini broke a silence of nearly two years on general foreign affairs to deliver a lengthy résumé of his policy, " from China to Peru ".[98]

Despite Beneš' statement that there existed no differences between Czechoslovakia and Italy and that both states desired friendly relations,[99] public opinion within the former continued to view with alarm the tendency of the latter to draw closer to the vanquished states. Was this the beginning of an attempted revision of the Peace Treaties? A large number of irritating " incidents " served to arouse more strongly the latent hostility. The so-called " Rothermere affair " was the first to reawaken the antagonism to Italy that had been

[96] Currey, *op. cit.*, pp. 205-206.

[97] *The New York Times*, January 22, 1928.

[98] *Cf.* Currey, *op. cit.*, pp. 234-255; *Corriere della Sera*, June 5, 1928.

[99] *Corriere della Sera*, June 20, 1926.

dormant for several years.[100] Lord Rothermere, an influential British newspaper owner, expressed, on June 20, 1927, in his newspaper, the London *Daily Mail,* great concern for the minorities within the states of the Little Entente and pointed out the unfairness to Hungary of the Treaty of Trianon. Beneš retorted that Rothermere was very poorly informed on Central European affairs.[101] All the Czechoslovak newspapers, and even the German *Prager Tagblatt,* supported Beneš' stand. After an exchange of letters had failed to elicit any retraction from Rothermere, Beneš felt it necessary to ask the British government to disclaim Rothermere.[102] Premier Baldwin's statement of October 6, challenging Rothermere to prove his allegiance to the Conservatives,[103] was apparently accepted as a disclaimer by Czechoslovak public opinion.[104] The incident was explained at length to the Foreign Affairs Committee of the Czechoslovak National Assembly by Beneš on October 25, 1927.[105] Beneš pointed out that the British government had nothing to do with the Rothermere campaign which was directly contrary to British foreign policy, that Sir Austen Chamberlain, the British Foreign Secretary, had specifically disclaimed Rothermere in a personal conference with Beneš at Geneva, and that Rothermere's articles represented Hungarian revisionist propaganda masked as agrarian reform for Central Europe.

The affair might have ended here, had not Rothermere been received with great éclat by Mussolini in March, 1928. At once public opinion in Czechoslovakia was again aflame.

[100] *Cf.* Machray, *op. cit.,* pp. 322-326.

[101] *The New York Times,* August 7, 1927.

[102] *Cf.* Toynbee, *op. cit.,* 1927, p. 206.

[103] *The Times,* October 6, 1927; *The New York Times,* October 7, 1927.

[104] *Čas, Národní Listy, Národní Politika,* October 7-8, 1927.

[105] *Cf.* Beneš, *Boj o mír,* pp. 374-377.

The *Lidové Noviny* pointed out Mussolini's sympathy for Hungary, and stated that fairer boundaries than the present ones could not be drawn.[106] The *Prager Tagblatt* claimed that all except Rothermere must realize the bad feeling that would exist when Mussolini asked strategic boundaries for Italy and ethnographic ones for Hungary.[107] The *Právo Lidu* accused Mussolini of preferring war in Central Europe to an agreement.[108] The *Národní Politika* claimed that Hungary had refused a frontier rectification, but wanted her former boundaries intact.[109] All newspapers united in emphasizing the inviolability of the Treaty of Trianon. If possible, Czechoslovak feeling at the time was more bitter against Italy than against Hungary, for such hostile expressions were taken for granted from the latter but were unexpected from the former.[110] Beneš had perhaps the last word regarding the incident in an exposé of June 6, 1928, before the Foreign Affairs Committee of the National Assembly. Once again he pointed out that, on May 23, Chamberlain had stressed the fact that the British 'government "did not identify itself with the press campaign for the revision of the Treaty of Trianon." [111] Beneš concluded with the observation that the new status quo would be maintained because the constructive forces of Europe were greater than the destructive ones.[112]

[106] *Lidové Noviny*, March 29, 1928.

[107] *Prager Tagblatt*, March 29, 1928.

[108] *Právo Lidu*, March 29, 1928.

[109] *Národní Politika*, March 29, 1928.

[110] *Cf. Svornost*, April 1, 1928.

[111] *The Times*, May 23, 1928.

[112] Beneš, E., *La Situation internationale et la politique étrangère tchécoslovaque. Cf.* also, *Tisky* (Poslanecká Sněmovna), no. 1587, xii, June 6, 1928, 6 session, Beneš' answer to Chamber of Deputies' interpellation regarding Rothermere, for which *cf. Tisky* (Poslanecká Sněmovna), no. 1337, xii, November 16, 1927, 5 session.

In contrast with Italy, France remained on excellent terms with Czechoslovakia. Economically, the ties between France and Czechoslovakia were drawn closer by the conclusion, on July 2, 1928, of a new commercial treaty providing for most-favored-nation treatment and for reciprocal freedom of commerce and navigation.[113] Similarly, the military ties linking Paris and Praha were strengthened by discussions between the respective military authorities at periodic conferences which had followed the visit of Marshal Foch to Czechoslovakia in 1923.[114] Flattering to the military prestige of Czechoslovakia was the visit in 1929 of Marshal Pétain, who promised, in the presence of delegates from the two other states of the Little Entente, that France would always be on the side of Czechoslovakia whenever the need should arise.[115] After witnessing the manoeuvres in Moravia, Pétain complimented the Czechoslovaks upon the efficiency of their army.[116]

After Locarno, the cooperation of Czechoslovakia and France became particularly intimate, and, despite a prediction that the former would revert to the Soviet orbit whenever Europe would become normal,[117] continued to give every indication of permanence as long as the post-war status quo should endure.[118] In answer to wide-spread criticism that the Little Entente as a whole, and particularly Czechoslovakia, under the guidance of Beneš, had become a tool in the hands of France, might not the reverse be maintained with equal justification? In view of the mutual interde-

[113] *Treaty Series*, vol. xcix, pp. 105-257.

[114] *Cf. supra*, pp. 219-220.

[115] *The New York Times*, August 27, 1929; *Svornost*, August 28 and September 3, 1929.

[116] *Národní Listy*, September 4, 1929; *Svornost*, September 18, 1929.

[117] *Cf.* D'Abernon, *op. cit.*, vol. i, p. 237.

[118] For Franco-Czechoslovak relations during the depression, *cf. infra*, pp. 312 *et seq*.

pendence, could it not be said that " French policy was more the captive than the master of the Little Entente "[119] and that France had no alternative for her precarious system of alliances? In the estimation of the writer, the truth lies somewhere between these two extreme statements, in a tolerant appreciation of the similarity in the major interests of both, particularly as long as they remain guardians of the new status quo.

" Irreconcilable Hungary "

Within Central Europe, apparently irreconcilable Hungary remained the chief obstacle to any post-Locarno adjustment just as she had been formerly to reconstruction.[120] The successful reconstruction of Hungary, which had been completed by the end of June, 1926, when Mr. Jeremiah Smith, the Commissioner-General, left Budapest,[121] contributed less to the stability of Central Europe than had been anticipated. As early as 1922 or 1923, certain Hungarians, out of " patriotic " motives, had begun to forge French bank notes. By 1925 the spurious bills had appeared in large quantities in various parts of Europe. As the result of information that had been obtained at the time of the arrest, in Amsterdam, of three Hungarians who had attempted to pass forged 1,000 franc notes, the counterfeiters, led by Prince Ludwig Windischgrätz, were arrested on January 4, 1926.[122]

[119] *Cf.* Simonds, F. H., *Can Europe Keep the Peace?* (New York, 1931), p. 198.

[120] *Cf. supra*, pp. 205 *et seq.*

[121] For further details regarding the reconstruction of Hungary, *cf. Official Journal*, February, 1926, p. 131; July, 1926, pp. 876-878; September, 1926, pp. 1176-1188; *The Financial Reconstruction of Hungary*, General survey and principle documents, Geneva, 1926; *Termination of the Functions of the Commissioner-General*, resolution of the Council of the League of Nations of June 10, 1926.

[122] *The Times*, January 4-11, 1926.

In view of the financial interests involved, French apathy in not following the matter energetically was surprising. The Bank of France did make " due investigations ",[123] but, thereafter, France failed to make the anticipated protest to the Hungarian government.[124] Briand stated merely that, at the proper time, in cooperation with Czechoslovakia, his government would " draw the necessary conclusions from this affair of incredible brigandage ".[125]

Briand never explained his apparent inertia. Was his obvious reluctance motivated by fear that he could not prove the responsibility of the government of Bethlen? Or did he dread lest he throw Hungary automatically into the arms of Mussolini? Czechoslovak public opinion failed to relish the hesitation of France. The incident revived memories of Hungarian forgeries of Czechoslovak bank-notes to the amount of over 30,000,000 crowns between 1919 and 1921,[126] and was taken as fresh evidence of the impossibility of reconciliation between the two states.[127] While extremists demanded joint action with the two Little Entente partners, which had also suffered in the past from Hungarian forgeries of their currencies, the Czechoslovak government adhered to the view of the moderates, who desired a judicial inquiry.[128]

On May 26, 1926, Prince Windischgrätz and his accomplice, Nadosy, formerly Chief of Police of Hungary, were

[123] *Ibid.*, January 27-28, 1926.   [124] *Ibid.*, February 2, 1926.
[125] *Ibid.*, March 4, 1926.   [126] Machray, *op. cit.*, p. 273.
[127] *České Slovo, Prager Presse, Národní Listy, Národní Politika*, January 5-7, 1926.

[128] For Beneš' answers to violent interpellations in parliament on the question of the Hungarian forgeries and for debates on his speech, *cf.* *Zprávy* (Poslanecká Sněmovna), 7 meeting, February 16, 1926, pp. 279-290, 1 session; 9 meeting, February 18, 1926, pp. 304-341, 1 session; 10 meeting, February 19, 1926, pp. 410-446, 1 session. *Cf.* also, *Le Temps*, March 1, 1926, for the reply of Count Bethlen to Czechoslovak accusations.

sentenced to four years' imprisonment and fines of 10,-000,000 crowns, whereas lesser sentences were meted out to the minor conspirators. The Bank of France received damages of one franc as a vindication of its right to financial compensation, and the government of Hungary was absolved from all connection with the plot.[129]

When two appeals in August and October, carried ultimately to the Royal Curia (the highest court in Hungary), failed to change materially the original judgment, public opinion in both France [130] and Czechoslovakia [131] felt outraged over what it considered the inadequacy of the punishments. Beneš remained unconvinced of the innocence of the Hungarian government.[132] France, with the approval of Czechoslovakia, on June 5, 1926, presented officially the general question of international forgeries to the League of Nations.[133] The matter was referred to the Mixed Committee of the Council, which, on October 13, 1926, presented a report requesting closer cooperation among the authorities of all states. In order to prevent a repetition of the incident, it advised the establishment of a central international committee.[134] After due time had been allowed for a summary of the viewpoints of the various governments concerned (until December 6, 1928), there was prepared a draft convention for the suppression of counterfeiting currency.[135] In announcing her ratification, Czecho-

---

129 *The Times*, May 27, 1926; for full details *cf.* also, Toynbee, *op. cit.*, 1926, pp. 178-190; Machray, *op. cit.*, pp. 272-274, 294-296; Gedye, G. E. R., *Heirs to the Hapsburgs* (Bristol, 1932), pp. 148-153.

130 *Le Temps*, August 18-21, October 15, 1926.

131 *Prager Presse*, May 27, August 18-20, October 15, 1926.

132 *Cf. Official Journal*, July, 1926, pp. 871-873, for Beneš' discussion.

133 *Ibid.*, July, 1926, p. 950.

134 *Ibid.*, February, 1928, pp. 197-203.

135 *Ibid.*, February, 1929, pp. 275-304; June, 1929, pp. 886-912; April, 1930, pp. 308-317.

slovakia stated that " the competent organs of the Republic have declared themselves to be in favor of the draft convention, which forms a first step towards the effective prevention and the international suppression of counterfeiting currency ".[136]   Thus innocuously terminated the efforts of France and Czechoslovakia to hold Hungary responsible for the forgeries committed by some of her prominent citizens. Nevertheless, the incident was neither forgotten nor forgiven in either Czechoslovakia or Hungary, in both of which countries public opinion continued to attribute the most sinister motives to the actions of the other.

Before the matter of the Hungarian forgeries was ended, another incident, perhaps even more serious, again strained the relations of Hungary and Czechoslovakia almost to the breaking point, and brought about a general international tangle of no mean proportions.   On January 2, 1928, at the Austrian frontier railway station of St. Gotthard, Austrian railroad officials discovered five freight cars loaded with machine gun parts enough for five hundred guns which were being shipped from Italy across Austrian territory.   The cars, shipped from Verona and declared to contain machinery, were consigned ostensibly to Czechoslovakia, but were believed, in reality, to have been intended for Hungary [137] contrary to Article 180 of the Treaty of Trianon, which had specified that " the importation of arms, munitions and war material of all kinds is strictly forbidden ".   This allegation, if true, would constitute a violation of the treaty by both Italy and Hungary.   Austria was interested merely in the

---

[136] *Ibid.*, February, 1929, p. 276.

[137] To Berkovics Brothers, at Slovensko-Nové-Město (Satoralja-Ujhely or Satorlajaygtely).   It was shown subsequently that this firm, which denied all knowledge of the shipment, was actually located across the border in Hungary.   The Treaty of Trianon had awarded the railway station to Czechoslovakia, but most of the town to Hungary.   *Cf. Official Journal*, July, 1928, pp. 907, 910, 911 and 915.

violation of her regulations regarding arms and in the loss of revenue, since arms were charged higher rates than machinery. The discovery was an accident, the result of suspicions that had been aroused by the haste with which the cars were being connected to Hungarian engines. Since the cars were already in Hungarian hands, the Austrian officials did not attempt to stop them. The Austrian government was informed promptly of the incident, but it made no official protest, for it regarded the whole affair merely as a minor frontier question entirely within the competence of its Ministry of Railroads.[188]

The Little Entente was not willing to consider the St. Gotthard incident so lightly. Yugoslavia had been uneasy since April 5, 1927, the date of the signature of the Italo-Hungarian Treaty of Friendship, Conciliation and Arbitration,[189] a treaty which had almost surrounded her with states within the orbit of Italian influence. To Yugoslavia, and to Czechoslovakia as well, Italian and Hungarian efforts to minimize the importance of the affair at St. Gotthard seemed clear indications of guilt. Beneš announced that Czechoslovakia did not desire to make a great international issue of the affair, but that such an attempt must not be repeated. He warned Hungary that, in such an event, the Little Entente could not remain inactive.[140] On February 1, 1928, all three members of the Little Entente brought the matter up before the League Council in order to fix the responsibility for the

---

[188] *The Times* and *The New York Times*, January 3, 1928; Toynbee, *op. cit.*, 1928, pp. 161-162; Machray, *op. cit.*, pp. 330-331.

[189] *Treaty Series*, vol. lxvii, pp. 399-409.

[140] The Czechoslovak Chamber of Deputies, by a vote of 165 to 44, passed a proclamation considering the St. Gotthard incident as an attempt to detach Slovakia and to destroy the integrity of the Republic. *Zprávy* (Poslanecká Sněmovna), 123 meeting, January 24, 1928, pp. 29-39, 5 session; 124 meeting, January 25, 1928, pp. 3 *et seq.*, 5 session.

incident,[141] but Czechoslovakia and Yugoslavia were apparently distressed by the disinterestedness of Rumania.[142]

Before the League Council met, new developments took place. When no consignor appeared to claim the guns by the middle of February, Hungary announced that they would be sold at auction, after having been rendered useless for military purposes. In spite of the request of the League Council that Hungary delay the sale until due investigations could be made, the auction was held, according to Hungarian reports, on February 24, but the parts continued to remain in the hands of Hungarian officials. The truth soon came to light, that, on February 20, Hungary had destroyed the five carloads of arms that were to have been investigated. The Little Entente determined to probe the matter to the bottom. Italy's claim that the guns had been manufactured by a private firm which was also in charge of shipping them was shown to be false. A minute investigation proved that they were arms that Italy had captured during the War, and that, beyond all doubt, she still owned them. The Little Entente believed that, when Rome discovered that evasions were of no avail, she applied pressure upon Budapest to destroy the arms in defiance of the League, and the chief culprit, Italy, thus avoided responsibility and tried to make the League helpless by destroying the evidence.[143]

On March 5, 1928, began the forty-ninth session of the League of Nations. The Council decided to send to investigate the incident a group of neutral experts, a Committee of Three, representing the Netherlands, Finland and Chile,

[141] Cf. *Official Journal*, April, 1928, pp. 387-397, for texts of notes of Yugoslavia and Czechoslovakia, and pp. 545-549 for official communiqués on the incident from Austria, Hungary, Rumania, Yugoslavia and Czechoslovakia.

[142] *The New York Times*, January 27-28, 1928.

[143] *Official Journal*, July, 1928, pp. 906-907.

who were to make a study of the pertinent documents. Their report, originally due March 10, was not presented, because all the documents were not yet available. After further delays, it was decided to send investigators to Basel to examine the original way-bills (April 15-19), but even they could not discover what Czechoslovakia regarded the most important point, the ultimate destination of the machine-gun parts.[144]

The investigators finally made two reports on June 7, 1928. No satisfactory evidence had been unearthed. The ultimate destination of the weapons had not been ascertained, and consequently, Hungary, while censured severely for the illegal possession of war material and for its unduly precipitate destruction, was not held responsible for any intent to violate the Treaty of Trianon. Thus, the final judgment was inconclusive in that it neither acquitted nor convicted Hungary. The chief significance of the incident lay in the arousing of the suspicions of the Little Entente as to the motives of Italy and Hungary, and in the demonstration that the three partners gave of their relative solidarity.[145]

In view of the bitterness that characterized the relations of Hungary and Czechoslovakia, especially during this period of " incidents ", it might well be wondered whether any attempts to safeguard the new status quo would not be undertaken in vain and whether anything constructive could be accomplished. The commercial relations between the two countries, which through seven years of intermittent and apparently fruitless negotiations had been carried on practically without any treaty basis, were regulated by a treaty of May 31, 1927. For a long time both states had felt the need of a definitive commercial treaty, but the final impetus to the renewal of negotiations had been provided by the in-

[144] *Ibid.*, April, 1928, pp. 387-397.
[145] *Ibid.*, July, 1928, pp. 905-910.

creased duties that Czechoslovakia levied on agricultural products. According to the new treaty, Hungary was granted concessions on foodstuffs in return for similar concessions on Czechoslovak manufactured goods. Additional clauses clarified many other points ordinarily provocative of friction, such as the legal treatment of production and transportation quotas, railway traffic, mutual assistance in customs clearance, the prevention, prosecution and punishment of infringements of customs regulations, mutual legal assistance in criminal customs cases, and a veterinary convention concerning traffic in animals and animal products. The treaty was to be of indefinite duration, but could be denounced on six months' notice.[146] The treaty failed to produce all the beneficient results that had been anticipated because the bitterness between the two states was too deep-seated to be abated except in a limited degree even by the best of treaties.

The Austrian Problem Again

The other half of the former Dual Monarchy, Austria, felt less bitter towards the victor states, and, in the hope of assuring her own salvation, had even shown, periodically, a relatively high degree of cooperation with them. Her financial reconstruction was terminated successfully on June 30, 1926, at which time the Commissioner-General's office was abolished.[147]

Reconstructed Austria was no longer self-sufficient economically. Her extensive internal pre-war trade had become

[146] *Treaty Series*, vol. lxv, pp. 61-299; *Zprávy* (Poslanecká Sněmovna), 95 meeting, July 7, 1927, pp. 2370-2405, 4 session; 114 meeting, December 6, 1927, pp. 7-19, 5 session.

[147] *Cf. Monthly Summary*, August, 1925, p. 189; *Official Journal*, March, 1926, pp. 447-450; July, 1926, p. 916; special supplement, October, 1926, pp. 393-396; *The Financial Reconstruction of Austria*, Termination of the Functions of the Commissioner-General; *The Financial Reconstruction of Austria*, General Survey and principal documents; *supra*, pp. 192 *et seq.*

international trade. If she were to survive, she would have
to increase the efficiency of her production and obtain favorable tariff rates from her neighbors. Henceforth, as in the
cases of Belgium and Switzerland, foreign trade would be
her life blood. In appreciation of this fact, Article 222 of
the Treaty of St. Germain had granted Austria permission
to conclude, for a five-year period, special accords with Hungary and Czechoslovakia, but, because of mutual hostility,
no advantage had been taken of this concession. After the
initial bitterness of the post-war period had somewhat subsided, Austria did follow the recommendation of the League
Council that she conclude commercial treaties with her
neighbors,[148] and, during 1923-1925 concluded such treaties
with Italy, April 28, 1923; France, June 22, 1923; Germany,
July 12, 1924; Czechoslovakia, November 27, 1924; and
Spain, February 3, 1925. Treaties with almost all the other
states of Europe followed.[149]

The new tariff agreement with Czechoslovakia, signed at
Vienna on November 27, 1924, supplemented the commercial
treaty of May 4, 1921. Except for some minor exceptions
for which special licenses were still required, Austrian exports to Czechoslovakia were no longer subject to governmental control. About one-third of the items mentioned in
the Czechoslovak tariff—clothing, rubber, leather, paper,
textiles, wooden goods, tools, hardware, iron, machinery,
metal ware, electrical appliances, musical instruments, automobiles, and various chemicals—were conceded lower rates;
in most instances, the reductions amounted to fifty per cent
or more.[150]

[148] *Official Journal*, March, 1923, pp. 215-216.

[149] *Ibid.*, March, 1923, pp. 211-221; Basch and Dvořáček, *op. cit.*, pp.
88-89. *Cf.* also, p. 89 for chart of Austria's exports, 1923-1924.

[150] *Treaty Series*, vol. xlii, pp. 201-443.

The stimulation of Austrian exports to Czechoslovakia enabled Austria to remain also the latter's best customer among the small states of Central Europe.[151] On the whole, Czechoslovakia held a favorable balance of trade against Austria, but still had to make payments because of other items, such as interest on investments, transit trade, banking, insurance, profit on sales made on commission, tourist traffic and the export of articles of quality in the personal baggage of tourists.[152]

As both countries sought to eliminate the more obvious of the many unnecessary disadvantages that had resulted from their separation, there ensued a rapprochement which was confirmed by the treaty of arbitration and conciliation, which was signed on March 5, 1926, at Vienna amid profuse expressions of mutual friendship.[153] Arbitration was made practically obligatory in every instance. There was created a permanent board of arbitration, from which appeal might be made to the Permanent Court of Arbitration at the Hague. Similarly, disputes of a political nature which were not settled by regular diplomatic methods had to be submitted to this same Court, from which, however, a joint appeal might be made to the Permanent Court of International Justice. The treaty was to be effective for ten years, and might be renewed for another ten years.[154]

This rapprochement was hardly consummated before it was ruptured temporarily by a tariff war, which was caused by Austria's denunciation, in November, 1926, of the political agreement of December 16, 1921, and the commercial

---

[151] Cf. *Publications*, Economic and Financial, 1927 ii 68 ii, pp. 238-239, for statistics to 1927.

[152] Basch and Dvořáček, *op. cit.*, pp. 90-91 (charts).

[153] Cf. *Arbeiter Zeitung, Neue Freie Presse* and *The New York Times*, March 4-6, 1926.

[154] *Treaty Series*, vol. li, pp. 349-359.

treaty of May 4, 1921, together with its supplement.[155]
The tariff war would begin with the expiration of the treaty
on April 15, 1927. Because of the long years of unfavorable trade balances, Austria regarded it necessary to increase
her duties on certain Czechoslovak goods. Czechoslovakia
maintained that the Austrian adverse balance was superficial, not real, because Austria reexported many of the goods
she obtained from Czechoslovakia. The tariff war caused
severe losses to both states. In Austria, the worst sufferers
were the manufacturers of machine tools, women's dresses,
millinery and lingerie, whereas in Czechoslovakia, distress
was most prevalent among the producers of cotton and linen
goods, glassware and machinery.[156] On July 21, 1927, there
was signed a new treaty, favorable to the manufacturers of
both states, in the form of a supplementary agreement to the
treaty of May 4, 1921.[157]

The superficial nature of Austro-Czechoslovak hostility
was revealed by the negotiations that were taking place during this period of friction. At the time when the respective
manufacturers were at daggers drawn, the statesmen were
negotiating for the improvement of means of communication
between the two capitals. Two treaties of February 15,
1927, provided for air navigation and for the establishment
of regular air-ways.[158] About a year later, as a part of
her campaign against the visa nuisance, Czechoslovakia completed the negotiations for the mutual abolition of compulsory passport visas with both Austria and Germany.[159]

In spite of the efforts of Czechoslovakia to aid Austria
economically, the position of the latter remained desperate.

[155] *Ibid.*, vol. lxxviii, p. 437.
[156] *The New York Times*, April 9, 29, 1927.
[157] *Treaty Series*, vol. lxxxi, pp. 7-275.
[158] *Ibid.*, vol. lxxiii, pp. 349-385.
[159] *Ibid.*, vol. lxxiii, pp. 87-93.

The process of reconstruction under League auspices had been successful financially, but had failed to solve the major economic difficulties of Austria. Various interested neighboring states sought to advance solutions for the Austrian problem, such as the so-called Habsburg solution which might involve a reunion with Hungary, a so-called Italian solution, a German solution or Anschluss, a Danubian Confederation and continued independence. Of these alternatives, Czechoslovakia preferred the last, which in spite of its obvious difficulties, she thought practicable with a fair degree of cooperation from neighboring states, and which involved the least danger to herself. One of the chief objectives of Beneš' foreign policy was to prevent the consummation of one of the alternatives less favorable to his country, for, until some permanent solution was attained, stability could not be expected within Austria.

As has already been narrated, Beneš, with the aid of the Big and Little Ententes, had averted, for the time being at least, the Habsburg solution to the problem.[160] Similarly, any so-called Italian solution had been prevented when the Little Entente had opposed successfully an undue extension of Italian influence over Austria.[161] Of the proposed solutions, Anschluss was regarded as the most menacing by Czechoslovakia, as involving the greatest threat to her own existence. It was to be regretted that, at the time when Austro-Czechoslovak relations were becoming more friendly because of Czechoslovakia's active participation in the reconstruction of Austria, Germano-Czechoslovak relations were becoming more tense. Since 1924, there had been developing friction over the possibilities of an Austro-German union

---

[160] *Cf.* Beneš, E., *The Problem of Central Europe and the Austrian Question* (speech of March 21, 1934, before the Foreign Affairs Committees of parliament), pp. 49-54; *supra*, pp. 186-188.

[161] Beneš, *op. cit.*, pp. 40-46; *cf.* also, *supra*, pp. 193 *et seq.*

and over Germany's policy of economic penetration.[162] Since the middle years of the decade of the 1920's, Czechoslovakia had considered Anschluss as her chief single problem, in perhaps greater need of immediate solution than any other, an opinion particularly prevalent since 1927.[163] To quote J. O. Crane, " The two main causes of the recent revival of Anschluss agitation in Austria were economic maladjustment and the lack of a will to survive ".[164] Within Austria, there appeared to exist little national patriotism; some Clericals opposed the union and the Socialists advocated it, but both viewpoints might undergo rapid changes as the result of any one of several influences.[165]

Another alternative contemplated the possibility of replacing the Little Entente with a Danubian Confederation which would include also Austria and Hungary, and perhaps Poland as well. Such a grouping would subvert one of the basic ideas of the Little Entente, namely, that it was impossible to include friends and enemies within the same organization. The political fears of Czechoslovakia, Rumania and Yugoslavia had been greater than their desires for any increased economic advantages that might have resulted from a larger bloc. In this respect the interests of Czechoslovakia and Austria clashed. The former sought to preserve equally both her political and economic independence, whereas the

[162] Cf. Hudec, K., " Československá republika a Německo", Zahraniční Politika, vol. viii, pp. 425-433, 546-555, 681-696, 803-813.

[163] Beneš, op. cit., pp. 27-40; Chmelář, J., " Československá zahraniční politika v roce 1927", Zahraniční Politika, vol. vii, pp. 1-6; cf. also, Prager Presse, October 28, 1927 for speech of Masaryk.

[164] Crane, op. cit., p. 133.

[165] Ibid., pp. 134-135; Kleinwaechter, op. cit., pp. 34-35; Slosson, P. W., " The Problem of Austro-German Union," International Conciliation, no. 250, pp. 221-254; Chmelář, J., " Rakouský problem a střední Evropa", Zahraniční Politika, vol. vii, pp. 1147-1159; Bernus, P., " L'Autriche et l'Anschluss ", Le Journal des débats, vol. xxxv, pt. ii, pp. 312-314; cf. also, The Times, February 1 and 28, 1927.

latter sought the advantages of a larger organization, regardless of the loss of independence that might be involved. Czechoslovakia desired an extension of the existing commercial treaties into a system of preferential tariffs for the entire Danubian area, as the most desirable solution that was possible of attainment. Her experiences at Portorose [166] and subsequently had convinced her that an economically unified Danubian Confederation was an impossibility, that, if nothing else, the post-war development of industrial activity within the hitherto purely agricultural states of this area alone would have precluded such a solution.[167] Czechoslovakia's desire to draw Austria into the orbit of the Little Entente was consistent with her unwillingness to accept Austria as a member of the Entente or of any Danubian Union. To all appearances, Beneš drew a delicate distinction: he desired amity and economic preferences with both Austria and Hungary, but not their inclusion in the Entente. The Little Entente was to remain an exclusive group of victors, with dominating power.

During the autumn of 1924 there had been many rumors of the imminence of the formation of a Danubian Confederation.[168] Beneš, who had been the alleged author of the project, declared that it could never be realized because none of the Little Entente states desired it.[169] France and Great Britain apparently favored such a combination.[170] There began, during 1925, among the various Danubian states, a series of negotiations that envisaged the establishment of a system of preferential tariffs. Beneš, who welcomed such

---

[166] *Cf. supra*, pp. 190 *et seq.*

[167] *Cf.* Pasvolsky, *Economic Nationalism of the Danubian States*, p. 282.

[168] *Deutsche Allgemeine Zeitung*, September 28 and October 2, 1924; *Le Temps*, September 30, 1924; *Corriere della Sera*, October 1, 1924.

[169] *The Times*, May 13, 1925.

[170] *Ibid.*, June 8, 1925; *cf.* also, Beneš, *op. cit.*, pp. 47-49.

soundings initially, withdrew his approval when Italy insisted upon being included in the bloc,[171] and Austria, France and Great Britain experienced the same reaction.[172]

Austria, which still retained hopes of arriving at some satisfactory solution of her problem, called a Central European Economic Conference to meet at Vienna September 8-9, 1925. However, such differences of opinion resulted that little of a constructive nature could be accomplished. After recommending the formation of a permanent commission to examine the possibilities of a Central European Economic Union, the Conference adjourned with the platitude that " The Central European Economic Conference considers as one of the principal evils of the Central European economic situation the continuing isolation of the economic systems of the small States ".[173]

After this failure, the project of a Danubian Confederation lagged for a period of over two years and appeared to be overshadowed by the more imminent Anschluss. Since Czechoslovakia dreaded both alternatives, the visit of Chancellor Seipel of Austria to Praha on February 13, 1928, aroused speculation as to his real objectives. Talk of both Anschluss and the Danubian Confederation was revived. Seipel appeared to be concerned primarily over the continued independence of Austria, to which end he sought Czechoslovak support for his own project to have the League's place of meeting transferred from Geneva to Vienna. He stated that he already had the support of many Balkan and

[171] *Prager Presse, The Times,* July 27, 1925.

[172] *The Times,* August 31, 1925, and February 9, 1926; *Arbeiter Zeitung,* August 31, 1926; *Le Temps,* February 9-10, 1926. The Great Powers' disapproval was motivated largely by a realization that their own foreign trade might suffer if an economically efficient Danubian Confederation were created.

[173] Pasvolsky, *op. cit.,* pp. 90-91; *cf.* also, *Arbeiter Zeitung,* September 8-9, 1925.

East-European states, but that he was opposed by the Viennese Pan-Germans, who feared that such a transfer would prevent any future Anschluss. Czechoslovakia did not support his scheme. In Praha Seipel sounded the possibility of a Central European Locarno, of an alternative regional agreement among Austria, Hungary and Czechoslovakia, under the leadership of Czechoslovakia.[174]

Beneš, who had undergone, meanwhile, a change of opinion, was favorable to this last proposal, but apparently believed that a still larger unit would be even more advantageous. Beneš allegedly envisaged a Central European Locarno whereby the Little Entente was to be transformed into a Five- or Six-Power Entente by the addition of Austria and Hungary, and perhaps Poland as well. It appeared that he no longer feared the addition of Vienna and Budapest to the Little Entente, for he realized that the difference in strength between the vanquished and victor states was so great that the former could not hope to regain their pre-war hegemony over the latter. Purely economic considerations were becoming increasingly important. The fact that others were still unconverted to the new idea became evident from the hostile reception accorded to it.[175] Rumors arose that the Little Entente was doomed. Much was made of the fact that the Jachymov Conference of 1927 had adjourned dismally after failing to reach any economic agreement. Similar reports were aired when the Little Entente failed to call in 1928 the customary spring and fall conferences. Beneš was alleged to have suggested the return to Hungary of two small frontier areas overwhelmingly

[174] *The New York Times*, February 16, 1928; *Národní Listy, České Slovo*, February 15, 1928; *Svornost*, February 16, 20, 25, 1928.

[175] *Národní Listy, The New York Times*, February 23, 1928; *Svornost*, February 23, March 9, 1928.

Hungarian in order to induce Hungary to participate.[176] Hungary reacted unfavorably to the projected Federation, for she did not want to commit herself to any permanent recognition of her existing boundaries. Similarly, both Rumania and Yugoslavia felt no enthusiasm for the project, whereas public opinion within Czechoslovakia was also generally hostile. Italy would be certain to make secret, if not open, opposition because of her fears of a revival of a Great Power in Central Europe, and Germany would regard it as the deathknell of Anschluss. Under the circumstances, many feared that the project would be more apt to cause friction rather than prevent it, hence nothing was done at this time.[177]

To Czechoslovakia, the inclusion of Germany, or any other Great Power, in any Central European Federation would be unthinkable: an Austro-German union alone might threaten her both politically and economically. An economic approach to the problem did not blind Czechoslovakia to the fact that a political union might result. Such a union would render still more precarious Czechoslovakia's competitive position for the trade of the Danubian region. Czechoslovakia realized also that, despite her efforts, she was still compelled to seek the assistance of Austro-German foreign financial contracts, a dependence which would become enhanced by a unification of Austria and Germany. Finally, her chief fear was political—that an Austro-German economic union would develop inevitably into an Anschluss that might threaten her existence.[178] Therefore, out of the

[176] *The New York Times*, March 8, 1928. Four days later the Czechoslovak Consul-General in New York City, Novák, denied categorically any suggestion by Beneš to cede territory to Hungary. *The New York Times*, March 12, 1928.

[177] *České Slovo*, March 10-11, 1928.

[178] Cf. Pasvolsky, *op. cit.*, pp. 284-286; Slosson, P., "Problem of Austro-German Union", *International Conciliation*, no. 250, pp. 221-254;

instinct for sheer self-preservation, Czechoslovakia felt compelled to insist upon the independence and territorial integrity of Austria.[179]

Little Entente Conferences, 1925-1929

The three Little Entente partners agreed to hold at Sinaia, August 15-18, 1925, a Little Entente of the press for the purpose of coordinating the respective public opinions of their peoples. At this Conference, the official press bureaus of Czechoslovakia, Rumania and Yugoslavia created a central bureau, in which each country was represented by a committee and which was expected to meet regularly.[180]

Despite this new agency, the ties among the members of the Little Entente tended to become weaker rather than stronger. An indication of this new trend was furnished during February, 1926, at the Conference of Temesvar, a special meeting which had been called, ostensibly, for the purpose of arriving at a unified policy with regard to the Hungarian forgeries. During the discussion of February 10, the fact developed that Czechoslovakia alone was interested. Her two partners, apparently satisfied with the degree of security that had already been attained, determined to await the results of the regular judicial inquiry.[181] As a result, in the attempt to bring the forgery scandal home to the Hungarian government, Czechoslovakia had to proceed without the support of her Little Entente partners.[182] Beneš

Friedman, J., " Současna ọbchodně-politicka situace československé republiky ", *Zahraniční Politika*, vol. viii, pp. 7-17.

[179] Beneš, *op. cit.*, pp. 55-62. For the later renewal of Anschluss agitation, *cf. infra*, pp. 312 *et seq.*

[180] *České Slovo*, August 17-18, 1925; *Deutsche Allgemeine Zeitung*, August 25, 1925; *L'Europe nouvelle*, October 24, 1925; *cf.* also, Cosma, *op. cit.*, pp. 150-152; Codresco, *op. cit.*, vol. ii, pp. 269-272.

[181] *Prager Presse*, February 11, 1926; *The New York Times*, February 12, 1926.

[182] *The New York Times*, October 12, 1926; *Le Temps*, October 14, 1926.

indulged in no useless recriminations.   He merely stated his belief that, ultimately, Hungary would have to be added to the Little Entente, but only after the former had explored first every other possibility.[183]   There were also current rumors that, at Temesvar, a Balkan pact to include Greece was also discussed, but, in any event, nothing came of it.[184]

Regardless of the lack of cooperation in the affair of the Hungarian forgeries, the states of the Little Entente were willing to renew their treaties of alliance.   On June 13, 1926, Czechoslovakia and Rumania, at Bucharest, agreed to another extension of the alliance of April 23, 1921, which had already been prolonged for three years on May 7, 1923.[185]   In a like manner, in a protocol of the same date, Rumania and Yugoslavia renewed again their alliance of June 7, 1921, which had already been renewed on July 7, 1923.[186]   The third link, the Czechoslovak-Yugoslav treaty, did not require prolongation at this time.[187]

The regular Little Entente Conference for 1926 was held at Bled during June.   Once more there became apparent the tendency for the three states to drift further apart when the discussions were terminated rather abruptly as the result of Rumania's announcement that she had concluded with Poland, on March 26, 1926, a defensive treaty against th U.S.S.R.[188]   Beneš and Nincic, who desired Soviet friendship and complete freedom of action regarding the

---

[183] *The New York Times*, February 13, 1926.

[184] Toynbee, *op. cit.*, 1926, pp. 146-149; Cosma, *op. cit.*, pp. 142-149; Machray, *op. cit.*, pp. 274-277 ; Codresco, *op. cit.*, vol. ii, pp. 7-11.

[185] *Treaty Series*, vol. liv, pp. 253-255.

[186] *Ibid.*, vol. liv, pp. 257-265.

[187] *Le Temps*, June 15, 1926; *cf.* also, Chmelář, J., " Československá zahraniční politika v roce 1926 ", *Zahraniční Politika*, vol. vi, pp. 4-10.

[188] *Treaty Series*, vol. lx, pp. 161-167.

Soviet Union, disapproved of this treaty, not as anti-Bolshevik, but as anti-Russian.[189]

During the following year, 1927, the divergence among the three partners became even more apparent. The three Foreign Ministers, Beneš, Mitilineu and Marinković, held their regular Conference at Jachymov on May 13-14, 1927, to decide their future policies. After a discussion of five hours on the first day and another of three hours on the following day had demonstrated that solidarity still existed on few political issues, the three ministers decided to abandon, for the time being, all attempts to strengthen their alliance politically, and, instead, to turn their efforts towards a cultural, economic and commercial union. Some such conclusion was inevitable if the Little Entente was to be preserved as an efficient organization. Yugoslavia had failed to interest her partners, especially Rumania, in the dangers attending the Italo-Hungarian rapprochement. On the other hand, Rumania feared the Soviet Union. The interests and political alliances of Yugoslavia and Rumania clashed; it seemed as if the former would gravitate towards France and the latter towards Great Britain. Confronted with the conflicting objectives of her two partners, Czechoslovakia apparently preferred to evade the issue until the position of Germany should become clarified; what she considered at the time her chief problem, an Austro-German union, was of no particular concern to either Rumania or Yugoslavia.[190]

In this manner, the Foreign Ministers of the Little Entente determined to retain their union and to avoid any definite statements as to their respective foreign policies; but, by such

[189] *The Times*, June 18-19, 1926; Machray, *op. cit.*, pp. 286-291; Codresco, *op. cit.*, vol. ii, pp. 19-23; *cf. also*, Machray, R., " The Little Entente and its Policies ", *Fortnightly Review*, vol. cxxv, pp. 764-774.

[190] *The New York Times*, May 14-15, 1927; Machray, *The Little Entente*, pp. 308-313. *Cf.* also, *Prager Tagblatt*, May 18, 1927, for Beneš' views on the future of the Little Entente.

tactics, they let slip an opportunity to adopt a constructive policy that might have been followed by other Powers. All three Ministers sought to reduce friction with Hungary. Calling attention to the increased economic vitality of Austria, they agreed to unite with France in objecting to an Austro-German union. However, they refused to commit themselves on Poland's question whether German economic pressure upon Poland would not be a danger to all Europe, on the ground that this question was beyond their scope and a matter rather for the League. In concluding the Conference, the three members stated that the Little Entente was stronger than ever and necessary for the preservation of European peace.[191]

Beneš deplored current rumors regarding the imminent dissolution of the Little Entente and exerted himself to counteract them. To this end, on January 5, 1928, he granted a special interview to representatives of the *Chicago Daily News,* wherein he expressed his belief that it would be impossible for any great war to break out for the next ten years, by which time the older generation would have disappeared and the horror of war lessened. Beneš considered that any union of the defeated states would make for war, whereas a union of states led by France would tend to make for peace. The Little Entente was to be a vital part of any such union. In Beneš' opinion, the recent Franco-Yugoslav alliance was a great deterrent to Italian militarists and the expansion of such treaties might lead to total disarmament. Individual treaties might solve also the Russian question, a process in which the Little Entente might become the connecting link between the U.S.S.R. and the Western Powers. Beneš looked forward to a treaty uniting the

---

[191] *The New York Times,* May 16, 1927; *cf.* also, Codresco, *op. cit.,* vol. ii, pp. 33-37; Seton-Watson, R. W., "The Little Entente", *Contemporary Review,* vol. cxxxii, pp. 694-707.

Soviet Union, Poland, and the Little Entente, a treaty heretofore impossible because of the bitterness between Warsaw and Moscow, and between Rumania and the U.S.S.R. over Bessarabia. The main point to be noted was that the Little Entente was not on the verge of dissolution and that it had not already fulfilled its mission, but that it still had an important rôle to play in the affairs of Europe.[192]

The activities of the Little Entente during 1928 were prima facie evidence of the continued vitality of the organization. The St. Gotthard incident[193] did much to consolidate the bloc. In the spring the three states organized an air service to operate between their leading cities.[194] Early in April, Duca, the Rumanian Minister of Foreign Affairs, invited Yugoslavia and Czechoslovakia to a conference at Bucharest to consider the hostile attitude of Mussolini to the Little Entente, but the respective Foreign Ministers found it impossible to accept the invitation before June. The Conference of Bucharest, June 20-21, 1928, greatly strengthened the loosening ties of the Little Entente. As usual, Poland, without being formally a member, was also present, being represented by an observer. Beneš proposed the holding of a Central European Economic Locarno, without any attempts being made to convert it into a Danubian Confederation and suggested Austria as the first accession. His proposal was received favorably, but no active steps were taken at the time to make it effective. It was decided also that each state should remain free to adopt an independent policy concerning Italy and Italian anti-Slav agitation, a decision that did nothing to strengthen the bonds between Yugoslavia and

---

[192] Beneš, *La Situation internationale et la politique étrangère tchécoslovaque* (exposé aux Commission des affaires étrangères du Senat et Chambre, le 6 juin, 1928).

[193] Cf. *supra*, pp. 274 et seq.

[194] Cf. *Svornost*, December 27, 1927, for plan.

her two partners. The main pronouncement of the Conference was to the effect that the Little Entente, although desirous of friendly relations with Hungary, had not changed its earlier attitude, and still stood as a unit in opposing any attempts to revise the Peace Treaties and thereby to threaten anew the peace of Europe.[195]

Yugoslavia and Czechoslovakia, during the autumn of 1928, negotiated a series of treaties that cemented even more firmly their long-standing friendship. Still unsettled was the question of mutual claims and debts contracted before and during the World War. A treaty of September 29, 1928, prohibited legal procedure for all claims and debts in former Austro-Hungarian crowns contracted before February 26, 1919, in which the currency was contestable,[196] and relegated such questions to a later treaty, which was signed at Praha on November 7, 1928.[197] On the same date, the two states also signed a consular convention.[198] In the meantime, the negotiations for a new commercial treaty were threatened by a " pig war " between the two countries.[199] The new treaty of commerce and navigation was signed at Praha on November 14, 1928. Yugoslavia won her point for reciprocal most-favored-nation treatment, but prohibitions might be imposed on trade for purposes of public health, safety, morality or finance. It was agreed that any restrictions on state

[195] *Prager Tagblatt, Prager Presse,* June 20, 1928; *Svornost,* June 21-23, and July 8, 1928; Machray, *op. cit.,* pp. 342-346; Codresco, *op. cit.,* vol. ii, pp. 59-64.

[196] *Treaty Series,* vol. xcvi, pp. 421-425.

[197] *Ibid.,* vol. xcv, pp. 101-111.

[198] *Ibid.,* vol. xcviii, pp. 297-317.

[199] *The New York Times,* December 2, 1928. Yugoslavia produced more hogs than all the other Balkan countries combined, and had been able to undersell all European competitors. The farmers of Czechoslovakia demanded protection against Serbian pigs, but Yugoslavia insisted upon most-favored-nation treatment in return for similar privileges that had been granted to Czechoslovak industrial products.

monopolies would be mutual. Citizens of either state would be exempt from military service in the other or from contributions in lieu thereof. Other clauses provided for numerous exemptions from duties, for freedom of transit by rail, for equal railway rates, for seagoing vessels to have equal rights in both countries and for postal communications to be as speedy as possible.[200]

The acts that specifically strengthened the Little Entente were the renewals of the treaties of alliance and of the defensive military conventions that supplemented them. The Czechoslovak-Yugoslav treaty of alliance was prolonged in September, 1928,[201] as a part of the series of treaties between the two states, and was ratified by Czechoslovakia on February 12, 1929.[202] The alliance was to remain effective until a year after notice of termination had been given. The regular Little Entente Conference for 1929 was held at Belgrade, May 20-21, at which time the prolongations of all the treaties of alliance were consummated. On May 21, Czechoslovakia and Yugoslavia changed the terms [203] of their recently prolonged alliance in order to make it the same as the similar treaties of the same date between Czechoslovakia and Rumania,[204] and between Rumania and Yugoslavia.[205] Each of the three treaties was prolonged for five years, with renewal automatic at the end of each such period unless the treaty should be denounced six months earlier.

During the course of the Conference of Belgrade there arose the conviction that the system of bilateral agreements, which had hitherto been employed and which Beneš, perhaps

[200] *Treaty Series*, vol. xcvii, pp. 9-59.

[201] *Ibid.*, vol. lxxxvii, pp. 309-311.

[202] *České Slovo*, February 12, 1929; *Svornost*, March 5, 1929.

[203] *Treaty Series*, vol. xciv, pp. 53-55.

[204] *Ibid.*, vol. xcvi, pp. 307-309.

[205] *Ibid.*, vol. xcviii, pp. 221-223.

from a sense of making the best of a semi-favorable necessity, had always defended as an element of strength rather
than of weakness, should be replaced by a tripartite alliance.
From the viewpoint of Czechoslovakia, the obvious increase
in the defensive strength and cohesion of the Little Entente
might be to a large degree offset by an increase of obligations
and by a decrease of freedom in the conduct of foreign
policy, particularly in questions that might concern the
Balkans.[206]   She obtained a compromise on May 21, 1929,
in the general treaty of conciliation, arbitration, and judicial
settlement, an act which reflected the basic principles of both
Locarno and of the Kellogg Peace Pact which the League
was then sponsoring.   By this new treaty, the three partners
agreed that all disputes, of whatever nature, were to be
either conciliated, arbitrated, or subjected to judicial decision.   There was to be no interference with already established judicial procedure.   All disputes as to the respective
rights of the three states were to be submitted to an arbitral
tribunal or to the Permanent Court of International Justice.
It was decided that all disputes might be submitted to conciliation before resorting to arbitration.   After three
months' notice, direct application by any party could be made
to the Permanent Court of International Justice to settle
any dispute.   At the request of one state, a Permanent
Conciliation Commission would be constituted within six
months.   This Commission was to be composed of five members, one from each disputant and the other three from three
different countries.   In conciliation procedure, the parties
might agree to invite a third Power to intervene, if the third
Power had an interest in the dispute.[207]   This general treaty
had the advantage that it strengthened the ties of the Little
Entente by providing for the peaceful solution of any dispute

[206] Cf. Crane, op. cit., pp. 185-186.
[207] Treaty Series, vol. xcvi, pp. 311-331.

without increasing the obligations of its members. The Conference of Belgrade closed with a resolution for a closer economic alliance among the three states. It had been one of the most constructive of the Conferences of the Little Entente, one which was expected to become significant in the safeguarding of the new status quo.[208]

On August 20, 1929, Czechoslovakia ratified the treaties which had been signed at the Conference of Belgrade.[209] On the same day, the *Ceské Slovo* created a sensation with the statement that the treaties were supplemented by a secret military treaty among the three countries of the Little Entente,[210] a statement that lost little force by spirited denials and by the retraction of such an assertion in the following issue.[211] Since the *Ceské Slovo* had always been considered Beneš' mouthpiece, and since the editor of its foreign news columns, Dr. Jaroslav Kopecký, had accompanied Beneš to the Conference of Belgrade, Czechoslovak public opinion refused to credit any denials of the existence of a secret military convention.[212] Added point was given to this opinion by the fact that no German member of the Czechoslovak cabinet had been present at the meeting that had ratified the treaties. If any additional confirmation was necessary, Czechoslovak public opinion considered it offered by the manoeuvres in Moravia, late in August, 1929, when there were present as observers Marshal Pétain of France, and the Chiefs of Staff of the armies of Rumania and Yugoslavia, with their assistants.[213]

[208] *The New York Times*, May 21-23, 25, 1929; *Svornost*, May 10, 22, 25, 26, 1929; *Le Temps*, May 24, 1929; Machray, *op. cit.*, pp. 359-362; Codresco, *op. cit.*, vol. ii, pp. 77-94.

[209] *Ceské Slovo*, August 20, 1929; *Svornost*, August 26, 1929.

[210] *Ceské Slovo*, August 20, 1929.   [211] *Ibid.*, August 21, 1929.

[212] For the close cooperation of the Little Entente during 1929, *cf.* also, Chmelář, J., "Československá zahraniční politika v roce 1929", *Zahraniční Politika*, vol. ix, pp. 1-8.

[213] *Národní Listy*, September 4, 1929; *Svornost*, September 18, 1929.

Germany and the League of Nations

Czechoslovakia held the highest hopes that the Locarno agreements would be followed by a period in which Europe as a whole, under the auspices of the League, would seek to establish upon a firm basis the new post-war status quo. To this end, one of the most important steps was to have been the entry of Germany into the League. However, this step, instead of promoting harmony, became rather the occasion for a fresh display of international rivalry. An extraordinary session of the League was called for March, 1926, to arrange for the admission of Germany, a matter that should have been relatively simple had it not been for other Powers. Spain, Brazil, Poland, China, Czechoslovakia and Persia requested permanent Council seats also, but all except the first two soon abandoned their demands. In order to save the situation by a compromise, Czechoslovakia offered to resign her non-permanent seat to Poland, and Sweden made a similar offer. After considerable international intrigue, marked particularly by foreign pressure upon Sweden, both states resigned, to be succeeded by Poland and Holland, but Germany's admission was still blocked by Brazil, which resisted all pressure.[214] The March session proved to be entirely barren of results. When, largely because of German objections, Brazil and Spain were denied permanent seats, they submitted resignations from the League. The way was thus cleared for the admission of Germany by a unanimous vote at the meeting of September 8, 1926. The number of permanent seats was increased from four to five, and, at the same time, the number of non-permanent seats was increased from six to nine.[215]

[214] Toynbee, *op. cit.*, 1926, pp. 1-98; Cosma, *op. cit.*, pp. 248-251; Buell, *op. cit.*, pp. 111-118; Bassett, J. S., *The League of Nations* (New York, 1928), pp. 300-325.

[215] *Official Journal*, October, 1926, p. 1241.

While the prolonged struggle for seats was an undignified exhibition of national selfishness, the transaction as a whole strengthened the League by the substitution of one Great Power for two lesser ones and also accentuated the influence of Europe within that body. Czechoslovakia felt that her sacrifice of a seat on the Council was worth while in order to ensure a satisfactory solution of the German problem; the fact that her friend and ally, Poland, had succeeded her on the Council augured well for the adequate representation of her own interests within the League.[216] Even this sacrifice proved needless, for the elections of 1926 for the Council resulted in Poland, Rumania and Chile being designated to sit for three years; China, the Netherlands and Colombia for two years; and Belgium, Czechoslovakia and San Salvador for one year.[217]

Beneš stated,

I did not share the optimism of those who believed that the entry of Germany would solve everything, and I do not share the pessimism of those who think it will be disastrous. What we must face is the fact that, with Germany's inevitable inclusion, the League enters upon a new phase, also inevitable. The heroic period is over. We have to find the routine working level on which all human business must be conducted. Germany's presence will naturally add complications, though I am convinced the German delegation will move very slowly. They will watch and wait; they will make no attempt to change the Treaty—which without textual change, you know, is already a good deal modified!

Aside from Germany, it is going to be harder to work with a Council of fourteen than with a Council of ten. The more

[216] Chmelář, J., "Otazka rekonstrukce Rady Společnosti Národu", *Zahraniční Politika*, vol. v, pp. 777-783; Hobza, A., "Reorganisace Společnosti Národu", *Zahraniční Politika*, vol. v, pp. 863-867.

[217] *Monthly Summary*, vol. xi, p. 192.

seats, the less responsibility for each, and the more nations represented, the less international representation. . . . We who are making a new order must learn to adjust ourselves to it.[218]

Peace, Security and Disarmament

Beneš desired to ensure still-further the new status quo by embodying, in some general agreement, his efforts of almost a decade on behalf of peace, security and disarmament.[219] This ideal appeared to be on the eve of realization, when, on September 17, 1927, the League adopted two Czechoslovak proposals: (1) to render it obligatory for League members to facilitate the meetings of the Council in case of a crisis and the functioning of the organs of the League in times of emergency, and (2) to specify the methods of regulation which would enable the Council to make such decisions as might be necessary to enforce the obligations of the Covenant as expeditiously as possible.[220] To give force to the above resolutions, the League formed a new committee on Arbitration and Security, headed by Beneš.[221] Beneš urged all League members to negotiate regional security compacts on the Locarno model as the best practical means of obtaining security. He desired that each state be asked to halt existing rearmament programs.[222]

As chairman of the Committee on Arbitration and Security, Beneš had sent to all members of the League a questionnaire regarding their views. Norway, Sweden, Great Britain and Germany sent replies. The two Scandinavian states preferred a general treaty upon the Locarno model.

[218] Beneš, *Boj o mír* (speech of December 9, 1926), pp. 362-373.

[219] *Cf.* Kačer, K., "Deset let prace pro ideu odzbrojeni", *Zahraniční Politika*, vol. vii, pp. 1048-1064, 1159-1170; vol. viii, pp. 629-647, 776-790, 901-912, 1183-1197, 1455-1478; *L'Europe nouvelle*, January 15, 1927.

[220] *Official Journal*, special supplement, no. 57, pp. 42-43.

[221] *Ibid.*, May, 1928, pp. 610-611.

[222] Beneš, *Boj o mír* (speech of October 25, 1927), pp. 374-377.

Great Britain opposed the enforcement of the Peace Treaties by any system of guarantees based solely upon public opinion, and suggested instead a series of regional treaties. Germany advocated the removal of the causes for war by the adoption of conciliation procedure for non-justiciable disputes, and considered guarantees for the enforcement of treaties of arbitration unnecessary. With these views before them, Beneš and the three rapporteurs [223] who assisted him prepared a series of model treaties [224] at a conference at Praha beginning January 26, 1928. When these treaties were presented to the second session of the Committee (February 20-March 7, 1928) at Geneva, spirited discussions followed.[225] France wished each state to guarantee every boundary in Europe, a move that would spell the union of all against any aggressor, whereas Great Britain presented a plan of regional understandings. Both plans contemplated the aid of the United States in maintaining peace. In the dispute wherein Great Britain maintained that a " progressive reduction of armed forces could be the only true safeguard for world peace " and France that " military security would have to precede disarmament on land or sea ", the three states of the Little Entente shared the views of France.[226] Again Beneš wished to avoid a definite choice between Great Britain and France; his policy embraced elements of both plans, yet Czechoslovakia was bound so closely to her two Little Entente partners and to France that, had it come to a crisis, he would have had to follow the lead of France.[227] On September 26, 1928, the League Assembly

[223] Holsti of Finland, Politis of Greece, and Rutgers of the Netherlands.
[224] *Cf. Official Journal*, May, 1928 pp. 612-650.
[225] *Cf. ibid.*, pp. 651-706, for discussions and other proposals.
[226] *Cf.* Crane, *op. cit.*, p. 149.
[227] *České Slovo*, June 7, 1928; *Svornost*, June 20, 1928; Beneš, E., " Exposé Dra. Beneše, přednesené 4 října 1928 v zahraničním výboru

approved both a general act and the negotiation of special bilateral treaties of arbitration and conciliation.[228]

In the struggle for the attainment of pacific means for the settlement of international disputes, a prominent part was played by the Kellogg or Paris Peace Pact. After a year of international negotiations,[229] the Secretary of State of the United States, F. B. Kellogg, was successful in obtaining, on August 27, 1928, the signatures of fifteen of the leading countries of the world to the treaty. The contracting parties condemned recourse to war for the solution of international controversies and renounced it as an instrument of national policy. They agreed that the solution of all disputes or conflicts of whatever nature or origin would be sought only by pacific means. The treaty would be open for the adherence of every Power of the world and would become effective among the fifteen original signatories when ratifications by all fifteen were deposited at Washington, D. C.[230]

Beneš took the lead in his country in advocating the Kellogg Peace Pact,[231] a sentiment that was almost unanimous throughout Czechoslovakia,[232] which signed the treaty on August 27, 1928,[233] ratified it on January 23, 1929, and deposited the ratification with the League on March 2, 1929.[234] The Czechoslovak government interpreted the

poslanecké sněmovny", *Zahraniční Politika*, vol. vii, pp. 1006-1012; *cf.* also, Chmelář, J., "Československá zahraniční politika v roce 1928", *Zahraniční Politika*, vol. viii, pp. 1-6.

[228] *Official Journal*, special supplement, no. 67, pp. 34 *et seq.*

[229] *Cf.* Shotwell, J. T., *War as an Instrument of National Policy* (New York, 1929); Zimmerman, M. A., "Americký projekt paktu proti válce", *Zahraniční Politika*, vol. vii, pp. 427-432.

[230] *Treaty Series*, vol. xciv, pp. 57-64.

[231] *Cf.* Beneš, *Boj o mír* (speech of June 6, 1928), pp. 397-413.

[232] *Právo Lidu, Prager Presse, České Slovo*, June 9 and 18, July 1, 1928.

[233] *České Slovo*, August 27, 1928.

[234] *Ibid.*, March 2, 1929.

Kellogg Peace Pact in a note of July 20, 1928, sent to Lewis Einstein, United States' Minister at Praha. Beneš thanked the United States for the invitation to participate in the general negotiations and pointed out that for many months he had been stressing the importance of the Pact and the political necessity of associating other Powers in it. His representations to the Locarno Powers had been particularly urgent. He believed that any violation of a multilateral treaty by one contracting party would liberate the other signatories from obligations to that Power, and that the right of self-defense would be in no way restricted by the new Pact. Thus defined, the Pact, in the eyes of Czechoslovakia, had as its objective the maintenance of peaceful relations among the signatory Powers. Czechoslovakia gladly made renunciation of war an instrument of her national policy. Hence she accepted the explanations contained in the United States' note of June 23, 1928 (nothing in the Pact was incompatible with either the League Covenant, with the Locarno agreements or with other treaties that had been negotiated), and approved the Pact.[235]

By March 8, 1929, fifty-eight states had ratified.[236] Thereupon, the League Council at its session of January, 1930, appointed a committee which, meeting from February 25 to March 5, worked out an amendment to the Covenant in order to bring it into harmony with the Pact of Paris.[237] Since the texts of Articles 12 to 18 were not revised, Czechoslovakia was satisfied and made no comments.[238] However, the amendment was not adopted.

During the early years of the existence of the League, there had been established the Permanent Court of Inter-

[235] Cf. Wheeler-Bennett, J. W., Information on the Renunciation of War, 1927-1928 (London, 1928), pp. 166-168.

[236] Official Journal, May, 1930, p. 383.

[237] Ibid., May, 1930, pp. 353-383.   [238] Ibid., May, 1930, p. 381.

national Justice, the Protocol of which had been prepared, as early as December 16, 1920, for the signatures of adherence of the members of the League and of the other states mentioned in the Annex to the Covenant. Czechoslovakia had acceded on September 2, 1921.[239] The Protocol had also a so-called " optional clause " by the signature of which a state rendered the jurisdiction of the Court compulsory for the pacific settlement of certain international disputes. Adherence to the " optional clause " might be made unconditionally, or for a limited time, or through reciprocal agreements with other states. The core of the whole matter was stated in Article 36, paragraph 2, of the statute, which specified that, by its declaration, a state accepted the compulsory jurisdiction of the Court in (1) the interpretation of any treaty, (2) any question of international law, (3) the existence of any fact which, if established, would constitute a violation of an international obligation, and (4) the nature and extent of the reparation that was to be exacted for the aforementioned violation.

On September 19, 1929, Czechoslovakia accepted the optional clause. Beneš declared that, without any special agreement regarding any other state, Czechoslovakia accepted the jurisdiction of the Court under the optional clause for ten years from the date of the deposit of ratification in any future dispute except in cases where another method of pacific settlement had already been provided.[240] The fact remained that the ratification of Czechoslovakia had followed that of other Powers. In the 1929 Assembly of the League of Nations, Great Britain, France and Italy had continued

[239] *Ibid.*, November, 1927, p. 1533.

[240] *Cf. Permanent Court of International Justice*, series E, no. 6, pp. 481-482, for text of Beneš' note.

the drive for the acceptance of the optional clause, and Czechoslovakia had followed their example.[241]

Attention should also be called to the fact that Czechoslovakia has not ratified the general act,[242] even though it was virtually the child of Beneš' own Committee on Arbitration and Security. This apparent inconsistency was owing to adverse public opinion which balked at entrusting to any foreign agency questions vital to the existence of the Republic.[243] Nevertheless, Czechoslovakia continued to be one of the most ardent advocates of the basic principles of the League. Through Beneš, she had been extremely fruitful in constructive suggestions for the improvement of the organization, i. e. amendments expediting the procedure of the Council and Assembly, reinforcing the Covenant by a general non-aggression agreement (the Geneva Protocol), by special regional agreements like the Little Entente treaties, and by urging the League to exert effective jurisdiction over any question that might threaten general peace. Although Czechoslovakia has never regarded the League as a cure-all for her international troubles, for she has solved her most vital ones outside its scope, she has shown, on the whole, willingness to submit to that body such questions as fell within its proper jurisdiction, particularly minorities, the reconstruction of Austria and Hungary, security, disarmament, and the preservation of the new status quo upon the basis established by the Locarno agreements.

[241] Cf. *Official Journal*, special supplement, no. 75, pp. 74-76. Twenty-four states had accepted it before 1929.

[242] Cf. *supra*, pp. 299 *et seq.*

[243] Cf. *České Slovo, Národní Politika*, September 19, 1928.

CHAPTER VII

The Depression

ECONOMIC CONFERENCES

THE high hopes that had been prevalent throughout Europe as a result of the progress made in the various negotiations regarding the establishment of security failed to materialize. The feeling of optimism that had produced Locarno and the Pact of Paris was followed by a reaction that produced a feeling of pessimism as to the future and a general disinclination to follow the precedents of international cooperation. There resulted a marked revival of selfish nationalism that augured ill for the future success of such projects for international harmony as still felt the impetus of the preceding period of optimism. This new trend of events was an outgrowth of the world-wide economic depression which began in the autumn of 1929, and which soon attained such proportions that the major activity of almost every state was directed towards its mitigation. Instead of a unified international struggle, against the common menace, there developed a tendency for each individual state to go its own way, to seek its own salvation regardless of the consequences to the others. This revival of national selfishness tended to aggravate still further the trend towards international chaos, and produced a depression that existed not only in the sphere of economics, but in almost every other human activity. Amid the general distress, most of the nations of the world sought to alter those portions of the status quo that appeared detrimental to their own interests.

305

The transition from optimism to pessimism was fairly rapid. While the various Powers were still desirous of attaining a greater degree of international cooperation and stability, they called at Geneva, under the auspices of the League of Nations, a World Economic Conference, which met on May 4, 1927, with fifty states being represented by 194 delegates. After a debate of four days, the Conference was divided into three Commissions: on commerce, industry and agriculture. The first Committee (commerce) advocated an immediate general tariff reduction; the second (industry), of which the chairman was Dr. Hodač of Czechoslovakia, specified the circumstances in which international industrial combinations would be considered beneficial or harmful; and the third (agriculture) sought to adjust the prices of agricultural and industrial products, to form cooperative societies and to develop agricultural credit. After heated debates, it was decided to abandon all attempts to create an international agricultural credit bureau. The Conference terminated with the plenary session of May 21, at which time the reports of the three Committees were approved, the U.S.S.R.[1] alone dissenting.

The Czechoslovak delegates to the World Economic Conference issued an official statement to explain their views: (1) Czechoslovakia has not yet overcome the economic results of the World War; (2) Czechoslovakia has devoted all her energies to coordinate a national economic system; (3) Czechoslovakia has always tried to avoid inflation and to balance her budget; (4) Czechoslovak agricultural and industrial production has been handicapped by the results of the War; (5) Czechoslovak industry was in a difficult position owing to a complete change in the fundamental conditions ruling output and markets; (6) the above factors had determined the trend of Czechoslovakia's trade policy after

[1] *Publications*, Economic and Financial, 1927, ii, 13, 33 p.

the War; and therefore (7) Czechoslovakia was pursuing a national economic policy which was still in a condition of transition.[2] Czechoslovakia's viewpoint was further clarified by one of her delegates, Dr. Stodola, who, on May 7, stated that his country had made untiring efforts to better her own economic situation without relying to any great extent upon foreign assistance. Czechoslovakia was willing to cooperate loyally with other countries to revive international trade. For several years it had been her policy to reduce customs duties. As evidence of this fact Stodola pointed out that Czechoslovak duties in 1927 were only five per cent higher than the Austrian duties of 1913. He promised that Czechoslovakia would try to decrease still more internal obstacles to the maintenance of a large agricultural and industrial output, and would press for the adoption of the same policy upon an international scale.[3]

On June 16, 1927, Beneš stated in a meeting of the League Council that the great merit of the Conference had been to throw impartial light upon the origins, causes and nature of present economic problems. He believed that many confused and mistaken ideas had been set right. He issued also a warning that the cure that had been prescribed (i. e. international cooperation) would be slow and would require much patience, but would be sure. He pledged the full adherence of Czechoslovakia in principle to the work of the Conference, but again pointed out the need for patience. Certain ideas and principles that had been formulated, particularly in regard to commercial policy, would require more thorough examination in order that their consequences might be fully appreciated. On behalf of his country, Beneš announced his intention of adopting immedi-

[2] *Ibid.*, 1927 ii 31, pp. 4-9.
[3] *Ibid.*, 1927 ii 52, vol. i, pp. 124-125.

ately a policy conforming with the principles approved by the Conference.[4]

A special Conference was called to meet at Geneva on October 17, 1927, to deal with the abolition of import and export prohibitions and restrictions, thirty-five states being represented. Dr. Ibl, speaking for Czechoslovakia on October 18, 1927, referred to Beneš' speech of June 16, and pointed out that no change had taken place in the views of his country.[5] After three weeks of debate, this second Conference approved a convention of eighteen articles which was based upon the recommendations of the Economic Committee of the League. The treaty specified that, except for restrictions imposed for the sake of public safety, public health, the protection of national currencies, or for curtailing the traffic in arms, all export and import prohibitions or restrictions would be abolished within six months of the coming into effect of the treaty, but that, under abnormal circumstances, each signatory might adopt temporarily whatever measures might be deemed necessary to protect its vital interests.[6]

At once fifteen states submitted extensive exceptions which were intended to safeguard interests that they considered vital. Only eight states agreed to sign immediately, among them Czechoslovakia,[7] but eighteen ratifications were necessary to render the treaty effective. Since the required ratifications were slow in coming, a Protocol was prepared in Paris on December 20, 1929, whereby Poland and Czechoslovakia were allowed until May 31, 1930, to submit their

---

[4] *Ibid.*, 1927 ii 50, pp. 8-9. Cf. *Zprávy* (Poslanecká Sněmovna), 128 meeting, February 7, 1928, pp. 19-22, 5 session, for Deputy Horpynka's explanation of how Czechoslovakia's activities at the World Economic Conference differed with the economic ideas of parliament.

[5] *Publications*, Economic and Financial, 1928 ii 7, pp. 64-65.

[6] *Treaty Series*, vol. xcvii, pp. 391-462.

[7] *Národni Listy*, November 8, 1927.

ratifications, whereupon the treaty would go into effect.[8] Subsequently, in the hope that other ratifications might be forthcoming, Poland was granted an extension of time to June 20, 1930, and Czechoslovakia to June 26, 1930. Czechoslovakia ratified the treaty the day before her time limit expired,[9] but Poland still postponed ratifications until all artificial import barriers would be lifted from what she considered her natural markets.[10] Thereupon, on June 25, Czechoslovakia announced that she would wait for other ratifications, particularly Poland's, before she would consider the treaty effective.[11] Czechoslovakia's attitude in waiting for Poland before ratifying the treaty for the abolition of import and export prohibitions, and thereby inaugurating a widespread repudiation of the agreement, appeared reactionary and contrary to her general policy.[12] The explanation would be found in the fact that Czechoslovakia, in spite of her readiness to sign the treaty at once, had been but lukewarm to the agreement because of her internal political situation; the Agrarian Party, although not in a majority, still retained a considerable influence which, for economic reasons, had been wielded relentlessly against the treaty, and the indecision of the other states had furnished the Agrarians with the necessary weapons to make their policy prevail.[13] Czechoslovakia's action induced eight other states to proclaim in disgust that, after July 1, 1930, they would also cease to regard the treaty as binding upon themselves.[14]

[8] *Le Temps, The New York Times,* December 20, 1929.

[9] *The New York Times,* June 25, 1930.

[10] *Gazeta Warszawska,* June 27, 1930.

[11] *České Slovo,* June 28, 1930.

[12] *Cf.* McClure, W., *World Prosperity* (New York, 1933), p. 368.

[13] *Cf. Publications,* Economic and Financial, 1930 ii 13, p. 23, for Czechoslovak explanation (Ibl) of December 6, 1929.

[14] *The New York Times,* June 30, 1930.

Only Great Britain, the United States, Japan, Portugal, the Netherlands, Denmark and Norway continued to adhere to the treaty.[15]

Another effort to promote international cooperation was inaugurated by Aristide Briand, who, on April 17, 1930, sent to twenty-six nations memoranda regarding a vast new project.[16] His draft plan, completed on May 11, 1930, envisaged a United States of Europe upon an economic basis.[17] To support his project, Briand cited the League's approval of regional understandings.[18] The general response was favorable.[19] Czechoslovakia's reply was handed to the French Minister in Praha on July 14. The Czechoslovak government pointed out that its foreign policy, as evinced by membership and work in the Little Entente, by Locarno, and by efforts generally on behalf of European peace, had always been favorable to any plan that would tend to promote a greater degree of cooperation among the nations of Europe. Briand's plan was of the type of regional agreement which had been approved by Article 21 of the League Covenant and which Czechoslovakia had been sponsoring. Czechoslovakia was willing to enter into any federation provided that the national sovereignty of the states participating remain unimpaired, that European states with overseas interests be included, that the organization be not aimed against any overseas state, and that the principles of the League prevail. Czechoslovakia considered it expedient that the eleventh League Assembly institute a Committee of Research which would assemble the replies of the various states, and

[15] Toynbee, *op. cit.*, 1929, p. 111.

[16] *The New York Times*, April 17, 1930.

[17] *Ibid.*, May 11, 1930.

[18] *Ibid.*, May 18, 1930 (text of plan).

[19] *Cf. Publications*, Political, 1930 vii 4, pp. 17-65, for the texts of the various replies.

prepare for next year's meeting a draft statute of organization. The Czechoslovak note suggested also that this statute include only fundamental rules in order to ensure harmony between political and economic factors.[20]

Lengthy debates took place between Briand and Henderson over the respective French and British viewpoints over the details of the plan: France desired first a federation, which was to bring about disarmament, whereas Great Britain wished disarmament first, and believed that a federation would follow. On September 16, 1930, the French delegates proposed the creation of a Commission of Inquiry on European Union.[21] The suggestion was adopted on the following day by the forty-five delegates of the various states, the response of the Czechoslovaks being favorable.[22] The general approval induced Schober, the Austrian delegate, to point out that a United States of Europe should be preceeded by regional understandings and, that in view of this fact, Austria and Germany were projecting a Customs Union, which other states might join.[23] As a result of this new development, which raised the question of the revision of the Peace Treaties, Briand gave up his plan for a United States of Europe and sought merely "a decent orthodox Geneva burial for his idea".[24]

Beneš still persevered. At the third session of the Commission of Inquiry on May 19, 1931, he proposed three economic remedies: (1) a system of customs unions; (2) systems of agrarian preferences and industrial understandings coupled with customs truces; and (3) a system of

[20] Cf. ibid., Political, 1930 vii 4, pp. 45-46; cf. also, Beneš, E., La Situation de l'Europe, la Société des Nations, et la Tchécoslovaquie, speech of October 15, 1930, Sources et documents tchécoslovaques, no. 15.

[21] Official Journal, special supplement, no. 84, pp. 117-118.

[22] Ibid., p. 126.

[23] Cf. Monthly Summary, vol. xi, pp. 117-118.

[24] The New York Times, September 6, 1931.

special bilateral treaties. Beneš issued a warning that the question was primarily political, regardless of the intention of the delegates to regard it as essentially economic. The formation of one European group would consolidate a rival group and produce economic war. In his estimation, the present exaggerated protectionism would have to be replaced gradually. The first step might well be tariff stabilization, followed by reductions later. Haste might ruin the entire program. He suggested a system of bilateral treaties which would preserve intact most-favored-nation clauses and which would restrict preferences to agricultural products. Czechoslovakia was willing to study all phases of the problem and would do her share to bring about a general improvement.[25] On September 12, 1931, Beneš praised the Commission of Inquiry as practical, justifiable and necessary. He emphasized the fact that Czechoslovakia had placed high hopes in it. The League Assembly, largely as the result of this plea, prolonged indefinitely the life of the Commission of Inquiry,[26] and on September 26, at the fifth session of the Commission of Inquiry, Czechoslovakia was given a place on a special committee to examine a draft pact of economic non-aggression.[27] It was not to be. Briand died on March 7, 1932,[28] and the Commission, at its next meeting (September 30-October 1), accomplished nothing.[29] Thereupon the idea was abandoned.

The Proposed Austro-German Customs Union

The long proposed Anschluss assumed a concrete form in the spring of 1931 in the project for an Austro-German

[25] *Publications*, Political, 1931 vii 7, pp. 46-50.

[26] *Official Journal*, special supplement, no. 99, pp. 11-12.

[27] *Publications*, Political, 1932 vii 8, p. 1.

[28] *The New York Times*, March 8, 1932.

[29] *Publications*, Political, 1932 vii 13, pp. 7-11.

Customs Union. The question was broached by Curtius, the German Foreign Minister, early in March, 1931, during a visit to Vienna.[30] A communiqué of March 22, 1931, announced officially that the economic unity of the two countries was contemplated by a Protocol on March 19.[31] This announcement proved to be a test of the sincerity of France, Czechoslovakia, etc., in a United States of Europe. Although the Customs Union might be joined by others, it was construed by some of the victor states as an evasion of the Peace Treaties and as the first step towards a political union. On the following day the representatives of France, Italy and Czechoslovakia lodged at Vienna a protest that the proposed union constituted a breach of the Geneva Protocols of October 4, 1922 [32] (the reconstruction of Austria). The protest was unheeded by Austria; rather, she appeared to be furthering the project by announcing on March 25 that she would consider as denounced from July 1, 1931, her existing commercial treaties with Hungary, Yugoslavia and Czechoslovakia.[33] Her dissatisfaction with the treaty of July 21, 1927, with Czechoslovakia, had been caused by what she had considered its excessive rates. Despite her impending Customs Union with Germany, Austria, on July 22, 1931, signed at Vienna a new commercial treaty with Czechoslovakia, whereby tariff rates were readjusted, generally at lower figures, mutual most-favored-nation clauses of earlier treaties were retained, and neither country, except with the consent of the other, was to levy export duties under whatever name.[34]

[30] *Arbeiter Zeitung, The New York Times*, March 4, 1931.

[31] *The New York Times*, March 22, 1931; text, March 24, 1931.

[32] *Ibid., Arbeiter Zeitung*, March 23, 1931.

[33] *The New York Times, Svornost*, March 25, 1931.

[34] *Treaty Series*, vol. cxxviii, pp. 59-305.

The projected union met with diverse responses. Great Britain decided not to oppose the move.[35]   Italy studied the project with a view to acceding.[36]   The U.S.S.R. was sympathetic.[37]   France objected to the union, which was expected to kill prospects of a long-term loan by her to Germany.[38]   Curtius explained the whole matter to the Ambassadors of France, Great Britain and Italy,[39] and requested that the still broader question of a European customs union be placed upon the League agenda.[40]   The tension was relieved somewhat when Briand obtained from Austria a promise not to resume negotiations until after the May meeting of the League.[41]   The Little Entente, after the most serious internal crisis in its history, also pronounced itself definitely opposed to the project.[42]

From the outset, Czechoslovakia was bitterly opposed to the union, and affected to disbelieve Austro-German denials of any political aspects of the proposal.   Beneš voiced repeatedly the viewpoint of his country,[43] and called upon the German minority to prove itself loyal to Czechoslovakia in the crisis.[44]   To avert the union, Beneš, on April 23, 1931,

[35] *The New York Times*, March 25, 1931.

[36] *Ibid.*, March 26, 1931.   [37] *Ibid.*, March 28, 1931.

[38] *Ibid.*, March 26 and 28, 1931.   [39] *Ibid.*, March 24, 1931.

[40] *Ibid.*, April 16, 1931.   [41] *Ibid.*, April 18, 1931.

[42] *Ibid.*, May 6, 1931; for full details, *cf. infra*, pp. 323 *et seq.*

[43] Beneš, *Boj o mír*, pp. 551-553 (speech of March 26, 1931); pp. 554-600 (speech of April 23, 1931, summarizing the whole situation before the Foreign Affairs Committees of both houses of parliament); *Official Journal*, vol. xii, pp. 1075-1077.   Through March, April and May, 1931, practically every issue of every Czechoslovak newspaper printed columns on the union, only with the coming of summer was there any marked decrease in public interest.   *Cf.* Beneš, E. (Argus), *The Economic Aspect of the Austro-German Customs Union* (Prague, 1930), for a semi-official summary of Czechoslovakia's economic reasons for opposing the project; also, Bitterman, M., *Austria and the Customs Union* (Prague, 1931).

[44] *The New York Times*, May 8, 1931; *České Slovo*, May 10, 1931; *Svornost*, May 11, 1931.

proposed a counterplan embracing all Europe, a customs union based upon most-favored-nation principles with agrarian preferences.[45] Beneš had had this plan in mind for some time, but had not announced it earlier out of deference to Briand's projected United States of Europe.[46] If successful, Beneš' scheme would have been a practical compromise between the exigencies of the European economic situation and the demands of the Czechoslovak Agrarians, but, failing to attract sufficient support, it became but one of many suggestions that led to no practical results.

The campaign against the Austro-German Customs Union acquired added momentum as the result of the denunciation of the project by France in a memorandum of May 18, 1931,[47] which was reinforced by a report that the French bankers would be willing to aid Austria if the projected union was dropped.[48] On September 3, 1931, in order to save face by anticipating an adverse opinion of the World Court, the agency to which the project had been referred for an advisory opinion, both Austria and Germany stated that they had renounced it voluntarily.[49] Many within Austria deemed this renunciation merely temporary, to be revoked at some more favorable occasion in the future.[50] The only permanent factor in the situation was that the future relations of Austria and Czechoslovakia would depend largely upon the sincerity of the renunciation. The official death-knell of the Austro-German Customs Union was sounded, apparently, on Sep-

---

[45] *The New York Times*, April 24, 1931; *České Slovo*, April 23, 1931; *Svornost*, April 24, 1931.

[46] *Cf.* Beneš, *Boj o mír*, pp. 529-550 (speech of October 15, 1930).

[47] *Official Journal*, vol. xii, pp. 1168-1169.

[48] *The New York Times*, May 18, 1931.

[49] *Arbeiter Zeitung*, September 3, 1931.

[50] *Ibid.*, *Neue Freie Presse*, September 3, 1931; *Svornost*, September 4, 1931.

tember 5, 1931, when the World Court by a vote of eight to seven pronounced it contrary to the international agreements already entered into by Austria.[51]

Czechoslovakia's contacts with Germany, potentially her most dangerous enemy, remained " correct ", indeed almost cordial for many years, a condition of affairs that reflected creditably upon the statesmen of both countries. The mutual cooperation between the two states, which had been engendered by close economic ties, reached perhaps a climax in two treaties which were signed at Praha on April 29, 1931,[52] regarding the establishment and operation of regular airways, both with and without landings in the territories of both countries.

Despite these two treaties, relations between Czechoslovakia and Germany became strained as the result of the active part which had been taken by the former in aiding the frustration of the Austro-German Customs Union. Beneš, in his desire to maintain relations with both Austria and Germany upon the former cordial plane, stressed the point that Anschluss was not merely a problem for Czechoslovakia, but was continental in scope. He sought to substitute for the defunct Customs-Union a new project. On October 20, 1931, he proposed, specifically, a tentative customs union of Austria and Hungary with Czechoslovakia. To this bloc would be added eventually Yugoslavia, and perhaps Rumania also. In his estimation, nothing of permanent value could be accomplished without the approval of France, Italy and Germany, but, on the other hand, no plan could be imposed successfully by the Great Powers upon the

---

[51] *Permanent Court of International Justice*, series A/B, no. 41; *The World Court's Advisory Opinion on the Austro-German Customs Union*, the American Foundation, Foreign Relations Bulletin no. 9, September 5, 1931.; *Official Journal*, vol. xii, pp. 2069-2070; *Monthly Summary*, vol. xi, pp. 117-118, 167-168, 190, 213 and 226.

[52] *Treaty Series*, vol. cxxxiii, pp. 347-367.

small states of Central Europe without the consent of the latter. Above all, there must be no secret negotiations.[53]

Through a leakage which developed from Beneš' informal conversations with the Austrian Minister at Praha, to whom he had outlined his project, Czechoslovak public opinion became aware of the plan before Beneš delivered his exposé. Much agitation resulted when the Czechoslovak government saw fit to censor the October 7 edition of the *Prager Tagblatt* because of an article wherein a Dr. B. Jelinek, in approving Beneš' plan too forcibly, stated that, if the proposed Danubian Union was not consummated, Czechoslovakia would revert to the condition of Bohemia after the Thirty Years' War.[54] In spite of a generally favorable reaction within Czechoslovakia, Beneš' plan drew little support elsewhere: the other Little Entente states were cool, Germany, Austria, Hungary and Italy were hostile,[55] and France alone approved [56]—in fact, disapproval was so general that Beneš felt it advisable to deny rumors that his project had been inspired by France.[57]

The lack of support encountered by Beneš' plan could be accounted for in part by a German counter-project for relieving to some degree the economic distress of Central Europe. Germany sought to aid the agricultural states of Southeastern Europe by granting special preferential tariffs to their wheat. To this end, treaties were drawn up between Germany and Hungary, and between Germany and Rumania, despite the fact that such special privileges violated the most-favored-

[53] *Národní Listy, The New York Times*, October 21, 1931; *Svornost*, October 14 and 23, 1931.

[54] *Cf. The Central European Observer*, October 9, 1931.

[55] *Berliner Tageblatt, Arbeiter Zeitung, Corriere della Sera*, October 21, 1931; *Svornost*, March 17 and April 8, 1932; *The Times*, April 8, 1932.

[56] *Le Temps*, October 21-22, 1931.

[57] *The New York Times*, December 11, 1931; *Svornost*, December 15, 1931.

nation clauses of treaties with many other countries. These two treaties, to become effective, required the approval of all the states with which Germany had negotiated commercial treaties that contained most-favored-nation clauses. Twenty countries, including the United States,[58] failed to protest because of the diminution˜of their treaty rights, but three others, namely, Czechoslovakia, Argentina and Turkey, sent Germany vigorous protests immediately, and demanded privileges similar to those which Germany was offering to Hungary and Rumania. These protests caused the German project to be dropped, and strained also future relations between Germany and Czechoslovakia.[59]

Austria, disappointed in being excluded from some larger customs organization and apparently despairing of her future as an independent entity, seethed with rumors regarding the imminence of desperate action. Dr. F. Soukup, President of the Czechoslovak Senate and one of the leaders of the Social Democratic Party, returned to Praha from Austria, where he had attended a convention of Austrian Social Democrats, and brought with him an alarming report of the activities of the Austrian Fascists, who were charged with desiring the destruction of the Austrian Republic and the restoration of a monarchy. In Soukup's opinion, Czechoslovakia could never tolerate such a change within Austria.[60]

Politics vs. Economics within the Little Entente

One of the best examples of the interplay of politics and economics was offered by the negotiations that Czechoslo-

[58] The United States, the Soviet Union and Denmark reserved the right to suspend judgment until a later time.

[59] *Berliner Tageblatt, Národní Listy*, November 17, 1931; *Neue Freie Presse, Prager Presse*, November 20, 1931; *Svornost*, November 18 and 21, 1931.

[60] *The New York Times*, November 19, 1931; *Svornost*, November 21, 1931.

vakia conducted with her two Little Entente partners during 1930 and 1931. The 1930 conference of the Little Entente was held on the plateau of Štrba (Štrbské Pleso), in the Tatra Mountains of Slovakia, June 25-28, 1930. There were present the three Foreign Ministers: Beneš, Marinkovič and Mironescu. The Conference centered its attention upon Hungary, where rumors were rife of a coup d'état on the part of Otto on the model of Carol II's in Rumania. Again the Little Entente deemed it necessary to warn Hungary against attempting the restoration of the Habsburgs and against attempting any revision of the Treaty of Trianon. Other questions concerned the application of the Pact of Paris and the decision of the recent Hague Conferences. Concern was felt that Poland sent no observer to the Conference, and the menace of Franco-Italian rivalry was also felt keenly. Beneš stated that he desired a renewal of Franco-German friendship. The high degree of economic nationalism still extant caused him to be sceptical of the success of an economic Little Entente.[61] The Praha *Večer* of June 26, 1930, created a sensation at the Conference by publishing a statement of Dr. Viškovský, the Czechoslovak Minister of National Defense, to the effect that Central Europe was in more danger of war than it had been at any time in the past ten years because of Italian and Hungarian intrigues and because of the increase in armaments in Europe as a result of such threats. Nevertheless, the Conference closed on an optimistic note,[62] caused primarily by the signing of a new Czechoslovak-Rumanian commercial treaty [63] in spite of domestic objections in both states,[64] and by the

[61] *České Slovo*, June 29, 1930; *Svornost*, June 30, 1930.

[62] *Svornost*, July 2, 1930; *Prager Presse*, July 1, 1930.

[63] *Treaty Series*, vol. cxix, pp. 73-159.

[64] Cf. *The New York Times*, June 28, 1930.

evidences of solidarity of the major interests of the three members.[65]

On July 21, 1930, there opened at Bucharest a conference between Rumania, Yugoslavia and Hungary for the purpose of creating an agricultural bloc in Central Europe. Very early a limited degree of cooperation was attained on the questions of erecting grain elevators and of financing harvests. For a time the Praha newspapers displayed a measure of resentment over the exclusion of Czechoslovakia.[66] Nothing of note was accomplished, because no agreement could be reached upon the question of a unified monopoly of exports, to which neither Rumania nor Yugoslavia would assent, owing to fears that the agency might be controlled by Hungary.[67]

Of relatively greater importance were the Conferences of Sinaia and Warsaw. On July 22, 1930, representatives of Rumania and Yugoslavia met at Sinaia in order to attempt to render the Little Entente as efficient economically as it was politically. It was hoped also that Rumania and Yugoslavia could establish economic contacts with the U.S.S.R. on the order of those of Czechoslovakia. On August 1 the Conference recommended a more complete agreement between their agriculturalists and the Czechoslovak manufacturers,[68] but any such attempt would be certain to encounter the hostility of the powerful Agrarian Party within Czechoslovakia.[69] Although much could be accomplished by long-termed bilateral commercial treaties, the states concerned doubted whether the concessions that would be required

[65] *Národní Listy, Lidové Noviny,* June 26, 1930; *Svornost,* June 25–July 2, 1930.

[66] *Cf. České Slovo, Národní Politika, Národní Listy,* July 21-22, 1930.

[67] *Cf.* Crane, *op. cit.,* p. 158.

[68] *Cf. ibid.,* p. 158.

[69] *Cf. Svornost,* August 2, 1930.

might not be greater than the benefits that would be received.[70]

The Conference of Warsaw, which met on August 28, 1930, was attended by representatives from Poland, Estonia, Bulgaria, Hungary, Rumania, Yugoslavia and Czechoslovakia, and by observers from Finland and from the League. There were signed a whole series of international agreements between the agricultural and industrial states, as well as agreements based upon collaboration between states economically similar.[71] The Conference decided to advocate the formation of an economic United States of Europe based upon mutual preferential tariffs on agricultural products. It recommended an immediate abolition of export bounties and of discriminations that tended towards indirect protection. However, the objections of overseas states, coupled with the unwillingness of the industrial states to grant concessions to the agricultural states, precluded the possibility of creating a successful economic combine that might have any pretensions of being continental in scope.[72]

Perhaps the chief problem of the Little Entente in 1930 was the fact that its members were at odds economically, although in accord politically. The conflict of economic interests had been demonstrated by the fact that, before 1930, Czechoslovakia had had no tariff treaties with either of her diplomatic partners. To the inherent difficulty of creating an economic unit of industrial yet semi-agricultural Czechoslovakia and of predominantly agricultural yet industrially ambitious Rumania and Yugoslavia, must be added the fact that the exigencies of the geographical position of the states of the Little Entente would demand the inclusion of Austria and Hungary as well in any really efficient economic bloc—

[70] Crane, *op. cit.*, p. 162; *cf.* also, *Prager Presse*, August 13, 1930.

[71] For text, *cf. L'Europe nouvelle*, September 13, 1930.

[72] *Cf.* Crane, *op. cit.*, pp. 159-160.

a combination apparently impossible for nationalistic and political reasons.[73]

The spring of 1931 witnessed fresh rumors of the imminent dissolution of the Little Entente. The visit óf Prince Nicholas of Rumania to Budapest early in April gave rise to reports that he had been sent there by his brother, King Carol II, for the purpose of sounding Hungary on the possibility of a union of the crowns of Hungary and Rumania under Carol, in which event Nicholas would become Governor of Transylvania.[74] The visit of Nicholas was merely the occasion for one of many rumors that Carol was considering the withdrawal of Rumania from the Little Entente and that he would carry his country from the French to the Italian camp.[75] On the other hand, Yugoslavia and Czechoslovakia cemented still more firmly their existing friendship by a new commercial treaty signed on March 30, 1931.[76]

Beneš won his point to have the regular 1931 conference of the Little Entente held at Bucharest early in May, before the May meeting of the League Council, in order to ascertain the views of the three states regarding the proposed Austro-German Customs Union.[77] He was surprised to receive from Rumania an evasive answer as to her viewpoint on the question, for fear lest the discussions might give rise to economic questions delicate to the susceptibilities of the members of the Little Entente! The new Rumanian Minister of Foreign Affairs, Ghika, went on to state that, in view of the recent cabinet crisis, Rumania had not been able to come to a definite viewpoint on the question.[78]

---

[73] *Cf.* Hanč, J., "O Středoevropské hospodářské dorozumění", *Zahraniční Politika*, 1932, pt. i, pp. 108-118.

[74] *Svornost*, April 10, 1931.   [75] *Cf. ibid.*, June 9, 1930.

[76] *Treaty Series*, vol. cxxv, pp. 273-335.

[77] *Cf. Svornost*, May 1, 1931.

[78] *České Slovo*, April 30, 1931.

The Conference of Bucharest, which was held in the utmost secrecy behind closed doors, confronted the Little Entente with the greatest internal crisis it had ever faced. At the end of the first day's proceedings, May 3, 1931, it was announced that the object of the Conference was the winning over of Hungary to the Little Entente in an effort to prevent the accession of Hungary to the Austro-German Customs Union, an event which it was feared would have spelled complete German hegemony over Central Europe. To avert such a calamity, the Little Entente proposed to Hungary considerable reductions in tariff rates to permit the importation of Hungarian wheat into the states of the Little Entente, a cooperative pooling of Hungarian, Rumanian and Yugoslav wheat, and a uniform system of credits for farmers. Desperate as was deemed the situation of the Little Entente, further reports of the offering of full membership in the organization to Hungary were discredited—the Little Entente was fundamentally a defensive alliance against Hungary and would lose its raison d'être by such a step. Baffling indeed was the secrecy of the Conference and the refusal of admission to reporters.[79]

After the final session of May 6, 1931, definite statements were issued: there had been passed resolutions of hostility to the Austro-German Customs Union and others urging Czechoslovakia to forego the collection of duties on Rumanian and Yugoslav agricultural products in return for preferential duties on Czechoslovak manufactures.[80] In spite of the secrecy surrounding the Conference, it may be assumed that a great clash of interests took place between Czechoslovakia on the one hand and her two partners on the other, a conflict from which the former emerged victorious,

[79] *České Slovo, The New York Times*, May 4, 1931; *Svornost*, May 5, 1931.

[80] *The New York Times*, May 6, 1931.

and in which political considerations triumphed over economic ones. The alignment of Yugoslavia and Rumania against Czechoslovakia was revealed by the meeting at Temesvar, of Kings Alexander and Carol, during the crisis of the Conference, a meeting which caused anxiety in both Czechoslovakia and France, which was supporting her against her two partners.[81]

Czechoslovakia, predominantly industrial, had interests diametrically opposed to those of Rumania and Yugoslavia; for instance, she had a well-developed agricultural system as a result of which she could not consume more than a small part of the agricultural exports of her two partners.[82]   In the search of the latter for other markets, the large and hungry population of Germany appeared the most promising. The two agricultural members of the Little Entente felt the need of protecting themselves against becoming the dumping ground for Czechoslovak manufactured goods.   The projected Austro-German Customs Union, the bugbear of Czechoslovakia and France, was no menace to Rumania and Yugoslavia; if anything, they welcomed it as a step in the abolition of tariff barriers against their agricultural products —with such a Union, trade would flow both ways and under conditions more advantageous to them than would trade with Czechoslovakia and the Soviet Union, both of which had a relatively lesser need for agricultural products.   Rumania and Yugoslavia had little fear of the results, even if the Austro-German Customs Union were the first step to Anschluss.   Their strength and geographical position were such that they deemed that the economic advantages far outweighed any remote political dangers that might result.

[81] Ceské Slovo, Le Temps, May 4, 1931; Svornost, May 5, 1931.

[82] Cf. Svornost, January 24, 1932, for the influence of the Czechoslovak Agrarian Party upon Beneš' negotiations.

It was a great tribute to the influence of Czechoslovakia and of Beneš personally that Rumania and Yugoslavia were induced to continue the policy of preserving the status quo economically as well as politically. The important part played in Czechoslovakia's diplomatic triumph by unstinted French support could hardly be overestimated, and was appreciated accordingly by the recipient, in spite of the realization that France had an equally vital interest in the preservation of the Little Entente. The crisis served to show the interdependence of international politics and economics. Rumania and Yugoslavia were subjected to a cruel choice— in the crisis they preferred to preserve the friendships and policies of the War, which were of unquestioned value even if they were not entirely an unmixed blessing, rather than adopt the untried road which might lead to possibly greater economic advantages with perhaps attending perils.[83] Czechoslovakia did her utmost to minimize the points of divergence with her partners, hence the policy of secrecy. At the close of the Conference of Bucharest, Ghika asserted anew the absolute solidarity of the Little Entente.[84] It had weathered successfully the most severe crisis in its history; as long as the same enlightened policy of mutual tolerance and understanding would guide its statesmen, it promised to continue " sitting on the lid " and preventing any alteration of the status quo. However, nothing could last forever and, amid the increasingly insistent attempts of discontented states to revise the Peace Treaties, it became more and more open to question how long such a policy could be maintained.

[83] For a comprehensive account of both the domestic and the foreign problems of the Little Entente, *cf.* Malynski, E., *Les Problèmes de l'est et la Petite Entente* (Paris, 1931).

[84] *České Slovo,* May 5, 1931; *Svornost,* May 6, 1931.

Hungarian Revisionism

Hungary continued to make renewed attempts to alter the status quo. Since Hungarian resentment might be considered practically permanent, there remained the question of the tactics that Czechoslovakia should use to counteract Hungarian agitation. For many years it had been rumored that Masaryk and Beneš had held widely divergent viewpoints regarding the attitude Czechoslovakia should adopt towards attempts to revise the Treaty of Trianon. In the belief that Czechoslovakia could not continue to resist indefinitely hostile pressure from both Germany and Hungary, Masaryk allegedly had, in recent years, asserted repeatedly in public his willingness to negotiate with Hungary the question of a boundary revision, whereas Beneš did not believe in yielding a square, inch of soil to Hungary. The Czechoslovak Chamber of Deputies went on record as opposed to any revision.[85]

On October 8, 1929, it was rumored that President Masaryk was willing to negotiate with Hungary for all territory granted to Czechoslovakia by the Treaty of Trianon, and, except for Bratislava, to return all regions in which the Hungarian population totalled fifty per cent or more.[86] Beneš officially denied the authenticity of Masaryk's offer, but political opponents remained sceptical.[87] For about a year nothing more was heard of the matter, but in the fall of 1930 the question was revived. The Vienna *Neue Freie Presse* stated that one of its reporters had been granted an interview by Masaryk wherein the President had stated his

[85] *Zprávy* (Poslanecká Sněmovna), 198 meeting, May 23, 1929, pp. 31-33, 8 session.

[86] *The New York Times, České Slovo, Prager Presse*, October 8, 1929; *Svornost*, October 9, 1929.

[87] *The New York Times, České Slovo*, November 17, 1929; *Svornost*, November 18, 1929.

willingness to negotiate modifications of the existing frontier with Hungary if the latter would abandon its traditionally hostile attitude towards Czechoslovakia.[88]   Again there came official denials to the effect that the President had not granted any such interview, that he realized that a problem of such magnitude could not be decided by Czechoslovakia alone without consulting both the Big and Little Ententes, and that he had no intention of arousing the question of an entire revision of the Peace Treaties.[89]   Great indeed was the agitation within Czechoslovakia and widespread the protest against any concession to the traditional foe.   Pronouncements of Hungarian revisionists to the effect that a plebiscite in Slovakia would result in union with Hungary were given the lie by Father Andrew Hlinka, the political leader of the Slovaks and their spokesman in the Chamber of Deputies, when he stated that the Slovaks would never consent to any voluntary revision of the boundary, but would rise to the defense of their existing frontiers whenever the need might arise.[90]   Thus ended, for the time being at least, any talk of revising the frontiers of Slovakia.

On September 28, 1930, the Czechoslovak government proclaimed its intention to begin the construction of a navy.[91] The keel of the first patrol boat, the " Masaryk ", was laid at Komarno on October 15, 1930.[92]

Another question that disturbed the quiet of Czechoslovakia, as well as that of the other members of the Little Entente, was the constantly haunting menace of the restoration of a Habsburg to the throne of Hungary.   After the exile and death of Emperor Charles in 1922, his eldest son,

[88] *Neue Freie Presse*, September 28, 1930.
[89] *Národní Listy*, October 1-2, 1930; *Svornost*, October 3 and 16, 1930.
[90] *Prager Presse*, December 8, 1930; *Svornost*, December 9, 1930.
[91] *České Slovo*, September 28, 1930.
[92] *Ibid.*, October 15, 1930.

Otto, had been recognized as "King" by the Hungarian legitimists. Otto, a boy of ten at the time, was brought up in exile by his mother, Zita, to regard himself as the true ruler of Hungary. Although forced by poverty to accept the hospitality of King Alfonso and of various noblemen in Spain and later in Belgium, he nevertheless continued to greet regularly delegations of Magyars and to indicate in every possible way his dissatisfaction with the existing condition of affairs. Since 1922, ex-Empress Zita had left little undone that might hasten a Habsburg restoration, and had increased her activities as Otto grew older, to the increasing uneasiness of the states of the Little Entente. A sigh of relief went up in Czechoslovakia when November 20, 1930, the date of Otto's eighteenth birthday and of his majority, passed without action.[93] Nevertheless, the so-called "King Question" still remained unsolved and continued to be regarded by Hungary as an open wound. Zita and Otto continued their quest for foreign support. Beneš stated that the position of Czechoslovakia remained unaltered, and that a restoration of the Habsburgs would mean war.[94]

The Czechoslovak-Hungarian commercial treaty of 1927, which expired on December 15, 1930, again had the effect of leaving the commercial relations between the two states without any treaty basis. The cause of the difficulty had been Czechoslovakia's dissatisfaction with certain of the tariff provisions of the treaty. As early as April 30, 1930, she had requested Hungary to revise these certain items [95] and, when no satisfaction was forthcoming, on June 15, 1930, she denounced the treaty,[96] which was to expire six

[93] *Ibid., Národní Listy, Prager Presse, Svornost,* November 20, 1930.

[94] *České Slovo,* July 3, 1930; *Svornost,* July 4, 1930.

[95] *Národní Listy,* April 30, 1930.

[96] *Sbírka zákonu a nařízení státu československého,* ročník 1930, částka 83 ze dne 13 prosince, čis. 177.

months later. At once a tariff war broke out; from the date of the expiration of the treaty, both countries proceeded to levy on the goods of the other duties far higher than those in effect during the validity of the recent treaty. Hungary suffered particularly from the Czechoslovak boycott on wheat. Late in December, 1930, a delegation of Hungarian business men visited Praha in the hope of saving the situation by some compromise,[97] but, owing primarily to the opposition of the Czechoslovak Agrarian Party, no agreement could be reached.[98] Hungary replied to Czechoslovak restrictions on agricultural products by decreeing that henceforth, except by special permission, certain manufactured goods, including shoes, textiles and woolens, could not be imported from countries with which Hungary had no trade agreements.[99] Thus the tariff war raged on. Its immediate result was closer economic ties between Czechoslovakia and Yugoslavia, whereas Hungary turned to Germany, Austria and Italy.[100]

Another evidence of the depth of hostility between Czechoslovakia and Hungary was the verbal clash between Beneš and Premier Bethlen of Hungary. Beneš had granted an interview to a reporter of the Paris *Midi* in which he had made statements which Bethlen had deemed unwarranted interference in the internal affairs of Hungary.[101] In self-defense Beneš replied that he asked nothing better than eco-

[97] *Prager Presse*, December 17, 1930.

[98] *Zprávy* (Poslanecká Sněmovna), 96 meeting, December 16, 1930, p. 42, 3 session.

[99] *Národní Listy*, December 26, 1930.

[100] *Cf. Svornost*, January 31, 1931. Commercial relations between Czechoslovakia and Hungary had no treaty basis until June 4, 1934, but the agreement of that date was changed several times during 1934 and 1935. For full details, *cf.* Chmelář, J., "Československá zahraniční politika v roce 1935", *Zahraniční Politika*, vol. xv, p. 679.

[101] *Cf. The New York Times*, February 15, 1931.

nomic and political cooperation with Hungary. He considered Bethlen's violent attack nothing more than propaganda against his, Beneš', comparison of the treatment of the respective minorities by Hungary and Czechoslovakia, a comparison unfavorable to the former.[102] He ignored completely Bethlen's personal remarks. As usual, the Czechoslovak press took up the issue. From the protest of February 21, 1931, of Ghiczy, the Hungarian Minister to Praha,[103] it appeared that the comments of the *Právo Lidu* were the most irritating, but again, as in the case of earlier protests of Italy which will be considered shortly, Czechoslovakia refused to place any restrictions upon the freedom of the press.[104] Czechoslovakia's relations with Hungary remained far more embittered than those with any other country.

Italo-Czechoslovak Friction

Since the so-called " Rothermere incident " of 1927-28,[105] Czechoslovak public opinion continued to associate Italy with Hungarian attempts to revise the Peace Treaties. After this outburst, there ensued a period of two years of silent resentment of Italian foreign policy on the part of Czechoslovakia, until the year 1930 witnessed a series of new crises. Italian foreign policy appeared tortuous, opportunistic and hard to understand. Its apparent contradictions might be best explained perhaps by the fact that Italy desired to preserve the status quo in regard to her gains during the War, and yet sought to revise those portions of the post-war settlement which had failed to bring her the rewards to which she felt herself entitled. Unsatisfied colonially, and playing

[102] *České Slovo*, February 15, 1931; *Svornost*, March 1, 1931.

[103] *České Slovo*, February 21, 1931.

[104] *Ibid.*, February 23, 1931; *Svornost*, February 24, 1931.

[105] *Cf. Le Temps*, March 30, 1928, for Mussolini's speech on the necessity for a revision of the Peace Treaties; also *supra*, pp. 267-269.

a losing game against France and the Little Entente for preponderance in Central Europe, Italy, to avoid isolation, felt
that any future improvement in her international status
might well depend upon the success with which she could
hold the balance of power between the victor and the vanquished states of the World War. Thus, Italy sought to
revive the game that she had played so successfully before the
War—of having one foot in each camp.[106]

The April visit of Premier Bethlen of Hungary to Rome
aroused the apprehensions of all the members of the Little
Entente, particularly when it was reported that Mussolini
had promised to second Hungarian attempts to revise the
Treaty of Trianon.[107] In June it was rumored in Praha
that Otto would ascend the Hungarian throne in the fall,
primarily through the assistance of Italy, which would con-
front France and the Little Entente with the fait accompli.[108]

September, 1930, witnessed a severe Italo-Czechoslovak
crisis. On June 6, 1930, there circulated throughout Yugoslavia reports of the summary execution of several Yugo-
slavs, charged with high treason, by a Fascist tribunal at
Trieste. The report filtered through in spite of strict censorship.[109] Without exception, Czechoslovak newspapers
condemned the bloody deed, calling attention to the possibility of a world-wide conflagration as the result. Czechoslovak public opinion was incited still further by Italian concern for defenseless Hungary, whose capital, Budapest, lay
within range of Czechoslovak guns from across the
frontier.[110]

---

[106] *Cf.* Simonds, *op. cit.*, pp. 212-213.

[107] *Svornost*, April 20-21, 1930; *Národní Listy*, April 20, 1930.

[108] *Právo Lidu*, June 22, 1930; *Svornost*, June 23, 1930.

[109] *Svornost*, June 8, 1930.

[110] *Ibid.*, September 10, 1930; *Národní Listy*, August 21, 1930.

On September 10, 1930, Kramář, the leader of the National Democrats, openly called the executions at Trieste barbarous,[111] a statement echoed throughout the Czechoslovak press. The next day, Signor Pedrazzi, Italian Minister to Praha, protested to Dr. Krofta, acting for Beneš while the latter was at Geneva, against the hostile tone of the Czechoslovak press, but received the answer that the Czechoslovak press was independent and enjoyed freedom of expression, hence the government regretted that it could do nothing about the matter.[112] Czechoslovak anger grew apace at the outrage to a Slav minority.[113] The *Právo Lidu*, as usual the most radical, led the way, followed by the *České Slovo*, in demanding in the name of Slavdom a cessation of Mussolini's interference in the internal affairs of other states —that it was high time he understood that his sovereignty did not extend to Czechoslovakia.[114] On the same day a mass meeting at Praha ended in a march to the Italian Legation, the windows of which were broken by stones.[115] A committee was organized to boycott Italy and Italian goods as a further protest.[116] Dr. K. Viškovský, Czechoslovak Minister of National Defense, pledged Yugoslavia military assistance in the event of an emergency.[117] The Czechoslovak Legion, composed of war veterans, pledged similarly their loyalty to Yugoslavia.[118] Czechoslovak and Yugoslav Sokols, protesting in union against the Trieste executions,

[111] *Národní Listy*, September 10, 1930; *Svornost*, September 11, 1930.

[112] *The New York Times, Národní Listy*, September 11, 1930; *Svornost*, September 12, 1930.

[113] *Cf. The New York Times*, September 12, 1930.

[114] *Právo Lidu, České Slovo*, September 13, 1930; *Svornost*, September 14, 1930.

[115] *The New York Times*, September 13, 1930.

[116] *Ibid.*, September 17, 1930; *Svornost*, September 20, 1930.

[117] *Svornost*, September 20, 1930; *České Slovo*, September 19, 1930.

[118] *České Slovo*, September 23, 1930; *Svornost*, September 24, 1930.

drew in response heated Italian criticism of their interference.[119]   Another Italian protest against the sentiments of the Czechoslovak press, this time by Signor Francesco Palmieri, Italian Consul at Bratislava, had an effect entirely opposite to what had been intended.[120]

Mussolini aroused apprehensions throughout Europe by a provocative speech of October 27, 1930, wherein he called attention to the future of Italy and of Fascism.[121]   Abroad, his utterances were considered more cynically brutal than any of Bismarck's; the chorus of disapproval resounded from London, Paris, Berlin and Praha.[122]   The statement that a general revision of the Peace Treaties would be to the interest of all Europe and would tend to prevent war was subjected to particular criticism.[123]

Early in 1931 there took place the celebrated flight of the Italian air squadron to Brazil.   After the official report of the flight had been published, it was discovered that, among the casualties, were some Hungarians, who had come to Italy to be trained in aviation.   At once the *Právo Lidu* called attention to the fact that Italy was conniving in Hungarian evasion of the Peace Treaties by training Hungarian officers in Italy.[124]   Signor Pedrazzi again protested to Beneš, who expressed his regret about the article in the *Právo Lidu*, but no steps were taken to prevent the paper from publishing further anti-Italian articles.[125]

[119] *Corriere della Sera*, September 24, 1930; *Svornost*, September 25, 1930.

[120] *Právo Lidu, Lidové Noviny, Národní Listy, České Slovo*, September 10, 1930; *Svornost*, September 28, 1930.

[121] *Corriere della Sera*, October 27, 1930.

[122] *The Times, Le Temps, Deutsche Allgemeine Zeitung, Národní Listy*, October 28, 1930; *Svornost*, October 29, 1930.

[123] *Cf. The New York Times*, November 2, 1930.

[124] *Právo Lidu*, February 18, 1931.

[125] *The New York Times*, February 19, 1931; *Svornost*, February 20, 1931.

The U.S.S.R. and Poland

Czechoslovakia's neighbors to the East sought to allay rather than to enhance the friction that existed within Central Europe. Hand in hand with closer economic contacts, there became marked also between the U.S.S.R. and Czechoslovakia a steady diminution of political friction. The former had long abandoned any hopes of successful interference in the internal affairs of the latter. The once formidable Communist Party within Czechoslovakia, which had been founded in 1921 by Czechoslovak radicals, dwindled and was torn by internal dissensions,[126] until on August 14, 1930, its members agreed to merge by September 1, 1930, with the Social Democratic Party.[127] Although revived later, it no longer represented a threat to the stability of the Republic.

The question of de jure recognition of the Soviet Union received renewed impetus during the summer of 1931 through the active efforts of Czechoslovak manufacturers, who insisted that such recognition of Russia was a vital necessity to the recently improved business relations between the two states and more important to the welfare of the Republic than any purely political considerations. Within, Czechoslovakia, the Socialists were favorably inclined, but the National Democrats, led by Kramář, were as always bitterly opposed to the move. On September 3, 1931, Jan Šeba, former Czechoslovak Minister to Belgrade and at the time a member of the Czechoslovak parliament and an intimate friend of Beneš, admitted that he was conducting, at Moscow, negotiations for de jure recognition.[128] Despite the infer-

---

[126] *Svornost*, April 13, 19, 1929.

[127] *Ibid.*, August 15, 1930. *Cf.* also, Reimann, P., *Dějiny komunistické strany československé* (Praha, 1931), for a detailed account of the history of the Czechoslovak Communist Party.

[128] *Národní Listy, České Slovo, Svornost,* September 3, 1931.

ence of Fischer that Beneš, since 1929, might be using Kramář's opposition as a mere excuse for withholding de jure recognition,[129] no evidence had been produced that Beneš had not been sincere on every occasion that he had advocated Soviet recognition. In 1931, the opposition within Czechoslovakia was still so strong that there existed little chance for a successful outcome of any Soviet negotiations that were not strictly economic in nature.[130] Nevertheless, the initialing of the treaty of friendship and non-aggression between France and the U.S.S.R.[131] had a marked effect upon Czechoslovak public opinion, which hoped for similar agreements between the Soviet Union and Poland and the Soviet Union and Czechoslovakia. It created within the Republic a sentiment more favorable to recognition than ever before, a steadily growing conviction that de jure recognition of the Soviet government on the part of Czechoslovakia was merely a question of time and circumstances.[132]

The outlook on Czechoslovakia's eastern horizon appeared still more favorable as a result of Poland's conciliatory attitude. Poland, which had already, on January 15, 1931, concluded with Rumania a five-year treaty of mutual guarantee,[133] renewed again, for three more years, the secret treaty of military alliance with France which had been drawn up during June, 1922, for ten years.[134] Still feeling insecure,

[129] Cf. Fischer, op. cit., vol. ii, p. 507.

[130] Cf. Chmelář, J., " Československá zahraniční politika v roce 1931 ", Zahraniční Politika, vol. xi, pt. i, pp. 101-107.

[131] The Times, The New York Times, August 20, 1931. The treaty was signed November 29, 1932. Cf. Nouveau recueil, iii série, vol. xxix, pp. 28 et seq.

[132] Národní Politika, České Slovo, August 20, 1931; Svornost, August 21, 1931; cf. also, Fierlinger, Z., Sovietské Rusko na nové dráze (Praha, 1932).

[133] Treaty Series, vol. cxv, pp. 171-175.

[134] Le Temps, May 19, 1932; Svornost, May 20, 1932.

Poland, despite the almost frantic objections of Rumania, signed, on July 25, 1932, in Moscow, with the Soviet Union, a non-aggression pact with regard to which the two countries had been negotiating since January.[135] The only satisfaction that Rumania could secure was a promise that Poland would withhold ratification of the treaty until Rumania would bring to a satisfactory termination her own dispute with Moscow over Bessarabia.[136] During the summer and early fall of 1932 Poland sought to cultivate also warmer friendship with Czechoslovakia, a campaign which perhaps reached its climax early in October when Czechoslovak public opinion reacted favorably to a much publicized statement attributed to the Polish Minister of Foreign Affairs, Zaleski, that the preservation of peace and the maintenance of a balance of power in Central Europe were dependent upon the cooperation of Poland and Czechoslovakia.[137]

Revisionism vs. the Status Quo

It appeared that Europe was again threatened with a division into two armed camps over the question of the Peace Treaties: into a revisionist bloc which included Germany, Italy, Austria, Hungary and Bulgaria, and into an anti-revisionist bloc composed of France, Belgium, the Little Entente, Poland, and possibly Great Britain,[138] an alignment which had been predicted several years in advance by Viscount D'Abernon, the British Ambassador to Germany.[139] France, which continued to uphold the principle of the inviolability of the Peace Treaties, met the challenge subtly

[135] *Cf. Izvestia, Gazeta Warszawska,* January 30, 1932; *Svornost,* January 31, 1932.

[136] *Svornost,* July 25-26, 1932; *Gazeta Warszawska,* July 24-25, 1932.

[137] *Národní Listy,* October 1, 6, 1932; *Svornost,* October 13, 28, 1932.

[138] *Cf.* De Balla, V., *The New Balance of Power in Europe* (Baltimore, 1932).

[139] D'Abernon, *op. cit.,* vol. ii, p. 108.

in 1931; by means of granting foreign loans judiciously and by exerting thereby political pressure upon the recipients of her favors, she not only strengthened greatly her own bloc, but hoped to disrupt, eventually, the opposing alignment. The first of these so-called political loans was made on March 10, 1931, $42,000,000 to Rumania. By means of two agreements of March 30 and April 17, France loaned Poland $40,000,000, most of which was to be spent for the construction, by French engineers, of a railroad connecting the coal fields of Upper Silesia with Gdynia, Poland's only seaport. On April 23, the day of Beneš' denunciation of the Austro-German Customs Union, Czechoslovakia was granted a loan of $50,000,000 to help liquidate frozen assets. On May 8, Yugoslavia was loaned $42,000,000 for public works and for the stabilization of her finances. After protracted negotiations, the last of this particular series of loans was made in August, $25,000,000 to Hungary,[140] in return for control of Hungarian finances, a lease on Hungarian railroads, and a Hungarian promise to renounce revisionism, an act which may have had some influence in inducing the latter to adopt a reserved attitude towards the proposed Austro-German Customs Union.[141]

In spite of the loan from France, Czechoslovakia's finances remained in a strained situation. Her foreign trade greatly declined between 1930 and 1932.[142] The depression was caused by several factors. The civil war in China and the

[140] Cf. The New York Times, September 13, 1931, for article by R. L. Buell, "The Weight of France's Gold on the Scales of Diplomacy"; Toynbee, op. cit., 1932, p. 36; Rouček, op. cit., p. 146; Langsam, op. cit., p. 208.

[141] Cf. The New York Times, April 17, 1931.

[142] For the years 1930, 1931 and 1932, respectively, Czechoslovakia's imports amounted to 15,715,000, 11,801,000 and 8,155,000 crowns, respectively; her exports, 17,474,000, 13,149,000 and 7,399,000 crowns, respectively. Cf. Publications, Economic and Financial, 1933, ii A 7, p. 165.

series of bankruptcies in various South American states had crippled Czechoslovakia's textile exports, the decline of the pound sterling had affected adversely the export of glassware, porcelain, gloves, and other small manufactured articles and, worst of all, about twenty-five per cent of Czechoslovakia's foreign trade had been conducted with her immediate neighbors, Germany, Austria, Poland and Hungary, states which were on the verge of bankruptcy. In these states, Czechoslovak merchants had granted extensive credits which had become frozen assets, owing to moratoria and other factors. During the several years in question, the Republic had also made considerable payments on its foreign debts.[143] Hence, negotiations were opened for a second loan. When Dr. V. Pospíšil, Governor of the Czechoslovak National Bank, sounded France in December, 1931, the terms were so severe that he declined even to consider them. They were not made public, but were resented by Czechoslovakia, whose financial distress was but temporary and owing to a lack of liquidity rather than to excessive deficits.[144] However, the negotiations were continued. On January 22, 1932, an agreement for a new French loan of one billion Czechoslovak crowns (about $30,000,000) was approved by the Czechoslovak government,[145] and signed by Osuský, the Czechoslovak Minister to Paris, and by Flandin, at the time the French Minister of Finance, but again the specific terms were not made public.[146] It might be safely inferred that the new loan, which was considered the culmination of the

[143] *Cf. Státní zaverečný účet republiky československé za rok 1930*, pp. 286-289; *1931*, pp. 312-313; *1932*, pp. 330-331; *1933*, pp. 332-333.

[144] *Svornost*, January 22, 1932.

[145] *Zprávy* (Poslanecká Sněmovna), 165 meeting, January 22, 1932, pp. 3-6, 5 session.

[146] *Národní Listy*, January 21, 25, 1932.

French system of political loans, bound Czechoslovakia more closely to France than before.[147]

Another of these so-called political loans was granted by France to Austria, $14,000,000 on December 29, 1932. Voted in the French Chamber of Deputies 325 to 188, and in the French Senate 144 to 68, this loan to an enemy state two weeks after France defaulted on $19,000,000 of war debts due to the United States was an act which even Flandin characterized as " monstrous ".[148]

Beneš' project for an economic Danubian Confederation comprising, as a nucleus, Czechoslovakia, Austria and Hungary, a project which as late as January 6, 1932, was reported abandoned by France because of the opposition of Germany and Italy,[149] was revived during March, and embodied in the so-called Tardieu plan for a Danubian Confederation of Austria, Hungary and the Little Entente. In general, Czechoslovak public opinion was favorable. The *Národní Listy* desired that the bloc be truly a new Confederation and not merely a resurrection of the Dual Monarchy,[150] whereas the *České Slovo* recommended that the plan be studied first by economic experts, then by the various Czechoslovak political parties, and finally by the May conference of the Little Entente.[151] In an exposé of March 25, 1932, Beneš approved the project in the hope of improving Central Europe's economic status, but felt that the united support of the Great Powers would be essential for its success.[152] On the same day France secured the approval of Great Britain for the

---

[147] *Cf. Svornost*, January 26, 1932.

[148] *Le Temps*, December 29, 1932.

[149] *The New York Times*, January 6, 1932.

[150] *Národní Listy*, March 11, 1932.

[151] *České Slovo*, March 11, 1932.

[152] *Ibid., Národní Listy*, March 25, 1932; *Svornost*, March 26, 1932.

plan.[153] On April 6 a four-Power conference of France, Great Britain, Germany and Italy met at London in an attempt to prevent the economic collapse of Central Europe. Britain and France recommended that the five states in the projected Confederation lower their tariffs against one another by ten per cent, that they abolish all other agencies that hindered trade, that other states renounce most-favored-nation clauses in treaties with the states of the bloc, that $40,000,000 be loaned to the states in the bloc, and that the agricultural produce of these five states be given a unilateral preference by all other countries. Germany and Italy remained unalterably opposed to the plan, on the ground that their own exclusion would complicate unnecessarily their existing economic difficulties without affording sufficient relief to the five small beneficiaries.[154] As a result, the London Conference collapsed within two days, and with it went all hopes for the success of the Tardieu plan.[155] In vain did Hungary, Rumania and Yugoslavia accept the Tardieu plan in principle,[156] and in vain did Hungary support the Little Entente against Germany, Italy and Austria.[157]

The regular Conference of the Little Entente was held at Belgrade, May 13-15, 1932, with the Foreign Ministers of Poland (Zaleski) and of Greece (Michalakopoulos) present as observers. The chief significance of the meeting was a pronouncement against supernationalism as expressed in the tendency for each state to adopt its own selfish economic policy: as the best antidote, the five-Power Danubian Confederation was again recommended temporarily, until a more

[153] *Le Temps*, March 25, 1932; *cf.* also, Chmelář, J., " Tardieuuv plán středoevropské spoluprace ", *Zahraniční Politika*, vol. xi, pt. i, pp. 185-192.

[154] *The Times, The New York Times*, April 6-9, 1932.

[155] *Národní Listy*, April 11, 1932.

[156] *The New York Times*, April 20, 1932.

[157] *Ibid.*, April 21, 1932.

extensive agreement could be reached.[158]   This recommendation was denounced by Premier Bethlen of Hungary, who
had apparently been converted to a viewpoint that the best
interests of his country lay in the continuation of a policy
of revisionism,[159] and by both Italy and Germany.[160]

Reparations and Debts

The problem of Central European reparations, which had
been for a decade one of the bitterest of controversies, had
arisen again in 1929.   The Succession States had been com-
plaining that the League had been so interested in the problem of German reparations that it had neglected to pay adequate attention to problems of a similar nature in Central
Europe.   The supposedly final settlement [161] of the question
of German reparations renewed the desire of the Succession
States for an equally definite solution of their corresponding
problems, hence Beneš' activity in the interim.   Beneš became
the spokesman for all the Succession States when he urged
the Little Entente to adopt a unified attitude regarding the
question.   He went on to state his opinion that all the states
of Central Europe would be wise if they associated their
respective financial and political problems with the issue of
German reparations and with the Young Plan.[162]   At the
Little Entente Conference of Belgrade of May 20-21,
1929,[163] the three partners came to an agreement, in which

[158] *Ibid.*, May 15-16, 1932.

[159] *Ibid.*, May 23, 1932.   [160] *Ibid.*, June 12, 1932.

[161] The Young Plan for German reparations, after being threshed over
by a committee of experts at Paris from February, 1929, to June 7,
1929, stated the definite amount that Germany would be compelled to pay.
The plan was also referred, for final approval, to a conference of governments, to meet at the Hague on August 6. Cf. *The Times, Le Temps,*
June 6, 1929.

[162] *České Slovo*, May 15, 1929; *Svornost*, May 16, 1929.

[163] Cf. *supra*, pp. 294-296.

they were joined later by Poland and Greece, that they would withhold their approval of the Young Plan and of the reduction of German reparations until after their own reparations problems with Austria, Hungary and Bulgaria had also been solved. The five states formed a bloc that acted as a unit at the Hague Conference in August, 1929, and at the second session in January, 1930, until its essential demands had been conceded. The same stand was taken at the Paris Conference on non-German reparations during September-November, 1929.[164]

The agreements signed at the Hague Conference on January 20, 1930, represented one of the most important events in post-war Europe since the Peace Treaties. Austrian reparations to Poland and Czechoslovakia (Article 177 of the Treaty of St. Germain) were abrogated. Czechoslovakia objected to being burdened by the Powers with a debt of approximately $150,000,000 for " Costs of Liberation " until Hungarian reparations were fixed at a figure which she approved. All in all, the " Costs of Liberation " for the Succession States totalled approximately $2,000,000,000. The thorny problem was not direct reparations, but the claims which arose for former crown properties of Austria-Hungary and for the estates which were being broken' up as the result of the new policies of agrarian reform which the states of the Little Entente were enforcing. Italy cooperated with the Little Entente in the adoption of a compromise, the " Brocchi Plan ", for Hungary, whereby there were created two separate funds: fund A, about $45,000,000, for land claims, and fund B, about $20,000,000, for the claims of the Habsburgs, of churches, of railroads, and of industrialists. The operating capital for these funds was to be raised, until 1943, partially through deposits from Hungarian payments

[164] *Cf. Le Temps*, January 24, 1930, for the declaration of Mironescu regarding the intimate collaboration of the states of the Little Entente.

made by Great Britain, France and Italy, but, from 1943 to 1966, entirely by deposits of the states of the Little Entente from Hungarian payments which would accrue to their benefit. The Mixed Tribunals (Hungarian-Czechoslovak, Hungarian-Rumanian and Hungarian-Yugoslav) might exercise merely juridical functions, but could no longer be the vehicles for financial claims directed against these three states.[165] The reparations that Czechoslovakia had been expected to contribute to the Allied fund for crown property, about 25,000,000,000 Czechoslovak crowns, were cancelled. The "Costs of Liberation" were cut to about one-fourth and were to be represented by thirty-seven annual payments of 10,000,000 Reichsmarks each (a little over 80,000,000 Czechoslovak crowns). Czechoslovakia was granted also a share of Bulgarian and Hungarian reparations, about 25,-000,000 Czechoslovak crowns.[166] In addition to the sacrifices that Czechoslovakia had made for independence, she could point to the fact that her national pride could not permit others to bear the entire cost of the war that had freed her.[167] The agreements reached at the second Conference were signed at Paris by the Commission for Eastern Reparations, composed of Bethlen, Beneš, Marinkovič and Titulescu, on March 31, 1930, and by the representatives of the Great Powers on April 28, 1930. They took the form of four conventions concerning (1) the reparations agreements between Hungary and the Creditor Powers, (2) the settlement of land reform, (3) the settlement of Mixed Arbitral Tribunal questions, and (4) the Powers of the Special Funds.[168]

[165] *Cf.* Crane, *op. cit.*, pp. 163-169.

[166] *Cf. Agreements Concluded at the Hague Conference, January, 1930* (London, 1930).

[167] *Cf.* Krofta, K., " Haag a Pařiž ", *Zahraniční Politika*, vol. ix, pp. 497-500; Chmelář, J., " Československá zahraniční politika v roce 1930 ", *Zahraniční Politika*, 1931, pt. i, pp. 12-19.

[168] *Treaty Series*, vol. cxxvii, pp. 95-101.

The settlement represented for Czechoslovakia a total liquidation of the reparations question. She also took advantage of her cooperation with France and Italy during the reparations negotiations to settle her debts with them. For the equipment and maintenance of the Czechoslovak Legions during the war, France was to receive for fifty years an annual payment of 10,000,000 paper francs, and Italy, for a like period of time, an annuity of 20,000,000 Czechoslovak crowns.[169]

It remained for the sequel to demonstrate how illusory had been any hopes for a final settlement of the general question of reparations. The post-war loans, primarily of the United States and of Great Britain to Germany, added to the already immense burden of reparations, created for Germany in the summer of 1931 a very precarious financial situation. In the emergency came the proposal of President Hoover of July 1, 1931, of a moratorium of one year in the payment of reparations and all inter-governmental loans.[170] It was well received in most countries with the exception of France, which objected lest it be especially favorable to Germany, and lest it militate against the inviolability of the Peace Treaties and of the subsequent reparations settlement. Nevertheless, after a struggle, France fell in line with the other Powers to avoid isolation.[171] Hoover's plan was welcomed by the Little Entente and especially by Czechoslovakia, to which it would mean relief from the annual payment of

[169] For Beneš' two exposés of January 30 and May 20, 1930, *cf.* Beneš, *Boj o mír*, pp. 438-490 and 491-528; also Beneš, E., *Les Problèmes des réparations et la liquidation de la guerre mondiale à la Haye* and *Vers la liquidation de la guerre: traités de la Haye et de Paris*, Sources et documents tchécoslovaques, nos. 12 and 13.

[170] *The New York Times*, June 19-30, 1931.

[171] *Ibid., Le Temps*, June 19-30, 1931; *cf.* also, Armstrong, H. F., " France and the Hoover Plan ", *Foreign Affairs*, vol. x, pp. 23-33.

$3,000,000 in interest due on her debt to the United States,[172] but the political situation, especially the fear of offending France, dictated a reserved acceptance of the proposal until France had accepted as well.[173] However, the moratorium failed to improve the situation.

The three states of the Little Entente desired to have discussed further before the League the questions of disarmament, war debts and German reparations.[174] In this attempt, they seconded the initiative of Great Britain, which had attempted to call an economic conference at Lausanne, Switzerland, on January 18, 1932.[175] Throughout the year, Beneš worked on the question of world disarmament,[176] but, without much success. The negotiations on disarmament took him far afield in their almost labyrinthine details, not only into every European political conflict of importance, but even to a declaration against the activities of Japan in China. Beneš was not concerned in the intricacies of the Manchurian situation on its own merits, but solely because Japan's headlong course in defying the opinion of the rest of the world had, in his estimation, contributed greatly towards reducing the prestige and influence of the League.[177]

By the middle of the summer of 1932, France had apparently begun to lose hope of obtaining extensive German rep-

[172] Regarding Czechoslovakia's debt settlement of October 13, 1925, with the United States, cf. supra, pp. 248-249.

[173] *České Slovo*, June 25, July 2, 15, 1931; *Národní Listy*, July 15, 1931; Beneš, *Boj o mír*, pp. 601-619 (speech of October 20, 1931, before Foreign Affairs Committees of Senate and Chamber of Deputies).

[174] *Svornost*, February 4, 1932.

[175] *The Times*, December 30, 1931.

[176] *Cf. The New York Times*, February 13, 28, March 2, July 19, 1932; *Svornost*, January 1, 4, February 4, 13, 14, 26, 29, March 3, 5, 16, 19, April 24, June 15, 24, July 14, 20, 29, August 7, 1932. For full details, cf. Kraus, J., *Světové odzbrojení* (Praha, 1933). Cf. also, infra, pp. 352-354.

[177] Beneš, *Boj o mír*, pp. 620-652 (speech of March 22, 1932).

arations. At the Lausanne Conference, on July 9, 1932, there was signed an agreement whereby the Young Plan for German reparations, which had envisaged an amount of 34,000,000,000 gold marks, payable in annuities until 1988, was scrapped and replaced by a new obligation of merely 3,000,000,000 gold marks (about $714,600,000). Other parts of the agreement concerned the extension of the moratorium on inter-Allied debts, financial assistance to the distressed states of the Danubian area, the appointment of a commission to examine the agricultural problems of the Danubian area, and the calling of a world economic conference under the auspices of the League of Nations.[178] Clear-cut indeed was the inference that the United States was expected to reduce its debt claims against the former Allies in proportion to the reductions that they had accorded Germany.[179]

When the regular war debt payments to the United States again became due on December 15, 1932, after the one year interval of the Hoover moratorium, the resumption of payments was irksome to the nations of Europe. As has already been mentioned, France took the lead in defaulting. Czechoslovakia, which with Poland asked the United States on November 22, 1932,[180] for a revision of her debt agreement and for a suspension of the payment due on December 15, 1932, paid her instalment of $1,500,000 under protest, after the United States had declined her request. This action was explained by Dr. Kamil Krofta, Under-Secretary

[178] Anon., *The Lausanne Agreement*, Carnegie Endowment for International Peace, no. 282; *Final Act of the Lausanne Conference*; cf. also, Lippmann, W. and Scroggs, W. O., *The United States in World Affairs* (New York, 1933), pp. 132-153; Moulton and Pasvolsky, *War Debts and World Prosperity*, pp. 344-366.

[179] Cf. Langsam, op. cit., p. 193, regarding the "gentlemen's agreement" of Great Britain, France, Italy and Belgium.

[180] *Národní Listy*, November 22, 1932.

of Foreign Affairs, as an evidence of Czechoslovakia's sincere desire to honor all her international obligations, regardless of the actions of other states.[181] The Czechoslovak Minister to the United States, Dr. Ferdinand Veverka, while presenting the payment expressed the hope that the United States would participate in an international conference for the solution of the problem of war debts,[182] and, on January 21, 1933, asked for a reconsideration of Czechoslovakia's war debt by the United States.[183]

Another part of the Lausanne agreement, the promise to convene a general economic conference, was fulfilled by the Conference of Stresa, which was attended by eighty delegates representing fifteen states. During the Conference, which met from September 5-21, 1932, a united front was presented by delegates from the Little Entente, supported by Austria, Hungary, Poland and Bulgaria. France proposed a plan to grant the five states of the rejected Danubian Confederation preferential tariffs on their agricultural exports for at least three years. This scheme was to be financed by a sum of 75,000,000 Swiss francs which was to be raised by contributions from each state participating, in the proportion to which each adherent failed to grant preferences by a system of bilateral commercial treaties. The Conference struck a snag when Great Britain refused to contribute to the fund as an alternative to the granting of tariff preferences. In the last analysis, only Germany, Austria, Czechoslovakia and Switzerland were willing to grant preferences; Italy preferred to contribute to the fund; whereas France was amenable to both alternatives. The

[181] *Ibid., Prager Presse,* December 15, 1932.

[182] *Svornost,* December 16, 1932. For details of the debt correspondence between Czechoslovakia and the United States, *cf.* Chmelář J., "Zahraniční politika v roce 1932 a Československo", *Zahraniční Politika,* vol. xii, pp. 1-10.

[183] *The New York Times,* January 22, 1933.

final report of September 20 represented a compromise of the views of France, Italy, Germany and the bloc of small states, since Great Britain still continued to hold aloof. Embodied in nine general resolutions, the final agreement established an administrative committee of the adhering states, with headquarters at Basel and with supervisory powers over such matters as grain preferences, bilateral treaties and the special fund. The actual value of the new set-up was open to question. Considerable disappointment was expressed over the lack of agreement upon a second fund for the stabilization of currencies.[184] In this manner were dashed the ambitious plans of the Lausanne Conference.

Throughout 1932, the states of the Little Entente had been watching with concern the growth of revisionist sentiment, both among their own discontented minorities and in the members of the revisionist bloc. The success of the hastily called special Little Entente Conference of January 22-23, at Montreux, Switzerland,[185] for the purpose of evolving a unified policy with regard to the questions of disarmament, reparations and revisionism, convinced the three Foreign Ministers of the advisability of a second special Conference late in the year. Beneš, Titulescu and Yeftič met at Belgrade on December 18-20, 1932, to discuss primarily a common line of action regarding the threats of revisionists. Other questions concerned disarmament, reparation payments of Germany's former Allies, and an economic reorganization of the Little Entente. The fact that the Lausanne agreement had altered the financial clauses of a Peace Treaty, that military clauses of all the Peace Treaties were being subjected to threats of revision, and that the territorial clauses alone seemed to retain any indications of permanence, caused alarm which was not allayed by the fact that the disarmament con-

---

[184] Cf. *Publications*, Political, 1932, vii ii.
[185] *The New York Times*, February 2, 1932.

ference of the Powers had been a failure thus far and had
been adjourned until January 19, 1933. The Conference
of Belgrade closed with an official communiqué that again
revealed the solidarity of the Little Entente. It proclaimed
the creation at Geneva of a permanent committee of the three
Foreign Ministers and of a permanent secretariat, but no
declaration was issued against the propaganda of revisionists, much to the disappointment of Yugoslavia, which desired some such declaration against Italy. On the other
hand, the solidarity of Rumania was welcome to her two
partners, who had feared that Italian influence might have
had a weakening effect upon the organization.[186] Shortly
after the close of the Conference, Beneš summarized both
the future hopes and fears of his country when he warned
the Great Powers that the Little Entente would continue to
advocate disarmament and to oppose any revision of the
Peace Treaties.[187]

The tendency to default the debts due to the United States
found its echo also in the question of the so-called " Eastern
reparations ". Before the special Conference of the Little
Entente met at Belgrade, the three partners were informed
by the Great Powers that the latter would no longer continue
to advance the deposits that would be necessary to administer
the special funds that had been created by the agreements of
the Hague and Paris. By this decision, Hungary and Bulgaria, on the one hand, would receive no longer any money
payments in compensation for the territories that they had
lost by the Peace Treaties, but, on the other hand, would
deem themselves absolved also from further reparation payments. Thereupon, the three states of the Little Entente,
in paying their January instalments of $10,000 each, agreed

---

[186] *Ibid.*, December 18-20, 1932; *Svornost*, December 17, 1932.

[187] *České Slovo*, December 24, 1932; *The New York Times*, December
25, 1932.

that this payment would be their last, and that they also would consider themselves released from any further reparations obligations.[188]   In this manner was the general disrespect for treaty obligations enhanced and the chaotic condition of Europe aggravated, until, by the winter of 1932-1933, the disintegration of any " Concert of Europe " appeared complete and pessimism seemed to be the order of the day.[189]

[188] *Cf. Prager Tagblatt*, January 6, 1933; also, *Svornost*, January 7, 1933.

[189] For a detailed discussion of the desperate financial plight of Central Europe, *cf.* Chappey, J., *La Crise de la monnaie et la restauration des Pays Danubiens* (Paris, 1933).

CHAPTER VIII

The Nazi Crisis

The Causes and Importance of Hitlerism

DURING the winter of 1932-1933 the world-wide depression still endured: although there was improvement in some respects, in others lower depths were reached. The ensuing pessimism, coupled with a high degree of nationalism, created for the whole world problems which represented a composite picture of almost every aspect of human activity. Of such problems Central Europe had perhaps more than its share: certainly among the states of the revisionist bloc at least there grew stronger the tendency to blame the Peace Treaties for the major portion of the evils that they had to endure. These states came to advocate, more and more forcibly, revisions of the Peace Treaties that were considered too drastic by the states of the status-quo bloc. The dangers of the situation were appreciated by Beneš, who, on November 7, 1932, before the Foreign Affairs Committee of the Senate and the Chamber of Deputies, delivered an address entitled "Will Europe decide for Peace or War?" In this exposé, after a thorough review of the situation, he pointed out how recent events had created, particularly in Germany, a condition of affairs ominous to the future peace of Europe.[1]

The Reich was seething with discontent because of numerous frustrations of the national will. Too weak to rebel directly against the terms of the Treaty of Versailles during the years immediately after the termination of the War, Germany had already tried twice in vain to evade indirectly

[1] Beneš, *Boj o mir*, pp. 653-681.

certain of its provisions.[2]   Many Germans had accepted the Locarno agreements reluctantly, and with misgivings.[3]   The final blow to the status quo was dealt by the failure of the disarmament conference of 1932.   From February 3 to December 11 the delegates from the German Republic pleaded almost frantically that, in order to avert a domestic upheaval, Germany be allowed to arm to a degree consistent with her own security, if the other Powers could not agree to disarm to the German level.[4]   The only concession that Germany could obtain was the agreement of December 11, 1932, whereby, in principle, she was granted equality of rights in arms matters to prevent her from leaving the conference which adjourned on December 14, 1932, to meet again on January 19, 1933.[5]

Beneš worked hard to try to save the 1932 disarmament conference.   The viewpoint of Czechoslovakia was stated officially on February 12: the Czechoslovak government (1)

[2] For seeking a complete moratorium, the Cuno government had been punished by the French occupation of the Ruhr, which had lasted from January, 1923, to August, 1925, and which, by ruining the German middle classes, had paved the way for the later Nazi movement; whereas the second attempt, the proposed Austro-German Customs Union, had been frustrated through the use of the financial power of France, which, in 1931, had hastened financial crashes in both Austria and Germany, results that, in the eyes of patriotic Teutons, justified fully the most drastic countermeasures. *Cf.* Simonds, F. H. and Emeny, B., *The Great Powers in World Politics* (New York, 1935), pp. 196-197; Einzig, P., *World Finance, 1914-1935* (New York, 1935), pp. 217-223.

[3] *Cf.* Simonds and Emeny, *op. cit.*, p. 197.

[4] France and Germany blamed one another for the failure to reach an agreement: France accused Germany of "calculated encroachments" on the Treaty of Versailles, and Germany blamed France for the "calculated withholding" of rights that she, Germany, believed her just due morally according to the same Treaty. *Cf. The Times, The New York Times,* February 3, December 11 and 12, 1933; *cf.* also, Procházka, R., " Nová tvář problému bezpečnosti ", *Zahraniční Politika,* vol. xiv, pp. 82-83; Toynbee, *op. cit.*, 1933, p. 136.

[5] *Publications,* Disarmament, 1933, ix 10, p. 208.

accepted the guiding principles of the conference as a basis for discussion; (2) expressed the opinion that the final convention should establish the principle of a definite and explicit limitation of armaments; (3) was prepared to adopt supervision of effectives, of armaments, and of arms manufacture and trade in a more complete and effective manner than that in present operation or that proposed thus far in the conference; (4) favored the establishment of a more complete system for the prohibition of chemical and bacteriological warfare, and was prepared to extend this prohibition to other means of offensive warfare, particularly to aerial bombardments of the civil population, of cities, and especially of the capitals of the belligerents; (5) was convinced that the above suggestion should be supplemented by a system of penalties; (6) intended to support the view of France; and (7) believed that the final convention should bring about genuine disarmament by a series of graduated stages. At the same time the Czechoslovak government reasserted its belief in the necessity of a progressive and scientifically organized policy of peace with a view to strengthening the authority and augmenting the powers of the League Council.[6]

Beneš became rapporteur of the General Commission of the conference on February 24. In this capacity, on April 20 he explained the organization of the national civilian forces of his country. He pointed out particularly that civil aviation was controlled by the Ministry of Public Works and had received a subsidy of 38,600,000 crowns in the budget of 1932.[7] The preliminary phase of the conference terminated in the meetings of July 20-22,[8] whereupon the Technical

[6] *Ibid.*, 1932, ix 25, p. 52.

[7] *Ibid.*, 1932, ix 31, pp. 66, 103-104.

[8] *Cf. ibid., Records of the Conference for the Reduction and Limitation of Armaments*, Series B, Minutes of the General Commission, vol. i (February 9-July 23, 1932), pp. 153-185, for details of Beneš' work as rapporteur.

Committee of the National Defense Expenditure Commission of the conference sought to obtain from each member of the League all facts and figures pertinent to its national defense expenditures.[9] After this information had been assembled, no agreement could be reached. In vain did Beneš seek to set an example by pledging Czechoslovakia's continued adherence to a disarmament truce.[10] Amid the conflicting opinions regarding security and disarmament, one fact stood out prominently, namely, that in refusing the demands of Germany, the other Powers became in a large measure responsible for the fall of Chancellor Brüning and for the rise of Hitlerism.[11]

Germany's third revolt against the terms of the Treaty of Versailles was direct. The Austrian-born Adolf Hitler, who had long been considered harmless and later merely a threat to the internal tranquillity of Germany, became Chancellor of the Reich on January 30, 1933.[12] Taking his stand upon an unqualified condemnation of the Peace Settlement, Hitler arrogated to himself more and more power. The aging President of the Republic, Von Hindenburg, could not stem the tide, with the result that long before his death at the age of eighty-six years on August 2, 1934,[13] he had

[9] *Cf. ibid.*, 1933, ix 3, vol. ii, pp. 131-137, for facts and figures regarding Czechoslovakia.

[10] A disarmament truce, i. e. a pledge not to increase armaments, which had been proposed by Italy and advocated by Denmark, Norway, the Netherlands, Sweden and Switzerland, had been accepted by Czechoslovakia for one year as from November 1, 1931. Upon its expiration, Beneš renewed his country's pledge for another four months. *Cf. Official Journal*, special supplement, no. 96, p. 46 (Beneš' statement of September 24, 1931); January, 1932, p. 148 (Beneš' statement of October 27, 1931); January, 1933, p. 128 (Beneš' statement of September 14, 1932).

[11] *Cf.* Wheeler-Bennett, J. W., *The Pipe Dream of Peace* (New York, 1935), pp. xiii-xv.

[12] *The New York Times*, January 30-31, 1933.

[13] *Ibid.*, August 2, 1934.

become a mere figure-head and Germany had been transformed from a republic to a dictatorship with Hitler in full control. Many of the German people, with whom any leader who would dare to condemn openly the Treaty of Versailles would become popular, acquiesced willingly in the change in government. In this manner there came to pass the reaction that Dr. Vlastimil Tusar, as Czechoslovak Minister to Germany, had predicted as early as March 21, 1922.[14]

The ultimate result of the Nazi revolution can not be foreseen at this writing. It was unquestionably the most important single event of the year 1933, and certainly one of the most important events of the whole post-war era. It might be considered even as marking the end of the immediate post-war period [15] and as inaugurating an entirely new period, one in which Germany no longer accepted more or less supinely the dictates of the victor states of the World War, but began to reassert herself actively. Conscious of her own reviving strength, she sought to abolish all the existing distinctions between victor and vanquished states, and to regain a position of equality with the other Great Powers. Of the small states of Central Europe, Czechoslovakia was perhaps the most endangered by the rise of Hitlerism. She was aware of her peril, but, in the early days of the movement at least, regarded it as a menace that would necessitate vigilance on her part, but one that she need not necessarily fear.[16]

---

[14] *Cf.* D'Abernon, *op. cit.*, vol. i, pp. 296-297. Tusar, whom Beneš allegedly thought unduly pro-German (*cf. ibid.*, vol. ii, p. 58), considered "insane" the French policy of pressing Germany too hard, and predicted that the ultimate result would be a revolution which would cause a general collapse and the rise of a labor party which would pay no reparations.

[15] *Cf.* Toynbee, *op. cit.*, 1933, p. 111.

[16] For this attitude of Czechoslovakia, *cf.* Bauer, F., *Hitlerová třeti riše a naš stát* (Praha, 1933).

Strengthening the Little Entente

There arose again the question of the illegal shipment of arms to Hungary. On January 9, 1933, forty carloads of arms (40,000 to 50,000 rifles and 200 machine guns) were shipped from Italy to Hirtenberg in Austria, allegedly to be repaired there in order to furnish labor for unemployed machinists, since the weapons represented pre-war Austrian equipment. If the charges of the *Arbeiter Zeitung* were true, the weapons were not repaired at Hirtenberg, but, with the connivance of the Austrian government, were merely loaded into trucks and transshipped into Hungary.[17] At once the Little Entente was aroused. Czechoslovak public opinion questioned whether this move did not represent a verification of rumors of a secret alliance between Italy, Austria and Hungary.[18] Benes seized the occasion to issue again a warning against any propaganda aimed at revising the Peace Treaties.[19] On January 20, France decided to support the protest of the Little Entente against the shipment of arms from Italy to Hungary.[20] Beneš, as spokesman for the Little Entente, demanded action, either by the League of Nations or by a cooperative effort of Great Britain and France.[21] He pointed out that the Hirtenberg affair was not an isolated incident, but that, in all, Italy had shipped to Hungary 180,000 rifles, 200 machine guns, and unknown numbers of aeroplanes and trucks, the latter of which could be transformed into tanks. He pleaded for a cessation of Italo-Magyar intrigues,[22] but again, as in the case of earlier inci-

---

[17] *Arbeiter Zeitung*, January 9, 1933; *Svornost*, January 10, 1933.

[18] *Národní Listy*, January 15, 1933.

[19] *The New York Times*, January 15, 1933.

[20] *Ibid.*, January 20, 1933.

[21] *Ibid.*, January 27 and February 9, 1933.

[22] *Svornost*, February 12 and March 5, 1933.

dents,[23] in vain. Nothing effective was accomplished to check such activities, probably because Italy, a Great Power, was involved.

Germany's new challenge to the status quo was answered promptly by the Little Entente. On February 16, 1933, the three Foreign Ministers—Beneš, Titulescu and Yeftič—signed, at Geneva, a new treaty whereby their mutual ties were again strengthened. In order to ensure unity in the prosecution of a common foreign policy, there was created a Permanent Council of Foreign Ministers, which, by unanimous vote, would have to approve the negotiations of any new treaty or the adoption of any new unilateral policy of international significance on the part of any member. The Permanent Council would meet obligatorily three times a year. One of these meetings would rotate among the three states, another would be held at Geneva at the time of the meeting of the League Assembly, and the place of the third was not specified. The presiding officer would be the foreign minister of the state wherein the first obligatory conference was held. He would select the date, place and agenda, and would continue to preside until the first obligatory conference of the following year. All three states would enjoy equality upon all questions. The Permanent Council could decide whether any question should be entrusted to one delegate or to the delegation of one country. It would also have the right to establish other commissions on special questions. An economic council would be created. The Permanent Council would be aided by a secretariat, one section of which would work permanently at Geneva. The policy of the Permanent Council would be guided by the League Covenant and by the important post-war treaties. Treaties already negotiated with other states would be coordinated to the greatest degree possible. Eventually, full

[23] *Cf. supra*, pp. 267-269, 274-277.

membership might be extended to other states " on conditions to be decided in each specific case ". The three existing
bilateral treaties of alliance and the tripartite treaty of conciliation, arbitration and judicial settlement were renewed in
perpetuity, an action which was intended to give the Little
Entente the force and cohesion of a Great Power.[24]

In a lengthy exposé of March 1, 1933, before the Foreign
Affairs Committees of the Czechoslovak Senate and of the
Chamber of Deputies, Beneš stated the reasons why the new
pact had been negotiated. In his estimation, some stronger
union had become inevitable for two reasons: because of the
chaotic condition of Central Europe, particularly since each
of the three Great Powers that were immediate neighbors of
the states of the Little Entente were undergoing internal
political revolutions, and because the Little Entente dreaded
the outcome of the 1933 disarmament conference. He
stressed particularly the fact that the reorganized Little
Entente was not directed against Italy.[25]

The reorganized Little Entente was indeed a powerful
entity, but not without weaknesses. Although the military
provisions of the new agreement remained unpublished and
unknown, the Little Entente was known to have, at the time,
the third largest military establishment in Europe (after
the U.S.S.R. and France). Its area, among Continental
Powers, was second only to the U.S.S.R., whereas its population, approximately 48,500,000, exceeded that of either
France or Italy. On the other hand, there might be pointed
out, as weaknesses, the following facts; approximately one-
fourth of the population consisted of minorities; Czechoslovakia was the only industrial member; her Škoda works, the

[24] *Treaty Series*, vol. cxxxix, pp. 233-239.

[25] Beneš, E., *Le Pacte d'organisation de la Petite Entente et l'état
actuel de la politique internationale*, Sources et documents tchécoslovaques,
no. 20; *Boj o mír*, pp. 688-691; for the whole exposé, *cf.* pp. 682-713.

only arms manufacturing establishment, lay, in time of war, in an extremely exposed position; and finally, the armaments of the three partners, particularly those of Rumania, were fast becoming obsolete. In view of these facts, the actual efficiency of the Little Entente, in the event of a major war, remained problematic.[26]

The closer union of the Little Entente states met with diverse responses in the foreign press. It was approved most heartily by France,[27] and also, but with less cordiality, by Great Britain.[28] Both Moscow [29] and Warsaw [30] considered it a constructive step, one that would increase materially the prospect of preserving the peace of Central Europe. Austria [31] and Germany [32] disapproved, whereas Italy and Hungary were violent in their objections. The Italian press denounced certain alleged secret clauses in the Little Entente treaty.[33] Perhaps the most bitter denunciation of all was the Berlin speech of March 8 of ex-Premier Bethlen of Hungary, who, in the course of calling attention to the common interest of Germany, Italy and Hungary in trying to prevent too intimate a union between Northern and Southern Slavs, stigmatized the Peace Treaties as a " rotting status quo which could not be maintained ".[34] The chorus of disapproval and of false allegations mounted so high that it provoked, within Czechoslovakia, parliamentary interpellations and heated re-

[26] *Cf. The New York Times*, March 5, 1933.

[27] *Le Temps*, February 17, 1933.

[28] *The Times*, February 17-18, 1933.

[29] *Izvestia*, February 18, 1933.

[30] *Gazeta Warszawska*, February 17, 1933.

[31] *Neue Freie Presse*, February 17-20, 1933.

[32] *Vossische Zeitung*, February 17-19, 1933.

[33] *Cf. Corriere della Sera* and *The New York Times*, February 26, 1933, for reprints of a series of earlier allegations by *Giornale d'Italia*.

[34] *Vossische Zeitung*, March 9, 1933.

torts from high officials of the government. Beneš denied the authenticity of a French allegation that, on August 7, 1932, Germany, Italy and Hungary had drawn up a secret military alliance, and branded as " idiotic " current Hungarian-sponsored rumors that the new Little Entente treaty had called for a joint Czechoslovak-Yugoslav occupation of Hungary in the event of a Soviet-Rumanian war; [35] whereas Dr. Bradač, the Czechoslovak Minister of National Defense, responded to a parliamentary inquiry by stating that he had " full confidence in the army's power of resistance ".[36]

Italy and Poland

By March, 1933, among the more interesting aspects of the Nazi crisis were the reorientations of foreign policy on the parts of Italy and Poland. In order to enhance the prestige of Italy, Mussolini sought to play the part of an arbiter, to hold the balance of power between the status quo and revisionist blocs, between France and Germany, whereas Poland determined to continue her support of the status quo bloc only in return for specific new advantages.[37] Czechoslovakia believed that, in order to attain his objective, Mussolini desired to dominate Central Europe, and that, to this end, in the eyes of Italy, a strong Little Entente or an extension of either French or German influence into this area were equally undesirable.[38]

On March 22, Mussolini had made public the details of a Four Power Pact, whereby, through an agreement among Great Britain, France, Germany and Italy, necessary revisions would be made and the peace of Europe safeguarded for

[35] *Svornost*, February 11, 1933; *The New York Times*, March 4, 1933.

[36] *Národní Listy*, March 15, 1933.

[37] *Cf.* Toynbee, *op. cit.*, 1933, pp. 184-186, 206-208; also, Krofta, K., *Československo v mezinárodní politice* (Praha, 1934), p. 15.

[38] *Cf.* Krofta, *op. cit.*, pp. 8-9.

the next decade.[39]   Great indeed was the indignation of the small victor states at being excluded from consultations so momentous to their future.   Poland was particularly angry that her pretensions were ignored, and considered for a time the acceptance of full membership in the Little Entente,[40] a sentiment that was echoed within that organization.[41]   However, time brought reflection, and Poland turned again to her policy of prestige which would be shattered by such a move. The Polish Dictator, Pilsudski, who had long opposed such a step as an abandonment of Polish pretensions to the status of a Great Power, came to the conclusion that intimate co-operation with the Little Entente would insure adequate security against the German menace.[42]   During April, 1933, the Polish Foreign Minister, Beck, made a series of visits to the capitals of the Little Entente states in order to sound their policies.   As a result of this trip, there arose a rumor that France, Poland and the Little Entente had signed an agreement against Mussolini's Four Power Pact,[43] a rumor that the Polish Foreign Office denied.[44]   Nevertheless, Mussolini's threat of reviving the Triple Alliance,[45] intended to hasten French acceptance of his plan, had, perhaps, some influence in crystallizing public opinion in the status quo bloc.

On March 25, 1933, after a lengthy discussion in its Permanent Council at Geneva, the Little Entente lost no time in taking a firm stand in denouncing Mussolini's plan and in warning against any attempted revision of the Peace

[39] *The New York Times*, March 22, 1933.

[40] *Ibid.*, March 24, 1933.

[41] *Ibid.*, March 26, 1933; *Národní Listy*, March 28, 1933; *Svornost*, March 30, 1933.

[42] *Gazeta Warszawska*, April 25, 1933.

[43] *The New York Times*, April 25, 1933.

[44] *Gazeta Warszawska*, April 25, 1933.

[45] *The New York Times*, April 12, 1933.

Treaties.[46]   Confident that France would fully protect its interests during the four Power conferences, the Little Entente sent Titulescu as its representative to Paris, where he received assurance that France would continue to oppose unreservedly all revisions, particularly those territorial in nature.[47]

Czechoslovakia's attitude regarding the Four Power Pact was presented to a plenary session of parliament by Beneš in another lengthy exposé of April 25, 1933. After a summary of the evolution of revisionism, Beneš pointed out how Mussolini's project represented the culmination of a decade of efforts to dominate Central Europe and to reduce the small states of that region to the status of pawns of the Great Powers.   Should such a condition come to pass, it would be a backward step, a major tragedy for Europe as a whole. In his estimation, a strong Little Entente functioned as a balance-wheel that helped stabilize Europe: it was neither a purely anti-Hungarian concept, nor was it a mere satellite of France.   Any territorial alterations at Czechoslovakia's expense would mean war.   Revisions of the Peace Treaties were possible only under the terms of Article 19 of the League Covenant.   Czechoslovakia might accept certain minor frontier rectifications, provided that there would be no threat of foreign pressure, no reign of terror, but a mutual agreement arrived at peaceably after due negotiations, and that adequate compensation be given her in return.   Otherwise, in sheer desperation, she might feel compelled to leave the League of Nations!   Finally, Beneš advocated the doctrine of the equality of states—the abolition of all distinctions between the Great Powers and other states, and between the victors and vanquished of the World War; for, as long as these distinctions remained, no reconciliation was possible,

[46] *Ibid.*, March 27, 1933.
[47] *Ibid.*, March 30-31, 1933.

nor could any European Directorate function satisfactorily without the consent or the participation of the small states.[48]

As the negotiations regarding the Four Power Pact continued, it came to be realized generally that the result would be a synthesis of the views of the Great Powers.[49] On May 18, Hitler pledged his support to Mussolini's plan to preserve peace and stated his belief that no war would improve existing conditions.[50] Four days later, the four Powers agreed to the plan in principle,[51] news that was received calmly by the Little Entente,[52] which also gave its approval on May 30. The Little Entente communiqué accepted the Four Power Pact on the strength of French assurances that the original proposal had undergone drastic revision, particularly that unanimous consent by the League Council would continue to be required for any treaty revision. It stated further that the Little Entente could not tolerate any organization that would entitle any Great Power to make any decisions regarding the interests of other states. In reply to these objections, France promised that the Four Power Pact would concern only the signatory Powers, and that it would exert no pressure for frontier revisions upon the Little Entente.[53]

The final draft, a compromise of the views of France and Italy, was initialed on June 7, and signed on July 15. Italy and Germany were denied colonial compensation by Great Britain and France. France insisted on several points: that the four Powers deal only with their own interests and aban-

[48] Beneš, E., *La Question du directoire européen et la revision des frontières*, Sources et documents tchécoslovaques, no. 21; *Boj o mír*, pp. 714-769.

[49] *Cf. The New York Times*, May 22, 1933; Fiša, P., "Pakt čtyř velmoci", *Zahraniční Politika*, vol. xii, pp. 305-312.

[50] *Völkischer Beobachter*, May 18, 1933.

[51] *The New York Times*, May 22, 1933.

[52] *Ibid.*, May 24, 1933.

[53] *Ibid.*, May 31, 1933.

don all pretensions to determine any territorial revisions, and that the prestige and authority of the League be permitted to remain intact.   As a result, the final draft of the Pact retained vague provisions for revision of the Peace Treaties, and, in the event of the failure of the Disarmament Conference, for a gradual attainment of armament equality by Germany.[54]   On June 7, France sent almost identical notes to the Little Entente and to Poland, explaining her attitude and promising again that nothing in the Pact would affect their existing treaties with her.   The notes called particular attention to the fact that Article 2 of the new Pact permitted revisions only under Article 19 of the Covenant.[55]   Nevertheless, France had not asked the other three Great Powers to accept her interpretation of the Pact, and she could not bind them by her own action.[56]   In this manner did France keep her faith with her small Allies.   Of all the small victor states of Europe, Poland alone nursed a grievance—that France did not support adequately her claims to recognition as a Great Power.[57]

1933 Little Entente Conferences

On June 20-22, 1933, the three Foreign Ministers of the Little Entente met in London in order to ascertain the British viewpoint regarding the practicability of a Danubian Confederation as a means of weaning Austria and Hungary from the influence of Germany.[58]   Despite the support of Great Britain, France and Italy,[59] the plan failed.   The

[54] *Nouveau recueil,* iii série, vol. xxviii, pp. 4 *et seq.*

[55] *Le Temps,* June 7, 1933.

[56] Wheeler-Bennett, *op. cit.,* p. 145.

[57] *Cf.* Toynbee, *op. cit.,* 1933, p. 218; Wheeler-Bennett, *op. cit.,* pp. 127-146.

[58] *The New York Times,* June 22, 1933.

[59] *Ibid.,* August 26, 1933.

German Vice-Chancellor, Von Papen, and the Reich Minister without Portfolio, Göring, preferred instead, and in fact had already predicted,[60] a new Central Europe, dominated by a revisionist bloc under the joint leadership of Germany and Italy. Premier Gömbös of Hungary considered unsatisfactory the proposed Danubian Confederation,[61] or any other project that would perpetuate the status quo,[62] and maintained that a drastic revision of the Peace Treaties alone could restore Central Europe to economic health.[63] When Chancellor Dollfuss of Austria visited Mussolini on August 20,[64] rumors arose of a plan for a new Danubian Confederation of only Austria, Hungary and Italy, to the exclusion of the Little Entente.[65] These rumors of the rivalry of Italy and the Little Entente for predominance in Central Europe became so persistent that, on October 15, Beneš felt compelled to issue a statement that he would oppose any Danubian Confederation that would not include Czechoslovakia.[66]

Mussolini had probably intended to crown his Four Power Pact with another project, an economic and political union of the Little Entente, Austria, Hungary and Italy.[67] The visits of Premier Gömbös of Hungary to Vienna on July 9, and to Rome on July 25, were interpreted as steps preliminary to the formation of the new bloc. The fact that the states of the Little Entente had shown more interest in, than opposition to, the new project, seemed to indicate that France, although excluded from the contemplated new bloc, had given it her approval. Beneš, to whom any territorial strengthen-

[60] *Ibid.*, April 14, 1933. [61] *Ibid.*, July 2, 1933.

[62] *Ibid.*, September 17, 1933. [63] *Ibid.*, July 10, 1933.

[64] *Cf. ibid.*, August 21, 1933, for the official communiqué of the visit.

[65] *Ibid.*, August 23, 1933; *cf.* also, *Právo Lidu* and *České Slovo*, August 22, 1933.

[66] *The New York Times*, October 15, 1933.

[67] *Cf. Nouveau recueil*, iii série, vol. xxx, pp. 7 *et seq.*, for the Italian memorandum of September 29, 1933, regarding Danubian affairs.

ing of Austria and Hungary or any union between them alone would be as distasteful as Anschluss, favored the new plan as a practical consummation of the Danubian Confederation that he had long been advocating. In order to safeguard the economic future of Central Europe, he advocated the restoration of an economic equivalent of the former Austro-Hungarian Empire.[68]

The Permanent Council of the Little Entente met in Praha early in June, 1933. The chief purpose of the Conference was economic, to create an Economic Council of three sections, one for each country and each with five members and technical advisers. Its main duty was to create a preferential tariff system for the three states and to investigate how a quota system could be employed to increase the exchange of goods. The Economic Council would meet four times annually, alternately in the three capitals, and would concern itself with such questions as general commercial policies, agriculture, industry, credits, banking and finance, and transportation. It would create immediately a special committee to " normalize " all branches of commerce and of industrial life. Interesting was the statement that " this normalization process will naturally extend to all branches of military equipment ".[69] The discussions also waxed political. It was agreed that the dangers of revising the frontiers of Hungary had been overestimated. Many complaints were made that the official communiqué failed to mention the status of relations with Poland, whose relations with both France and the Little Entente were cooling as the result of the Powers having disregarded Poland's wishes regarding the negotiations of the Four Power Pact.[70] The activities of the Economic Council made such progress that, on Oc-

[68] *Prager Tagblatt*, June 17, 1933; *The New York Times*, June 18, 1933.
[69] *The New York Times*, June 2, 1933.
[70] *Národní Listy, Národní Politika*, June 4, 1933.

tober 31, Beneš predicted that the next few years would witness the transformation of the Little Entente into a compact economic unit. He stated that Czechoslovakia would have to prepare for new developments by controlling private capitalism under a nationally planned economy. She would have to specialize in products her Little Entente partners could not supply, and would have to make adjustments to import their cattle and grain. At the same time Beneš desired close relations with both Austria and Hungary, but admitted that the attainment of any great degree of friendship with the latter would be difficult, particularly since Hungary's revisionist campaign was again revived.[71]

Another Little Entente Conference met at Sinaia for four days beginning September 24, 1933. All precedents were shattered by the presence not only of the three Foreign Ministers—Beneš, Yeftič and Titulescu—but of Kings Alexander and Carol, since this was the first Conference ever attended by the titular heads of more than one state. On the agenda for discussion were the recent visits of Gömbös and Dollfuss to Rome, the prospects of a Danubian Confederation, the general problem of increasing still further the solidarity of the Little Entente, and its relations with France and Poland. The result of the Conference was a declaration against the inclusion of Austria and Hungary in any bloc with the Little Entente. Beneš was selected to represent the organization on a diplomatic mission to Rome, where, by means of a conference with Mussolini, it was hoped that better cooperation with Italy could be attained.[72] No immediate agreement resulted. On October 19, Beneš paid a visit to Vienna, where he pointed out to Dollfuss his conviction that a system of bilateral treaties would be Austria's best protection, both economically and politically, and warned him against adopt-

[71] *The New York Times*, November 1, 1933.
[72] *Ibid.*, September 27, 1933.

ing any radical policy that might endanger relations with Czechoslovakia.[73]

The Franco-Soviet Non-Aggression Pact

The potential menace of Hitlerism created a Franco-Soviet non-aggression pact which was approved by Moscow on February 17,[74] 1933, and by the French parliamentary committee on foreign affairs on March 16;[75] in fact, the friendship between these two countries became so marked that, late in the year, Paris was rumored to have offered Moscow a defensive alliance.[76] On July 4, at London, the U.S.S.R., Czechoslovakia, Rumania, Turkey and Yugoslavia signed a non-aggression pact, which clearly defined both an act of aggression and an aggressor.[77] The Little Entente considered this pact an " Eastern Locarno ",[78] a consolidation of Eastern Europe against Germany.[79] Czechovakia was overjoyed that the U.S.S.R. had apparently broken definitely with Germany and had come over to the status quo bloc: as for herself, she determined to follow the example of the United States in recognizing the U.S.S.R. de jure. The Czechoslovak Foreign Affairs Committee of the Senate, on October 24, 1933, approved a memorandum wherein it began to prepare the way for recognition by a restoration of normal relations whenever practicable.[80] When the United

[73] *Ibid., Prager Tagblatt, Prager Presse, Svornost*, October 19, 1933.

[74] *The New York Times*, February 17, 1933.

[75] *Ibid.*, March 16, 1933.

[76] *Ibid.*, December 17, 1933.

[77] *Treaty Series*, vol. cxlviii, pp. 211-219.

[78] *The New York Times*, July 9, 1933.

[79] *Ibid.*, July 16, 1933. *Cf.* Padelford, N. J., *Peace in the Balkans* (New York, 1935), pp. 96-98 and 107-108, for the sequel. The Balkan Entente (Greece, Rumania, Turkey and Yugoslavia) represented an attempt to extend to the Balkans the philosophy of the Little Entente.

[80] *Tisky* (Senát), no. 1134, October 24, 1933, 9 session.

States recognized the Soviet Union on November 17, it was merely a question of time before Czechoslovakia would do the same.[81] The long delay, so strange for a state ostensibly as Slavophil as Czechoslovakia, had been caused, as related earlier,[82] primarily by political antipathy to the principles of communism.

Disarmament Negotiations

At the disarmament conference at Geneva, Great Britain took the lead in vain efforts to reconcile the German demands for arms equality with the French thesis of security first.[83] In this controversy, as might be expected, the sympathies of Czechoslovakia lay entirely with the latter. The nature of Hitler's foreign policy was clearly evinced when, following the example of Japan, Germany defied the public opinion of the world on October 14, 1933, by withdrawing from both the disarmament conference and the League of Nations.[84] Almost as a unit, the Nazi press welcomed the move as " an escape from the trap which had been set for Germany at Geneva ".[85] Nevertheless, Baron von Neurath, German Minister for Foreign Affairs, left open the possibility of further negotiations by stating that, if German demands for equality were met adequately, Germany might reconsider her recent decision.[86]

As a result of Neurath's hint, there ensued secret negotiations at Berlin between the French Ambassador, François-

---

[81] Chmelář, J., " Československá zahraniční politika v roce 1933 ", *Zahraniční Politika*, vol. xiii, pp. 85-93. For the Czechoslovak de jure recognition of the U. S. S. R. cf. *infra*, p. 387.

[82] Cf. *supra*, pp. 259 et seq.

[83] *Publications*, Disarmament, 1933, ix 1-2.

[84] *Ibid*., 1933, ix 11, p. 15; *Official Journal*, January, 1934, p. 16.

[85] Cf. *Vossische Zeitung, Frankfurter Zeitung, Deutsche Allgemeine Zeitung*, October 15, 1933.

[86] *Deutsche Allgemeine Zeitung*, October 15, 1933.

Poncet, and Hitler. Apparently, the latter desired to negotiate a series of bilateral agreements with certain individual states, and was reported to have offered non-aggression pacts to both France and Czechoslovakia.[87] Hitler insisted that Germany be permitted 300,000 men, 200 aeroplanes, six-inch guns and tanks. If this were conceded, Hitler expressed his willingness to agree to internationalize commercial air transportation whenever all other states would destroy their bombardment and combat aviation.[88] These negotiations were viewed with distrust by the French, who feared that they had much to lose and little to gain by a bilateral agreement. Largely because of this sentiment, the French Ministry of Foreign Affairs announced, on November 28, 1933, that it would negotiate with Germany no bilateral agreement, but would insist upon conducting such negotiations either at Rome or at Geneva. Since France and Germany were but two of the states that had signed the Versailles Treaty, France maintained that, to abrogate any of its provisions, there would be required also the assent of the other signatories, particularly of Great Britain, Italy, Poland and the Little Entente.[89] As a result of this insistence, little was accomplished.

Czechoslovakia's official attitude towards the Nazi rearmament threat was voiced by Beneš on October 31, 1933, in a speech before the Foreign Affairs Committee of both the Senate and the Chamber of Deputies. After summarizing the effect of the Nazi revolution upon the general European situation, he denied the imminence of any general catastrophe. He professed to find nothing particularly new in the Hitler variety of Pan-Germanism. The tenor of Czechoslovakia's foreign policy would remain unchanged: as for-

[87] *Le Temps*, November 26, 1933; *Svornost*, November 27, 1933.
[88] *Deutsche Allgemeine Zeitung*, November 28, 1933.
[89] *Le Temps*, November 28, 1933.

merly, it would be guided by a desire to maintain the status quo that had been established by the Peace Treaties, to further attempts at general disarmament, to strengthen the Little Entente, particularly by an economic union, to preserve " correct " relations with Germany, to remain on intimate terms with France, to continue existing friendships with Poland and Austria, to seek still closer relations with the Soviet Union, to attempt to reconcile Hungary, and to oppose every effort to destroy the principle of the equality of states which the League was striving to uphold.[90] Although the address of Beneš met with general domestic approval, he felt urged to defend himself against sporadic accusations that he had placed too much faith in the League. On November 8, he stated, " While treaties are being made, Czechoslovakia will make treaties. If machines guns are fired, it will be ready to fire machine guns, and if cannon, it will be ready to fire cannon also ".[91] Among Beneš' enemies, much was made of the alleged chauvinism of this speech, but, as Beneš' long record had indicated, this outburst must have been owing to extreme provocation, and its belligerent tone should be discounted. Within Czechoslovakia, the fifteen years of peace and internal consolidation had produced a general feeling of faith in the future of the Republic.[92]

The Economic Council of the Little Entente, under the presidency of Beneš, at Praha on January 9, 1934, sought to devise ways and means whereby the three partners might retain at least one-half of their foreign trade among them-

[90] Beneš, E., *La Revolution allemande et la nouvelle phase de la politique européenne*, Sources et documents tchécoslovaques, no. 23; *Boj o mír*, pp. 770-802.

[91] *Národní Listy*, November 8, 1933.

[92] *Ibid.*, November 20, 1933; *Svornost*, November 27, 1933, for summary by President Masaryk; *cf.* also, Ripka, H., *Patnact let československé demokracie* (Praha, 1933).

selves.[93] The regular Conference, which had been called originally for January 8, did not assemble until January 20, because of the assassination of Duca, the Rumanian Prime Minister. At Zagreb, January 20-24, the Conference came to a general agreement with regard to the future. United opposition was expressed against Mussolini: both as to his supposed project to replace the League with a " Concert of Europe ", and as to his suggestion for a Danubian Confederation based upon an economic alliance of Austria and Hungary. A firm stand was taken against Hungarian revisionist propaganda. Despite the wishes of France, the Little Entente states refused de jure recognition to the Soviet Union immediately, but insisted first upon further negotiations as to the terms she would offer in return. The sole discordant note was the desire of Yugoslavia for a rapprochement with Hitler. To Yugoslavia, Hitlerism represented no direct menace, whereas, in an emergency against Italy, the support of Germany might, conceivably, be of more value than that of France. There was also suggested a five-year Balkan non-aggression pact which was to be attempted immediately after the Conference.[94]

A Balkan Pact was initialed at Belgrade on February 4 and signed on February 9 by the Foreign Ministers of Greece, Turkey, Yugoslavia and Rumania. It was but partially successful, because Bulgaria refused, quite naturally, to agree to a perpetuation of her own dismemberment and Albania, presumably because of Italian pressure, also refused to join. The new agreement, in Articles 1-3 respectively, guaranteed the security of existing Balkan frontiers for five years, provided for mutual consultation of the member states upon all questions of common interest, and left open future

[93] Cf. *Právo Lidu*, January 10, 1934.
[94] *The New York Times*, January 24, 1934.

membership to the other Balkan states.[95]   Czechoslovakia welcomed the new organization as an additional guarantee of the stability of the Balkans and of Southeastern Europe.[96]

The Germano-Polish Rapprochement

Other aspects of Hitler's policy—opposition to Catholicism, Judaism and Communism—troubled still further the diplomatic waters of Europe.   At first, the threat of a resurrection of German military power had produced in Poland a feeling of dismay that had caused her to desire closer relations with the victor states and even with Moscow.[97]   Rumors of a secret military alliance between Germany and Lithuania [98] aroused Pilsudski to the point where he opened negotiations with the U.S.S.R. and Rumania for a united anti-German eastern bloc.[99]   However, he soon realized that Hitler's opposition to Communism had destroyed Poland's greatest fear of the past—of a Germano-Soviet combination against her—and that, correspondingly, she had, for the time being at least, lesser need of French support.

The long months of tortuous negotiations between Germany and Poland resulted in the signing, at Berlin, of a ten year non-aggression pact on January 26, 1934, and in its ratification on February 24.   This treaty, regarded by Poland as a diplomatic triumph of the first magnitude for her Foreign Minister, Beck,[100] was modelled on the Briand-Kellogg Peace Pact.   By its terms, both countries agreed not to resort to war as a means of settling disputes, regardless of circumstances.   Each state promised to prohibit,

---

[95] *Treaty Series*, vol. cliii, pp. 153-159.

[96] *Národní Listy*, February 5, 1934.

[97] *Gazeta Warszawska*, May 11, 1933; *Svornost*, May 12, 1933.

[98] *Svornost*, May 27, 1933; *Gazeta Warszawska*, May 26, 1933.

[99] *Gazeta Warszawska*, September 7, 1933; *Svornost*, September 8, 1933.

[100] *Gazeta Warszawska*, January 27-28, 1934.

within its territory, propaganda unfavorable to the other. The pact was to endure for ten years, and indefinitely thereafter unless denounced by a notice of six months. Purely domestic questions and earlier treaties with other Powers were to remain unaffected by this new agreement.[101] Beyond the mere text of the pact there remained many implications. The pact represented a private agreement between Hitler and Pilsudski, some of which was perhaps secret. The fact that the League had been omitted seemed to indicate the permanence of Germany's withdrawal from that organization; and the failure to mention a new frontier, the absence of further German territorial designs upon Poland for the next decade. A new protocol of March 7 terminated a tariff war of eight years' duration. Both states abandoned, against one another, their maximum tariff rates and adopted fixed quotas instead. Nevertheless, much still remained to be clarified: did the new pact have secret military and commercial clauses; was not Poland playing too dangerous a game; did the new agreement represent Poland's adherence to the revisionist bloc; and, if so, did it not spell a temporary, rather than a permanent, settlement for the Corridor, Posen and Upper Silesia? [102]

European reactions to the new pact were varied. Great Britain could see no harm in it.[103] The French Foreign Minister, Paul-Boncour, " rejoiced " over the treaty, at least for publication.[104] Germany deemed the Allied cordon around her broken.[105] Italy thought it a great blow at the

---

[101] *Nouveau recueil*, iii série, vol. xxviii, pp. 643 *et seq.*

[102] *Cf.* Duranty, W., *Europe: War or Peace?* (New York, 1935), pp. 27-28.

[103] *The Times*, January 27, 1934.

[104] *Le Temps*, January 27, 1934.

[105] *Deutsche Allgemeine Zeitung, Frankfurter Zeitung*, January 28, 1934.

French system of alliances.[106]   The U.S.S.R. approved it as a supplement to her own non-aggression pact with Poland,[107] which was reported prematurely as extended for another ten years also.[108]   Czechoslovakia greeted the new agreement without cordiality; to her it indicated another Polish desertion of the principles of intra-Slav cooperation.[109]   Rumors that Germany contemplated extending to her also an amity pact [110] failed to alter her opinion.   During March, 1934, Czechoslovak-Polish relations became tense as the result of several irritating frontier incidents, particularly in Těšin.[111] With considerable success, France, and Beneš also, exerted themselves to minimize friction and restore friendly relations prior to the visits of the new French Minister of Foreign Affairs, Barthou, to Warsaw and Praha.[112]   The French government desired particularly to strengthen the loosening ties with Poland and Czechoslovakia.   Barthou's trip to the two Slavic capitals, begun on April 21, was a success.   It confirmed the Franco-Polish alliance and the desire of all three countries to collaborate loyally in attempting to preserve the peace of Europe.   Poland was flattered because Barthou promised that France would treat her as an equal and insist upon her participation in all future conferences of the Great Powers.   Finally, the influence of Barthou brought to fruition the Soviet-Polish non-aggresion pact and eased Polish friction with Lithuania.[113]

[106] *Corriere della Sera,* January 28, 1934.

[107] *Izvestia,* January 30, 1934.

[108] *Gazeta Warszawska,* February 11, 1934.

[109] *Národní Listy, Národní Politika, České Slovo, Čas,* January 27-30, 1934.

[110] *The New York Times,* February 21, 1934.

[111] *Ibid., Národní Listy, Svornost,* March 18, 22, 26 and 27, 1934.

[112] *Svornost,* March 31, 1934.

[113] *Ibid.,* April 25, 1934; *Gazeta Warszawska,* April 24, 1934.   The Soviet-Polish non-aggression pact was signed at Moscow on May 5 and

On April 26, 1934, Barthou arrived in Praha, where he was greeted with much more cordiality than he had been at Warsaw.[114] Negotiations with Beneš began at once. The two statesmen soon agreed that the maintenance of peace in Central Europe depended upon the preservation of the independence of Austria. They agreed further upon a united front against Germany's demands at the disarmament conference, for they felt that they could never approve a policy which, in the name of arms equality, tended to encourage general rearmament. In all probability, Barthou might have pointed out also to Beneš the advisability of a speedy recognition of the Soviet Union.[115]

Debt Default

Czechoslovakia was compelled to turn her attention also to the problem of international finance. What should be her policy regarding her debt to the United States? Should she default like France, offer a token payment like Great Britain, or pay in full like Finland? The depression had caused serious doubts as to her ability to continue payments, yet considerations of honor and of gratitude rendered default distasteful. Ultimately, Czechoslovakia decided to follow the example of Great Britain: therefore, on June 15, 1933, she offered also a token payment ($180,000 instead of $1,500-000),[116] and, a half year later, when the United States

ratified at Warsaw on June 15. By this agreement the earlier treaty of July 25, 1932, was extended to January 1, 1946, thereupon to be renewed automatically every two years unless denounced by six months' advance notice.

[114] Beneš met Barthou immediately upon his arrival in Praha, and upon his departure, escorted him to the frontier. In contrast, when Barthou had arrived in Warsaw, no representative of the Polish foreign office had been on hand to greet him.

[115] *Cf. Národní Listy, Národní Politika*, April 26-30, 1934; *The New York Times*, April 30, 1934; Wheeler-Bennett, *op. cit.*, pp. 224-229.

[116] *Publications*, Economic and Financial, 1933, ii a 16, p. 261.

decided that token payments were defaults, she again followed the example of England in ceasing payments and in asking for a new debt arrangement.[117]   No new agreement was reached.[118]   When the devaluation of the dollar threatened to curtail exports to the United States, Czechoslovakia, on February 10, 1934, decided to desert the French gold bloc of which she had been a member and devaluate her crown also, by 16.6 per cent, or from a nominal value of $.0501 (exchange value $.0485), American post-devaluation, to $.041783 (exchange value $.040449), post-devaluation,[119] yet, even so, her crown remained far above its earlier nominal value of $.0296375, American pre-devaluation.[120]

The Revival of Hungarian Revisionism

Czechoslovakia had to face also a revival of a movement for the autonomy of Slovakia, to which the Magyars sought to give the appearance of spontaneity.   At the same time, Hungary continued her outspoken condemnation of the Treaty of Trianon.[121]   The direct attacks of the Magyars

[117] *The New York Times*, December 16, 1933.

[118] According to the Washington correspondent of *Le Temps*, Czechoslovakia sought to pay her debt to the United States with her savings in cotton.   On the average, she purchased annually from the United States about $18,000,000 worth of cotton, through German middlemen, whose annual profits on the transaction averaged about $600,000.   If this amount could be saved by purchasing directly through its own government buyers, it, plus manufactured exports, might, with the consent of the United States, pay Czechoslovakia's debt.   However, nothing further was heard of the project.   *Cf. Le Temps, Svornost*, January 5, 1934.

[119] *Svornost*, February 13, 1934; *The New York Times*, February 11, 1934.

[120] *Cf. supra*, p. 76.

[121] *Cf. Neue Freie Presse*, January 17, 1933, for speech of Gömbös. Revisionist agitation within Hungary was revived largely by Julius Gömbös, who became premier on October 1, 1932.   *Cf.* also, Bethlen, I., *The Treaty of Trianon and European Peace* (New York, 1934), for four lectures delivered by the author in London during November, 1933.

were relatively easy to answer, and drew responses in kind. On April 25, 1933, Beneš proclaimed before the Czechoslovak parliament that whoever might desire to wrest from Czechoslovakia any of her territory would have to come for it with an army,[122] and, on December 11, 1933, the Rumanian Minister of Foreign Affairs, Titulescu, in a speech at Košice while visiting Czechoslovakia, announced that, after a conference with Beneš, both had agreed that any revision of the Peace Treaties would mean war.[123]

The reiteration of the Magyar thesis that Slovakia and Subcarpathian Ruthenia did not desire to be component parts of the Czechoslovak Republic required refutation. Czechoslovakia set out to prove that most Slovaks and Ruthenes were satisfied with union with the Czechs and that the real dangers to the peace of Europe were neither intra-Slav cooperation nor the imminence of French hegemony, but rather a revision of the Peace Treaties and a restoration of pre-war Hungary.[124] The *České Slovo* maintained that the renewal of Hungarian agitation represented a desperate effort to prevent a domestic revolution by the exaction of some revision of the Treaty of Trianon.[125] Beneš' speech of April 25, 1933, was followed by two days of parliamentary interpellation in the course of which Senator Václav Klofáč on behalf of the Czechs, and Deputy Igor Hrušovský on behalf of the Slovaks, enthusiastically approved Beneš' viewpoint against revision.[126]

[122] *Zprávy* (Poslanecká Sněmovna), 263 meeting, April 25, 1933, pp. 3-25, 8 session; *ibid.* (Senát), 211 meeting, April 25, 1933, pp. 9-34, 8 session.

[123] *Svornost*, December 12, 1933.

[124] *Cf.* monograph of K. Krofta, *The Substance of Hungarian Revisionism* (Prague, 1934).

[125] *České Slovo*, October 12-13, 1933.

[126] *Zprávy* (Senát), 212-213 meetings, April 26-27, 1933, pp. 2-40 and 3-22 respectively, 8 session; *ibid.* (Poslanecká Sněmovna), 266 meeting, April 27, 1933, pp. 77-80, 8 session.

Many Ruthenes dreaded a return to the yoke of Hungary.[127] Beneš made a trip to Slovakia in December, 1933,[128] and to Ruthenia in May, 1934.[129] Upon both occasions he was greeted with enthusiasm when he summarized the domestic policy of the Republic as one of " progress, consolidation and unity ".[130] A cruel blow was dealt to Magyar hopes on April 12, 1934, when Father Andrew Hlinka, in a letter to the editor of the *České Slovo,* pledged unqualifiedly the support of the Slovak Peoples' Party, of which he was chairman, to the maintenance of the Czechoslovak Republic.[131] In vain did Father Jehlička [132] presume to represent truly the wishes of the Slovaks when he advocated a return of Slovakia to Hungary.[133] Equally ineffective were the pleas of another Magyarized Slovak, Unger, to divide Slovakia between Hungary and Poland.[134] This particular phase of Magyar revisionism came to an inglorious end in Slovakia itself during August, 1934,[135] but an echo of it persisted among certain dissatisfied individuals in the United States early in 1935.[136]

[127] *Cf.* Svornost, September 14, 1933.

[128] *Ibid.,* December 24, 1933.   [129] *Ibid.,* May 17, 1934.

[130] *Ibid.,* May 20, 1934; *cf.* also, Beneš, E., *Reč o problému podkarpatoruskem* (Praha, 1934).

[131] *České Slovo,* April 14, 1934; reprinted also in *Svornost,* April 29, 1934.

[132] *Cf. supra,* p. 95.

[133] *Národní Listy,* August 7, 1934; Svornost, August 22, 1934. *Cf.* Svornost, September 11, 1933, and May 14, 1934, for refutations of Jehlička by Dr. Osuský. An excellent monograph exposing Hungarian propaganda is that by R. W. Seton-Watson, *Treaty Revision and the Hungarian Frontiers* (London, 1934), particularly, pp. 72-74. *Cf. Slovenski poslanci a revizia mierových smluv* for the repudiation of Jehlička by the various Slovak political parties on December 20, 1933.

[134] *Cf.* Svornost, July 18, 1934.

[135] *Cf. ibid.,* October 2, 1934, for reprint of article found in various Praha newspapers of August 18, 1934.

[136] *Cf.* "Autonomist", *Slovakia's Plea for Autonomy.* This anonymous

Austria

The situation of Austria again attracted the attention of the whole world. Several years of interference on the part of German Nazis had produced a critical situation. The Fascist government of Chancellor Dollfuss felt compelled to resist pressure from both Nazis and Socialists. During February, 1934, in Vienna, there broke out, between the Fascist authorities and Socialists, an armed conflict in which several hundred lives were lost.[187] Since certain members of the Czech minority in Vienna had become implicated in the movement, the Czechoslovak Minister to Austria, Dr. Zdenek Fierlinger, deemed it necessary to intervene in an attempt to obtain for them less drastic sentences.[188]

Beneš journeyed to Paris to confer with the French Premier, Doumergue, and the French Minister of Foreign Affairs, Barthou, regarding Austria.[139] It was decided that, in all probability, Dollfuss would not need armed support, but that warning to Germany not to interfere in the internal affairs of Austria would prove sufficient. On February 17, 1934, Great Britain, France and Italy issued a joint declaration in favor of the continued independence and integrity of Austria.[140] France and Italy were wondering whether a restoration of the Habsburgs might not be an excellent check

monograph attempts to point out how the Czechs have failed to carry out the terms of the Pittsburgh Agreement. Ostensibly, it is a plea for the safeguarding of the rights of the Slovaks by a grant of full autonomy, rather than a plea for separation from the Republic. The existence of a certain amount of Slovak dissatisfaction with the existing rule cannot be denied, yet its extent has often been exaggerated.

[187] *Arbeiter Zeitung, Neue Freie Presse, The New York Times,* February 12-16, 1934. *Cf.* Langsam, *op. cit.,* pp. 526-535, for a summary of events in Austria.

[188] *Neue Freie Presse,* February 16, 1934; *Svornost,* February 17, 1934.

[139] *The New York Times,* February 16, 1934.

[140] *Nouveau recueil,* iii série, vol. xxx, pp. 3 *et seq.*

against Anschluss, but again Beneš made clear the fact that such an event would mean war.[141]   The official attitude of Czechoslovakia was presented by Beneš on March 21, 1934, before the Parliamentary Foreign Affairs Committee. In this exposé, after analyzing at length the rival schemes of interested Powers, Beneš stressed the belief that the only solution that would guarantee permanent satisfaction would be a policy that " Austria must remain Austrian ".[142]

Nazi activities within Austria caused much concern also to Mussolini, who sought to revive his earlier project of a triple pact among Italy, Austria and Hungary.   The visits of Dollfuss (February 7)[143] and of Fulvio Suvich, Italian Under-Secretary of Foreign Affairs (February 20),[144] to Budapest to confer with Premier Gömbös of Hungary were interpreted as soundings.   On March 3, there followed an official announcement that, on the 14, Dollfuss and Gömbös would confer with Mussolini in Rome.[145]   The new bloc was actually formed on March 17, when the three Premiers signed three protocols : in the first, they agreed to negotiate, by May 15, a series of bilateral treaties to aid exports, to bolster the price of Hungarian wheat, to increase the amount of commerce passing through the various Adriatic ports, and to establish, on the model of the Little Entente, a permanent economic commission of experts ; in the second, Italy and Austria agreed to inaugurate, by April 5, negotiations for a new commercial treaty ; and, in the third, the three states agreed, in future, to consult mutually upon problems common to all.[146]   On May 14, a trade agreement was signed

[141] *Svornost*, March 10, 1934; *Národní Listy*, March 9, 1934.

[142] Beneš, E., *The Problem of Central Europe and the Austrian Question*, p. 56.

[143] *Neue Freie Presse*, February 8, 1934.

[144] *Ibid.*, February 21, 1934.

[145] *Corriere della Sera*, March 3, 1934.

[146] *Treaty Series*, vol. cliv, pp. 281-303.

whereby Austria agreed to import 2,200,000 quintals of Hungarian wheat, and Italy, 2,000,000 quintals—an arrangement that was intended to preserve the economic status quo.[147]

On March 23, 1934, in an exposé before the Foreign Affairs Committee of the Czechoslovak Senate, Beneš pledged his support to Mussolini's plan to stabilize economic conditions in the Danubian area. He did not wish to render more difficult any understanding regarding the problems of Central Europe. Italy, the Dollfuss régime in Austria, Hungary and Czechoslovakia were, in his estimation, united in their opposition to any Austro-German union. Beneš admitted the necessity of supplementing a political understanding with an economic agreement. On the same day, in another address before the Foreign Affairs Committee of the Czechoslovak Chamber of Deputies, Beneš stated that a solution of the Austrian question would automatically solve most of the other problems of Central Europe. He was convinced that the recent resurrection of a feeling of nationalism within Austria was a positive factor in European politics, and that Austrian independence would have to be maintained. Apparently, Beneš, in these two addresses, had expressed the general opposition of Czechoslovakia to revisionism, for, in the parliamentary discussion that followed, even some German delegates shared his views.[148]

The preservation of the status quo became increasingly difficult after the Nazi revolution, for it soon became evident that relations with Germany could not be maintained upon the basis that had prevailed prior to the advent of Hitler to power. Czechoslovakia was confronted with the self-imposed problem of saving not only Austria from the clutches

[147] *Nouveau recueil*, iii série, vol. xxx, pp. 10 *et seq.* A quintal equals 3.67 bushels.

[148] *Cf. Prager Presse, České Slovo, The New York Times*, March 24, 1934.

of Germany, but of assuring her own preservation as an independent entity. To the former threat of becoming almost an enclave whenever Germany might extend their common frontier by approximately three hundred miles by the annexation of Austria, was now added the even greater menace of direct German designs upon the integrity of Czechoslovakia herself, from which Hitler desired to detach the borderlands inhabited by over three million Germans. Nor was the Nazi threat merely territorial in nature: the approach was far more subtle. Since Czechoslovakia remained almost alone as a democracy in Central Europe and was virtually surrounded by dictatorships, her leaders faced the necessity of combating German-inspired rumors of the imminent rise of Fascism from within. Masaryk and Beneš discounted the immediate dangers of both foreign war and Fascism. They regarded such rumors as primarily propaganda intended for home consumption within the revisionist states themselves.[149]

Friction with Germany

Czechoslovak relations with Germany were also becoming more tense. As early as January 14, 1933, just prior to the Nazi revolution, Beneš warned his people that a war between Germany and Czechoslovakia over their own differences was improbable, but that both states might easily become involved in a general conflict.[150] When it became evident that Hitler's tenure of power threatened to become more or less permanent, the reaction against Nazism became more pronounced. In the estimation of the Czechoslovaks, Hitler had done the world a service in tearing the mask from the face of German militarism, but, in so doing, had nullified in

[149] For Masaryk on war, cf. Svornost, April 13, 1934; on Fascism, ibid., April 1 and December 11, 1933; for Beneš on war and democracy, ibid., February 21-22, 1934; on Fascism, ibid., May 29, 1934.

[150] České Slovo, January 15, 1933.

three months fourteen years of patient effort on the part of German Socialists.[151] On May 8, Czechoslovakia listed 334 foreign newspapers, most of them Hitlerite in nature, whose circulation was henceforth forbidden within her borders.[152]

Czechoslovakia extended assistance to such German exiles as sought her hospitality.[153] Her representative on the League Council, Osuský, on May 30, favored speedy League action on behalf of the Jewish minority in German' Upper Silesia.[154] On October 11, the League Assembly provided an international basis for the care of Jewish refugees.[155] In the interim, President Masaryk had come to the conclusion that the situation of the Jews in Germany was an international problem.[156] After he had assured a delegation of Czechoslovak Jews that anti-Semitism would not be tolerated by the Republic,[157] a World Congress of Zionists met in Praha during·August. The delegates, 332 in number, included many of the leaders of the Jewish world. The Congress planned to aid the emigration of 250,000 Jews from Germany. Before adjourning, the delegates put themselves on record as opposing revisionism.[158]

Czechoslovakia's deep-seated opposition to the Nazi movement was again revealed on October 4, 1933, when the government suspended the activity of the German National

[151] *Ibid.*, May 6, 1933.

[152] *Ibid.*, May 8, 1933.

[153] *Cf. Svornost*, May 23-24, 1933, for estimates that 6,000 members of the German intelligentsia had sought refuge in Czechoslovakia from the persecution of Hitler.

[154] *Official Journal*, July, 1933, pp. 842-843.

[155] *Ibid.*, December, 1933, pp. 1616-1618.

[156] *Svornost*, August 25, 1933.

[157] *Ibid.*, July 20, 1933. *Cf.* also *ibid.*, October 15, 1933, for Masaryk's further views.

[158] *Cf. České Slovo*, August 21-24, 1933; *Svornost*, August 22, 23, 28, 1933.

Socialists and the German Nationalists.[159] This move was precautionary and was intended to put an end to Fascism as an element in internal politics. The order was well timed, and coincided with a new series of " incidents ".

The anti-German feeling that had been provided with a fresh impetus in September by the discovery of a new Pan-German map which included, among other regions, a third of Czechoslovakia in the projected new " Third Reich ",[160] culminated, oñ the last day of the month, in an attack by a Praha mob on Baron von Bibra, the First Secretary of the German Legation, who was parading the swastika on the most crowded streets of the city.[161] The German Minister to Praha could obtain no satisfaction for the incident; [162] rather, the Czechoslovak police staged raids in order to arrest well-known Nazis.[163]

Czechoslovakia was amazed by Germany's " blood bath " of June 30, 1934, wherein, according to Nazi reports, seventy-seven persons lost their lives in a " purge ".[164] Hardly had this surprise passed, before there occurred on July 25, 1934, the assassination of Premier Dollfuss of Austria by one member of a band of 144 Austrian Nazis.[165]

[159] *Cf. Tisky* (Poslanecká Sněmovna), no. 2358, October 19, 1933, 9 session, for law suspending activity of political parties dangerous to the state. The three largest German parties (Social Demóerat, Agrarian and Christian Socialist) gradually abandoned their hostile attitude towards the Czechoslovaks. Two smaller parties (National Socialist and Nationalist) retained Pan-Germanic and anti-Semitic programs. The former closely imitated Hitlerism, whereas the latter, dating from the origin of Czechoslovakia, was composed of dissatisfied German radicals. *Cf.* Hoch, *op. cit.*, pp. 40-41.

[160] *Cf. Svornost*, September 19, 1933.

[161] *Ibid., The New York Times*, October 1, 1933.

[162] *The New York Times*, October 4, 1933.

[163] *Svornost*, October 9, 1933.

[164] *Völkischer Beobachter*, July 1-3, 1934.

[165] *The New York Times, Svornost*, July 26, 1934.

Amid such bloody scenes, Czechoslovakia reaped the reward for her years of tolerant rule, when even part of her German minority expressed its gratitude for being spared participation in such civil strife.[166] The bloody course of Nazism was accepted by Czechoslovakia as evidence of the difficulty of the establishment of cordial relations between Hitler and herself, another potential victim. In her estimation, the only recourse was the creation of an overwhelming coalition that would isolate Germany and impress upon her the utter hopelessness of any new conflict.[167] This viewpoint was similar to that of France, perhaps an echo of Barthou's statement that his country would " continue to tighten the screws of diplomacy until Hitler would be compelled to capitulate.".[168]

Attempts to Isolate Germany

In Beneš' opinion, the situation called for a new orientation of the Powers. Since the fall of 1931, when the Soviet Union had come to realize the danger of a war on two fronts —in Central Europe and the Far East—she had begun to face about in her foreign policy, from a revisionist to a status-quo viewpoint. By March of 1934, Moscow had proceeded so far in the new direction that she began to take soundings in London and Paris regarding the possibility of her entry into the League.[169] The question was discussed further at Geneva by Barthou and Litvinov on May 18,[170] and, ten days later, the Soviet government announced that it had been invited to join the League.[171] To Beneš, these

[166] Cf. *Prager Presse*, August 20, 1934.

[167] Cf. *Svornost*, August 17, October 22, 1934.

[168] *Le Temps*, May 26, 1934; *Svornost*, May 27, 1934.

[169] *Svornost*, March 18, 23, 1934.

[170] Cf. *Le Temps*, May 19, 1934.

[171] *Isvestia*, May 18, 1934. Cf. also, *Le Temps*, May 30, 1934, for Litvinov's Geneva speech.

motives indicated the advisability of the formation of a new bloc of France, the U.S.S.R., the Little Entente and the Balkan Entente, from which Czechoslovakia could not afford to be excluded.[172] He believed that the time had arrived, according to the agreement which had been made at the Little Entente Conference of Zagreb on January 22, 1934, to recognize the Soviet government.[173] On June 9, Czechoslovakia and Rumania, apparently with the approval of Yugoslavia, recognized the Soviet Union: the fact that Yugoslavia did not act similarly was explained by Beneš as merely an indication that she did not find that particular time convenient.[174] The enthusiasm with which Czechoslovakia received the announcement indicated what a great change in sentiment had transpired as a result of the events of the Nazi crisis.[175]

The Little Entente followed the recognition of Moscow with the Conference of Bucharest, June 13-20, 1934, at which meeting it was decided to continue mutual cooperation with a view towards the economic recovery of Central Europe, and to continue opposition to Hungarian revisionism and to any restoration of the Habsburgs.[176] Hardly had the Conference terminated, when Barthou arrived from Paris. That evening, June 20, he delivered an address in which he stressed the common interests of France and Rumania in opposing revisionism.[177] After tarrying in Belgrade June

[172] Beneš, E., *Une Nouvelle phase de la lutte pour l'equilibre européen* (speech of July 2, 1934), p. 32.

[173] *Cf. supra*, p. 372.

[174] Beneš, *op. cit.*, pp. 32-33.

[175] *Cf. Národní Politika, Národní Listy, České Slovo*, July 9-10, 1934; *The Central European Observer*, July 13, 1934; *cf.* also, Chmelář, J., "Československá zahraniční politika v roce 1934", *Zahraniční Politika*, vol. xiv, p. 95.

[176] *The New York Times*, June 20, 1934.

[177] *Le Temps*, June 21, 1934.

23-26,[178] Barthou departed homeward, via Vienna.[179]   His trip was highly significant.   France was worried over the future solidarity of the Little Entente, particularly over the attitude of Yugoslavia.   The failure of the Geneva disarmament conference, and the threatened Italo-German rapprochement, apparently foreshadowed by Hitler's conference with Mussolini in Venice on June 14-15,[180] had increased French uneasiness as to the future.[181]   Apparently, King Alexander of Yugoslavia had also decided to fish in troubled waters. Just as Poland had resented the fact that a Soviet rapprochement with France would reduce her own value to the latter, Alexander, who in view of Nazi interference within Austria discounted the possibility of a lasting Italo-German rapprochement, felt that an Italo-French rapprochement, which he believed inevitable if Anschluss was to be averted, might involve an abandonment of his own country by France.   Yugoslavia had nothing to fear either from Moscow or from Anschluss, but did fear a Habsburg restoration and the extension of Italian influence in Central Europe and the Balkans.   Might not a recognition of the U.S.S.R. antagonize Germany needlessly without any corresponding gain for herself?   Should not Yugoslavia keep open, against a possible Habsburg restoration and future war with Italy, the chance of obtaining German support, which, conceivably, might be more powerful and more willingly extended than that of France?   Obviously, Alexander must have been motivated by some such reflections, when, according to reports, he declined to take any further action regarding the Soviet Union and promised merely to pay a visit to France in autumn.[182]

[178] *Ibid.*, June 26, 1934.   [179] *Ibid.*, June 27, 1934.

[180] *Cf. Völkischer Beobachter*, June 15-16, 1934.

[181] *Cf. The Central European Observer*, July 13, 1934, for Barthou's own comment on his trip.

[182] *Cf.* Duranty, *op. cit.*, p. 22; Simonds and Emeny, *op. cit.*, p. 316.

Moscow continued her peaceful policy by offering to Germany an amity pact to include also Poland and Czechoslovakia, but her overtures were rejected by Hitler.[183] Undeterred by this rebuff, Litvinov suggested, as an alternative, an Eastern Locarno Mutual Assistance Pact embracing Germany, Poland, the U.S.S.R., Czechoslovakia and the Baltic states.[184] His project enlisted the support of Italy and Great Britain,[185] and, later, of France as well.[186] Both Germany and Poland professed to see no benefits for themselves in the new agreement.[187] The Soviet Union offered a compromise—she would adhere to the Western Locarno Pact if Germany would do the same for the East;[188] she demanded some Eastern agreement prior to her entry into the League.[189] Nevertheless, Poland continued to oppose the plan as too indefinite,[190] and Germany suggested instead a series of bilateral treaties.[191] At last France lost patience and demanded from Poland a clear-cut answer as to her stand, hinting broadly that a negative reply might create a Franco-Soviet alliance.[192] The exact contents of the Polish reply were not published.[193] On September 18, 1934, the Soviet Union became a member of the League.[194]

[183] *Völkischer Beobachter*, June 18, 1934.

[184] *The New York Times*, June 24, 1934.

[185] *Ibid.*, July 14, 1934.

[186] *Ibid.*, July 16, 1934.

[187] *Ibid.*, July 16-17, 1934.

[188] *Ibid.*, July 24, 1934; *cf.* also, *ibid.*, July 22, 1934, for a summary of the negotiations.

[189] *Ibid.*, September 2, 1934.

[190] *Ibid.*, July 29, September 9, 1934.

[191] *Ibid.*, September 11, 1934.

[192] *Ibid.*, September 2, 1934.

[193] *Ibid.*, September 28, 1934.

[194] *Official Journal*, November, 1934, pp. 1392-1396, and special supplement, no. 123, p. 18.

Czechoslovakia supported whole-heartedly the entry of the U.S.S.R. into the League, whose prestige would be enhanced by such an accession, and her attitude was supported by her Little Entente partners.[195]   Even Poland withdrew its opposition to a permanent Council seat for the Soviet Union.[196] On September 13, the Little Entente announced its approval of the proposed Eastern Locarno Pact.[197]   On the 26, Litvinov and Barthou agreed upon a Mutual Assistance Pact that would include not only their own countries, but the Little Entente, Turkey, Italy, Greece and Spain.[198]   So idealistic a project could not be realized.

The summer of 1934 witnessed further steps in the isolation of Germany, when both Great Britain and Italy, which had formerly looked askance at a Franco-Soviet rapprochement, came to welcome it, and even considered joining it, in order to curb the Nazi menace.   Within Great Britain there had been developing, even before the Nazi " blood bath ", sentiment against repeating the mistake of 1914, when a clear-cut stand might have averted the World War; and, after the " purge ", the ties with France became closer.[199] Similarly, Italy was aroused to action when a year and a half of Nazi interference within Austria culminated in the assassination of Dollfuss on July 25, 1934.   For Germany, this event represented a setback in that it alienated the only Great Power in Europe that might have been friendly, Italy, which was thereby almost compelled to seek the friendship of France.[200]

[195] *The New York Times*, September 1, 1934.

[196] *The Times*, August 30, 1934.

[197] *České Slovo*, September 14, 1934.

[198] *The New York Times*, September 26, 1934.

[199] *Cf.* Duranty, *op. cit.*, pp. 29-30.

[200] *Ibid.*, p. 19; Simonds and Emeny, *op. cit.*, p. 274.

At once, Mussolini ordered an army to the Austrian frontier to prevent Anschluss.[201] Italy's speedy action in turn alarmed Yugoslavia and Czechoslovakia, both of which took prompt military measures also, for, to them, the extension of Italian control over Austria would be intolerable. The situation became critical and complex. Whereas Yugoslavia sought particularly to prevent Austria's falling into the hands of Italy, Czechoslovakia sought to save Austria from both Italy and Germany.[202] Apparently, Prince Starhemberg, Austria's Acting Chancellor after the murder of Dollfuss, preferred to cooperate with the Little Entente and Italy, rather than join Germany.[203] Barthou frankly declared his opposition to any solution of the Austrian question which would make Italy preponderant in Central Europe.[204] It appeared that Yugoslavia, of the small states, held the key to the situation. Should she desert France for Germany, she might be followed by Rumania, and even by Hungary. Thus, not only would the Little Entente and the French system of alliances be threatened with disruption, but Italy would lose her friend, Hungary. Such an eventuality was not impossible, for neither Yugoslavia, Rumania, nor Hungary was threatened directly by German ambitions in Central Europe, but on the contrary, found her a better market for their agricultural products than either France or Italy. In this emergency, Barthou sought to clarify the situation by inviting King Alexander to visit France.[205]

Instead of clarifying the situation, Alexander's visit to France made matters worse when, on October 9, 1934, both Alexander and Barthou were assassinated in Marseilles by

201 *Corriere della Sera*, July 26, 1934.
202 *Česke Slovo*, July 30–August 2, 1934.
203 *The New York Times*, September 16, 1934.
204 *Ibid.*, September 26, 1934.
205 *Cf.* Simonds and Emeny, *op. cit.*, p. 275.

a Croatian terrorist. Barthou's death apparently was an accident, the result of his attempt to protect the King, whom certain dissatisfied subjects had sought to slay as part of a plot to disrupt the unity of Yugoslavia.[206]

On October 14 the Foreign Ministers of the Little Entente met at Belgrade to confer regarding their stand against Balkan terrorists,[207] and, on the 19, united in a protest in which they accused Hungary of abetting the assassins.[208] Large detachments of the Yugoslav army were concentrated on the Hungarian frontier, and it was decided to request the League to investigate the charges against Hungary. The general situation was explained to both houses of parliament by Beneš in an exposé of November 6, 1934.[209]

Assured of the support of her Little Entente partners, of Greece, Turkey and France,[210] Yugoslavia threatened to take matters into her own hands if no satisfaction was forthcoming from Geneva. Hungary demanded the withdrawal of Beneš as President of the League Council when the case would be tried.[211] Despite French requests for further delay in order that some agreement might be reached with Italy, Yugoslavia actually submitted her protest to the League on November 22.[212] Two days later a fresh crisis was reached when Hungary demanded immediate action regarding the charges, which she characterized as a threat to the peace of Europe.[213] Matters were embittered still further when

[206] Cf. *Le Temps, The Times, The New York Times,* October 10, 1934.

[207] *The New York Times,* October 14, 1934.

[208] *Ibid.,* October 19, 1934.

[209] Beneš, E., *Vers un regroupement des forces en Europe?,* Sources et documents tchécoslovaques, no. 26.

[210] Cf. Padelford, *op. cit.,* pp. 114-115 and 124-125.

[211] *Official Journal,* December, 1934, p. 1769.

[212] *Ibid.,* pp. 1765-1766.

[213] *Ibid.,* p. 1768.

Yugoslav troops drove across the frontier into Hungary several thousand Magyars who had resided in Yugoslavia since the War and who had not been naturalized.[214]

The League, which considered the dispute December 7-10, 1934, finally evolved a satisfactory compromise. In the course of the deliberations, the Little Entente again demonstrated its solidarity. Beneš, speaking for Czechoslovakia, threatened her resignation from the League Council unless that organization demonstrated sufficient courage and efficiency to prevent an armed conflict between Hungary and Yugoslavia. However, Beneš took care to explain that such a step would not mean that his country would withdraw from the League.[215] After denouncing the principles of revisionism, Titulescu, speaking for the Little Entente, pointed out that Hungary's national honor was in no way questioned, whereupon both Hungary and Yugoslavia accepted the draft treaty sponsored by France, whereby there was created a permanent international investigating committee of five members for the suppression of terrorism.[216] At the same time all further frontier deportations ceased. Upon his return to Praha, Beneš explained his strong stand by pointing out that the object of revisionism was to destroy the status quo in Central Europe, and that revisionism could never accomplish its ends in a peaceable manner.[217]

The outcome of the assassination crisis helped further the isolation of Germany. A sensation was created on November 23 when Leon Archimbaud, Reporter of the Budget, announced, in the course of a debate in the French Chamber of Deputies, that the Soviet Union had offered her army to

[214] *Ibid.*, p. 1755.

[215] *Ibid.*, pp. 1723-1728 and 1745-1748; Beneš, E., *Le Sens politique de la tragédie de Marseille*, Sources et documents tchécoslovaques, no. 27.

[216] *Official Journal*, December, 1934, p. 1760.

[217] *Národní Politika*, December 16, 1934.

France in the event of a war with Germany.[218] This statement of an alliance was in all appearances premature, yet, subsequent denials by the Quai D'Orsay failed to remove the impression that an alliance was imminent.[219] The signature, on December 5, by France and the U.S.S.R. of a protocol which called for joint negotiations regarding the completion of an Eastern Locarno agreement seemed to confirm the new trend of events.[220] Czechoslovakia adhered to this protocol on December 12.[221]

France and Italy, after protracted negotiations, also reached a rapprochement on January 7, 1935. Signed by the French Foreign Minister who succeeded Barthou, Laval, and by Mussolini, the new Rome accord specified: (1) a pact of consultation whereby the two countries agreed to consult with one another upon all European questions, particularly in the event that Austrian independence should be jeopardized; (2) a pact of non-intervention, to be signed by the Little Entente, Austria, Hungary and possibly Germany; (3) other powers might accede to the consultative provisions of the pact and (4) colonial concessions by France to Italy in Africa. Although both negotiators disclaimed that the new accord was aimed at any particular country, the specific guarantee of Austrian independence left no doubt that it was intended against Germany.[222]

In this manner was a new ring of nations created around Germany. Except for distant Japan, whose willingness and ability to engage in a war in Central Europe were alike inconceivable, and for Poland, whose military value and sin-

---

[218] *Annales de la Chambre des Députés*, 15 législature, session extraordinaire de 1934, 1 partie, 1 séance le 23 novembre, 1934, p. 2572.

[219] *Le Temps*, November 24, 1934.

[220] *Nouveau recueil*, iii série, vol. xxx, pp. 643-644.

[221] *The New York Times*, December 12, 1934.

[222] *Nouveau recueil*, iii série, vol. xxx, pp. 644 *et seq.*

cerity were alike open to question, Nazified Germany appeared deserted by all whose weight was of great value. Nevertheless, Hitler continued to reiterate his demands for absolute German equality with the other Great Powers, on land, on sea, in the air, and colonially.

Czechoslovakia welcomed enthusiastically the Franco-Soviet and the Franco-Italian rapprochements as ensuring the peace of Europe and her own safety.[223] Both rapprochements were viewed with almost equal cordiality by her Little Entente partners. On January 11, 1935, at Ljubljana, the three Little Entente Foreign Ministers—Beneš, Yeftič and Titulescu—met to discuss the new situation that had been created by the recent Franco-Italian accord and to formulate a unified policy regarding it.[224] The decision of the conference was made public by Titulescu, who stated that the Little Entente would enter negotiations regarding a Danubian Pact only as a unit.[225] He was reported to have demanded also four specific conditions upon which alone the Little Entente would consider accession: (1 and 2) the restoration of the Habsburgs and the minorities question, respectively, would not be considered as solely internal affairs of any signatory Power; (3) all revisionist propaganda regarding the territories of signatories would be dropped and (4) the exceptional privileges enjoyed by some citizens of certain signatory states within the territories of another state (i. e. the special economic privileges of Italians in Dalmatia) would terminate with the signature of the new pact.[226] Although the effect of Titulescu's reported demands upon France and Italy is not known, the fact re-

---

[223] Cf. *České Slovo, Čas, Národní Politika, Národní Listy*, January 8-9, 1935.

[224] *Svornost*, January 12, 1935.

[225] *The New York Times*, January 12, 1935.

[226] *Ibid.*, January 29, 1935.

mained that the Little Entente did not accede to the Rome accord of January 7, 1935.

Nazi success in the Saar plebiscite of January 15, 1935, increased Czechoslovak apprehensions regarding Hitler's ultimate objectives. Rumors spread that Hitler might attempt a series of other plebiscites unauthorized by the Treaty of Versailles, particularly in Memel, Danzig, the Belgian communes of Eupen and Malmedy, Austria, and the German regions of Bohemia.[227] Fears of German surprise air attacks and growing convictions that Anglo-French negotiations with Germany regarding an air pact of non-aggression would produce no concrete results induced the Czechoslovak government in February, 1935, to approve a comprehensive plan of aerial defense. The new enactment required the owners of all large domiciles to provide bomb and gas proof concrete basements for the inmates. Employers were to provide similar shelters for their employees. All citizens were required to purchase gas masks. The larger cities were to provide warning sirens and first-aid stations. Severe penalties were to be meted out for sabotaging any air defense equipment. The government could force the sale of any property needed for defense purposes. Such elaborate precautions might not be necessary, but, in view of the fact that the Republic was almost surrounded by more or less hostile neighbors, it was deemed best to take no chances.[228]

On March 16, 1935, Hitler proclaimed compulsory military service throughout Germany. By this decree the standing army was increased to thirty-six divisions (500,000-600,000 men). Although Hitler pleaded the necessity for self defense,[229] particularly against the Soviet Union which

---

[227] *Cf*, *Svornost*, January 21, 22, February 16, 1935.

[228] *Tisky* (Senát), no. 1436, February 22, 1935, 2 session.

[229] *Völkischer Beobachter, Deutsche Allgemeine Zeitung,* March 16, 1935.

maintained a standing army of 940,000 men,[230] his move aroused general apprehensions. On March 18 Great Britain sent a note of protest against Germany's unilateral abrogation of the Treaty of Versailles.[231] Three days later France and Italy sent similar protests,[232] all of which were unheeded by Germany. After this repudiation of the Treaty of Versailles, Czechoslovakia felt compelled to rearm also.[233] Within a week she was reported to have begun new fortifications on the German frontier.[234]

The Austrian government feared Hitler also.[235] Chancellor Schuschnigg and Foreign Minister Berger-Waldenegg visited Paris (February 21-23) and London (February 24-26) in an effort to obtain further assistance against German threats. They were received politely but without enthusiasm in both western capitals. The British and French governments agreed to help maintain Austrian independence, but refused Austria any further loans and renewed their bans against a Habsburg restoration.[236]

The question of Austria's future became also the subject of discussions between the Little Entente and Italy. On March 25, Titulescu, who was spokesman for both the Balkan and the Little Ententes, conferred with Yeftič at Belgrade in the course of a tour through the states of the Little Entente. An unofficial report from Belgrade indicated that a difference of opinion had developed between Italy and the Little Entente. The former was apparently willing to approve the reintroduction of compulsory military service

230 *Publications*, Disarmament, 1935, ix 5, p. 839.

231 *The Times*, March 19, 1935.

232 *Le Temps*, March 22, 1935.

233 *The New York Times*, March 17, 1935.

234 *Ibid.*, March 24, 1935.

235 *Cf. Neue Freie Presse*, January 16, 1935.

236 *The Times, Le Temps, Svornost*, February 22-27, 1935.

within Austria as essential to prevent ultimate annexation by Germany, whereas the latter opposed such a move as establishing a precedent for the rearming of both Hungary and Bulgaria. The rearming of Austria might not represent a threat to the Little Entente, but the rearming of either Hungary or Bulgaria would be met " in the most resolute manner " (i. e. mobilization) by the three partners.[237] Two days later Titulescu met Beneš at Bratislava enroute to Paris. Apparently, the two statesmen were in complete accord, for, on departing, Titulescu stated that " no power could separate Czechoslovakia and Rumania ".[238]

The Western Powers also decided to hold a Conference in order to try to agree upon a common line of action regarding Germany. To this end, Eden, British Lord Privy Seal, Layal, French Minister of Foreign Affairs, and Suvich, Italian Under-Secretary for Foreign Affairs, met at Paris on March 23 and decided to call a three-Power Conference at Stresa for April 11.[239] Thereupon, Eden, together with Simon, the British Secretary for Foreign Affairs, departed for Berlin to hold a series of " exploratory conversations ". On March 25-26 they conferred with Hitler and the German Minister of Foreign Affairs, Von Neurath.[240] Upon his return to London on March 27, Simon gave the press a summary of the results. According to Simon, Germany refused to join any " Eastern Locarno ", Pact of Rome, or other guarantee of existing Danubian boundaries. Allegedly, Hitler demanded also a navy of 400,000 tons, an air force equal to that of the Soviet Union, a reopening of the question of the Austro-German Customs Union together with an Austrian plebiscite upon the issue and the cession by Czecho-

[237] *Svornost*, March 26, 1935.
[238] *The New York Times*, March 28, 1935.
[239] *Ibid.*, March 24, 1935.
[240] *Ibid.*, March 25-26, 1935.

slovakia of territory said to contain 3,500,000 Germans.[241] However, it still remained a question whether Hitler had merely hinted or had expressed openly such views.

While Berlin newspapers printed columns regarding Hitler's " moderation " and denied any desire to dominate Europe or to seize territories beyond Germany's existing frontiers,[242] great indeed was the pessimism in London,[243] and the anger in Praha.[244] At Paris, Titulescu delivered to Laval what was virtually an ultimatum of the Little Entente. Unless France would take immediate measures to create an effective " ring of steel " around Germany, the Little Entente would be compelled to open negotiations with Germany itself. As a result of his conversations at Belgrade and Bratislava, Titulescu pointed out that the Little Entente expected unstinted French support, failing which it would seek a rapprochement with Germany. To avert a collapse in the existing system of alliances, Titulescu suggested that France attempt to draw Poland again within her orbit and that France negotiate as soon as possible a military alliance with the U.S.S.R. By the creation of an overwhelming coalition alone could Germany, in his estimation, be made to disarm.[245]

Eden embarked on another series of visits in an effort to isolate Germany. On March 29 he arrived in Moscow to confer with Stalin, who promised to do all in his power to cooperate with the Western Powers in attempting to preserve the peace of Europe.[246] On April 1, Eden came to Warsaw,

[241] *The Times,* March 27-28, 1935.

[242] *Vorwaerts, Vossische Zeitung, Völkischer Beobachter,* March 27-29, 1935.

[243] *Cf. The Times,* March 29-30, 1935.

[244] *Čas, Národní Politika, Právo Lidu, Svornost,* March 27-30, 1935.

[245] *Svornost, Le Temps,* March 30, 1935; *cf.* also, *The New York Times,* March 30-31, 1935.

[246] *Izvestia, Svornost,* March 30, 1935; *cf. The New York Times,* April 1, 1935, for joint statement of Eden and Litvinov.

where he was received coolly by Pilsudski and Beck. Poland remained firm in objecting to an " Eastern Locarno ", particularly since such an agreement might make her the battleground between Germany and the Soviet Union and, under certain conditions, might even obligate her to defend Soviet territory.[247] At Praha, on April 4, Eden received the warmest welcome. The similarity between the foreign policies of the two countries was brought out forcibly by Beneš' statement, " we pursue the same policies and objectives as Great Britain ", and by Eden's response, " we stand or fall together ".[248] Upon returning to London, Eden pointed out that his tour had convinced him of the impossibility of including Germany either in an " Eastern Locarno " or in any pact with Great Britain, France and Italy.[249]

Mussolini also regarded the situation as being critical. He warned Great Britain and France that the Stresa Conference must bring Germany's aggressive policy to a halt. To that end he made the following suggestions: (1) it is useless to make peaceful gestures towards Germany, (2) the three Great Powers—Great Britain, France and Italy—must clarify the fact that Germany cannot continue to break treaties without suffering the consequences, (3) Germany must be punished for violating the Treaty of Versailles, (4) new steps must be taken to guarantee the integrity of Austria, and (5) the rearming of Austria, Hungary and Bulgaria must be permitted under some compromise that remained to be negotiated.[250]

Beneš regarded the general situation more optimistically. In his estimation, the best basis for peace would be unity

[247] *The New York Times, Svornost, Gazeta Warszawska,* April 2-3, 1935.

[248] *Svornost, The New York Times,* April 5, 1935.

[249] *The New York Times, The Times,* April 6, 1935.

[250] *The Times,* April 4, 1935; *Svornost,* April 5, 1935.

among the three Great Powers of Western Europe.[251]   The
encirclement of Germany appeared more imminent when the
Balkan and Little Ententes stated that they not only approved
a Franco-Soviet alliance, but would join it eventually.[252]
On the other hand, according to a rumor emanating from
Vienna, Austria was on the verge of an alliance with Germany.   It was alleged that Austria would send to Stresa an
envoy who would demand a cancellation of the military
clauses of the Treaty of St. Germain in order that Austria
might have an army of 65,000 men, 30,000 of whom would
be " selected conscripts ".[253]

The Stresa Conference of April 11-14, 1935, established
a united front of Great Britain, France and Italy and rep-
resented a joint effort in defense of peace.   Again Great
Britain refused to accept any definite continental commit-
ments beyond those of Locarno.   The Conference decided
that Austrian independence could best be preserved by a
Danubian Pact which would include all the neighbors of
Austria.   In order that such a Pact might be consummated,
Mussolini invited all interested Powers to a Conference at
Rome, tentatively for May 20.   With regard to an Eastern
Pact, the three Great Powers concluded merely to continue
discussions for " the consolidation of security in Eastern
Europe ".   France had already decided to enter into such a
pact with the Soviet Union, and even Germany had agreed to
accede to it, at least to some limited degree.   With regard to
the question of the rearming of Austria, Hungary and Bulgaria, Italy and France expressed the conflicting views of
the three former enemy states and of the Little Entente

[251] *The New York Times*, April 8, 1935.

[252] *Ibid.*, April 11, 1935. *Cf.* also, Padelford, *op. cit.*, pp. 127-129, for
the cooperation of the Balkan and Little Ententes, both of whom were
represented by Titulescu.

[253] *Neue Freie Presse*, April 4, 1935.

respectively. Since the Stresa Conference had decided to bring before the League the question of Germany's violation of the Treaty of Versailles by rearming, the Little Entente did not intend to permit the approval of similar violations of the Peace Treaties by the smaller former enemy states. As the result of Laval's forceful pleading of the Little Entente's views, the Stresa Conference decided that any rearming of the small former enemy states would have to await a truly effective peace and security agreement negotiated under the contemplated Danubian Pact.[254] The condemnation of Germany as a violator of the Treaty of Versailles by the League Council on April 17 inferred that similar condemnation might follow any further violations of the Peace Treaties by other states.[255] Czechoslovakia received the results of the Stresa Conference enthusiastically. Her people looked forward to the approaching Conference of Rome and to the imminent Franco-Soviet pact of mutual assistance, which would be followed by a similar pact between the U.S.S.R. and Czechoslovakia.[256]

On May 2, at Paris, Laval and the Russian Ambassador to France, Potemkin, signed a Franco-Russian pact of mutual assistance. Negotiated entirely within the framework of the League, the new pact contemplated: (1) consultation in the event of any danger of aggression, (2) immediate aid in the event of " unprovoked aggression ", (3) " aid and assistance " in the event of unprovoked aggression by a nation which violated the League Covenant by such action, (4) this pact would not be interpreted in a manner which might restrict the duties or obligations of members of the League and (5) this pact would endure for five years, and would continue indefinitely unless denounced one year before

[254] *The Times, The New York Times,* April 12-15, 1935.
[255] *Official Journal,* May, 1935, pp. 556-571.
[256] *The Central European Observer,* April 19, May 3, 1935.

the end of the five year period.[257]   The protocol of signature
which accompanied the pact showed the true significance of
the rapprochement.   One clause specified that " undertakings
in this treaty refer only to cases of aggression against either
of the contracting parties' own territory ".   Although the
Locarno agreements were not mentioned specifically, they
were amply protected by the statement that the new pact
" shall not be carried out in any way which, being inconsis-
tent with treaty obligations undertaken by the contracting
parties, might expose the latter to sanctions of an international character ".   German accession to the pact might
ensue " although circumstances have not hitherto permitted
the conclusion of these agreements, which the two parties
still look upon as desirable, the fact remains that the understandings set forth in the Franco-Soviet treaty of assistance
are to be understood to come into play only within the limits
contemplated in the tripartite agreement (i. e. among the
U.S.S.R., France and Germany) previously projected ".   In
contrast with the pre-war alliance between France and
Russia, the new agreement was much more limited in scope.
An outgrowth of the desire for an Eastern Locarno, it was
aimed only at Germany (i. e. France would not be required
to aid the U.S.S.R. against Japan).[258]

The signature of the Franco-Soviet treaty of mutual
assistance was followed by a report that France would help
finance the construction of strategic roads and railroads along
the western frontiers of the Soviet Union.[259]   On May 13
Laval visited Moscow.[260]   Two days later he and Litvinov
issued a joint invitation that nations which objected to an

[257] *Nouveau recueil*, iii série, vol. xxxi, pp. 645 *et seq.* Ratifications
were exchanged at Paris, March 27, 1936.

[258] *Cf. The New York Times*, February 28, 1936, for article comparing
the two alliances.

[259] *Ibid.*, May 4, 1935.

[260] *Le Temps*, May 14, 1935.

"Eastern Locarno" should join a non-aggression pact which would have no military obligations.[261]

Czechoslovakia hastened to associate herself with France and the U.S.S.R. As a matter of fact, her relations with Moscow had become increasingly cordial since her recognition of the Soviet régime, and she had been waiting merely for France to take the initiative. An alliance between the Soviet Union and Czechoslovakia had been rumored early in January, 1935, when a delegation of Czechoslovak journalists was received in Moscow with acclaim so unusually cordial [262] as to draw the ire of both Germany [263] and Poland.[264] A further gesture of friendship was the signing, on March 25, of two new Soviet-Czechoslovak treaties. One was a simple patent agreement, whereas the other, a trade credit treaty, was of relatively greater importance. Czechoslovakia had organized recently an Export Institute to investigate foreign trade and had opened commercial negotiations with the U.S.S.R., Austria and Hungary. Upon the recommendation of the Export Institute, the new commercial treaty with the Soviet Union included mutual most-favored-nation clauses, equitable import quotas and foreign exchange regulations, and an extension of the state guarantee of export credits. When ratified, this treaty would extend to the U.S.S.R. a credit of 250,000,000 Czechoslovak crowns.[265]

The treaty of mutual assistance between Czechoslovakia and the Soviet Union, similar to that between France and the Soviet Union, was actually signed in Praha on May 16 by Beneš and by the Soviet Minister to Czechoslovakia, Alex-

[261] *Ibid.*, May 16, 1935.

[262] *Cf. Svornost*, January 15, 21, February 10, 1935.

[263] *Vossische Zeitung*, January 8, 1935.

[264] *Gazeta Warszawska*, January 8, 1935.

[265] *Prager Presse, Čas*, March 26, 1935.

androvský. The pact was to become effective whenever one of the signatories became the object of an unprovoked attack on the part of a European state, in which case the other would assist immediately. It was to be noted, however, that, as in the case of the Franco-Soviet treaty, aid to Moscow would not be forthcoming against a Japanese attack. The protocol of signature specified also that " both governments understood that the obligation of mutual assistance becomes effective only when it shall meet the foreseen conditions of the pact and when the victim of aggression shall receive also the aid of France ". Czechoslovakia would not be obligated to assist the U.S.S.R. if France should refuse to do so. Still another variation from the Franco-Soviet pact was represented by a so-called " neutrality clause ", whereby, in the event of an attack upon one of the signatories " by one or two states, under circumstances that could not be foreseen, the other signatory must not aid, directly or indirectly, the aggressor, and both signatories offer one another assurances that there exists no secret treaty which would invalidate the fulfillment of these understandings ".[266] At the same time the two states negotiated an air convention whereby service between Moscow and Praha was to be begun in August. The direct route would have been via Warsaw, but when Poland refused permission to fly across her territory, the route was projected via Kiev and Užhorod.[267]

The Soviet-Czechoslovak treaty of mutual assistance, which was negotiated with the approval of Rumania and Yugoslavia,[268] was followed by a visit of Beneš to Moscow, whither he had received repeated invitations. Enroute, at

[266] *Nouveau recueil*, iii série, vol. xxxi, pp. 327 *et seq.*

[267] *The Central European Observer*, May 31, 1935; *cf.* also, *The New York Times*, April 18, 1935.

[268] *The New York Times*, May 17, 1935.

Warsaw, he received a cool reception.[269]   At Moscow, Beneš and Litvinov exchanged ratifications of the mutual assistance pact, of the air treaty, of the patent agreement and of the trade credit treaty.   They agreed that the only way to preserve European peace was by an extension of the mutual assistance pact to other states.   Their three day conference terminated with a joint communiqué stating that Czechoslovakia's geographic position had been a dominant factor in the rapprochement with the U.S.S.R.[270]   The communiqué was followed almost immediately by a report that the Soviet Union and Rumania were also negotiating a pact of mutual assistance.[271]

The various states of Central Europe were looking forward also to the contemplated Danubian Pact.   At the Conference of Venice, which terminated on May 6, Austria, Hungary and Italy were reported to have reached a tacit understanding favorable to Hungarian rearming.   Italy was alleged to have promised her moral support to a " rectification " of Hungarian frontiers in return for a Hungarian guarantee of Austrian independence.[272]   An interesting sidelight to the Conference of Venice was the report that Suvich had induced Beck, the Polish Minister of Foreign Affairs, who was then visiting Italy, to participate in the Danubian negotiations and help counterbalance the influence of France and the Little Entente.[273]

The Foreign Ministers of the three Little Entente states and of Greece met at Bucharest May 10-11.   They viewed the situation realistically.   Since eventual Hungarian and Bulgarian rearming was perhaps inevitable, would it not be

[269] Ibid., June 9, 1935.

[270] Ibid., June 11, 1935.

[271] Ibid., June 14, 1935.

[272] The Times, Le Temps, May 7, 1935.

[273] The Central European Observer, May 24, 1935.

advisable to please the Western Powers by approving the recommendation of the Conference of Stresa? What price might be exacted from Hungary and Bulgaria for such consent? In view of these considerations, the Little Entente and Greece agreed that these states accede to a six-Power pact of non-aggression and of mutual assistance.[274] The Little Entente was willing to abandon its long opposition to the rearming of the former enemy states on condition that they guarantee the status quo and agree to terminate revisionist propaganda.[275] Both the Little Entente and the Balkan Entente were haunted by two fears: (1) Hungary and Bulgaria would probably refuse to perpetuate their own dismemberment in return for a right they assumed already theirs and (2) the whole conception of a Danubian Pact was jeopardized seriously by Mussolini's African policy.[276]

The Henlein Movement

In the midst of the Soviet and Danubian negotiations, Czechoslovakia held, on May 19, the fourth general elections to both houses of parliament. The elections were orderly and resulted in but few changes in the governmental coalition, in which seven parties divided 166 of the 300 seats in the Chamber of Deputies, and 82 of the 150 seats in the Senate. However, most striking was the rise of the Sudetendeutsche Partei of Konrad Henlein,[277] which polled over a million votes as against four million for the governmental coalition. Absorbing the German National Socialists and the German Nationalists, it obtained 67 seats in parliament. Never before had two-thirds of the German votes been con-

[274] *The New York Times*, May 11-12, 1935.

[275] *The Central European Observer*, May 24, 1935.

[276] *The New York Times*, May 24, 1935. For the Italo-Ethiopian war, cf. *infra*, pp. 420 *et seq*.

[277] Prior to his entry into politics, Henlein was an obscure gymnastics instructor.

centrated in one party. The fact that the governmental coalition had been weakened could not be disguised. Significant also was the fact that the new party was not given representation in the Malypetr cabinet.[278] Despite the pledge of loyalty Henlein made to Czechoslovakia and to the ideals of democratic government, he was distrusted by the Czechoslovaks, particularly after he had objected to the secondary position to which his party had been relegated politically.[279] The *České Slovo* took the lead in denouncing him as "Czechoslovakia's Hitler" and in alleging that he represented Pan-Germanism financed by the Reich. It pointed out in particular that, in the estimation of Germany, the rise of the new party justified calling Czechoslovakia "the appendix whose removal was necessary before Europe could be restored to political health".[280]

Despite the new fears that were aroused as a result of the consolidation of the Germanic opposition, the fact that a composite state like Czechoslovakia, with fourteen political parties, could enjoy five and one-half years of political peace without the necessity of new elections was definite proof of her political stability.[281] Since 1926, when Czechoslovakia's German minority had decided to cooperate politically with the various Czech and Slovak parties,[282] its leader, Dr. Spina, had advocated a cultural union with Germany to which no

[278] *Cf. The Central European Observer*, May 24, 31, June 14, 1935.

[279] *The New York Times*, June 21, 1935.

[280] *Cf. České Slovo*, May 23-25, 1935.

[281] Two other minor threats to the Czechoslovak Republic were deemed to be Hlinka's Slovak People's Party, which won twenty-two seats, and Gajda's Fascists, who won six seats. The smallest of Czechoslovak parties, the Fascist National Community was represented in parliament for the first time after the 1935 election. *Cf.* Hoch, *op. cit.*, pp. 35-36. Gajda had resumed political activity after the 1933 amnesty for all political offenses. For the law, *cf.* Tísky (Poslanecká Sněmovna), no. 2388, October 12, 1933, 9 session.

[282] *Cf. supra*, p. 258.

liberal Czechoslovak had objected. However, Henlein's new conception, " Volksgemeinschaft ", indicated more than mere cultural affinity, although the exact nature of this " more " has not been specified. Coupled with an avowed intention to influence the foreign policy of Czechoslovakia to the abandonment of its present world-wide orientation in favor of a narrow orientation as a satellite of Germany, it was calculated to arouse grave concern among patriotic Czechs and Slovaks.[283]

Czechoslovak mistrust mounted with the discovery that followers of Henlein were prominent in three different espionage " affairs " that had come to light during the year.[284] Beneš sought to extend the olive branch to Germany on June 19 when he pointed out, to a delegation of Berlin newspaper representatives visiting Praha, that the chief goal of his foreign policy was the attainment of a friendly understanding with Germany which would not contravene Czechoslovakia's existing obligations to France. In his estimation, a rapprochement with Germany would go far towards solving the problem of Czechoslovakia's German minority,[285] but no rapprochement with Germany resulted. A new sensation was created by Henlein on September 21 when he sued the *Prager Presse* for libel for having stated that his movement had been financed by 50,000 marks from the German Minister of Propaganda, Göbbels.[286] The disclosures caused two

[283] *Cf. The Central European Observer*, December 13, 1935, for article entitled " Konrad Henlein in a Vicious Circle "; Hoch, *op. cit.*, pp. 41-44. For contrasting accounts of what the Henlein movement means for Germans and Czechs, respectively, *cf.* A German Bohemian Deputy, " The German Minority in Czechoslovakia ", *The Slavonic and East European Review*, vol. xiv, pp. 295-300, January, 1936; Sobota, E., " Czechs and Germans: a Czech view ", *ibid.*, pp. 301-320.

[284] *Cf. Svornost*, April 17, August 15, November 4, 5, 21, 1935.

[285] *Ibid.*, June 19, 1935.

[286] *Cf. Prager Presse*, September 21-22, 1935.

of his followers in the Chamber of Deputies, Hans Krebs and Rudolf Jung, to flee into voluntary exile in Germany, an act which convinced Czechoslovaks of the their guilt and led to demands that the Henlein party be disbanded by governmental decree as a threat against the integrity of the Republic.[287] The Czechoslovak authorities were at a loss whether to oppose Henlein or to compromise with him,[288] for both alternatives were distasteful. Early in December Czechoslovak public opinion was somewhat mollified when Dr. Spina, in a public address in Most (Brüx), subjected Henlein's policies to severe criticism on the grounds that they aroused needlessly the antipathies and fears of the Czechs, whereas in reality, according to Spina, there was little probability that Germany would attempt to annex Czechoslovakia's Germanic borderlands.[289]

The fact that the foreign policy of Czechoslovakia would remain unchanged after the elections was made clear by several official pronouncements. In two press interviews, Beneš pointed out his belief that collective security compacts could best preserve peace, which might become threatened seriously in the critical years 1936-1937,[290] and that the creation of international friendships would be the chief goal of his foreign policy.[291] On June 18, the first full day's session of the new National Assembly, the Prime Minister, Malypetr, explained at length both his domestic and foreign policies. Domestically, he warned recalcitrant Germans, Slovaks and Fascists against attempting to weaken national

[287] Cf. *Svornost*, September 26, 1935.

[288] Cf. Hanighen, F. C., "Troubled Days in Czechoslovakia", *Current History*, vol. xliii, p. 583.

[289] *Svornost*, December 8, 1935; *The New York Times*, December 4, 1935.

[290] *The New York Times*, June 14, 1935.

[291] *Ibid.*, *Svornost*, June 19, 1935.

unity. In foreign affairs, Czechoslovakia would pursue the ideals of the League, under which, he stated, all her treaties of alliance had been negotiated. For the immediate future, Czechoslovakia, together with France, the Soviet Union, Great Britain, Italy and her Little Entente partners, would strive for the successful conclusion of both Eastern and Central European Pacts.[292]

Göring's Balkan Tour

Hitler decided to take advantage of successive postponements of the Conference of Rome, which had been scheduled originally for May 20, by sending his lieutenant, General Göring, on a Balkan tour to restore Germanic influence in that area. On May 27, Göring was in Sofia to return a recent visit that a Bulgarian delegation had made secretly to Berlin. The trip took him also to Rumania, Yugoslavia and Hungary. He made a particularly strenuous effort to attract Yugoslavia within the German orbit, and thereby to create a Germanic bloc across Central Europe. Although Göring's tour was termed in Czechoslovakia and elsewhere a diplomatic failure,[293] its sequel was a political crisis within Yugoslavia, whereby Yeftič was succeeded as Premier by the allegedly Germanophil Stoyadinovič.[294] As a result of the internal difficulties of Yugoslavia, the Little Entente Conference of Bled was postponed, and Rumania hastened to draw closer to both Czechoslovakia and the U.S.S.R.[295]

[293] *Cf. The Central European Observer*, June 28, 1935, for detailed summary of Malypetr's speech.

[293] *Ibid.*, June 28, 1935, for full details of Göring's trip; also, *The New York Times*, June 2, 8, 12, 1935. Hitler considered the trip a decided success. *Cf. Völkischer Beobachter*, May 25–June 8, 1935.

[294] *The New York Times, Svornost*, June 21, 1935.

[295] *Svornost*, June 26, 1935.

Amplification of the Modus Vivendi

The month of June, 1935, witnessed also an amplification of the modus vivendi of 1928 [296] between Czechoslovakia and the Vatican by the definitive settlement of the question of the boundaries of dioceses.   Czechoslovakia had long maintained that a diocese should lie entirely within one state. The Austrian Bishop of St. Hypolite held jurisdiction over the Czechoslovak parishes of Vitorázko and Valčicko, and the German Archbishop of Breslau over much of Czechoslovak Silesia.   On the other hand, the Archbishop of Praha had authority over the Prussian County of Glatz.   Of the six Slovak dioceses, only two (Nitra and Banska Bystrica) lay wholly within Czechoslovakia.   A part·of the Bishopric of Spíš was in Poland.   The other three (Rožnava, Košice and Ostřihom) were divided with Hungary.   Particularly acute was the question of Ostřihom, whose Archbishop was Primate of Hungary.   By the new agreement, the political and religious boundaries were made to coincide.   The Archbishop of Praha surrendered Glatz.   Similarly, the Archbishop of Breslau turned over his parishes in Silesia to the Archbishop of Olomouc.   On the Austrian, Hungarian and Polish frontiers the new dioceses lay entirely within Czechoslovakia.   The loss of territory to Ostřihom was particularly regretted by the Hungarians who had regarded ecclesiastical control as a symbol upon which to base hopes of revisionism. It might also be pointed out that the Holy See, in consenting to change boundaries which had existed since the Seven Year's War (1756-63), granted to the new Czechoslovak Republic a concession which it had refused to permit to the Austrian Monarchy.   The agreement embraced also two other points: two commissions, a state and an ecclesiastical, were to determine the property divisions that the revision of diocesan boundaries would necessitate; and bishops would

[296] *Cf. supra*, pp. 254 *et seq.*

be appointed by the Holy See, but the state could make confidential objections to any candidature.[297]

Solidarity of the Status-Quo Bloc

There arose again the question of a Habsburg restoration in Austria. Within Czechoslovakia, the *Prager Presse* took the lead in calling attention to the imminence of a restoration.[298] Some of its assertions received apparent confirmation when the Austrian Federal Chamber approved a law restoring to the Habsburgs their former property within Austria.[299] The Little Entente took immediate action. The Yugoslav Regent, Prince Paul, hastened to Sinaia to confer with King Carol II.[300] Their decision was announced by Titulescu, who stated that, on the day of an Austrian coup d'état, the three Little Entente states would recall their diplomatic representatives, inaugurate an economic blockade, terminate the transportation of goods and passengers, mobilize their three armies, and take immediate military measures. The action of the Little Entente would not be motivated by mere sentiment, said Titulescu, but by a desire to avert the confusion that a change in the Austrian status quo would produce in Central Europe.[301] Cooperation among the three partners was further confirmed when Beneš stated that his oft-repeated earlier views regarding a restoration remained unchanged.[302] The *Prager Presse* objected to the return of Otto or Zita to either Austria or Hungary even as private citizens.[303]

[297] *The Central European Observer*, July 12, 1935; *Svornost*, June 18, 29, 1935.

[298] *Prager Presse*, July 9-10, 1935.

[299] *The New York Times*, July 11, 1935.

[300] *Ibid.*, July 12, 1935.

[301] *Ibid.*, July 14, 1935; *The Central European Observer*, July 26, 1935.

[302] *The New York Times*, July 21, 1935.

[303] *Prager Presse*, July 16, 1935.

The relative solidarity of the Little Entente, together with its close cooperation with the Balkan Entente, was again evinced at the Little Entente Conference of Bled, August 30-31, which was followed immediately by a Conference of the Balkan Entente. The Little Entente's fifteenth anniversary was commemorated by Beneš, who characterized the organization as a " fruitful alliance . . . which had fully justified its existence ". Beneš also raised the question of the recognition of Moscow by the Little Entente as a unit, but no action was taken because of the opposition of Yugoslavia. At the termination of the Conference, an official communiqué expressed solidarity regarding all political questions. The Little Entente would strive to help preserve general peace and remain faithful to the League. It remained unalterably opposed to a Habsburg restoration in either Austria or Hungary. In its estimation, existing difficulties would be greatly lessened by the successful conclusion of Eastern and Danubian Pacts. The latter, negotiated perhaps under French and Italian auspices, should include a guarantee of Austrian independence, mutual pledges of non-aggression and non-intervention, and a general agreement for consultation rather than mutual assistance in the event of a threat against either the political or the territorial status quo. The communiqué closed rather pessimistically with the statement that, since the question of the revision of the Peace Treaties was not to be raised, Hungary alone would probably destroy all hopes for a general agreement.[304]

The successive French, Czechoslovak and Soviet army manoeuvres during the late summer and early fall of 1935 produced fresh indications of friendship among the three countries. Significant also was the choice of location for

---

[304] *The New York Times, Svornost,* August 29-31, 1935; *The Central European Observer*, September 6, 1935.

each: the French in the Champagne in July,[305] the Czecho-slovaks on the German frontier in August,[306] and the Soviets in the Ukraine in September.[307] The three states sent military missions to one another's manoeuvres. The Czechoslovak manoeuvres, which were witnessed also by Rumanian and Yugoslav military missions, developed more than a tinge of reality when the hostile German minority showed its sentiments by cutting wires and committing other acts of petty sabotage.[308] The round of military manoeuvres closed early in October with those of Rumania, to which observers from her Little Entente partners and from France were invited.[309]

Both friends and foes realized that, in the event of war with Germany, Czechoslovakia's strategic position would be critical. The value of Soviet military aid might be merely psychological. Germany might be aided by Austria and Hungary, and perhaps even by Poland. The corridor whereby Soviet troops could reach Czechoslovakia (i. e. assuming Rumanian consent for Soviet troops to cross her territory) would be, in all probability, cut off and Czecho-slovakia isolated before any Great Power could render effective aid.[310]

Late in September, 1935, the Little Entente denied a report that a Soviet-Rumanian pact permitting passage to Soviet troops across Rumania to aid Czechoslovakia in the event of war had been negotiated.[311] Nevertheless, the

[305] *Le Temps,* July 20, 1935.

[306] *The New York Times,* August 18, 20, 1935; *Svornost,* August 22, 1935.

[307] *Národní Listy,* September 18, 1935.

[308] *Cf. The New York Times,* September 12, 1935, for statement of the Czechoslovak Minister of War, Machník.

[309] *Ibid.,* October 6, 1935; *Svornost,* October 7, 1935.

[310] Buell, L. R., *The Dangerous Year* (New York, 1936), p. 14.

[311] *The New York Times,* September 27, 1935. *Cf. ibid.,* July 17, 1936,

report produced, among Germany, Hungary and Poland, counter-negotiations alarming to Czechoslovakia.[312] Soviet leaders felt convinced that the new bloc aimed at the isolation and eventual partition of Czechoslovakia as a prelude to a war of aggression against the U.S.S.R.[313] The Czechoslovak government planned more elaborate fortifications, particularly along the German frontier.[314] The general situation was summarized by Beneš in a lengthy exposé, which he delivered on November 5 before the Foreign Affairs Committee of the Senate and the Chamber of Deputies. Beneš again pointed out that Czechoslovakia stood for peace and international cooperation. She threatened no one and would never become a party to an aggressive war. In a general crisis, the League could not refuse its aid. In addition to this moral support, he stressed the increase in Czechoslovakia's own strength because of the military progress that had been made. Czechoslovakia's system of alliances and friendships promised her the maximum security then attainable. After admitting that Czechoslovakia's geographical position was dangerous, he added,

but it is so because that geographical position is so important and far-reaching for the whole of Europe. It means that our State is the key to the whole post-War structure of Central Europe. If it is touched either internally or internationally, the whole fabric of Central Europe is menaced, and the peace of Europe seriously infringed. It would not be long ere all Europe would be grievously conscious of the fact. It is for that reason that today and for all future our international position

for the report that Rumania permitted the U. S. S. R. the use of a strategic railway to be constructed and financed by Czechoslovakia. Such a railway would materially improve Czechoslovakia's military prospects and enhance the value of the U. S. S. R. alliance.

[312] *Svornost,* September 26-27, 1935.

[313] *Cf. The New York Times,* October 11, November 10, 1935.

[314] *Ibid.,* October 17, 1935.

and our internal stability are a matter of great interest equally to France and the Soviet Union, equally to England and Italy, and to the Little Entente as they ought to be to Germany and Poland. Thus, whenever we should be in danger the vital interest of all the constructive forces of Europe would be on the side of our integrity and our prosperity.[315]

Beneš' able exposé, which might be regarded as the keynote of almost two decades of foreign policy, was approved enthusiastically by both houses of parliament. It attracted several Opposition groups and drew favorable comment from almost every shade of political opinion. The Social Democratic *Právo Lidu* praised his consistent and peaceful policy as exemplified by adherence to the League.[316] The Czech Socialist *České Slovo* approved the Anglo-French and League policies.[317] The Independent *Lidové Noviny* of Brno lauded Beneš' candor.[318] The Independent *Národní Politika* labeled his League policy " a dictate of reason ".[319] The Liberal Opposition *Národní Listy* also praised his League and his Polish policies.[320] Even the Independent German *Prager Tagblatt* found praise for Beneš' collective security endeavors.[321] Abroad, Beneš' speech was also received with general approval. The *Neue Freie Presse* was pleased with Beneš' cordial words regarding Austria.[322] The *Deutsche Allgemeine Zeitung* reproduced Beneš' remarks regarding Germany in their entirety.[323] *The Times* deemed

[315] Beneš, E., *The Struggle for Collective Security in Europe and the Italo-Abyssinian War*, Czechoslovak Sources and Documents, no. 8, p. 58.

[316] *Právo Lidu*, November 6, 1935.

[317] *České Slovo*, November 6, 1935.

[318] *Lidové Noviny*, November 6, 1935.

[319] *Národní Politika*, November 6, 1935.

[320] *Národní Listy*, November 6, 1935.

[321] *Prager Tagblatt*, November 6, 1935.

[322] *Neue Freie Presse*, November 6, 1935.

[323] *Deutsche Allgemeine Zeitung*, November 6, 1935.

Beneš' words the best foreign tribute that British foreign policy had received during 1935,[324] and French [325] and Soviet [326] comment was almost equally flattering.

Renewed Friction with Poland

In the speech of November 5, Beneš also voiced regret over his inability to draw Poland into the Soviet-Czechoslovak rapprochement. Tension between Poland and Czechoslovakia had been mounting steadily since January, 1934, when the former had adopted the "new policy" of a rapprochement with Germany.[327] The death of the Polish dictator, Pilsudski, on May 12, 1935, at the age of sixty-seven, did not change materially the trend of Polish foreign policy.[328] Under the guidance of the Germanophil Minister of Foreign Affairs, Beck, Poland rejected a Slavophil policy. Over a period of several months, many sections of the Polish press waged a violent anti-Czech campaign on behalf of the Polish minority in Těšin, which, allegedly, was being mistreated and subjected to a process of denationalization.[329] These allegations could not be substantiated by facts. The Polish minority enjoyed all the privileges of citizenship. It had representation in the Moravian-Silesian Diet, and sent two representatives to the Chamber of Deputies at Praha. Most of its children attended schools in which Polish was the language of instruction. Czechoslovakia was equally tolerant religiously. Eleven of the twenty-eight Catholic parish priests in Těšin were Polish. During the depression Czechoslovakia did adopt the policy common

---

[324] *The Times*, November 6, 1935.

[325] *Le Temps*, November 6, 1935.

[326] *Izvestia*, November 6, 1935.

[327] *Cf. supra*, pp. 373 *et seq.*

[328] *Gazeta Warszawska*, May 13, 1935.

[329] *Cf.* reprints in *Svornost*, February 4, 23, May 14, August 11, 13, 1935.

to all European states—that of discharging foreign workmen —but the Poles affected were citizens of Poland and thus had no special cause for complaint.[330]

Irredentism among the Poles in Těšin was aroused not only by irresponsible agitators, but by Polish officials. In the Polish Sejm itself there was brought out the fact that Malhome, the Polish consul in Těšin, had openly organized opposition to Czechoslovakia. After his recall at the request of Czechoslovakia, his successor, Klotz, was equally provocative.[331] Poland retaliated by asking for the recall of Meisner and Doležal, the Czechoslovak consuls at Cracow and Posen respectively.[332] Within Těšin itself hostility between Poles and Czechs became so marked that since early September gendarmes and military detachments guarded the public schools.[333] A large section of Czech public opinion feared lest Poland attempt to seize Těšin by a coup similar to that in Vilna in 1920.[334]

In the speech of November 5, Beneš warned Poland that Czechoslovakia could not permit illegal activities within her territories. He offered to submit the question to a Czechoslovak-Polish arbitration commission, to the League, to the world Court or to the conciliation and arbitration procedure provided by the still valid Czechoslovak-Polish convention of 1925.[335] On the same day, the Czechoslovak government declared a " state of emergency " in Těšin. Three days later came the Polish refusal to arbitrate. The official statement made much of the alleged discrepancy between Beneš' words

[330] Cf. The Central European Observer, October 18, 1935.

[331] Ibid., October 18, 1935.

[332] Svornost, October 21, 1935.

[333] Ibid., September 8, 1935.

[334] The Central European Observer, October 18, 1935.

[335] Ibid., November 15, 1935; Svornost, November 6, 1935. For the agreement of 1925, cf. supra, pp. 244-245.

and Czechoslovakia's actions.[336]   On November 19, when
Beck conferred with Smutnv, the Czechoslovak chargé
d'affaires at Warsaw, hopes of a settlement of the dispute
were raised temporarily, only to be dashed again when nothing further resulted.[337]   The fact that Polish Germanophils
regarded Czechoslovakia as a " seasonal State " that would
be absorbed eventually by her neighbors hindered the realization of a Slavophil Polish foreign policy.

Italy vs. Ethiopia

Another major question of Czechoslovak foreign policy
concerned the attitude that should be adopted with regard to
Mussolini's African adventure.[338]   The necessity for a clear-
cut attitude on the part of Czechoslovakia became evident
when Beneš was elected President of the League Assembly
early in September, at the time when the League was faced
with the Italo-Ethiopian question.   In his first speech as
President of the Assembly, Beneš urged that the crisis be
considered with the proper reserve.[339]   The small states of
Central Europe, Austria in particular, were concerned lest
the new crisis preoccupy the Western Powers to the extent
that Germany be left a free hand in Danubian affairs.   Amid
the pessimism prevalent generally at Geneva, Beneš continued
to urge patience despite his conviction that Mussolini would
not pause short of a decisive military triumph.   With the
outbreak of actual hostilities in Africa on October 3, Beneš
announced that his government would remain strictly neutral,
but also faithful to the general principles of the League.[340]

[336] *Cf. Gazeta Warszawska*, November 8, 1935.

[337] *Cf. Svornost*, December 9, 1935.

[338] *Cf. infra*, p. 423.

[339] *Official Journal*, special supplement, no. 138, pp. 35-36.

[340] *Ibid.*, p. 97.

The Ethiopian crisis not only broke the so-called " Stresa front " of the three " Western Powers " against Germany, but demonstrated again the inability of the League to halt the headlong course of a Great Power. Following the example of Japan in Manchuria, Mussolini planned the conquest of a part of Ethiopia, another member of the League, while, throughout the spring and summer of 1935, that organization had done little to halt such procedure. It was only after the termination of the rainy season had permitted the actual outbreak of hostilities that the League, at the behest of Great Britain, took up the question seriously. Although the reasons for the gradually stiffening attitude of Great Britain lie outside the scope of this work, the fact remained that Mussolini had miscalculated when he thought he would have a free hand in Africa after his agreement of January 7, 1935, with France. In requesting that the League declare Italy an aggressor, Great Britain, in the person of her Foreign Secretary, Hoare, sought to avoid the implication of acting solely to preserve her own African interests.[341]

The League Council on October 7 by a unanimous vote proclaimed Italy an aggressor for having violated Article 12 of the Covenant.[342] Two days later the Assembly took up the question in plenary session and on October 10 ratified the action of the Council.[343] Austria,[344] Hungary[345] and Albania[346] alone supported Italy. The Assembly set up at once a coordinating committee of seventeen (of which Czechoslovakia was a member) to prepare sanctions against

[341] *Ibid.*, pp. 43-46.

[342] *Ibid.*, November, 1935, pp. 1217-1226.

[343] *Ibid.*, special supplement, no. 138, pp. 113-114.

[344] *Ibid.*, p. 101.

[345] *Ibid.*, pp. 101-102.

[346] *Ibid.*, p. 114.

Italy. From the comprehensive list that was submitted, petroleum, cotton and iron were omitted on the ground that Italy could obtain these articles in unlimited quantities from either Germany or the United States. With these exceptions, sanctions were approved, to go into effect on November 18.[347] Upon that date there became effective against Italy an arms embargo on the part of fifty states, a prohibition of financial transactions on the part of forty-seven, a refusal to purchase Italian products on the part of forty-three, and an embargo on certain raw materials on the part of forty-five.[348]

The firm stand of the League in declaring for the first time in its history that one of its members was an aggressor raised the question what would be the attitude of the various members if the application of sanctions should impel Italy to declare war on Great Britain. The small victor states of Central Europe stood squarely behind Great Britain and the League. In their estimation, the African crisis was a mere prelude to a much greater one in the future involving Germany.[349] If the League could be strengthened sufficiently to cope efficiently with an aggressive Great Power, a precedent might be established whereby the small states might find in the League a safe refuge against future threats to their own integrity. While France hesitated long before leaning in the direction of Great Britain, for she needed both Britain and Italy against Germany in the future, certain members in both the Little and the Balkan Ententes (Yugoslavia, Greece and Turkey) pledged armed support to Great Britain against Italy should war ensue.[350] After the annual

[347] *Ibid.*, pp. 113-114.

[348] *Cf.* Buell, *op. cit.*, p. 37.

[349] *Cf.* Stolfer, G., "European Kaleidoscope", *Foreign Affairs*, vol. xiv, pp. 216-226.

[350] *The Times*, December 22, 1935; *Svornost*, December 23, 1935.

military conference of the Little Entente at Belgrade,[351] Rumania and Czechoslovakia had agreed tentatively to follow the lead of their more aggressive partner, Yugoslavia, although the final decision to approve Yugoslavia's pledge of armed support to Great Britain was not made until January 22, 1936.[352] Czechoslovakia had no direct quarrel with Italy; in fact, the government permitted the shipment of coal, shoes and other products to Italy until sanctions became operative.[353] However, the Czechoslovak government did not falter in its support of League principles, for it regarded the question as vital to the future of the Republic: if Czechoslovakia should refuse to support the League against Italy, what right would she have to invoke League assistance against German aggression in some future crisis? Thus motivated, Czechoslovakia informed the League of her willingness to impose upon Italy an oil, coal and steel embargo, should the League so decree.[354] Rarely had any policy of Beneš commanded such general support, even from the Opposition.[355]

Masaryk's Resignation

President Masaryk attained the age of eighty-five on March 7, 1935. An illness during the summer caused him to decide to yield his office whenever he felt he would be no longer able to perform all its duties. Having made no secret of this decision, Masaryk, early in November, began to make quiet preparations.[356] The actual resignation was postponed to December 14, until after the termination of the debates

[351] *The New York Times*, November 25, 1935.

[352] *Ibid.*, January 23, 1936.

[353] *Ibid.*, November 6, 1935.

[354] *Svornost*, December 2, 1935.

[355] Cf. *The Central European Observer*, November 29, 1935.

[356] *Ibid.*, December 27, 1935.

regarding the 1936 budget.[357]   It had been Masaryk's dear-
est wish that his successor would be Beneš; in fact, Masaryk
was reported to have stated that he would not yield the office
to any other.[358]   In the address of resignation, he stressed
the fact that he had been motivated largely by a desire to
avoid the error of Hindenburg—of remaining in office too
long—and recommended Beneš as the successor who would
carry on most ably the policies upon which the future of
the Republic depended.[359]   Beneš was elected President on
December 18.   Of the 442 ballots, he obtained 340; his only
opponent, Dr. Bohumil Němec, received 24, and the rest were
blank.   Němec, a professor of botany, received the votes of
the parties led by Beneš' personal foes, Kramář and Štribrný.
Blank ballots were returned by the followers of Henlein, by
the Fascists and by the feeble National Unity Party.   Significant was the fact that Beneš was supported by most of
the large parties, by Right and Left, by Communists, Socialists and non-Socialists, by Catholics and Protestants, by
Czechs, Slovaks, Magyars and non-Henlein Germans.[360]
He was the logical successor to Masaryk, and his overwhelming triumph a guarantee that the foreign policy of the Republic would remain unchanged.   This impression received
fresh confirmation on March 1, 1936, when Beneš was succeeded as Minister of Foreign Affairs by Dr. Kamil Krofta,
his assistant since 1927.[361]   Dr. Milan Hodža, a Slovak and
Minister of Agriculture, who had succeeded Malypetr as

[357] *Svornost*, November 30, 1935.

[358] *The New York Times*, December 13, 1935.

[359] *Cf. ibid.*, December 15, 1935, for text of address.

[360] *Ibid.*, *Svornost*, December 19, 1935; *cf.* also, *The Central European
Observer*, December 27, 1935.

[361] *Cf. The Central European Observer*, March 6, 1936, for short
biography of Krofta; *Svornost*, March 2, 1936.

Premier on October 30, 1935,[362] retained his Premiership after the election of Beneš.

Czechoslovakia's tolerant and constructive policies, both domestic and foreign, have gained for her the respect and admiration of the rest of the world and have gone far to reconcile her own minorities: her stability has been demonstrated beyond any doubt. In the realm of foreign affairs, she was singularly fortunate to have enjoyed the services of Dr. Edward Beneš. In foresight, patience, energy, integrity and ability, his foreign policy was outstanding. At home and abroad, particularly among the allies and friends of Czechoslovakia, there existed great pleasure over the fact that two of the co-founders of the Republic had succeeded one another in the Presidency.[363]

---

[362] *Svornost,* October 31, 1935.

[363] *Cf. The Times, Le Temps, Izvestia,* December 19-20, 1935.

BIBLIOGRAPHY

DOCUMENTS

CZECHOSLOVAKIA

Documents diplomatiques relatives aux conventions d'alliance conclus par la République Tchécoslovaque avec le Royaume des Serbes, Croates et Slovènes et le Royaume de Roumanie, Prague, République Tchécoslovaque, Ministère des Affaires Étrangères, Recueil des Documents Diplomatiques no. 2, 1923, 198 p.

Documents diplomatiques concernant les tentatives de restauration des Hapsbourg sur le trône de Hongrie, Prague, République Tchécoslovaque, Ministère des Affaires Étrangères, 1922, 169 p.

Měsíční přehled zahraničního obchodu (Monthly survey of foreign trade) Praha, The Czechoslovak Government Statistical Office, Monthly.

Národní Shromáždění Československé v prvním roce Republiky (The Czechoslovak National Assembly during the first year of the Republic), Praha, Předsednictvo Národní Shromáždění, 1919, 377 p.

Obchodní smlouvy mezistátní (International Commercial Treaties), Praha, Orbis Pub. Co., 1923-1925, 1928 (J. Dvořáček and Z. Konečný, eds.), 3 vols.

Peace Conference Delegation, 1919, Memoirs (Official claims of the Czechoslovak Delegation), Paris, 1919.

> No. 1, Les Tchécoslovaques, leur histoire et civilisation, leur lutte et leur travail, leur rôle dans le monde.

> No. 2, Les revindications territoriales de la République Tchécoslovaque.

> No. 3, Le problème des Allemands de Bohème.

> No. 4, Le problème de la Silesie de Teschen.

> No. 5, La Slovaquie - le territorie revendique en Slovaquie.

> No. 7, Les Serbes de Lusace.

> No. 9, Le problème de la région de Glatz.

> No. 11, La République Tchécoslovaque et son droit à la reparation des dommages de guerre.

Republika Československá, Národní Shromáždění, Poslanecká Sněmovna, *Těsnopisecké zprávy o schůzích Poslanecké Sněmovny Národního Shromáždění Republiky Československé* (Stenographic Reports of the Meetings of the Chamber of Deputies of the National Assembly of the Czechoslovak Republic).

Republika Československá, Národní Shromáždění, Poslanecká Sněmovna, *Tisky k těsnopiseckým zprávam o schůzích Poslanecké Sněmovny Národního Shromáždění Republiky Československé* (Documents on the Stenographic Reports of the Meetings of the Chamber of Deputies of the National Assembly of the Czechoslovak Republic).

Republika Československá, Národní Shromáždění, Poslanecká Sněmovna, *Zápisy o schůzích Poslanecké Sněmovny Národního Shromáždění Republiky Československé* (Minutes of the Meetings of the Chamber of Deputies of the National Assembly of the Czechoslovak Republic).

Republika Československá, Národní Shromáždění, Senát, *Těsnopisecké zprávy ọ schůzích Senátu Národního Shromáždění Republiky Československé* (Stenographic Reports of the Meetings of the Senate of the National Assembly of the Czechoslovak Republic).

Republika Československá, Národní Shromáždění, Senát, *Tisky k těsnopiseckým zprávam o schůzích Senátu Národního Shromáždění Republiky Československé* (Documents on the Stenographic Reports of the Meetings of the Senate of the National Assembly of the Czechoslovak Republic).

Republika Československá, Ministerstvo Národní Obrany, *Osobní věstník* (Personnel Journal), annual.

Résultats préliminaries du recensement de la population du 15 février, 1921, Prague, L'Office de Statistique, ,1921, 63 p.

Ročenka Národního Shromáždění Republiky Československé (Yearbook of the National Assembly of the Czechoslovak Republic), Praha, " Politika " Pub. Co., annual.

Sbírka zákonu a nařizení státu československého (Compilation of Laws and Proclamations of the Czechoslovak State), Praha, Státní Tiskarna, annual.

Slovenskí Poslanci a revizia mierových smluv (Slovak Deputies and the Revision of the Peace Treaties), Slovenska odbočka Československej národnej rady v Bratislavě, 1934, 8 p.

Státní záverečný účet republiky československské za rok 1924– (The State Debt Account of the Czechoslovak Republic for the Year 1924–), Praha, Státní Tiskarna, Nejvyšši účetní kontrolni úřad, 1926–, annual.

Umluva a poštovních stycich mezi Rakouskem, Italií, Rumunskem, Kralovstvím Srbů, Charvátuv a Slovincú a Československem, sjednaná v Portorose 23 Listopadu, 1921 (Treaty concerning Postal Service between Austria, Hungary, Italy, Rumania, the Kingdom of Serbs, Croats and Slovenes and Czechoslovakia, negotiated at Portorose on November 23, 1921), Praha, Státní Tiskarna, 1923, 24 p.

Zahraniční Politika (Foreign Policy) (Sborník pro studium mezinárodních otázek politických, právních, hospodářských a sociálních), Uřední Věstník Ministerstva Zahraničních Věci, Praha, Orbis Pub. Co., monthly.

FRANCE

Annales de la Chambre des Députés.

Conference économique internationale de Gênes 9 avril-19 mai, 1922, Paris, Imprimerie Nationale, 1922 (Ministère des Affaires Étrangères, Documents diplomatiques), 186 p.

Documents diplomatiques relatives aux negociations concernant les garanties de sécurité contre une aggression de l'Allemagne (10 janvier, 1919-7 décembre, 1923), Paris, Imprimerie Nationale, 1924, 271 p.

Documents signés ou paraphés à Locarno le 16 octobre, 1925, précédés de six pièces relatives aux negociations préliminaires (20 juillet-16 octobre, 1925), Paris, République Française, Ministère des Affaires Étrangères, Pacte de Securité ii, Imprimerie des Journaux Officiels, 1925, 39 p.

Neuf pièces relatives à la proposition faite le 9 février, 1925, par le Gouvernement Allemand et la réponse du Gouvernement Française (9 février-16 juin, 1925), Paris, République Française, Ministère des Affaires Étrangères, Pacte de Securité i, Imprimerie des Journaux Officiels, 1925, 31 p.

GREAT BRITAIN

Agreement for Guaranteeing a Loan to Austria, signed by Representatives of Great Britain, France, Italy, Czechoslovakia and Austria, October 4, 1922, London, 1922, His Majesty's Stationery Office (Parl. Rep., 1922, Cmd. 1765), 29 p.

Agreements Concluded at the Hague Conference, January, 1930, London, 1930, His Majesty's Stationery Office (Parl. Pap., 1930, Cmd. 3484), 172 p.

Convention Instituting the Definitive Statute of the Danube, Signed at Paris, July 23, 1921, London, 1922, His Majesty's Stationery Office (Treaty Series no. 16, 1922, Cmd. 1754), 31 p.

Correspondence between His Majesty's Government and the French Government respecting the Genoa Conference, London, 1922, His Majesty's Stationery Office (Misc. no. 6, 1922, Parl. Pap., 1922, Cmd. 1742), 10 p.

Final Act of the Lausanne Conference, July 9, 1932, London, 1932 (Misc. no. 7, 1932, Cmd. 4126), 16 p.

Final Protocol of the Locarno Conference, London, His Majesty's Stationery Office, 1925, 61 p.

Papers relating to the Hague Conference, June-July, 1922, London, 1922, His Majesty's Stationery Office (Parl. Pap., 1922, Cmd. 1724), 18 p.

Papers respecting Negotiations for an Anglo-French Pact, London, 1924, His Majesty's Stationery Office (Parl. Pap. France no. 1, 1924, Cmd. 2169), 175 p.

Papers respecting the Proposals 'for a Pact of Security made by the German Government on February 9, 1925, London, 1925, His Majesty's Stationery Office (Misc. no. 7, 1925), 51 p.

Reply of the German Government to the Note handed to Herr Stresemann by the French Ambassador at Berlin on June 16, 1925, respecting the Proposals for a Pact of Security, London, His Majesty's Stationery Office (Misc. no. 9, 1925), 9 p.

Resolutions adopted by the Supreme Council at Cannes, January, 1922, as the Basis of the Genoa Conference, London, 1922, His Majesty's Stationery Office (Parl. Pap., 1922, Cmd. 1621), 7 p.

LEAGUE OF NATIONS

Arbitration, Security and Reduction of Armaments, Geneva, 1924, League of Nations, 378 p.

Arbitration and Security, Geneva, 1926, League of Nations Secretariat, 200 p.

Rapport sur les travaux de la commission de reparations, Paris, Librairie F. Alcan, 1923, vol. i (1920-1922).

The Financial Reconstruction of Austria, Agreement approved by the League of Nations on September 16, 1924, Geneva, 1924, 16 p.

The Financial Reconstruction of Austria, General Survey and principal documents, Geneva, 1926, 312 p.

Financial Reconstruction of Austria, Termination of the Functions of the Commissioner-General (League of Nations, 1926, ii, 22), 8 p.

The Financial Reconstruction of Hungary, General survey and principal documents, Geneva, 1926, 248 p.

Termination of the Functions of the Commissioner-General (Hungary), Resolution adopted by the Council of the League of Nations on June 10, 1926 (League of Nations, 1926, ii, 23), 8 p.

League of Nations Official Journal.

League of Nations Monthly Summary.

League of Nations Treaty Series, supplemented by *Nouveau recueil général de traités et autres actes relatifs aux rapports de droit international* (continuation du grand recueil de G. F. Martens par H. Triepel), Leipzig, Librairie H. Buske, iii série.

Permanent Court of International Justice, series A, B, C and E.

Publications of the League of Nations,
 ii, Economic and Financial
 vii, Political
 ix, Disarmament.

The World Court's Advisory Opinion on the Austro-German Customs Union, The American Foundation, Foreign Relations Bulletin no. 9, September 5, 1931, 8 p.

THE NETHERLANDS

Conference at the Hague, June 26–July 20, 1922, Minutes and Documents, Department of Foreign Affairs, Government Printing Office, the Hague, 1922, 235 p.

THE SOVIET UNION

Memorandum of the Russian Delegation to the Genoa Conference, Genoa, 1922.

Les Reclamations de la Russie aux États responsable de l'intervention et du blocus, Materiaux et documents sur l'intervention, le blocus et les dommages causés par eux à la Russie, vol. iv, Edition de la Delegation de Russie à la Conférence économique internationale de Gênes, 1922.

Reply of the Russian Delegation to the Memorandum of May 2, 1922, Genoa, 1922.

Soviet Russia (official organ of the Russian Soviet Government Bureau in New York).

UNITED STATES

Final Protocol of the Locarno Conference, 1925, and treaties between France and Poland and France and Czechoslovakia, New York, Carnegie Endowment for International Peace, Division of Intercourse and Education, 1926, 93 p.

Papers Relating to the Foreign Relations of the United States, 1917-1918, 1920, Washington, D. C., United States Government Printing Office,

    1917, Supplement 2, 2 vols., 1932;

    1918, Supplement 1, 2 vols., 1933;

    1918, Supplement 2, 1933;

    1918 (Russia), 3 vols., 1931-1932;

    1920, 3 vols., 1935.

" Reply of President Wilson to a Senate Resolution concerning the American Troops in Siberia, June 26, 1919", *State Department, Russian Series,* no. 4, p. 5.

Russian-American Relations, March, 1917–March, 1920, New York, Harcourt, Brace and Howe (League of Free Nations Association), 1920, 375 p.

United States Congress, Senate, 65 Congress, 1919, "Hearings on Bolshevik Propaganda before a Sub-committee of the Judiciary", p. 24.

NEWSPAPERS AND PERIODICALS

Allgemeine Zeitung, weekly, Litomerice.

Arbeiter Zeitung, daily, Vienna.

Berliner Tageblatt (Wochenausgabe für Ausland und Uebersee), weekly.

The Bohemian Review (later *The Czechoslovak Review*), Official organ of the Bohemian National Alliance of America, monthly, Chicago.

Čas, twice daily, Praha.

The Central European Observer, fortnightly, Prague.

České Slovo, twice daily, Praha.

Československé Korespondence, Paris, published irregularly during the Peace Conference.

Československá Samostatnost, Paris, published on behalf of Czechoslovak independence.

Corriere della Sera, daily, Milan.

Current History, monthly, New York.

Deutsche Allgemeine Zeitung, twice daily, Berlin.

Deutscher Reichsanzeiger und Preussischer Staatsanzeiger, daily, Berlin.

L'Europe nouvelle, weekly, Paris.

Frankfurter Zeitung, daily.

Gazeta Warszawska, daily.

La Gazette de Prague, semi-weekly.

International Conciliation, monthly, except July and August, Worcester, Massachusetts (Carnegie Endowment for International Peace).

Izvestia, daily, Moscow.

Lidové Noviny, twice daily, Brno.

Manchester Guardian, daily.

Le Matin, daily, Paris.

Le Monde slav, monthly, Paris.

Národní Listy, twice daily, Praha.

Národní Politika, twice daily, Praha.

La Nation tchèque, bimonthly, Paris.

Neue Freie Presse, twice daily, Vienna.

The New York Times, daily.

Prager Abendblatt, daily.

Prager Presse, daily.

Prager Tagblatt, twice daily.

Právo Lidu, twice daily, Praha.

Rovnost, daily, Brno.

Samostatnost, weekly, Olomouc.

Svornost, daily, Chicago.

Le Temps, daily, Paris.

The Times, daily, London.

Völkischer Beobachter, daily, Berlin.

Vorwaerts, daily, Berlin.

Vossische Zeitung, daily, Berlin.

BOOKS AND PAMPHLETS

D'Abernon, E. V., *The Diary of an Ambassador*, New York, Doubleday, Doran & Co., 3 vols.; *Versailles to Rapallo, 1920-1922*, 1929, 335 p.; *Rapallo to Dawes, 1922-1924*, 1930, 350 p.; *Dawes to Locarno, 1924-1926*, 1931, 317 p.

Anon., *Deset let československé zahraniční politiky* (Ten Years of Czechoslovak Foreign Policy), Praha, Ministerstvi Zahraničních Věci, 1928, 213 p.

——, Dr. *Edvard Beneš, spoluzakladatel nové svobody a tvůrce zahraniční politiky československé* (Dr. Edward Beneš, Co-founder of the New Freedom and Creator of the Czechoslovak Foreign Policy), Sborník Státi, Praha, Čin Pub. Co., 1924, 283 p.

——, *The Evolution of Socialism in Czechoslovakia*, Prague, Executive Committee of the Czechoslovak Social Democratic Workers Party, 1924, 45 p.

——, *The Lausanne Agreement*, New York, Carnegie Endowment for International Peace, no. 282, 1932, 43 p.

——, *Přehled činnosti z prve pětileti Republiky Československé* (Survey of the Activities of the First Five Years of the Czechoslovak Republic), Praha, G. Herman, ed., 1923, 141 p.

——, *President Masaryk in Paris, Brussels and London in October, 1923*, Prague, 1924, 141 p.

Ashmead-Bartlett, E., *The Tragedy of Central Europe*, London, T. Butterworth, 1923, 320 p.

Ausset, J., *La Question Vaticane*, Paris, Sirey, 1928, 175 p.

"Autonomist", *Slovakia's Plea for Autonomy*, Middletown, Pa., Jednota Printery, 1935, 120 p.

Baerlein, H., *The March of the Seventy Thousand*, London, L. Parsons, 1926, 287 p.

Baker, R. S., *What Wilson Did at Paris*, New York, Doubleday, Page & Co., 1920, 113 p.

——, *Woodrow Wilson and the World Settlement*, New York, Doubleday, Page & Co., 1922, 3 vols.

De Balla, V., *The New Balance of Power in Europe*, Baltimore, Johns Hopkins Press, 1932, 208 p.

Basch, A. and Dvořáček, J., *Austria and Its Economic Existence,* Prague, Orbis Pub. Co., 1925, 106 p.

Bassett, J. S., *The League of Nations*, New York, Longmans, Green & Co., 1928, 415 p.

Bauer, F., *Hitlerová Třeti Riše a naš Stát*, Praha, Osvěta, 1933.

Beaumont, A., *Heroic Story of the Czechoslovak Legions*, Prague, The Czechoslovak Foreigner's Office, reprinted from the *Daily Telegram*, 1919, 84 p.

Beneš, E., *The Foreign Policy of Czechoslovakia*, speech of January 27, 1921, Prague, edited by the *Gazette de Prague*, 1921, 35 p.

——, *Five Years of Czechoslovak Foreign Policy*, Prague, Orbis Pub. Co., 1924, 39 p.

——, *Problemy nové Evropy a zahraniční politika československá*, Praha, Melantrich Pub. Co., 1924, 306 p.

——, *The Diplomatic Struggle for European Security and the Stabilization of Peace*, speech of April 1, 1925, Prague, Orbis Pub. Co., 1925, 31 p.

——, *Les Accords de Locarno*, speech of October 30, 1925, Prague, Orbis Pub. Co., 1925, 30 p.

——, *My War Memoirs*, New York, Houghton Mifflin Co., 1928, 512 p. (trans. from Czech by Paul Selver).

——, *La Situation internationale et la politique étrangère tchécoslovaque*, exposé du 6 juin, 1928, Prague, Orbis Pub. Co., 1928, 25 p.

——, *Les Problèmes des réparations et la liquidation de la guerre mondiale à la Haye*, exposé du 30 janvier, 1930, Prague, Orbis Pub. Co. 1930 (Sources et documents tchécoslovaques no. 12), 67 p.

——, *Vers la liquidation de la guerre: traités de la Haye et de Paris*, exposé du 20 mai, 1930, Prague, Orbis Pub. Co., 1930 (Sources et documents tchécoslovaques, no. 13), 50 p.

——, *La Situation de l'Europe, la Société des Nations, et la Tchécoslovaquie*, exposé du 15 octobre, 1930, Prague, Orbis Pub. Co., 1930 (Sources et documents tchécoslovaques, no. 15), 32 p.

——, (Argus), *The Economic Aspect of the Austro-German Customs Union*, Prague, Orbis Pub. Co., 1931, 85 p.

——, *Le Pacte d'organisation de la Petite Entente et l'état actuel de la politique internationale*, exposé du 1 mars, 1933, Prague, Orbis Pub. Co., 1933 (Sources et documents tchécoslovaques, no. 20), 64 p.

——, *La Question du directoire européen et la revision des frontières*, exposé du 25 avril, 1933, Prague, Orbis Pub. Co., 1933 (Sources et documents tchécoslovaques, no. 21), 93 p.

——, *La Revolution allemande et la nouvelle phase de la politique européenne*, exposé du 31 octobre, 1933, Prague, Orbis Pub. Co., 1933 (Sources et documents tchécoslovaques, no. 23), 62 p.

——, *Boj o mír a bezpečnost státu* (The Struggle for Peace and the Security of the State) (compilation of Beneš' speeches, 1924-1933), Praha, Orbis Pub. Co., 1934, 833 p.

——, *The Problem of Central Europe and the Austrian Question*, speech of March 21, 1934, Prague, Orbis Pub. Co., 1934, 66 p.

——, *Reč o problému podkarpátoruskem* (Speech on the Problem of Subcarpathian Ruthenia), Praha, Orbis Pub. Co., 1934, 56 p.

——, *Une nouvelle phase de la lutte pour l'équilibre européen*, exposé du 2 juillet, 1934, Prague, Orbis Pub. Co., 1934 (Sources et documents tchécoslovaques, no. 25), 62 p.

——, *Vers un regroupement des forces en Europe?*, exposé du 6 novembre, 1934, Prague, Orbis Pub. Co., 1934 (Sources et documents tchécoslovaques, no. 26), 33 p.

——, *Le Sens politique de la tragédie de Marseille*, discours du 7 et 10 décembre, 1934, Prague, Orbis Pub. Co., 1935 (Sources et documents tchécoslovaques, no. 27), 47 p.

——, *The Struggle for Collective Security in Europe and the Italo-Abyssinian War*, speech of November 5, 1935, Prague, Orbis Pub. Co., 1935 (Czechoslovak Sources and Documents, no. 8), 60 p.

Bethlen, I., *The Treaty of Trianon and European Peace*, New York, Longmans, Green & Co., 1934, 187 p.

Bitterman, M., *Austria and the Customs Union*, Prague, Orbis Pub. Co., 1931, 118 p.

Borovička, J., *Ten Years of Czechoslovak Politics*, Prague, Orbis Pub. Co., 1929, 131 p.

Brož, A., *The Rise of the Czechoslovak Republic*, London, Twentieth Century Press, 1919, 31 p.

——, *The First Year of the Czechoslovak Republic*, London, Twentieth Century Press, 1920, 80 p.

——, *Three Years of the Czechoslovak Republic*, Prague, Orbis Pub. Co., 1921, 40 p.

Buell, R. L., *Europe: a History of Ten Years*, New York, Macmillan, 1929, 428 p.

——, *The Dangerous Year*, New York, Foreign Policy Ass'n.. 1936, 80 p.

Butter, O. and Ruml, B., *La République tchécoslovaque*, Prague, Orbis Pub. Co., 1921, 101 p.

Caldwell, R. J., *The Economic Situation in Czechoslovakia in 1920*, Washington, Government Printing Office, 1921, 48 p.

Čapek, T., Jr., *Origins of the Czechoslovak State*, New York, The Revell Press, 1926, 104 p.

Chaloupecký, V., *Zapas o Slovensko* (The Struggle for Slovakia), Praha, Čin Pub. Co., 1930, 251 p.

Chamberlain, J. P., *The Danube*, Washington, Government Printing Office, 1918, 122 p.

——, *The Regime of the International Rivers: Danube and Rhine*, New York, Columbia University, 1923, 317 p.

Chamberlin, W. H., *The Russian Revolution, 1917-1921*, New York, Macmillan, 1935, 2 vols.

Chanal, E., *Monnaie et économie nationale en Tchécoslovaquie, 1918-1928*, Paris, M. Giard, 1929, 322 p.

Chappey, J., *La Crise de la monnaie et la restauration des Pays Danubiens*, Paris, M. Giard, 1933, 234 p.

Chmelář, J., *Political Parties in Czechoslovakia*, Prague, Orbis Pub. Co., 1926, 102 p.

Chmelář, J., Klíma, S. and Nečas, J., *Podkarpatska Rus* (Subcarpathian Ruthenia), Praha, Orbis Pub. Co., 1923, 206 p.

Cippico, Count A., *Italy, the Central Problem of the Mediterranean*, New Haven, Yale University Press, 1926, 110 p.

Císař, J. and Pokorný F. (comps.), *The Czechoslovak Republic*, London, Adelphia Terrace, 1922, 218 p.

Cižmář, J., *Ruské a naše vojsko v revoluce* (The Russian Troops and Ours in the Revolution), Brno, Moravské Legionaře, 1926, 240 p.

Codresco, F., *La Petite Entente*, Paris, P. Bossuet, 1931, 2 vols.

Cosma, A., Jr., *La Petite Entente*, Paris, Jouve et Cie., 1926, 295 p.

Crabitès, P., *Beneš: Statesman of Central Europe*, London, G. Routledge & Sons, 1935, 293 p.

Crane, J. O., *The Little Entente*, New York, Macmillan, 1931, 222 p.

Currey, M., *Italian Foreign Policy*, London, I. Nicholson & Watson, 1932, 330 p.

Danubius, *La Petite Entente et l'Orient, un cri d'alarme*, Paris, 1922, 34 p.

Dědeček, V., *La Tchécoslovaquie et les Tchécoslovaques*, Paris, Bossard, 1919, 196 p.

Dennis, A. L. P., *The Foreign Policies of Soviet Russia*, New York, E. P. Dutton Co., 1924, 499 p.

Dillon, E. J., *The Inside Story of the Peace Conference*, New York, Harper & Brothers, 1920, 513 p.

Dominian, L., *The Frontiers of Language and Nationality in Europe*, New York, Henry Holt & Co., 1917, 375 p.

Drummond, Sir E., *Ten Years of World Cooperation*, Geneva, Secretariat of the League of Nations, 1930, 467 p.

Duranty, W., *Europe: War or Peace?*, New York, Foreign Policy Ass'n., 1935, 47 p.

Einzig, P., *World Finance, 1914-1935*, New York, Macmillan, 1935, 382 p.

Eisenmann, L., *La Tchécoslovaquie*, Paris, F. Rieder et Cie., 1921, 126 p.

Fierlinger, Z., *Sovietské Rusko na nové dráze* (Soviet Russia on a New Road), Praha, Ustřední Dělnické, 1932, 195 p.

Fischer, L., *The Soviets in World Affairs*, New York, Cape and Smith, 1930, 2 vols.

Fouques-Duparc, J., *La Protection des minorités de race, de langue, et de religion*, Paris, thèse, 1922, 369 p.

Gedye, G. E. R., *Heirs to the Hapsburgs*, Bristol, Arrowsmith, 1932, 290 p.

Giannini, A., *Les Documents de la Conférence de Gênes*, Rome. G. Bardi, 1922, 273 p.

Gibbons, H. A., *Europe since 1918*, New York, The Century Co., 1923, 622 p.

Glaise-Horstenau, E. von, *The Collapse of the Austro-Hungarian Empire*, London, J. M. Dent & Sons, 1930, 347 p.

Graham, M. W., *New Governments of Central Europe*, New York, Henry Holt & Co., 1924, 683 p.

Graves, W. S., *America's Siberian Adventure*, New York, Cape and Smith, 1931, 363 p.

Gruber, J. (ed.), *Czechoslovakia: A Survey of Economic and Social Conditions*, New York, Macmillan, 1924, 256 p.

Haskins, C. H. and Lord, R. H., *Some Problems of the Peace Conference*, Cambridge, Harvard University Press, 1920, 307 p.

Hazen, C. D., *Europe since 1815*, New York, Henry Holt & Co., 1923, vol. ii, pp. 804-831.

Hlinský, J., *Ruskem a Sibiři* (Through Russia and Siberia), Praha, Pam. Odboje, 1922, 185 p.

Hoch, C., *The Political Parties in Czechoslovakia,* Prague, Orbis Pub. Co., 1936 (Czechoslovak Sources and Documents, no. 9), 72 p.

Hoetzl, J. and Joachim, V., *The Constitution of the Czechoslovak Republic*, Prague, Edition de la Société L'Effort de la Tchécoslovaquie, 1920, 54 p.

House, E. and Seymour, C. (eds.), *What Really Happened at Paris*, New York, Charles Scribners' Sons, 1921, 528 p.

Huszár, K., *Proletarier Diktatur in Ungarn*, Regensburg, Kösel & Dustet, 1920, 212 p.

Jászi, O., *Revolution and Counter-Revolution in Hungary*, London, P. S. King & Son, 1924, 239 p.

Jolly, E., *Le Pouvoir legislatif dans la République Tchécoslovaque*. Paris, Jouve et Cie, 1924, 143 p.

Kaas, Baron A. and Lazarovics, F. de, *Bolshevism in Hungary*, London, Grant Richards, 1931, 411 p.

Kellor, F. A., *Security against War*, New York, Macmillan, 1924, 2 vols.

Klecanda, J., *Operace československého vojska na Rusi v letech 1917-1920* (The Operations of the Czechoslovak Armies in Russia during the Years 1917-1920), Praha, Orbis Pub. Co., 1921.

Kleinwaechter, F. F. G., *Self-Determination for Austria*, London, Allen & Unwin, 1929, 78 p.

Koloušek, J., *Rašínová reforma měny* (Rašín's Currency Reform), Prague, Orbis Pub. Co., 1921.

Koudelka, J., *Ženevský protokol, idea a organisace světového míru* (The Geneva Protocol, the Idea and Organization of World Peace), Praha, Čin Pub. Co., 1926, 252 p.

Kramář, K., *Die russische Krisis: Geschichte und Kritik des Bolschewismus*, München und Leipzig, Duncker & Humbolt (autorisierte Übertragung aus dem Tschechischen von A. Schebek), 1925, 689 p.

Kratochvil, J., *Cesta revoluce* (The Road to Revolution), Praha, Čin Pub. Co., 1922, 674 p.

Kraus, J., *Světové odzbrojení* (World Disarmament), Praha, Orbis Pub. Co., 1933, 316 p.

Krofta, K., *Les Nouveaux états dans l'Europe centrale*, Prague, Orbis Pub. Co., 1930, 147 p.

——, *The Substance of Hungarian Revisionism*, Prague, 1934, Orbis Pub. Co., 31 p.

——, *Československo v mezinárodní politice* (Czechoslovakia in International Politics), Praha, Orbis Pub. Co., 1934, 28 p.

——, *A Short History of Czechoslovakia*, New York, R. M. McBride, 1934, 198 p.

Křovák, R., *Věčný úkazovatel k zákonu a nařízením o pozemkové reformě* (Permanent Index to the Law regarding Agrarian Reform), Praha, 1922, 85 p.

Langsam, W. C., *The World Since 1914*, New York, Macmillan, 3 ed., 1936, 888 p.

Lippmann, W. and Scroggs, W. O., *The United States in World Affairs*, New York, Harper & Bros., 1933, 355 p.

Liscová, Mrs. M., *The Religious Situation in Czechoslovakia*, Prague, Orbis Pub. Co., 1925, 60 p.

Lloyd George, D., *War Memoirs of David Lloyd George*, Boston, Little, Brown & Co., 1934, 4 vols.

Macartney, C. A., *National States and National Minorities*, London, Oxford University Press, 1934, 553 p.

Machray, R., *The Little Entente*, London, Allen & Unwin, 1929, 394 p.

Malynski, E., *Les Problèmes de l'est et la Petite Entente*, Paris, Cervantes, 1931, 560 p.

Masaryk, T. G., *Sur le Bolchevisme*, Geneva, Sonor, 1921, 38 p.

——, *Les Slaves après la guerre*, Prague, Orbis Pub. Co., 1923, 20 p.

——, *Světová revoluce za války a ve válce, 1914-1918* (The World Revolution during the War, 1914-1918), Praha, Orbis Pub. Co., 1933, 640 p.

——, *The Making of a State*, New York, A. Stokes Co., 1927, 518 p.

McClure, W., *World Prosperity*, New York, Macmillan, 1933, 613 p.

Mercier, M., *La Formation de l'état tchécoslovaque*, Chartres, F. Laine, 1922, 195 p.

Miller, D. H., *My Diary at the Conference of Paris*, n. p., Appeal Printing Co., 1926, 21 vols.

——, *The Drafting of the Covenant*, New York, G. P. Putnam's Son's, 1928, 2 vols.

——, *The Geneva Protocol*, New York, Macmillan, 1925, 279 p.

——, *The Peace Pact of Paris*, New York, G. P. Putnam's Son's, 1928, 287 p.

Mills, J. S., *The Genoa Conference*, New York, E. P. Dutton & Co., 1922, 436 p.

Mirkine-Guetzevich, B. and Tibal, A., *La Tchécoslovaquie*, Paris, Librairie Delagrave, 1929, 119 p.

Molisch, P., *Die Sudetendeutsche Freiheitsbewegung in den Jahren 1918-1919*, Vienna, Braumüller, 1932, 191 p.

Moulton, H. G. and Pasvolsky, L., *World War Debt Settlements*, New York, Macmillan, 1926, 448 p.

——, *War Debts and World Prosperity*, Washington, D. C., The Brookings Institution, 1932, 498 p.

Mousset, A., *La Petite Entente*, Paris, Bossard, 1923, 192 p.

Mowrer, P. S., *Balkanized Europe*, New York, E. P. Dutton & Co., 1921, 349 p.

Nicolson, H., *Peacemaking*, New York, Houghton Mifflin Co., 1933, 378 p.

Nosek, V., *Independent Bohemia*, London, J. M. Dent & Sons, 1918, 190 p.

O'Higgins, H. J., *March of the Czechoslovaks across Siberia*, New York, The Czechoslovak Arts Club, 1918, 28 p.

Opočenský, J., *The Collapse of the Austro-Hungarian Monarchy and the Rise of the Czechoslovak State*, Prague, Orbis Pub. Co., 1928, 216 p.

Padelford, N. J., *Peace in the Balkans*, New York, Oxford University Press, 1935, 209 p.

Papánek, J., *La Tchécoslovaquie, histoire politique et juridique de sa création*, Prague, thèse, 1922, 97 p.

Pasvolsky, L., *Economic Nationalism of the Danubian States*, New York, Macmillan, 1928, 609 p.

Piot, A., *La Couronne tchécoslovaque jusqu'au mort de Rašín, 1918-1923*, Paris, thèse, 1923, 260 p.

Přibram, A. F., *The Secret Treaties of Austria-Hungary*, Cambridge, Harvard University Press, 1920, 2 vols.

Przybylski, A., *La Pologne en lutte pour ses frontières* (translated from the Polish), Paris, Gebethner and Wolff, 1929, 172 p.

Rádl, E., *La Question religieuse en Tchécoslovaquie*, Prague, the Gazette de Prague, 1922, 62 p.

——. *Der Kampf zwischen Tchechen und Deutschen*, Reichenberg, Stiepel, 1928, 208 p.

Rašín, A., *The Financial Policy of Czechoslovakia during the First Year of its History*, Oxford, Clarendon Press, 1923, 160 p.

——, *Muj finanční plán* (My Financial Plan), Praha, Orbis Pub. Co., 1921.

——, *Inflace a Deflace* (Inflation and Deflation), Praha, Orbis Pub. Co., 1922.

Reimann, P., *Dějiny komunistické strany československé* (History of the Czechoslovak Communist Party), Praha, Borecký, 1931, 280 p.

Ripka, H., *Patnact let československé demokracie* (Fifteen Years of Czechoslovak Democracy), Praha, "Pokrok", 1933, 51 p.

Rist, C., *La Deflation en pratique*, Paris, Delagrave, 1924.

Ross, E. A., *The Russian Soviet Republic*, New York, The Century Co., 1923, 405 p.

Rouček, J. S., *Contemporary Rumania and her Problems*, Palo Alto, Stanford University Press, 1932, 422 p.

Schacht, H., *The End of Reparations*, New York, J. Cape and H. Smith, 1931, translated by L. Gannett, 248 p.

Schmidt-Friedlander, R., *Die Währungspolitik der Tschechoslowakei*, Reichenberg, Stiepel, 1929, 211 p.

Schuman, F. L., *War and Diplomacy in the French Republic*, New York, McGraw-Hill Book Co., 1931, 452 p.

Scott, A. P., *An Introduction to the Peace Treaties*, Chicago, University of Chicago Press, 1920, 292 p.

Scott, J. B., *Official Statements of War Aims and Peace Proposals, December, 1916 to November, 1918*, Washington, D. C., Carnegie Endowment for International Peace, 1921, 515 p.

Šedivý, K., *Sept années de politique intérieure tchécoslovaque, 1918-25*, Prague, Orbis Pub. Co., 1925, 69 p.

Selsam, J. P., *The Attempts to Form an Anglo-French Alliance, 1919-1924*, Philadelphia, University of Pennsylvania Press, 1936, 85 p.

Seton-Watson, R. W., *The New Slovakia*, Prague, F. Borový, 1924, 130 p.

——, *Slovakia, Then and Now*, London, Allen & Unwin, 1931, 356 p.

——, *Treaty Revision and the Hungarian Frontiers*, London, Eyre & Spottiswoode, 1934, 76 p.

Seymour, C. (ed.), *The Intimate Papers of Colonel House*, New York, Houghton Mifflin Co., 1926, 4 vols.

Shotwell, J. T., *War as an Instrument of National Policy*, New York, Harcourt, Brace & Co., 1929, 310 p.

Simonds, F. H., *How Europe Made Peace Without America*, New York, Doubleday, Page & Co., 1927, 407 p.

——, *Can Europe Keep the Peace?*, New York, Harper & Bros., 1931, 360 p.

Simonds, F. H. and Brooks, E., *The Great Powers in World Politics*, New York, American Book Co., 1935, 644 p.

Slosson, P. W., *Twentieth Century Europe*, Cambridge, Houghton, Mifflin Co., 1927, 747 p.

Stanoyevich, M. S., *Slavonic Nations of Yesterday and Today*, New York, H. W. Wilson Co., 1925.

Steidler, F. V., *Československé hnutí na Rusi* (The Czechoslovak Movement in Russia), Praha, Pam. Odboje, 1921, 113 p.

Stewart, G., *The White Armies of Russia: a Chronicle of Counter-Revolution and Allied Intervention*, New York, Macmillan, 1933, 469 p.

Stone, J., *International Guarantees of Minority Rights*, London, Oxford University Press, 1932, 288 p.

Strauss, E., *Tschechoslowakische Aussenpolitik*, Prague, Orbis Pub. Co., 1936, 165 p.

Street, C. J. C., *Slovakia, Past and Present*, London, P. S. King & Son, 1928, 64 p.

Temperley, H. W. V., *A History of the Peace Conference of Paris*, London, Froude, 1920, 6 vols.

Thompson, C. T., *The Peace Conference Day by Day*, New York, Brentano's, 1920, 423 p.

Toynbee, A. J., *Survey of International Affairs, 1920-23, 1924-*, London, Oxford University Press.

Vinacke, H. M., *History of the Far East in Modern Times*, New York, F. S. Crofts & Co., 1933, 503 p.

Werkmann, Baron C. von, *The Tragedy of Charles of Hapsburg*, London, P. Allan & Co., 1924, 297 p.

Wheeler-Bennett, J. W., *Information on the Renunciation of War, 1927-1928*, London, Allen & Unwin, 1928, 192 p.

——, *Disarmament and Security since Locarno, 1925-1931*, London, Allen & Unwin, 1932, 383 p.

——, *The Pipe Dream of Peace*, New York, W. Morrow & Co., 1935, 302 p.

Zmrhal, K., *Vlada Sovĕtu a Ĉeskoslovaci* (The Soviet Government and the Czechoslovaks), Praha, *Socialistické Listy*, 1919, 46 p.

ARTICLES

A German Bohemian Deputy, "The German Minority in Czechoslovakia", *The Slavonic and East European Review*, vol. xiv, pp. 295-300, January, 1936.

Anon., "In the matter of cessions by Germany to Czechoslovakia under Article 339 of the Treaty of Versailles", *The American Journal of International Law*, vol. xviii, pp. 186-198, January, 1924.

——, "Modus vivendi mezi Ĉeskoslovenskem a Vatikánem", *Zahraniĉní Politika*, vol. vii, pp. 97-98 (Beneš to Gasparri, text of Czechoslovak note of January 29, 1928), 1928.

Armstrong, H. F., "France and the Hoover Plan", *Foreign Affairs*, vol. x, pp. 23-33, October, 1931.

Aubert, L., "Security: Key to French Policy", *Foreign Affairs*, vol. xi, pp. 122-136, October, 1932.

Avennier, L., "Mezinárodní právo řiĉni a režim na Dunaji", *Zahraniĉní Politika*, vol. i, pp. 106-110, 189-194, 294-300, 1922.

Beneš, E., "Exposé Ministra Dra. Beneše o modu vivendi mezi Ĉeskoslovenskem a Vatikánem", *Zahraniĉní Politika*, vol. vii, pp. 200-203 (Text of speech of February 1, 1928), 1928.

——, "The Little Entente", *Foreign Affairs*, vol. i, pp. 66-72, September, 1922.

——, " Les Sens de la revolution tchécoslovaque ", *Vie des peuples*, vol. x, pp. 293-351, 1923.

——, " O sníženi zbrojeni " (speech of September 29, 1923, during the plenary session, as rapporteur for the Third Commission at the Fourth Assembly of the League of Nations), reprinted in *Zahraniční Politika*, vol. ii, pp. 1257-1264, 1923.

——, " The Foreign Policy of Czechoslovakia ", *Nineteenth Century*, vol. xcv, pp. 483-490, April, 1924.

——, " European Security ", *International Conciliation*, no. 212, September, 1925.

——, " Le Problème des petites nations après la guerre mondiale ", *Le Monde slav*, December, 1925, pp. 413-435.

——, " Les Slaves et l'idée slave pendant et après la guerre ", *Le Monde slav*, March, 1926, pp. 321-381.

——, " Exposé Dra. Beneše, přednesene 4 řijna, 1928, v zahraničním výboru poslanecké sněmovny ", *Zahraniční Politika*, vol. vii, pp. 1006-1012, 1928.

Bernus, P., " L'Autriche et l'Anschluss ", *Le Journal des débats*, vol. xxxii, pt. 2, pp. 312-314, August 24, 1928.

——, " Le Gouvernement tchèque et le Vatican ", *Le Journal des débats*, vol. xxxii, pt. 2, pp. 86-87, 130-132, July 18-25, 1925.

Binkley, R. C., " New Light on the Paris Peace Conference ", *Political Science Quarterly*, vol. xlvi, pp. 335-361, 509-547, 1931.

——, " Ten Years of Peace Conference History ", *Journal of Modern History*, vol. i, pp. 607-629, 1929.

Brailsford, H. N., " Prague and Vienna ", *New Republic*, vol. xxxi, pp. 223-226, August 2, 1922.

Buell, R. L., " The Vatican and the New World ", *Current History*, vol. xvi, pp. 977-984, September, 1922.

Chmelář, J., " Československá zahraniční politika v roce 1924 ", *Zahraniční politika*, vol. iv, pp. 1-6, 1925. Similar annual summaries follow in the first number of *Zahraniční Politika* each year.

——, " Otázka rekonstrukce Rady Společnosti Národu ", *Zahraniční Politika*, vol. v, pp. 777-783, 1926.

——, " Rakouský problem a středni Evropa ", *Zahraniční Politika*, vol. vii, pp. 1147-1159, 1928.

——, " Tardieuův plán středoevropské spoluprace ", *Zahraniční Politika*, vol. xi, pt. 1, pp. 185-192, 1932.

Chopin, J., " Les Tchécoslovaques en Russie ", *Révue de Paris*, vol. xxv, pt. 4, pp. 777-796, August 15, 1918.

Dumont-Wilden, L., " Les Difficultés intérieures de la Tchécoslovaquie ", *Révue politique et littéraire*, vol. lix, pp. 156-159, March 5, 1921.

Dvořáček, J., " Jánovská konference ", *Zahraniční Politika*, vol. i, pp. 165-170, 1922.

Fenwick, C. G., "The Legal Significance of the Locarno Agreements", *The American Journal of International Law*, vol. xx, pp. 108-111, 1926.

Fiša, P., "Pakt čtyř velmoci", *Zahraniční Politika*, vol. xii, pp. 305-312, 1933.

Fisher, L., "What the Sokols Stand for", *The Bohemian Review*, vol. i, pp. 1-4, June, 1917.

Friedman, J., "Současná obchodně-politická situace československé republiky", *Zahraniční Politika*, vol. viii, pp. 7-17, 1929.

Hajn, A., "Ochrana národnostních menšin—otázkou mezinárodní", *Zahraniční Politika*, vol. i, pp. 88-92, 1922.

Hanč, J., "O středoevropské hospodářské dorozumění", *Zahraniční Politika*, vol. xi, pt. i, pp. 108-118, 1932.

Hanighen, F. C., "Troubled Days in Czechoslovakia", *Current History*, vol. xliii, pp. 578-583, February, 1935.

Hejn, E. T., "The Czechoslovak Viewpoint", *The American Review of Reviews*, vol. lxv, pp. 490-491, May, 1922.

Hobza, A., "Reorganisace Společnosti Národu", *Zahraniční Politika*, vol. v, pp. 863-867, 1926.

Hodža, M., "Mala Dohoda, jej tradicie a jej dnešný úkol", *Zahraniční Politika*, vol. i, pp. 6-10, 1922.

Hudec, K., "Československá republika a Německo", *Zahraniční Politika*, vol. viii, pp. 425-433, 546-555, 681-696, 808-813, 1929.

Janin, General M., "Fragments de mon journal siberien", *Le Monde slav*, December, 1924, pp. 221-240; March, 1925, pp. 339-355; April, 1925, pp. 19-24.

——, "Au G. Q. G. russe", *Le Monde slav*, January, 1926, pp. 1-24; May, 1926, pp. 161-185.

Jeden Svědek, "Beneš a Mala Dohoda", *La Révue de France*, année ii, tome v, pp. 595-623, October 1, 1922.

Jonescu, T., "The Future of the Little Entente", *The Living Age*, vol. cccxi, pp. 699-703, December 17, 1921.

——, "How the Little Entente Began", *The Living Age*, vol. cccxi, pp. 627-632, December 10, 1921.

Jorga, N., "Les Fondements géographiques et historiques de la Petite Entente", *Le Monde slav*, March, 1925, pp. 439-461.

Kačer, K., "Deset let práce pro ideu odzbrojéní" *Zahraniční Politika*, vol. vii, pp. 1048-1064, 1159-1170, 1928; vol. viii, pp. 629-647, 776-790, 901-912, 1183-1197, 1455-1478, 1929.

Kadlec, K., "Magyars and the Czechoslovak Republic", *The Czechoslovak Review*, vol. iv, pp. 58-64, 1920.

Krčmář, J., "Přispěvky k výkladu o oceněni locarnských smluv", *Zahraniční Politika*, vol. iv, pp. 1334-1355, 1925.

——, "Československopolská hranice v území spišskem (Javorina) před Stalým Dvorem v Haagu a před Radou Společnosti Národu", *Zahraniční Politika*, vol. iii, pp. 7-20, 102-118, 186-196, 600-603, 1924.

Krofta, K., "Haag a Paříž", *Zahraniční Politika*, vol. ix, pp. 497-500, 1930.

Kučera, B., "Československá pozemková reforma s hlediška mezinárodního práva", *Zahraniční Politika*, vol. iii, pp. 444-454, 1924.

Lockhart, R. H. B., "Central Europe and Czechoslovakia", *Edinburgh Review*, vol. ccxxxviii, pp. 209-229, October, 1923.

Loiseau, C., "The Vatican and the New States of Central Europe", *New Europe*, September 25, 1919, pp. 241-247.

Loubal, F., "Slovenská declarace z 30 října, 1918, s hlediška mezinárodního", *Zahraniční Politika*, vol. ii, pp. 1435-1440, 1923.

Machray, R., "The Little Entente and Its Policies", *Fortnightly Review*, vol. cxxv, pp. 764-774, June, 1926.

Orbach, C. L., "Czechoslovakia's Place in the Sun", *Current History*, vol. xiv, pp. 944-945, September, 1921.

Paličkář, S. J. and Brož, A., "Czechs and Slovaks at Odds", *Current History*, vol. xxii, pp. 784-788, August, 1925.

Papoušek, J., "Základy Masarykový koncepce zahraniční politiky", *Zahraniční Politika*, vol. i, pp. 349-350, 1922.

Pergler, C., "Minorities in Czechoslovakia", *Current History*, vol. xvii, pp. 310-311, November, 1922.

Pichon, J. E., "Les Frontières de l'état tchécoslovaque", *Travaux du Comité d'Études*, Paris, Imprimerie Nationale, 1919, vol. ii, pp. 105-120.

Pinon, R., "La Réconstruction de l'Europe danubienne", *Révue des deux mondes*, 6 période, tome li, pp. 557-582, June 1, 1919.

——, "The Franco-Slovakian Treaty of Alliance", *Current History*, vol. xx, pp. 748-753, August, 1924.

Procházka, R., "Nová tvář problému bezpečnosti", *Zahraniční Politika*, vol. xiv, pp. 75-84, 1935.

Rankovitch, J., "France and the Little Entente", *The Living Age*, vol. cccxvii, pp. 7-13, April 7, 1923.

Ryan, J. H., "The Vatican's World Policy", *Current History*, vol. xvii, pp. 429-438, December, 1922.

Seton-Watson, R. W., "The Little Entente", *Contemporary Review*, vol. cxxxii, pp. 694-707, December, 1927.

——, "The Psychology of the Succession States", *New Europe*, vol. xvii, pp. 62-64, October 28, 1920.

——, "The Czechoslovak Republic", *Contemporary Review*, vol. cxix, pp. 310-321, March, 1921.

Slosson, P., "Problem of Austro-German Union", *International Conciliation*, no. 250, pp. 221-254, May, 1929.

Smith, C. B., *The Independent*, December 3, 1921, pp. 226-227 (editorial on Portorose Conference).

Sobota, E., "Czechs and Germans: a Czech View", *The Slavonic and East European Review*, vol. xiv, pp. 301-320, January, 1936.

Šrom, J. E., "Sovětské Rusko a Jánov", *Zahraniční Politika*, vol. i, pp. 429-434, 1922.

Stolfer, G., "European Kaleidoscope", *Foreign Affairs*, vol. xiv, pp. 216-226, January, 1936.

Vochoč, V., "Naš spolek s Francii", *Zahraniční Politika*, vol. iii, pp. 1-6, 1924.

Williams, M. O., "The Fighting Czechoslovaks", *Asia*, vol. xviii, pp. 722-728, September, 1918.

Winkler, M., "The Investor and League Loans", *Foreign Policy Association*, vol. iv, supplement 2, pp. 15-18, June, 1928.

Young, R. F., "Czechs and Slovaks", *New Statesman*, vol. xiv, pp. 155-156, November 8, 1919.

Zimmerman, M. A., "Americký projekt paktu proti válce", *Zahraniční Politika*, vol. vii, pp. 427-432, 1928.

INDEX

Albania, 25, 248, 266, 372, 421
Alexander I, 198, 324, 367, 388, 391-392
Alexandrovský, 404-405
Allied High Command, 33, 35
Anschluss, 47-49, 148, 173, 177, 282-283, 285-286, 287, 290, 312, 324, 366, 381, 388, 391
Apponyi, 164n.
Archangel, 115, 127, 128, 132
Archimbaud, 393
Austria,
    Armistice of November, 1918, 34
    Bank of Austria-Hungary, 50, 53, 63-69, 76
    and Little Entente, 174, 193, 284-287, 312-318, 380-383
    Protocol of Venice, 104, 183
    reconstruction of, 192-197, 278
    Republic recognized, 52
    Treaty of St. Germain, 32, 43n., 52, 56, 58, 59, 68, 71, 82, 173, 224, 225, 279, 342, 401
    war debts, 50-54
    war finance, 62-63, 64
    and Western Powers, 173-174, 175, 192, 195, 196, 284-285, 314, 380-381, 397
    see also, Anschluss, Austro-German Customs Union, Danubian Confederation
Austro-German Customs Union, 287, 311, 312-318, 322, 323, 324, 337, 398

Baldwin, 268
Balfour, 127
Balkan Entente, 368n., 372-373, 397, 401, 407, 414, 422
"Balkanization of Europe", 44-45, 58
Banffy, 182, 185
Baranya, 183-184
Barthou, 375, 376, 380, 386, 387-388, 390, 391-392, 394
Beaumarchais, de, 267

Beck, 361, 373, 400, 406, 418, 420
Belgium, 211, 212, 232
Beneš,
    and Austria, 173-178, 194-197, 282-288
    becomes Foreign Minister, 16
    and Central European economic cooperation, 79, 189-192
    and disarmament, 44, 181, 210-211, 299-394, 345, 352-354, 370-371, 398
    early life of, 14-15n.
    elected President, 423-425
    and France, 24, 105, 141, 211, 212-216, 217, 220-224, 228, 231, 236-240, 265, 376
    and Germany, 298-299, 316-317, 409
    and Great Britain, 24, 105, 127-128, 141, 211
    and Hungary, 163, 164-165, 169-170, 181-189, 204, 205, 207-208, 286-287, 326, 329-330, 356-357, 360, 392
    and Italy, 24, 104, 211-212, 223, 224-227, 265, 356-357, 362-363, 367, 420-423
    and League of Nations, 105, 106, 107, 111-113, 209-211, 227-229, 229, 307, 311-312, 352-354
    and Little Entente, 162-173, 198, 201, 202-203, 211, 221-222, 224, 226-227, 230, 260, 289, 291-292, 296, 319, 322, 325, 339, 341-342, 348-350, 357-358, 371-372, 395, 414
    and Peace Conference, 26-27, 37n., 45, 59
    and Poland, 134-135, 150, 152-154, 155-160, 178, 242-246, 263
    and reparations, 50, 207, 343, 345, 349-350
    and Rothermere, 267-269
    and Russia (U. S. S. R.), 113-

114, 114-129, 131-135, 136-138, 145-146, 241, 259-260, 261-262, 386-387, 404-406, 414
speeches :
September 30, 1919, 59, 60
January 31, 1920, 134
March 11, 1920, 136, 260
April 2, 1920, 137
August 4, 1920, 158-159
September 1, 1920, 166-167
January 27, 1921, 190
April 1, 1925, 244
October 30, 1925, 239
January 5, 1928, 291-292
April 23, 1931, 314-315
October 20, 1931, 345n.
March 25, 1932, 339
November 7, 1932, 351
January 14, 1933, 383
March 1, 1933, 358
April 25, 1933, 362-363, 378
October 15, 1933, 365
October 31, 1933, 367, 370-371
March 21, 1934, 381
March 23, 1934, 382
November 6, 1934, 392
November 5, 1935, 416-417, 418, 419
and war debts, 51
and Wilson, 44
Berger-Waldenegg, 397
Bethlen, 230, 329-330, 331, 341, 343, 359, 377n.
Bibra, von, 385
Bradač, 360
Bratiano, 198
Bratislava, 32, 37, 40-41, 82, 85, 190
Brest-Litovsk, treaty of, 115-116
Briand, 140, 232, 272, 310-311, 315
Brüning, 354
Bulgaria, 172, 203, 230, 248, 266, 321, 336, 347, 349, 406-407
Neuilly treaty of, 204n., 224, 225
Burgenland, 182-183, 184

Cannes, 140
Carol II, 319, 322, 324, 367, 413
Catholic Church,
and Beneš, 251, 257
Concordat of 1855, 91
Czech national revival, 91
Czechoslovak National Church, 93-94
Free-Thinkers, 95

and Hus, 92, 250, 253
land reform, 90-91, 251
and Masaryk, 92, 96, 250, 256-257
Modus Vivendi with Czechoslovakia, 254-257, 412-413
Praha riot, 92
separation of Church and State (Czechoslovakia), 96
and Slovaks, 96-97, 249-250, 255-256
St. Václav, 251
see also, Hlinka
Cecil, 127, 209
Čeljabinsk, 117, 119
Čermak, 117
Chamberlain, 231, 268
Charles, ex-Emperor-King, *see* Habsburgs
Chicherin, 121-122, 135-136, 137, 145, 154
China, 107-108, 337, 345
Ciriaci, 256
Clemenceau, 152
Conference of Ambassadors, 158n., 159-161, 182, 183, 186-187
Council of Four (Big Four), 30, 31, 32, 40, 153
Curtius, 313, 314
Czechoslovakia,
Allied recognition of, 15
area of, 78
army in World War, 22n.
bankruptcies in, 86
commercial treaties of, 87-89, 102, 103, 171-172, 176, 178-179, 205, 244, 247-248, 260-263, 263-265, 277-278, 279-281, 293-294, 319-320, 328-329, 404
conduct of foreign affairs, 21, 22-23
constitution :
permanent, 20-21n., 112-113
provisional, 20
cooperation of Beneš and Masaryk, 21, 326
" costs of liberation ", 53, 342-343
customs duties, 80-81, 84-85, 88
Czechoslovak National Council, 14
Declaration of Geneva, 16
disarmament, *see* Beneš, and disarmament
and Fascism, 90, 257-258, 385, 408n., *see also*, Gajda

Foreign Affairs Committees, 23
Foreign Trade Bureau, 81, 84, 87
Import and Export Commission,
    80, 81
industrial inheritance of, 77
land reform, 90-91
Liberty Loan, 64
military policy, 19-20, 414-415,
    416, *see also*, Little Entente,
    military conventions
minorities, 17, 18, 45, 46-47, 61-
    62, 71, 79, 108-113, 240,
    314, 384-385, 407-411
navy, 327
occupation of Slovakia, 18-19
at Peace Conference:
    Anschluss, 47-49
    boundaries:
        Austrian, 31-32
        Bohemian, 24, 28-31
        Hungarian, 32-42
        Polish, 43, 150-154
        Ruthenian, 42
    corridor, 31-32
    Czechoslovak territorial com-
        mission, 27
    economic outlets, 54-58
    Inter-Allied Commission for
        Těšín, 27
    Lusatian Sorbs, 32
    reparations, 49-51
    summary of, 58-59
    war debts, 51-54
political form of, 15
political parties of:
    Agrarian, 69, 137, 241, 252, 253,
        309, 320, 329, 385n.
    Christian Social, 258, 385n.
    Clerical, 252, 253
    Communist, 334, 424
    Fascist, 408, 410, 424
    German Agrarian, 258
    German National Socialist,
        384-385, 407
    German Nationalist, 385, 407
    National Democrat, 253, 332,
        334
    National Socialist, 251, 253
    National Unity, 424
    Pětka, 74, 250, 252-253
    Popular (Slovak Catholic),
        258, 379, 408
    Socialist, 70, 251, 252, 424
    Sudetendeutsche Partei, 407-
        411
population of (1921), 78
Provisional National Assembly,
    16
religions of, 94n.
return of Legions, 16, 129, 133
social reform, 89-90
stability of, 97, 408
tariff barriers against, 87-89
see also, France, Great Britain,
    Italy, League of Nations,
    Little Entente, Russia,
    United States

Danubian Confederation, 58, 180,
    282, 283-288, 292, 316-317,
    339-341, 347, 364-368
Davidović, 227
Diderichs, 119
Dmowski, 153
Doležal, 419
Dollfuss, 365, 367, 380-382, 385,
    390, 391
Doumergue, 380
Dousmanis, 203
Duca, 198, 201, 227, 292, 372

Eden, 398, 399-400
Einstein, 302
Engliš, 71-73, 74
Estonia, 134, 248
Ethiopia, 407, 420-423

Fierlinger, 380
Finland, 248, 321, 376
Flandin, 338, 339
Foch, 38, 130, 216, 219-220, 270
Four Power Pact, 360-364, 400
France,
    and Czechoslovakia, 22, 24, 31,
        34, 37, 102, 122, 211-220,
        231-239, 270, 338-339
    debt default, 339, 376-377
    at Peace Conference, 24, 25, 30,
        41
    and Poland, 135, 152, 179, 212,
        216, 233, 236-238, 243, 335,
        337, 364, 366-367, 389, 399
    see also, Italy, Little Entente,
        Russia
François-Poncet, 369-370

Gajda, 118-119, 123, 125, 129, 257-
    258, 408n.
Garbai, 35
Gasparri, 254

Gažik, 258

Geneva Protocol, 227-229

Genoa Conference, 140-145, 199, 200-201

Germany,
  and Czechoslovakia, 18, 88, 98-99, 215, 382-383, 397, 407-411, 416
  reparations, 341-342, 345-346
  Saar plebiscite, 396
  Versailles, treaty of, 43n., 48-49, 49-50, 56, 57, 59, 79-80, 80-81, 351-352, 355, 396, 397, 400, 402
  Weimar constitution, 48-49
  see also, Anschluss, Austro-German Customs Union, Hitler, Locarno, Poland, Russia

Ghiczy, 330

Ghika, 164n., 322, 325

Göbbels, 409

Gömbös, 365, 367, 377n., 381

Göring, 365, 411

Gratz, 181-182

Great Britain,
  and Czechoslovakia, 88, 100-101, 122, 248, 422-423
  at Peace Conference, 24, 25, 30, 31
  see also, League of Nations, Little Entente, Russia

Greece,
  and Italy, 113, 266
  and Little Entente, 168, 203, 248, 289, 340, 342, 390, 392, 406
  Politis, 228
  see also, Balkan Entente

Habsburgs:
  Charles, 52, 73, 169-170, 181-182, 184-186, 187-188, 327
  Joseph, 163
  Otto, 319, 328, 331, 413
  Zita, 328, 413

Hainisch, 177

Helmer, 252

Henderson, 311

Henlein, 407-411

Herriot, 228, 231

Hillerson, 133-134, 139

Hindenburg, von, 232, 354, 424

Hitler, 354-355, 363, 369-370, 372, 373-374, 382-383, 386, 389, 396-399, 411

Hlinka, 23, 95, 253, 258, 327, 379

Hoare, 421

Hodač, 306

Hodža, 424

Hoover, 44, 344-345, 346

Horthy, 39, 169-170

Hotowetz, 84

House, 120

Hrušovský, 378

Hungary,
  ex-prisoners in Russia, 117, 119
  forgeries, 271-274
  Hirtenberg affair, 356-357
  and Italy, 183, 266, 274-278, 290, 319, 331, 333, 356-357
  reconstruction of, 205-208, 271
  revisionism, 17, 18, 42, 134, 165, 259, 268-269, 326-330, 336-341, 372, 377-379, 392, 406, 414
  St. Gotthard affair, 274-278
  Trianon, treaty of, 43n., 56, 164n., 173, 182, 183, 201, 205, 206, 207, 224, 225, 230, 269, 274, 319, 326, 331, 377-378
  see also, Habsburgs, Little Entente, Slovakia

Hus, see Catholic Church

Hymans, 232

Ibl, 308

International rivers:
  Danube, 32, 33-35, 40-41, 54, 56-58, 82
  Elbe, 29, 54-55, 56, 81, 98
  Oder, 30, 54-55, 56
  Vistula, 54-55

Irkutsk, 119, 129

Italy,
  Corfu incident, 113
  and Czechoslovakia, 101-102, 103, 104, 108-109, 207, 268-269, 330-333, 341, 423
  at Peace Conference, 24, 30, 31, 50
  rivalry with France, 100, 220-224, 226, 265-271, 394-395
  see also, Hungary, Little Entente, Mussolini, Yugoslavia

Janin, 126-127

Japan, 120-121, 122, 126, 248, 345, 369, 394, 403, 405, 421

Jehlička, 95, 379

Jelinek, 317

Jews, 18, 46-47, 384

Jonescu, 108, 162, 167, 168, 179
Joseph, *see* Habsburgs

Karolyi, 34, 35
Kellogg Peace Pact, 295, 301-302, 373
Kerensky, 121
Klofáč, 19, 378
Klotz, 419
Kolchak, 126, 127, 128, 129, 132
Kopecký, 296
Košice, 37, 42
Kramář, 15n., 16-17, 19, 23, 45, 54-55, 69, 123, 130, 137, 152n., 154, 241, 332, 334-335, 424
Krofta, 254, 256, 332, 346, 424
Kujtun, treaty of, 129
Kun, Bela, 19, 35-39, 163

Laroche, 41
Latvia, 134, 248
Lausanne Conference, 346-348
Laval, 394, 398, 399, 402, 403
League of Nations,
    Amendments to Covenant of, 106-113
    and Austria, 193, 195-197
    Czechoslovak minorities treaty, 45
    early sessions of, 25, 46, 107
    and Ethiopia, 420-423
    and Germany, 297-299, *see also*, Hitler
    and Hungary, 205-206, 207, 271-278
    and Russia (U. S. S. R.), 386, 389-390
    "Treaty of Mutual Assistance", 209-211, 227
    see also, Little Entente
Lithuania, 375
Little Entente
    conferences of, 197-204, 211, 221-222, 224, 226-227, 229-230, 260, 286, 288-296, 318-325, 339, 340, 341-342, 348-350, 361-362, 364-368, 371-372, 387-388, 395, 406-407, 411, 414, 423
    extensions of, 201-202, 204, 289, 294-296, 357-360
    formation of, 162-173
    and France, 197-198, 212, 220-224, 265-266, 270, 290, 291, 325, 336-341, 364, 399, 414-415

    and Great Britain, 197-198, 290, 422-423
    and Hungary, 164-165, 169-170, 184-189, 199, 221, 243, 246, 272-277, 293, 323, 349-350, 356
    and Italy, 103, 188-189, 193-194, 195-196, 222-223, 266-267, 274-278, 363, 365, 397, 422-423
    and League of Nations, 107, 108
    military conventions of, 172-173, 204
    and Russia (U. S. S. R.), 138, 198, 199-200, 221-222, 230, 260, 289-290, 320, 335-336, 368-369, 387-390, 415
    see also, Anschluss, Austria, Balkan Entente, Bulgaria, Danubian Confederation, Greece, Habsburgs, Poland
Litvinov, 261, 386, 389, 390, 403, 406
Lloyd George, 128n., 130, 140
Locarno, 229-240, 352

MacDonald, 228
Magyars, *see* Hungary
Malhome, 419
Malypetr, 408, 410, 424
Marinković, 227, 290, 319, 343
Marmaggi, 250, 251, 254, 256, *see also,* Catholic Church
Masaryk, 14n., 16, 18, 19, 41, 110, 115, 118, 123, 124, 126, 131-132, 135, 155, 167, 177, 212-213, 224-225, 239, 326-327, 423-425
Mastný, 216
Mayr-Harting, 258
Maxa, 117
Meisner, 419
Michalakopoulos, 340
Millerand, 157, 212
Mirbach, 116
Mironescu, 319, 342n.
Mitilineu, 290
Mussolini, 204, 211-212, 222-223, 224-226, 266-267, 269, 332-333, 336-341, 360-364, 365, 367, 381-382, 388, 391, 394, 401-402, 407, 420-423

Nadosy, 272
Nationalism, 13 and n.
Němec, 424

Neurath, von, 369, 398
Nicholas, Prince, 322
Ninčič, 165, 198, 200, 221. 223, 224,
 227, 240, 289

Omsk, 115, 119, 128
Osuský, 107, 164n., 338, 379n., 384
Otto, *see* Habsburgs

Paderewski, 157, 158, 159
Palmieri, 333
Papen, von, 365
Pašič, 163, 198, 201, 227
Paul, Prince, 413
Paul-Boncour, 374
Pedrazzi, 332, 333
Peidl, 39
Pétain, 270, 296
Pichon, 41
Pilsudski, 361, 373-374, 400, 418
Piltz, 201
Pittsburgh Agreement, 17
Poincaré, 140
Poland,
 Amendments to League Covenant,
  109-113
 and Baltic states, 179, 200, 389
 boundary disputes:
  Javorina, 159-162, 242
  Orava, 43, 159-162, 244
  Spiš, 43, 159-162, 244
  Těšin, 43, 149-159, 244, 418-420
 and Germany, 155-157, 200, 242-
  243, 373-376, 394, 395
 and League of Nations, 106-113,
  309
 and Little Entente, 144, 168, 179-
  180, 189, 194, 199-201, 222,
  242, 246, 289, 291, 292, 319,
  342, 366-367
 and Russia, 130, 134, 135, 139,
  154-156, 222, 243, 336
 see also, France
Politis, 228
Portorose Conference, 190-192, 194
Pospíšil, 338
Potemkin, 402

Rašin, 50, 63-69, 70, 71, 74, 75-
 76, 79
Renner, 174
Requin, 209
Rothermere, 267-269, 330
Rumania,

war against Hungary, 34, 36-39
 see also, Carol II, Little Entente
Russia (U. S. S. R., Soviet Union),
 and Czechoslovakia, 114, 133, 138-
  139, 144-146, 260-263, 334-
  336, 368, 386-387, 388-389,
  395, 402, 404-405, 415-418
 and France, 100, 118, 125, 136,
  139, 221n., 243, 335, 368-
  369, 390, 393-394, 402-404
 and Germany, 115-116, 120, 142-
  143, 368, 386
 and Great Britain, 100, 118, 125,
  140, 221n.
 New Economic Policy of, 140
 see also, Little Entente, Poland
Ruthenia, 17, 18, 42, 378, 379

Sacharov, 262
Salgo-Tarjan, 36, 41, 206, 208
Sapieha, 179
Satoralja-Ujhely, 41, 274n.
Schanzer, 104, 193, 195
Schober, 178, 182, 192, 311
Schuschnigg, 397
Šeba, 334
Seipel, 192-193, 285-286
Serbian Orthodox Church, 94
Simon, 398
Sirový, 128
Skirmunt, 179-180
Škoda munition works, 36, 358-359
Skrzynski, 232, 242, 246, 263
Slaviček, 164n.
Slovakia, 16, 17, 61, 95-96, 163, 165,
  255, 377-379
 provincial government inaugur-
  ated, 19
 war over, 34-42, 77
 see also. Hlinka, Hungary, re-
  visionism
Smith, 207, 271
Smutný, 420
Smuts, 41
Sokols, 257, 332
Soukup, 318
Soviet Union, *see* Russia
Spain, 161, 248, 297, 390
Spina, 258, 408, 410
Stalin, 399
Starhemberg, 391
Štefánik, 15n., 16, 43n., 101, 126-127
Stodola, 307
Stoyadinovič, 411

Stresemann, 230
Stříbrný, 424
Succession States,
    economic and financial relations
    of, 63, 65, 67n., 68-69, 71,
    85, 87, 189-192
    and the peace settlement, 44-45,
    46, 50-54
    and reparations, 341-350
    see also, Austria, Czechoslovakia,
    Hungary, Poland, Rumania,
    Yugoslavia
Supreme Council, 26-27, see also,
    Council of Four
Suvich, 381, 398, 406
Švehla, 253, 258

Tardieu, 339-340
Teleki, 181-182
The Hague, conferences of, 143
Tiso, 258
Tittoni, 109, 110-111, 113
Titulescu, 343, 348, 357, 362, 367,
    378, 393, 395, 397-398, 399,
    413
Tokaj, 33, 41
Trotsky, 117
Trumbič, 163
Turčanský Sv. Martin, 17n.
Turkey, 203, 248, 266, 318, 368, 390,
    392, see also, Balkan
    Entente
Tusar, 70, 355

Ukraine, 139, 146, 265
Unger, 379
United States,
    and Czechoslovakia, 101, 105, 122,
    248-249, 344-345, 346-347,
    368-369, 376-377, 379
    and Germany, 318
    at Peace Conference, 24, 30-
    31, 41
    and war debts, 248-249, 339, 344-
    345, 346
U. S. S. R., see Russia

Vaida-Voëvod, 164
Veverka, 198, 261, 347
Vienna, 32, 36, 48n., 60-61, 165, 176,
    197, 279, 285, 286, 313, 380
Viškovský, 319, 332
Vladivostok, 115, 117, 119, 127,
    128, 129

"Western orientation", 82, 85, 86,
    98, 105, 113, 129, 137
Weygand, 154
Wilson, 30, 44, 101, 120-121, 122,
    123, 130, 158n., 160
Windischgrätz, 271-273
Wiseman, 121
World Economic Conference, 306-
    307

Yeftič, 348, 357, 367, 395, 397, 411
Yugoslavia,
    and Austria, 177
    friction with Italy, 100, 103, 168,
    391
    see also, Alexander I, Little
    Entente

Zaleski, 336, 340
Zimmerman, 196
Zita, ex-Empress, see Habsburgs
Zolger, 164n.

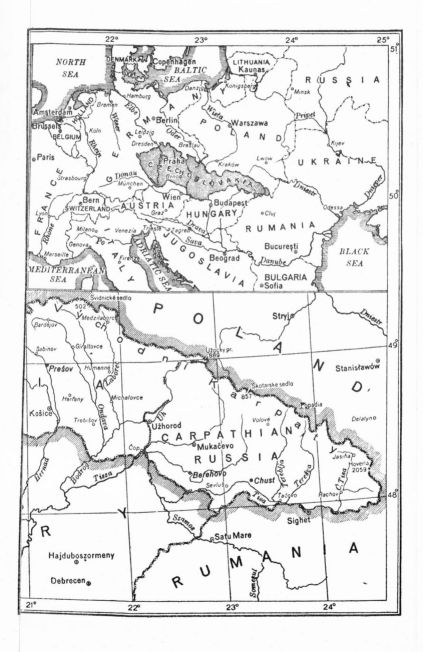

VITA

THE writer was born in Cedar Rapids, Iowa, on September 3, 1901. He was graduated from Washington High School of that city in June, 1919, and in September received a scholarship from Coe College. At that institution he was a Reader in American History for Professor S. G. Pattison. After two and a half years at Coe College, he transferred in January, 1922, to the State University of Iowa, where he obtained his A.B. in 1923 and his A.M. in 1924. At Iowa he was Undergraduate and, later, Graduate Assistant to Professor Louis Pelzer in the freshman classes in American History. In September, 1924, he went to Columbia University, New York City, 'for graduate work and research for the Ph.D. degree. Here, he had three seminars under Professor Carlton J. H. Hayes. Since September, 1928, he has been at the University of North Dakota as Assistant and Associate Professor of American History.